Allen Partridge

Real-Time Interactive 3D Games:

Creating 3D Games in Macromedia Director 8.5 Shockwave Studio

A Division of Pearson Technology Group
201 West 103rd St. • Indianapolis, Indiana, 46290 USA

Real-Time Interactive 3D Games

International Standard Book Number: 0672322854

Library of Congress Catalog Card Number: 2001092345

Printed in the United States of America

First Printing: November 2001

04   03   02   01   4   3   2   1

Trademarks

Warning and Disclaimer

Executive Editor
Jeff Schultz

Acquisitions Editor
Kate Small

Development Editor
Maryann Steinhart

Managing Editor
Charlotte Clapp

Project Editor
Heather McNeill

Copy Editor
Bart Reed

Indexer
Ginny Bess

Proofreader
Rowena Rappaport
Jody Larsen

Technical Editor
Robert Walch
Matthew Manuel

Team Coordinator
Amy Patton

Media Developer
Dan Scherf

Interior Designer
Gary Adair

Cover Designer
Bill Thomas

Page Layout
Rebecca Harmon
Lizbeth Patterson

Contents at a Glance

Table of Contents

About the Author

Dr. Allen Partridge teaches Dramatic Media, specializing in interactive entertainment, at the University of Georgia and runs Insight Interactive, an online game-development company. Allen is the co-host of dirGames-L, the largest online e-mail discussion community centered on game design and creation using Macromedia Director.

Allen's game and interactive CD-ROM credits include *Art Car Crazy*, *Word Wacky*, *Camp Scamp*, and *Virtual Silly Puttie*. Recently he released ICE-T, network conferencing software designed specifically for theatre preproduction teams to hold interactive production meetings.

Allen has been working with Macromedia Director since 1995. He is the founder of the recently created Director-3D.com, the first online community created for the sole purpose of sharing information regarding the use of Macromedia Director and 3D.

Dedication

For Mary, my friend, my muse, and my rock.

Acknowledgments

I cannot remember when I've had so much fun doing anything. Writing this book has been a joyful, educational, and satisfying experience.

It would not have been so without the constant love and support I have felt from my beautiful wife, Mary, my enchanting daughter, Lily, my endearing and generous mother, Ethel, and my inspirational father, Eldon. They taught me to dream, to savor, and to persevere.

I have been blessed with business partners who are also my dearest friends. I maintain my sanity thanks to the wisdom, knowledge, art, and advice of Nathan Rhuby, Brad Cushman, Sophia Varcados, Matt Kew, and Mark Dolney.

Several people have helped me enormously as I struggled to perfect, or at least stabilize, the dozens of demos and games in this book. They tirelessly poured over thousands of lines of code in the hope that they might help me make my ideas as clear as possible for you.

Robert Walch, a talented and successful game programmer and head of Entermation Game Design Studios, has been a constant voice of encouragement and has worked tirelessly to ensure that the book is technically sound.

Paul Catanese, author of *Director's Third Dimension*, granted me amazing opportunities to learn. My book has been substantially improved by the lessons I learned through reading and responding to Paul's fantastic book.

Several of my Ph.D. and MFA students have spent months evaluating the work and the code at my request. I am forever grateful for the sage advice of my students who have often taught me more than I could ever hope to teach them.

Katherine Hammond, Lee Smith, and Vincent Argentina have taught me to be respectful and generous in my writing. They've given me a better understanding of the responsibilities of authorship.

I could not have even conceived of a book like this without the amazing sharing, patience, and creativity that emerges from the dirGames-L mailing list. It is the finest list community I have ever had the honor of participating in, and I would be remiss if I didn't thank all of its members. They have given me constant support and intelligent feedback and have led me to a much more complete understanding of game development.

I owe most of my understanding of the nuances of Director's 3D engine to Swerve, Barry, Danny, NoiseCrime, Ullala, Christophe, Jerry Charmilund, and the whole Tron gang.

I would not have been able to write this book at all were it not for the intellectual and emotional support of Dr. Stanley Longman, Dr. Charles Eidsvik, Mr. B. Don Massey, and Dr. Farley Richmond.

The University of Georgia has provided support for my research, equipment for my creative development, and a home for my family and myself. I want to thank each member of the Drama and Dramatic Media Faculty at the University of Georgia.

There have been several people in my life who have unwittingly contributed to this book and to your ultimate enjoyment of it:

Dr. Tom Hart encouraged me to pursue whatever path interested me, and this is exactly where I landed. Tim Frank and Keith Miller gave me tools, toys, and faith when I had yet to demonstrate any talent.

Barbie Dickensheet taught me to be patient, to write carefully, and to trust in the ultimate goodness of people. I would not be Dr. Partridge without her, and this book would not exist without her.

Dr. Dan Hannon and Dr. Dean Wilcox, both visionaries and dreamers, helped shape and define my interests and creative vision. They were mentors, and for that I am forever grateful.

The wonderful support, generosity, and professionalism of the many editors and experts at Sams Publishing must be applauded. I want to specifically thank Kate Small, who had faith in me, encouraged me, and gave me room to grow.

Tell Us What You Think!

As the reader of this book, *you* are our most important critic and commentator. We value your opinion and want to know what we're doing right, what we could do better, what areas you'd like to see us publish in, and any other words of wisdom you're willing to pass our way.

As an Executive Editor for Sams, I welcome your comments. You can e-mail or write me directly to let me know what you did or didn't like about this book—as well as what we can do to make our books stronger.

Please note that I cannot help you with technical problems related to the topic of this book, and that due to the high volume of mail I receive, I might not be able to reply to every message.

When you write, please be sure to include this book's title and author as well as your name and phone or fax number. I will carefully review your comments and share them with the author and editors who worked on the book.

E-mail: m3feedback@samspublishing.com
Mail: Jeff Schultz, Executive Editor
            Sams
            201 West 103rd Street
            Indianapolis, IN 46290 USA

Introduction

This is a book about making 3D games in Macromedia Director Shockwave Studio. Expect it to be a book about code, interface tricks, and wacky game ideas. Along the way, I will share my experiences, life, and attitudes about games and game development. I have always tended to swim upstream, so I doubt that much of this will seem comfortable or familiar. I don't like things to be too comfortable. It spawns mediocrity.

This is a desperately needed book. The rapid improvement of Macromedia Director coupled with the exponential increase in the speed of computers and the massive popularity of real-time 3D games are creating a tremendous opportunity in the information market. As I write this book, Macromedia Director 8.5/Shockwave Studio is about to go public, and when it does, its influence will be astounding. I know this because I've seen what it can do, and it is hardly difficult to see the opportunities such power will provide.

Thousands of software developers (both traditional Director developers and developers accustomed to other languages) will want to learn how to use these new tools as well as learn strategies for creating 3D games. They will want to learn to use the tool because Macromedia has produced a mind-blowing Internet-enabled 3D engine. The potential and range of the tool is unparalleled. No other 3D engine supports the depth of features for developers within the context of a drag-and-drop authoring environment.

The stage has been set. Shockwave Flash has enjoyed unprecedented popularity and is drawing an ever-growing pool of converts over to the Macromedia camp. Shockwave 3D is the feature that will motivate these enormous audiences to investigate Director.

Although other books are available that can help you learn these new features, this book is specifically geared toward game development. It is a sad fact that after nearly a decade of Director books, only one book has ever dealt with games, and none deal with the topic of 3D game development in Director.

In this text, I give you a model for simulating the behavior of people that is phrased in the language of the traditional stage, and as such, inherently dramatic. What the heck does that have to do with Shockwave 3D games? Everything.

I describe the manner in which intelligent agents interact and negotiate in order to resolve conflict within games and interactive performances. I come to all of this from the live theatre, so as you might expect, I'm going to bring a lot of live theatre to my interpretation of Director.

This book holds some interesting insights for people who want to gain an understanding of the traditional theatre. It will appeal to the vast audience of Macromedia Director developers because of its unusual and detailed free source code as well as the interesting approach to complex 3D games.

User Skill Requirements

This book is written in common language and includes simple descriptions and definitions of the computing concepts introduced along the way. It does not presuppose awareness of game design, but it does operate on the assumption that you are already somewhat familiar with Macromedia Director. The book should not be considered a primer. It delves deeply into the theory of character and environment design for interactive games, and it presents a substantial set of tutorials on the use of 3D Lingo. It is an intermediate to advanced text on these subjects. Although I include some information and tutorials using 3D Studio Max, you do not need to be familiar with 3D Studio Max in order to follow the text and use its resources.

User Skill Development

After finishing the book, you may expect to have gained a better understanding of games and game design. You should be able to create virtual environments, Web sites, kiosks, CD-ROMs, and other interactive 3D products using Director and the knowledge that you have acquired from this book.

You will develop a stronger understanding of object-oriented programming, behaviors, and 3D environments in general. You will have the tools to plan and create a game based on the methods explained in the book, and you will gain a general understanding of the advantages and disadvantages of using Director on any proposed 3D project.

In addition, you receive copies of some of my more enticing prebuilt behaviors and Lingo, enabling you to instantly create sophisticated 3D cameras and other cool toys.

Who Should Read This Book?

Intended for anyone who is interested in the gadgets, games, and gizmos that feed our imaginations, this book is an examination of our actions and of our amusements. I explain how "the way that people behave" can form a model by which to program interesting simulations. This book was created for the artists and entertainers who play parts in our many entertainment forms. It may hold interest for the thinkers and tinkers who imagine the way minds work and the way people behave. It provides some structures to build on for those mad men and women who crunch polygons and crank out killer code.

This is a book about some fundamental changes in the way we amuse ourselves. As I write it, I am aware of a single pending wave in the torrent of waves that have made up the many technological advancements of the past decade. On the surface, it seems small enough. The newest release of Macromedia's Director Shockwave Studio supports 3D graphics. It is in fact a tsunami, waiting to form.

The wave draws its power from several places. Shockwave has an installed user base of nearly 60 percent of all Web browsers. Its evil cousin, Flash, holds a user base well into the 90-percent range. When 3D Shockwave is introduced, millions of users will have fully cross-platform, high-power 3D plug-ins installed onto their computers via automatic update. Virtually overnight, Shockwave 3D will support a user base larger than any previous 3D Web delivery mechanisms, such as VRML, could ever imagine.

Why Buy This Book?

You will learn to use Director 3D through hands-on experience.

Programmers and multimedia developers are impatient for results. We don't like to wade through a bunch of garbage trying to find gems. We want to see examples of programs that remind us of (perhaps even inspire) the projects we plan to work on. We want to see results and then explanations of those results.

I've put this book together in a way that matches the learning style of many programmers, game developers, and multimedia developers better than more conventionally organized texts.

What Tools Will You Need?

You will probably gain more from reading this book if you have version 8.5 of Macromedia Director. Optionally, you might enjoy following along with the references to 3D Studio Max, version 3.1 and Character Studio Version 1.2.

You will find it easier to work with the materials covered if you have Director 8.5 and a computer with hardware-accelerated 3D graphics, although this is not necessary.

PART I

The Dramatic Structure of Games

Investigate and understand the nature of games and their fundamental dramatic structures. Explore the limitations of these correlations to other dramatic forms and learn what makes games an alternative entertainment medium.

CHAPTER 1

The Story: How Much Is Too Much?

Understanding the nature of dramatic structures and stories will help you to create more exciting games. I don't mean to suggest that an electronic game is the same thing as a story. It isn't. It is not exactly like a play, or a film, or a nonelectronic game. It is an entertainment form in its own right. Although games are not mutant dramatic forms or alternative delivery vehicles for stories, they do take advantage of many of the traits, methods, and forms found in stories, plays, and films. They also take advantage of many of the traits of nonelectronic games.

After reading this chapter, you should

- Know the fundamental parts of a plot
- Know the principles of a challenge-reward system
- Know the kinds of games that use stories as vehicles
- Understand the limitations of stories in games
- Understand how to create conflict between the player and other parts of the game
- Understand how to make a game's story get more interesting over time
- Have brainstormed plots for several games
- Have evaluated proposed stories and fixed the snoozers
- Have written logical descriptions of events that might happen in the game

Getting Started

I'm going to kick things off with a discussion of the similarities and differences between games and dramatic narratives. This is hardly a new discussion. Hal Barwood and other game developers have been fueling an ongoing discussion/debate over the relationship between games and stories for many years now. You can take a cue from the recurring nature of the discussion that there must be some interrelation between games and narratives. I'm going to try to pin that relationship down a bit.

Although some common threads exist between games and dramatic narratives, there are some fundamental differences between the structure of stories and the structure of interactive narratives. In the first part of this chapter, "Getting a Grip on Narratives", I'll walk you through many of those differences.

Once you've seen the various methods of creating stories for games, you'll have a chance to brainstorm some game and story ideas of your own. I'll give you some helpful hints to avoid developing games that would bore even Al Gore, and I'll help you learn to identify those pitfalls before you go to the trouble of making the world's dullest game.

Now don't panic. I know that brainstorming game ideas threatens to be the sort of touchy-feely exercise that you've managed to avoid since your freshman Human Communication class. I promise not to get flaky on you. I'll give you some good strategies for preparation and some solid code for execution. Use the bits that you like, but give brainstorming a chance. You might find that it's a fairly painless way to plan—and planning almost always saves you money.

In the "Games That Make Stories Happen" section later in the chapter, we'll explore some methods of using simulated intelligence (code objects that try to find the best solution) to create a story-management system. I'll go over the ideas here and then show you some working examples in Part III of the book, "Putting Strategies into Action."

When I talk about games in this book, I'm generally talking about real-time 3D games. Even within that narrow group, there are several types of games. The one people usually associate with the medium is the first-person shooter. Games such as Quake have enjoyed some popularity, but I should point out that these are not the most popular game titles on the market today. Variations on the first-person shooter have generally involved adding a story and challenges or mystery to the basic premise (that you walk around and shoot everything that moves). There are many other sorts of real-time 3D games. I've painted with fairly broad strokes as I described these varied real-time 3D games; therefore, you will be able to apply many of the concepts discussed to most 3D games, regardless of the specific style they embrace.

One common thread that binds most 3D games together is that the increased and varied potential to move objects around in the game space often leads to a reduced ability to predict the actions of the player. Because we can't always control what the player does in our games, I'll talk about ways to make the game adapt to the choices the player makes. Even though our game will adapt and change, we'll give it (the intelligent agent that controls the story within the game) some skills so that it can fight to inject the coolest parts of the narrative back into the game. I'll walk you through some necessary steps in breaking an idea down into something that you can turn into a game, and you'll get to write that idea in a way that will lead you one step closer to making your dream game a reality.

Getting a Grip on Narratives

Stories are about conflict, and games are about conflict. This similarity is one of the elements people point to when they are trying to convince you that games are stories. However, if you've seen many games, you've probably noticed that there is something a little screwy about this notion.

In some ways the differences created by the interactivity in electronic entertainment and the carefully crafted escalation of tension found in good stories seem mutually exclusive rather than analogous. Game addicts will tell you that a game may have an awesome story, but that doesn't mean it will work as interactive entertainment. Likewise, interactive entertainment can be very engaging without really offering the audience any sort of narrative.

Thinking about games and stories as the same thing doesn't work. Thinking about them as opposites, where one prevents the other, doesn't work. So what does work? It is far better to think of these two elements as complementary ingredients of the game. They are independent features, each of which brings something desirable and engaging to the entertainment experience (see Figure 1.1). It is important that developers recognize and respect the relationship between these elements.

FIGURE 1.1

The interactive elements and narrative of any electronic game may be visualized as complementary ingredients rather than mutually exclusive components.

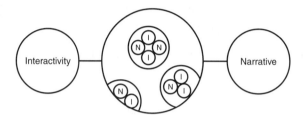

In order to write and design stories for games, you will need to learn all you can about dramatizing conflict and throw out some basic assumptions you may already have about stories. The really difficult pattern to discard in the transition from traditional narratives to game narratives is the paradigm introduced by your sixth grade English teacher. You remember when she drew Freytag's pyramid, that funny mountain shape, on the chalkboard and said, "Now here is the exposition, followed by rising action and then a climax…" (see Figure 1.2). At this point, you started giggling and stopped paying attention. Your teacher was reinforcing a literary tradition that pushes a very specific Western-European/American plot onto virtually every story you've ever read or movie you've ever seen.

FIGURE 1.2

A typical linear analysis of a plot diagram, which you may well remember from your youth.

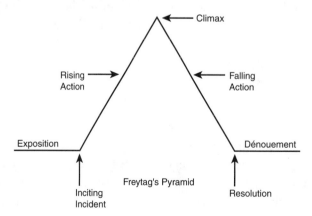

It's so deeply stuck inside the heads of most Americans (thanks to television) that thinking of stories that don't adhere to these rules can be a very taxing experience. To write stories that will work with games, you're going to have to figure out either how to disregard your old teacher's lesson or how to convince your audience that they really don't want to play a game that allows them to choose what happens next.

The assumption that events must happen in a predetermined order, and that these events feed into an overall structure with crisis, climax, and so on is often difficult for citizens of Western cultures to abandon. Let it go. Loosen up. You don't need tightly constricted structures to experience conflict. Great games tell great stories regardless of the choices the player makes. They are epic journeys and eventful adventures. They cannot be created in the way one might craft a play or a screenplay because interactivity rapidly renders the planned plot either irrelevant or at least substantially less relevant.

If the player gets to choose the next course of action, then either you have to predict and provide media and solutions for an exponentially widening tree of branched narrative structure, as shown in Figure 1.3, or you need to abandon some of the traditions of narrative structure you learned back in sixth grade. (It's okay; you never really liked sixth grade anyway.)

The problem with branching narratives is bipartite. The developer has to produce an exponentially increasing amount of media in order to accommodate each successive branch, and the player has an ever-narrowing field of choices because each choice that the player makes eliminates an ever-widening number of possible actions.

You cannot predict the order of events in your games unless you are going to remove nearly all the interactive choices from the people who play them. If the game is going to happen in 3D space, the problem becomes even more immediately apparent. Consider any 3D role-playing game. The characters will move wherever the player directs them. Preplanned structure is immediately thrown out the window. Or is it? Certainly we are no longer authors of the narrative structure in the manner that we would be if we were writing a screenplay or a short story.

FIGURE 1.3

Branching narratives quickly grow too complex and costly.

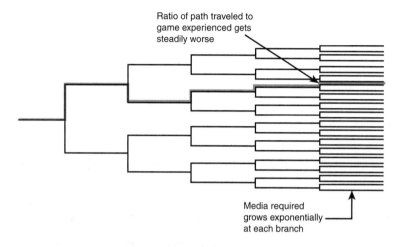

Ratio of path traveled to
game experienced gets
steadily worse

Media required
grows exponentially
at each branch

The Branching Narratives Model

In a typical electronic game, branching narratives are used to enable the user
to make choices at predetermined junctions within the game. The inherent
problem with this method is that the user's choices are very limited and
ultimately the solutions to puzzles are limited as well. When the audience sees
that these are in fact rather limited branches that they are able to follow, the
puzzle becomes a linear maze rather than a genuinely interactive simulation.

Even a fairly simple example using this branching option demonstrates how
goofy this model can be. Imagine, for example, a game that simulates life as a
teenager. We'll assume that the primary goal of our game's lead character is to
persuade his mom to let him go out for the evening (see Figure 1.4).

Working within this branching paradigm, the player might be given three
optional phrases to "speak" to the virtual mother in order to con his way out
of the kitchen. Mom will fall for one line, half-fall for another, and reject the
third. The average player will likely try all three at some point.

Suppose, however, that the player's instinctive choice is to escape by climbing
through the window rather than talking to mom. The programmers, having
failed to consider this option, will not have included the consequences of this
option, and the game could easily break. Certainly the result would not be
graceful. Considering every conceivable strategy may well prove impossible.

FIGURE 1.4

The limitations of the branching narrative can sometimes even seem idiotic.

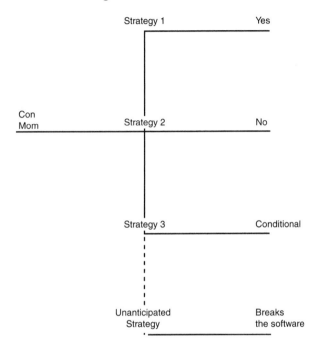

Programming special responses for every imaginable solution is a time-intensive and ultimately futile effort. In short, the game will be really hard to make, and really dull to play. A huge time investment and a minimal appeal do not make up a formula for successful game development.

The Object-Oriented Model

In our simple game example, each point of conflict resolution is a junction with several branches dictating the available options. You could approach each such point from a different angle. You could see points of conflict resolution as infinitely solvable if you were able to create the response to a proposed solution on-the-fly. If you can adapt to any action the user chooses, you don't design and create static media to respond to the player's choices—you program the computer to create responses dynamically.

This approach imbues the environment with certain simulated physical, spiritual, and psychological properties, and it lends intelligence to the simulated characters that encounter those environments. To put it simply, in the branching model, the developer has to work really hard to create a few moments of game play. The branching content will be the same every time you walk down those paths. The object-oriented model is ultimately less time consuming to make and offers the player a virtually unlimited number of choices. It can be designed so that gameplay is never the same, even if the player makes the same choices.

There is a continuum between stories and interactivity. Interactivity is at one end of the continuum and structured narrative is at the other end. It may be visualized as two glasses of water that must share a single volume of fluid. You cannot have more in one glass without sacrificing some from the other (see Figure 1.5). The ironic part is that the players will bring narrative structure to the game even when none is present. That's right. They'll supply the story structure, as long as there are well-developed environments, plausible interesting characters, and complex, engaging conflicts.

FIGURE 1.5

The continuum between narratives and interactivity.

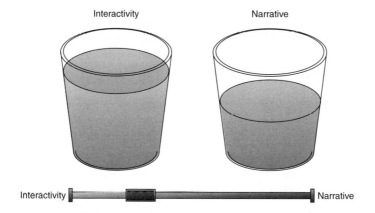

In Part III of this book, I'll walk you through the creation of a 3D computer role-playing game called *17 Keys*. Although you will see the specific strategies involved in programming and media creation for *17 Keys* in a later chapter, it will help at this point to begin discussing the game as an example of the object-oriented model of game construction.

Because the code objects that create the game are independent of any linear organizational structure, each of the objects is able to communicate directly with any other object. This makes the structure of the game nonlinear (see Figure 1.6).

FIGURE 1.6

A narrative-management object decides dynamically whether a proposed solution to a given puzzle is acceptable.

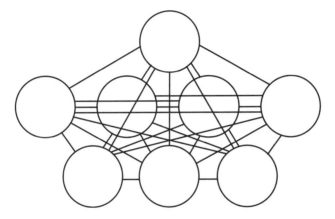

There is a path from every
object to every other object.

Introducing *17 Keys*

As *17 Keys* begins, players are dropped into the world with no information about where they are or what they should do. The fact is, there's a tremendous amount to be said for letting players discover what is going on in a game, and it reduces the need for rambling and stupid instruction screens.

Soon logical players find themselves investigating the world. They immediately identify the fact that each of them has control over one of the characters, and the players are able to learn things about their characters by the way they look, move, and sound. The players also make some assumptions: "We must be looking for something," or "We are supposed to discover or defeat something." "Can we shoot?" they ask themselves—because everyone likes to shoot things. No, they determine. The players roam around a bit and notice a large stone near the center of what they feel fairly certain is an island. They tinker with it a bit, but it doesn't seem to do anything at this point.

The players could just as easily not find the stone at this point. If they do, they'll see the intricate carvings of spinning kaleidocycles and dragon wings, but they might just as easily be off investigating the inside of one of the caves.

The players build and design the narrative. They determine how the game/level will end. In general, the more open ended you can make your games, the better off you will be in terms of the immersion enabled by the interaction of the players.

Adding Conflict

All good stories have conflict. Conflict, like it or not, is a type of violence, and violence is the invasion of another person's (or character's) personal space. It may be physical, intellectual, or psychological. We'll create conflict for the characters in *17 Keys* by establishing rules that govern personal space in each of these categories. We'll examine the degree of violation as well as the timing of the incident and the goals of each character in order to determine how the characters should react to such conflict.

Invasion of another character's or object's space can be evaluated in terms of the severity of the violation, the goals of the characters, the level of tension desired at this moment in the game, and the type of violation (see Figure 1.7.)

FIGURE 1.7

Each of the criteria for evaluation filters the stimulus event in order to narrow the potential reactions.

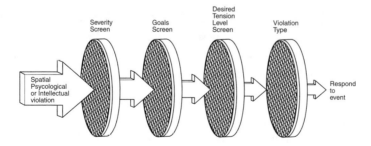

So our story will have interesting, intelligent characters, rich unusual environments, and variable degrees of conflict—physical, intellectual, and psychological. But a good game has one more critical ingredient: It is fun to experience. This is, in fact, the single most important element to any game. Fun comes from each of these areas in a game, but it is also intrinsic to the game's challenge-reward system.

The Challenge-Reward System

When we overcome a conflict in a game, we are rewarded. At its most basic level, this reward is internal. We are gratified that we have resolved the conflict. In many cases, that reward is reinforced, with external rewards. You may be able to use the money you gather to purchase items in the local town.

You might find that the characters you have cooperated with during gameplay reward you with amulets, magic charms, or helpful information. Your efforts might be rewarded with celebratory whistles, bells, chirps, and fanfares. Any of these elements can contribute to the enjoyment people feel while playing a game. However, having them in your game does not guarantee that it will be fun, but this does provide a good base on which you may build.

A lot of people will pretend that they can define fun within computer games for you. I don't buy it. Games are the result of acts of creation. Although certain methods have worked in the past, copying those techniques does not guarantee your game will be fun to play. In fact, it is often no fun at all to play a game that is a poor copy of a previously established one.

I think that the best advice is to play lots of games, not just computer games. Read lots of books, not just computer manuals. See lots of plays, movies, and good television. Live. Ask why of everyone and everything. Don't be afraid to fail. If you have joy, and enjoy creating games, the games you craft are a lot more likely to be fun.

Along those lines, don't be too quick to accept criticism. Some people won't like your game. They'll complain about how it's this or isn't that on public listserves, and you'll feel frustrated and unappreciated. People are all different. There is no reasonable way that everyone could be expected to like the same sorts of games. Write your games for yourself. I'm a firm believer that compromise breeds mediocrity. If you try to please everyone, you'll end up with a very dull game.

Brainstorming a Story

I look to all sorts of places for inspiration for my stories and games. The only place I try not to look is to other games. I think that other games are a great resource, and I'm certainly not suggesting that you should stop looking at games once you decide to design them. I am saying that there is not really much substance required for simply copying or cloning games someone else has already created. Besides the obvious legal implications of cloning, I think that it dulls your imagination. So my best advice for finding inspiration for your games is to go out and live a little.

If you are interested in a topic, chances are that someone else is interested in the same topic. It doesn't matter what the topic is—you can always use it as a leaping-off point for a game. Later, we'll run ideas such as this through a series of tests in order to see whether they have some of the fundamental qualities that are needed for a game. For now, just write down ideas, places, characters, and situations as they pop into your head.

The Idea Web

Once I've collected some ideas, I like to start creating an idea web. I don't think in a very linear pattern, so outlines and I don't get along very well. Linear thinking generally leads to limited thinking and very limited software programming. To create associatively organized tools and toys, it helps to have an associatively arranged brain. So for those of you who have never created an idea web (or story web), take a glance at Figure 1.8, which shows a brainstorming session that I had for *17 Keys*.

In Figure 1.8, I'm freely associating the fundamental game concepts with whatever ideas pop into my head. It gives me a way to explore as many variations of the story as I want and then I'm free to pick and choose the ideas that I think will make the most engaging game.

Aside from providing a peek into the bizarre manner in which my brain works, the figure can give you some sense of the way that ideas feather together when you are first imagining a game space. In this case, I started with a distinct image of a man and a dragon in a forest. I didn't know much of anything about the man or the dragon at that point, and that is perfectly fine. You can tell that I started with them because they are basically in the center of the web. I usually begin in the center of the page and then work outward. Arrows are used to indicate that one thought is related to another.

FIGURE 1.8

This brainstorming image was created in order to evolve the basic ideas for 17 Keys.

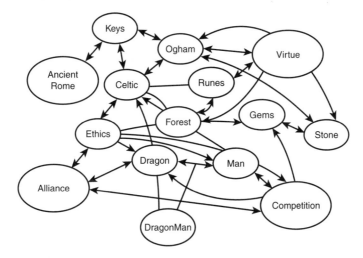

As I reviewed the idea web I realized that, although very romantic, a man and a dragon wandering through the forest is not going to make for very interesting or engaging characters.

Conflicts and Complications

The next step was to ask some questions. What does the man want? What does the dragon want? How are these wants in conflict with each other's needs? Why this forest? Why do the events of this game happen now as opposed to any other time?

Answering these questions provided me with a clearer vision of a story that might have the qualities to make a good game. There will be conflict if the man and the dragon are competing to get to the resources on the island.

Although the purpose of the brainstorming is primarily to generate new ideas, it is really important to think from the starting gate forward about the potential for conflict within those ideas. Most of the time when an idea is falling flat, it is because it didn't have much conflict to begin with. Run each of your ideas through this simple test:

   1. Is the idea exaggerated enough to be more engaging than a walk to the grocery store?

2. Is the idea full of enough conflict and enough potential for complication to give the player a good long game?

3. Do I care about the characters?

If your answer to any of these questions is negative, then your audience will probably not enjoy your game. In Figure 1.9, I've taken the diagram a bit further and asked myself a few more of these questions. I'm searching for conflict and trying to add a few more filters to the mix. Eventually I'll put this all down in neatly organized specs, but at this point I don't want to miss opportunities or shut down my imagination too early.

FIGURE 1.9

The conflict-centered brainstorming document demonstrates the creation of a web of associated ideas.

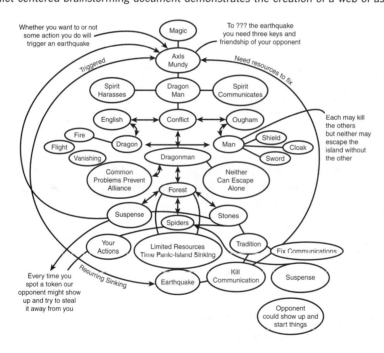

The next phase for me usually involves a little sketching, a little story writing, and a little fantasizing (see Figure 1.10). If you can imagine gameplay in your head, you can be pretty certain that you are headed in the right direction.

FIGURE 1.10

A sketch for 17 Keys.

Exercise 1.1:   Brainstorming Stories for Games

Now that you have a better idea of how I brainstorm the story for a game, try to brainstorm a game of your own. I've prepared a series of questions that should help you get underway. Just answer each question by adding as many elements to your diagram of the story web as you can imagine:

- Who is this game about? (This is usually the character that the player will find himself or herself representing.)

- What does this character want?

- What is stopping this character from getting what he wants?

- List a bunch of steps the character will have to take in order to get what he is after.

- For each step, list some things that could prevent the character from getting the stuff he is after.

- For each thing that prevents the character from getting what he is after, list ways that the same problem could also impede other steps.

- Is there anything about the character's struggle that your audience will relate to?

- Is the struggle exaggerated enough to make it more engaging than simply going back to work at the quickie-mart?

- Where is this story happening?

- Is the location conducive to action?

You should now have a diagram that looks a bit like Figure 1.8 or Figure 1.9, but with your own ideas, characters, and setting. In the next section, we'll look at each of the major elements of a real-time 3D game and separate the dull game ideas from the winners.

Stripping Away the Snoozers

There are many ways to bore your audience to tears. I'm going to describe a few of the more obvious methods in the hope that you'll use this knowledge for good and not for evil. There are plenty of dull games in the world already.

If I don't care about the characters or situations in a game I play, I'll get bored. First-person shooters are a great example of this. Sure, we all like to blow things up for a while. Heck, we even enjoy the challenge of blowing things up in new and interesting ways. Unfortunately, a good old-fashioned killing spree is really not sufficient to entertain most intelligent audiences for more than a couple of hours.

Shooters, jumpers, leapers, duckers, racers, or roamers are all dull without something else to keep our attention. What is the point of wandering around a landscape? Even if there are tokens to acquire, without specific goals, there is really very little to hold a user's attention. It doesn't really matter what the nature of the game is, if there is not some sort of substance, players will grow tired of overcoming obstacles and eventually stop playing—not because they are ready to move on to a more pressing activity or because they have won the game on some level, but because they are bored.

If the puzzles in the game are too difficult to understand or decipher (see Figure 1.11), the player will lose interest and abandon the game. It is important to remember that puzzles should scale their difficulty to match the amount of gameplay experience the player has had with the game.

FIGURE 1.11

A game with a puzzle that is absurdly difficult. The puzzle asks the player to decipher a message based solely on complex icons. Perhaps cryptographers would be amused, but most of us would just be frustrated.

This brings to mind a variation on boredom. The finger-twitch game (one that requires rapid manipulation of the interface through keyboard or joystick input) can become a genuine source of boredom if there isn't enough to the story to keep the audience engaged. Several games use an ever-escalating difficulty scheme to increase tension over the course of the game. This is good practice as long as something of interest is evolving in the story line as well. Conversely, if the game is simply a self-escalating series of finger exercises, the game will ultimately be less than perfectly satisfying.

Clearly, by these standards, a lot of well-paid and successful game designers have unleashed some seriously bad games on the rest of us. How on earth can we prevent these paralyzing mistakes in our own work? The best way to avoid boring your public to tears is to put your game ideas through the ringer.

Exercise 1.2:   Putting Your Ideas Through the Ringer

At every step of the process, treat your game like it is someone else's idea. Imagine that it is not just the idea of a colleague or stranger, but the work of your mortal enemy. Wish with all your might to find the flaws in this game plan. You'll find them, because your enemy is a dufus. Now write that sorry sad sack a scathing memo that lists every single one of his or her game's flaws and advises the right way to handle the problems. After all, you want your boss to know how much smarter you are than the moron who came up with this lame-brained game idea.

Figure 1.12 shows the principle elements you will want to check in your game ideas.

FIGURE 1.12

A diagram of the basic filters. Ask yourself about each of these elements.

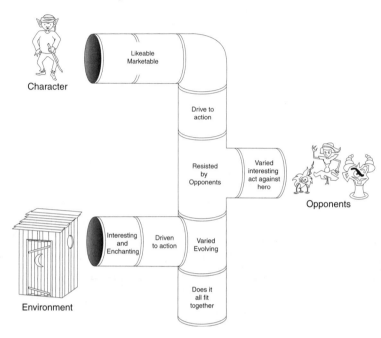

Start with the basics. Here's a checklist to help you evaluate your game idea:

- Is the central character likeable, marketable, and driven to action by nearly impossible-to-achieve objectives? If not, how could that character be changed in order to reach this level?

- Are the main character's opponents varied, strong, and driven to actions that work directly against the goals of your main character? If not, how should they be modified to meet these standards?

- Is the environment interesting, engaging, and conducive to action? Is there enough variety to the environment to keep players' attention through several stages of gameplay? Does it evolve or progress? Does it echo the messages found in the story? If it does not, how might you change it so that it does?

If your story makes it this far, you are ready to tease it with some even tougher standards:

- Will there be a market for this game? Who is likely to buy it or download it online? Are there ways you can make the existing story more marketable without changing the basic composition?

- Is the game too complex to complete given your time and your budget? Are you implementing more than one new complex feature? Adding a bunch of innovative features to your game can make you top dog for a day or two, but is it going to cost you in every other area of your game? No one will care whether your game has the greatest new feature in the world if there is nothing to challenge the player once the game has started.

- Are you capable of producing or procuring the media for the game? Do you have enough personnel to complete the project in the timeframe you are envisioning?

Made it through all of these? Then you are likely ready to move on. If not, keep revising your diagram until you think the story idea for your game is able to withstand the torrent of criticism. Be hard on yourself. It is much easier to make changes at this stage than it will be at any other stage along the way.

Games That Make Stories Happen

It is possible to craft games that create stories dynamically rather than rely on a preplanned plot. The trick is that you need to understand the foundational principles of a plot and take advantage of the properties of a plot to plant narrative potential.

A plot is essentially a staircase of events that generate escalating, unresolved tension (see Figure 1.13). Let's break that down. A plot has many events. The events happen over time. Each event is more tense than the previous one. The tension is usually left unresolved. The tension may be resolved, but if it is, it should either be the end of the story or replaced immediately by a new, even bigger problem.

FIGURE 1.13

A plot is a staircase of unresolved or partially resolved events creating escalating tension.

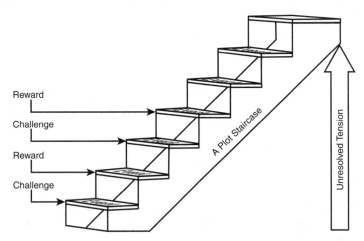

If we think about this model logically, we could say that there is *stasis* (a time when everything is working in balance). Stasis is interrupted by an event (often called an *inciting incident*) that sets things in motion (see Figure 1.14). This event irritates the player or intelligent agent (the character inside the game that responds with behaviorally driven actions to any stimulus). The response of either intelligence is to try different strategies to remove the stimulus. In a drama, the process of attempting to remove the stimulus triggers new events that in turn cause new stimuli that in turn cause irritation.

Just as the force of a rock falling into a still pond is eventually depleted, the force of the inciting stimulus eventually loses power unless a steady stream of additional stimuli feeds it. These additional interruptions are called *complications*.

One of the most reputable authorities on dramatic structure and playwriting, Sam Smiley, uses this model to analyze plays. Both Smiley and I are referencing the model created by behavioral psychologist Edwin Guthrie. We'll talk more about Guthrie's psychological theory of motivation as it relates to the actions of characters in the next chapter.

Another way to look at the escalating nature of plot is to use the simplified expression "somebody wants _____ but _____ so _____." Just fill in the blanks with appropriate goals and obstacles and repeat as needed. For example "Joe wants wealth but Harry has all the money in the land so Joe attacks

Harry's Castle." In electronic games, the *somebody* is generally the player. Sometimes the player is motivated to want something for a higher purpose; regardless, he or she is usually the one actively pursuing the goal.

FIGURE 1.14

Stimulus interrupts stasis. The object attempts to restore stasis and triggers more events, more stimuli, and more interruptions in stasis.

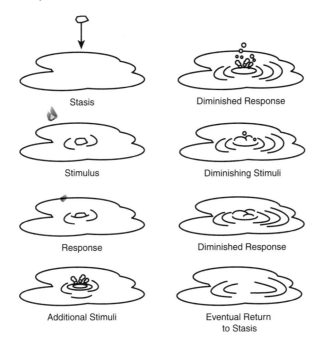

Stasis	Diminished Response
Stimulus	Diminishing Stimuli
Response	Diminished Response
Additional Stimuli	Eventual Return to Stasis

The *wants* part of the expression is a manifestation of the desire to return to stasis, which is sometimes hard to see. Consider Joe's dilemma. He wants money. On the surface, this may seem like it defies the "return to stasis" theory, but you should realize that Joe's goal (to get money) is really an abstraction of a more fundamental goal: Joe wants money so that he can buy food and shelter. The need for food and shelter are internal stimuli that are nagging at Joe and disrupting his stasis. He is hungry and cold. To remove the stimuli of cold and hunger, Joe decides to get money.

The *wants* and the *but* of a character go hand in hand. If there were no obstacle (*but*) for the character, he'd already have whatever it was he wanted and we could call it a day. The obstacle is the source of the conflict for him.

The last element in the expression is the *so* (the outcome). This is the resulting action attempted by the primary character. You might express a plot as follows: "Gerald wants a drink but he has no clean glasses so he goes to the sink to wash one, but the water is green so he grabs a bottle of milk out of the refrigerator and takes a big swig right out of the bottle, but the milk has soured." Repeat and escalate as needed.

The formula is nearly identical for a game. The player wants to save the princess, slay the dragon, or win the race. Unfortunately, there are obstacles of every imaginable sort in the path of the player. Sometimes these are literal obstacles, physical puzzles that must be solved. They may also be psychological obstacles or intellectual challenges; the goals of the players may change as they evolve a more sophisticated understanding of their situation. It doesn't really matter what the obstacles are or how they manifest themselves in the game. It only matters that the players may overcome them.

This is what led to the challenge-reward model you see in so many games today. Give the player a small obstacle to overcome. Once the player succeeds, give him a small reward. Ideally, the reward assists the player in overcoming the next challenge. Before the player has had a chance to revel in his success, present the next challenge. Challenge and reward is simply another way of expressing the concept of a plot as escalating, unresolved tension.

We cannot force the user to follow a preplanned story line. However, we can plant things that will cause escalating tension in our games. To do this, we need to know the following:

1. How much tension the player is currently experiencing
2. Which resolution strategies have already been attempted
3. How much to increase the tension each cycle
4. When to allow the player to resolve the ultimate conflict

Half of the work of making games that incorporate stories is making widgets that cause escalating tension. The other half of the puzzle is planting expositional information within those events that is logically driven by the events.

If I start a play or screenplay with a monologue voiceover, you can be relatively certain that I have serious exposition problems in my writing. Any time that you deliver exposition (the stuff game designers call *backstory*) as unmotivated information, you risk losing your audience's interest.

Players don't want to read about the traditions of battle between the ancient interplanetary races that led up to the moment of the game—they want to play the game. Teach them about the traditions of battle, the history of cruelty, and the expectations of their character's people by setting forth some task that reveals information about the gamescape via the conflict. If this information comes as part of the game's action, players will view it as an integral part of the story, but if exposition comes in a canned cinematic interlude or text-only backstory, they'll give up on the game before they get started.

Integrated exposition is designed into the game in every challenge and in every reward. In Chapter 3, "Managing Your Story On-the-Fly," I'll walk you through some Lingo that actually implements these concepts in the creation of a narrative-management system. These fundamental concepts provide the basis for the narrative manager.

Leaving the Decision in the Player's Hands

The important thing to note about the narrative-management model is that at no point do we take the decisions out of the hands of the player. We encourage conflicts of a given intensity at appropriate moments during gameplay, but we don't ever limit the choices that the player may make. The goal of this model is to provide solid and challenging obstacles to the player regardless of the direction that the player travels or the goals the player pursues.

You accomplish this by making the entire model out of independent, interrelated objects rather than chronologically dependent events. In the theater, this structure is called *episodic*. Ironically, it is the typical mode of presentation for epic stories and romantic legends.

To create an episode, you need an obstacle and a player willing to try to overcome that obstacle. You cannot force players to work against a given obstacle, but you can help guide them toward the obstacles that are the most appropriate for their entertainment experience at any time within the game.

If everything is working well, players will want to overcome the obstacles that we present and, upon doing so, will be rewarded with a combination of genuine rewards, personal satisfaction, and a new set of obstacles.

You sacrifice control in this model. However, you gain flexibility and minimize the amount of specific media that must be created. You add some peculiar new rules that suggest that any dialog or exposition must not rely on the other episodes.

This narrative-management model is oriented around conflict events and conflict-resolution strategies as objects. Each conflict event is an object, and every attempted resolution is generated by an intelligent agent (also an object) or the player.

The conflict event object checks the attempted action for specific property values and commands and then submits a recommended course of action to the narrative-management object. That object compares its memory of the player's previous actions to the table defining appropriate reactions created by the game developer. It then approves, denies, or modifies the action. I'll expand on this model and give you some examples that implement these concepts in Chapter 3.

Close Enough to Care About

It is important to keep in mind that Shockwave 3D is Macromedia's multi-purpose solution for Web delivery of real-time 3D graphics. It is not meant to compete with the Quake or Unreal engines. It is a multiplatform, flexible, all-purpose 3D-delivery system. It will never run as fast as a comparable 3D engine that is compiled in C. As a result, optimization is the lifeblood of the Director 3D game programmer. We must optimize everything we do.

One of the single most important things that we can do to optimize our game engines is to remember one central rule when planning the conflict events for our games: It only matters if it's close enough to matter. Lingo is fast. It is really, really fast. I have seldom written a handler that even came close to slowing down the system via calculations. Drawing things in 3D space is slow. The more things you draw, the slower the frame will animate. If you draw too much stuff, your animation will play too slowly, and people will not enjoy your sluggish game. The moral of this story is that it is almost always better to simply calculate something than it is to calculate and draw that thing.

It is nearly always better to have a less realistic image than to have choppy, erratic animation. Therefore, there are several ways to reduce the quality of the image, limit the number of models that are drawn, and reduce the complexity of the images rendered. As you begin thinking about what needs to happen in your game, you should keep your mind focused on simplification, especially in regard to the reduction of events to the immediate sphere of influence of the player.

NOTE

> The concept of *spheres of influence* comes largely from the work of Will Wright on *The Sims*. It is a modified form of world cognizance, making the objects aware, in a sense, of their surroundings. This is not artificial intelligence. It is simulated intelligence. That's why I use the phrase *intelligent agents* to describe the AI objects in the various projects.

For example, the `sphereOfInf.dir` file on the accompanying CD-ROM contains a forest of trees. In its original form, each tree is 68 polygons. There may be up to 10,000 trees in the forest, but if there are that many trees, most machines will balk under the weight of all those polygons. Think about it: 10,000 trees would be built from 680,000 polygons. There aren't many desktop computers that can handle drawing more than half of a million polygons at once.

Let's say that there are only 100 trees created when the movie is started. That would cost us 6,800 polygons. This is not an unreasonable request for most of today's computers. We could further optimize the trees by pasting cutout images of trees onto two polygon planes, but this looks really cheesy. There is a low end to optimization. I like to think of it as the "what's the point?" place. If I look at a proposed solution and it is clear that virtually all the work could be done using two-dimensional graphics, I know that I've gone too far. I'll talk more about optimizing polygons in our models in Chapter 8, "Low Polygon Modeling and Third-Party Exporters."

Drawing 3D images isn't the only performance killer. Modifiers will generally slow down performance. This effect is almost imperceptible if only a handful of models are using modifiers. However, the effect is painfully obvious if you apply a modifier to large numbers of models.

If you were to add collision modifiers to every tree in the forest and the giant ball that rolls through the forest, playback would slow down dramatically.

If we were able to sense when a collision modifier were actually necessary, we'd save ourselves thousands of calculations per frame. The animation would be much smoother and play much better on slower machines.

Example: Spheres of Influence

This checking only what's around us is the foundational principle behind the sphere of influence. A *sphere of influence* is the volume surrounding a game entity. In Figure 1.15 the dragon and the man from *17 Keys* are illustrated with visual representations of these spheres of influence. These spheres are actually virtual objects, but visualizing them in this manner can aid in understanding the way in which they work. You create a virtual sphere around the object by checking for intersection with other nearby objects before they actually move close enough to cause us any trouble, and we enhance the properties and modifiers of objects as they get close enough to care about.

FIGURE 1.15

A visualization of spheres of influence interpenetrating for multiple objects in 3D space.

On the CD-ROM you'll find a file called sphereOfInf.dir associated with this chapter. Open this movie now and click the Play button in Director. Think of it as forest pinball if you like. I haven't given you any control over this ball, so sit back and watch. The camera is set up to follow the ball's movements, as are some lights. The forest is created at random, so if your ball escapes the forest without bouncing, just click rewind and play again.

The point here is not to make the forest into a glorified pinball set, but to demonstrate how much optimization can be accomplished and how to dynamically adjust the properties of individual models based on their spheres of influence.

Imagine that you are standing inside that forest. Imagine that you are the ball. You'll need to be able to see where the trees are if you are to aim for them or to avoid them. There are several ways to accomplish this, but we want to do it in a way that uses as little CPU power as possible.

Now the time-consuming, processor-intensive way to do this would be to check the distance between yourself and every tree—or worse yet, to have every tree check all the items around it and see whether you are within a given distance.

That's not what you'd do in real life. You'd look around and approximate your distance from the trees that you see are close to you. If you can't see a tree, it must not be close enough to matter. If a tree is too far away, by definition it is not close enough to matter.

The most efficient way to do this would be to ask Director politely for a list of the models that the camera is displaying right now and then use a camera as a sort of virtual vision. Unfortunately, this feature is not yet available, but there is a close approximation.

TIP

Using many `modelsUnderRay()` calls when there are a lot of objects in the scene can substantially slow down your performance. Remove extraneous models from the scene before casting any rays in order to maximize playback speeds.

We'll use a function called `modelsUnderRay()` to broadcast a beam in any given direction until it runs into something. Then we'll look at how far away that something is, and if it is close enough to matter, we'll add it to the things we plan to tinker with.

NOTE

If you don't speak Lingo yet, this may be a bit heavy for your first encounter. There are several great resources online that can help you gain a greater understanding of Lingo. Consult Appendix C, "Online Resources," for a list.

Take a look at the first few lines of code for a typical ray casting:

```
m = member(1).model("GeoSphere01")
-- member(1) is the member that contains the 3D world.
wp = m.getWorldTransform().Position
-- world relative coordinate position of the model
md = vector(1, 0, 0) — model-relative direction forward.
```

```
wd = ( m.getWorldTransform() * md ) - wp
-- world relative direction vector (the direction to cast the ray.)
ttCollisions = member(1).ModelsUnderRay(wp, wd, 1, #detailed)
-- cast the ray and store the resulting list in the variable ttCollisions
```

NOTE

Part II of this book, "Building Blocks of Shockwave 3D Games" explains the basic methods and properties that are used in 3D Lingo. I have included some examples in this section in order to introduce you to broader concepts. If you are struggling to follow the code, you may find it helpful to read the overview of Director 3D in Chapter 5, "An Introduction to Director 3D," before moving on.

The first line creates a variable, m, which will serve as a quick reference to the ball model. We're going to shoot that little ray out from somewhere after all, and the center of our ball is a perfectly sensible place to begin.

Line 3 of this algorithm asks Director to give us the world-relative position of the model. Later, we will use this vector to calculate the position offset of the ball from the center of the world. We put the value into the variable named wp (for world position).

Line 5 simply places the direction we want to cast the ray, relative to the model, into a variable called md (model direction). Remember that each object in 3D space has its own transform and with it, its own orientation. Envision a car on a racetrack. If the racetrack is your world, you could easily gain an understanding of which direction is north and which is south.

If a car were heading north, the front of the car and north would both be aligned, but as soon as the car began to turn to the left, the car would be heading northwest. This wouldn't change the fact that the car is going forward. Forward is relative to the car, whereas the geographic directions are relative to the world. In our case, the front of the ball is facing the positive x-axis. Therefore, the direction vector (vector(1,0,0)) represents model-relative forward.

Now we're ready for a little math magic. If you multiply a model's world-relative transform by a model-relative direction vector and then subtract the world.position offset, you will get a new direction vector that contains the world-relative direction vector pointing the same way.

We first gathered the world-relative position of the model. In our sample movie, this begins at vector(1374.3325,-1219.2494,99.6645). Next, we multiply the transform of the ball by the direction vector representing the direction that we want to go and subtract the offset (the world position of the ball). That step looks like this:

```
wd = (member(1).model[2].getWorldTransform() * vector(1,0,0))\
  - vector(1374.3325,-1219.2494,99.6645)
```

Depending on the rotation of the ball, wd will be set to a world-relative direction vector that is equal to the model-relative direction vector.

NOTE

When you put vectors in Director, you will often see strange numbers, such as vector (1.37433e3, -1.21925e3, 99.6645). These numbers have been converted to scientific notation, and the system hasn't retranslated them to standard floating-point numbers. The e is used to represent the number of spaces that the number's decimal point has been moved. The preceding vector is actually vector(1374.33, -1219.25, 99.6645). In this form of scientific notation, the e followed by a number represents 10 to the power of the number following the e.

The last line of code casts the ray and loads the results of the call into the variable ttCollisions. The modelsUnderRay() function expects four arguments. The first argument is the world-relative position from which the ray will be broadcast. The second argument is the world-relative direction of the beam. The third argument is the number of models you want to know about. The function will return information about as many models that are in its path, up to this number. The final argument allows you to specify whether you want #simple or #detailed information returned.

Now the variable ttcollisions contains the resulting list. If the ray encounters a model, the returned list may look something like this:

```
 put ttCollisions
[[#model: model("GeoSphere01"), \
#distance: 31.2539, \
#isectPosition: vector( 1.40079e3, -1.21925e3, 44.7773 ), \
#isectNormal: vector( 0.4773, -0.3560, 0.8034 ), \
#meshID: 1, \
#faceID: 3, \
```

```
#vertices: [vector( 1.37502e3, -1.21925e3, 60.0819 ), \
vector( 1.39654e3, -1.28312e3, 18.9962 ), \
vector( 1.44283e3, -1.21925e3, 19.8040 )], \
#uvCoord: [#u: 0.0000, #v: 0.3800]], \
[#model: model("Plane01"), \
#distance: 1314.2787, \
#isectPosition: vector( 118.5371, -1.21924e3, 0.0000 ), \
#isectNormal: vector( 0.0000, 0.0000, 1.0000 ), \
#meshID: 1, \
#faceID: 2, \
#vertices: [vector( -4.78142e4, 4.80957e4, 0.0000 ), \
vector( -4.78142e4, -5.18926e4, 0.0000 ), \
vector( 5.21741e4, 4.80957e4, 0.0000 )], \
#uvCoord: [#u: 0.4932, #v: 0.4794]]]
```

If you break this down, it's pretty simple. The main list describes the two models that the ray intersected with. The first is the ball itself, GeoSphere01. The second is the ground, Plane01. For each model, #distance is the number of units between the origin of the ray and the point of intersection on the surface of the model. The #isectPosition property is a vector defining the point of intersection in world-relative terms.

The #isectNormal property is a direction vector describing the direction that the intersected face's normal is facing. The #meshID property tells you which mesh within the model was hit, and the #faceID property tells you which face on that mesh. The #vertices property lists the world position of each vertex that comprises the face that was intersected by the ray. The last property, uvCoord, lists the u and v position where the ray hit the texture on the face.

This ray-vision technique will make us very efficient, but it still doesn't quite handle everything we need handled. Therefore, we'll want to create a more robust version of this handler. We'll add some detail to the modelsUnderRay() function by making a new global handler called castRay().

We want our new handler to take in all the information necessary to cast a ray from a given point in a given direction. We know that we're always going to use model-relative directions for our castRay() function, so the first argument we need to feed it is the model-relative direction vector of the ray. Consider this handler:

```
-- This handler simplifies the process of casting the ray
-- it accepts the model relative direction vector

on castRay(whichWorld, whichDirection, whichModel, howMany, detail)
```

```
   m = whichModel
   wp = m.getWorldTransform().position
   md = whichDirection — model-relative direction forward.
   wd = ( m.getWorldTransform() * md ) - wp
   tCollisions = whichWorld.ModelsUnderRay(wp, wd, howMany, detail)
   return tCollisions
end
```

The new handler also needs a reference to the model from which we will cast the ray. Just like the modelsUnderRay() function, we need to say how many models we care to know about (two is a good number in most cases) and how detailed we'd like the information returned to be.

To use the new function, we just call castRay(vector(1,0,0), w.model[2], 2, #detailed). If you compare this to our first algorithm, you'll see that it simplifies the process quite a bit. In a nutshell, we've placed all the work that we know we'll be repeating many times into a handy little handler that will do it for us. This reduces typing and ultimately saves us all kinds of trouble. Now, to cast rays in all directions, we need only call the handler with each directional vector. Casting rays is only one of several possible ways to determine whether models have invaded the proximal space of one another. Our narrative manager will also track the intellectual and psychological events during the game in order to determine whether the characters and objects have violated one another's intellectual or psychological space.

The first step to writing code for any such project involves writing the events, properties, and commands that you want to occur in your game in a purely logical and widely dynamic way. It is handy to limit your description of events using the Boolean limiters: if, then, else, and, or, and not. In the last section of this chapter, we'll do an exercise that allows you to test this skill.

Exercise 1.3:   Writing Logical Descriptions of Dynamic Events

I might describe any aspect of my proposed game in all sorts of ways. If I ever want it to become a playable game, I need to first describe it in a very logical way.

For this exercise, begin with the story web that you assembled during Exercise 1.1. Look at the web and ask yourself, Is there anything about this story that I could describe logically? In my story web there are two primary characters.

They both want the same resources in the game space. I could say, "When the man sees a valuable object, the dragon may sense it and will teleport to the nearest tree in order to race toward that object. Either the man or the dragon will get the object, and if they get too close to one another, there may be a conflict." That tells me a good bit about the story and the game, but it would be a pain in the keister to write code for this sentence.

If I write the same thought in logical pseudocode, I get the following:

```
if model[man] castRay() returns object[x] then
--when the man sees an object
  if value(object[x]) > y then
--valuable object
    if dragonSense = random(z) then
--the dragon may sense it
      dragonTeleport(closestTreeToObject[x])
      -- the dragon will teleport to the nearest tree
      dragonRaceTo(object[x])
      -- the dragon will race toward that object
      if firstToObject[x] = dragon then
      -- if the dragon is the first one to the object then
        dragonTokenCount = dragonTokenCount + 1
      else
        manTokenCount = manTokenCount + 1
      end if
      if model[man].distanceTo(model[dragon] < xx then
      -- if the man and dragon are too close together then
      analyzeConfict()
      -- there may be a conflict.
    end if
  end if
end if.
```

This may look like Lingo, but it is not. It is just a logical expression of the events in the previous sentences. The important part is breaking the ideas down into logical parts and understanding where there are mathematically logical expressions. It is imperative that you do this sort of thing in order to ensure that your ideas can be translated into something that the computer can do.

Now try writing some of these on your own. Just write down some of the ideas from your idea web in sentences and then break the sentences down into logical expressions. Remember to focus on questions like these:

- Can the computer resolve this expression?

- Is this dynamic?

- Would it work in many different instances?

- Could this be reduced (simplified) further?

- Is there a way to make all or parts of this expression reusable in other circumstances?

- Is the language I'm using mathematically logical?

Do this exercise for as many ideas in your web as you can. You'll find it a huge advantage when we move on to writing the specs for the game. It is always helpful to plan these things ahead, and writing the ideas logically will both improve your sense of how to implement the game and encourage your imagination to reexamine some of the ideas you've already had.

There are several major influences to keep in mind when designing real-time 3D games. The traditional association between stories and games is still appropriate, but it is more important in 3D games to work within an object-oriented design model in order to maximize your ability to respond to the unpredictable navigational choices of the player. These increased demands suggest that much of your time should be dedicated to planning the story and functions of your game.

In Chapter 2, "Making Plans," I'll explain some additional techniques that game developers use to plan and engineer their games. You'll have a chance to see examples of these planning tools, and I'll show you some handy ways to make your own plans using these methods.

CHAPTER 2

Making Plans

One of the most important things you can do to build a better game than your competitor is to plan ahead. Planning your game will help you anticipate problems. Every problem you anticipate and avoid during planning will save you from a much more chronologically costly repair during development.

After reading this chapter you should

- Know how to write a treatment and spec
- Know how to plan the visual appearance of a game
- Understand the relationship between the story and the interface
- Understand the ways the interface encourages player interaction
- Have created your own treatment and spec for a game
- Have considered the impact of different visual images on the playability and entertainment value of a game

In the section titled "Planning the Story," I'll show you a typical treatment and spec and talk about why they can be a huge contributor to the success of a game. I'll discuss ways to integrate the ideas about immersive (player-engaging) stories from the first chapter into your plans for the game. I'll give some tips and tricks for reacting to the player's choices in a game, even if you have no clue what that player may choose to do.

I'll explain how to think of the events and conflicts your character will encounter as steps in a staircase. Each step makes the game more exciting, and you'll learn how to keep the player feeling both rewarded and challenged to continue. You'll have a chance to try your hand at writing your own game treatment, and I'll give you a bunch of ideas for keeping it on track.

Planning the interface is the final subject of this chapter. You'll learn about the various visual, physical, and mental mechanisms that affect the way people interact with your games. I'll talk about the process of designing your game's appearance. We'll investigate the elements that make games look polished, regardless of their individual style. I'll describe ways to integrate the story and the interface in order to help people understand how to control the user-input widgets they find in your game. Finally, you'll create your own spec for a game.

Planning the Story

Teams of 30 or more developers flooded with hundreds of thousands of dollars create commercial 3D games. Chances are that you don't have either a huge team of developers or hundreds of thousands of dollars. Your best hope of catching an audience in the world of online game design is through wise use of limited resources. This strategy always begins with planning your game carefully before you invest huge portions of your time into the creation of basic game functions.

In addition to the obvious timesaving reasons for detailed planning, there are substantial commercial motivations. Your client (whoever is paying the bills) will want to know what you plan to do. After all, how can he possibly water down your content and force your game into the realm of mediocrity if he doesn't have a clear understanding of your plans for the game.

Your plans can be divided into two major parts: the treatment and the spec. You need both if you are going to avoid getting sucked into the black holes of feature creep (adding new features on a whim) and media obsession (spending all your time fidgeting with sound, graphics, and 3D models).

A *treatment* is a document in which you describe your game and define the parameters for gameplay. It ensures that you've given some thought to playability and design issues in your game. A *spec* is a specific technical guideline you create for scheduling tasks, anticipating programming and media-creation conflicts, and tracking your progress.

Example: *n-Virae* Treatment and Spec

Over the next several pages, you'll find portions of a combination treatment/spec I've prepared for a proposed game called *n-Virae*. This has been clipped down substantially in order to help you see the underlying structure of the document. You'll find the entire treatment and spec for *n-Virae* in Appendix A, "Treatments and Technical Specifications." Throughout the treatment and spec, I'll comment in the margins on the various reasons for including each item and talk a bit about the category.

n-Virae Treatment and Spec

n-Virae is a multiplayer real-time/role-playing and strategy game set in a fantastic world of bizarre and colorful images. It bears some faint resemblance to the things we experience every day. *n-Virae* has a painted, surreal look. Buildings, trees, landscapes, and skies all seem almost possessed with personalities and faces to express them; in the right situation, these things will come to life.

Overview

Aimed at the upper-elementary and junior high–aged teen, *n-Virae* is a nonviolent community experience. Players assume identities within the environment, which are partially of their own design and partially predetermined. The identity the player takes on becomes a sort of virtual costume and character. A player's entire experience may be dramatically altered depending on the character he becomes. Certainly his perception of this world will be altered depending on the character he becomes.

There is no real limit to the number of characters that will be assigned to players in the *n-Virae*, although it should be noted that it seems at this point more practical to plan for groups of fewer than 50. A character is generated when the player starts the game. There is so much room for genetic variety and mutation that the resulting character cannot really be predicted. Advanced players will be able to influence and design the genetic makeup of new characters, and most players will be able to conceive children.

This game has some similarities to Mindscape's *Creatures*, although the multiplayer aspect as well as some fundamental differences in the look and feel, interface design, and goals of the game set it apart from *Creatures*. *n-Virae*'s closest cousin in the contemporary game landscape is Sony's *Everquest*. Like *Everquest*, *n-Virae* is a multiplayer online role-playing game (RPG). Think of either one as a sort of 3D Multiuser Dungeon (MUD). The similarities between the games end there. Most notably, *Everquest* is often violent and has artwork of a notably different style.

TITLES

Your treatment starts with a working title. This is really no small matter. Your title is a reflection of the game's style, its story, its audience, and its interactive approach. The title may echo the theme, point to a central character, or even define an audience. Try to come up with several titles so that you are sure you are working with the best one for this game. Don't get too attached to it. There is a good chance you'll throw it out in favor of something that works better.

OVERVIEWS

This is a sort of executive summary. You want to put all the import information about your game right up front in this section of the treatment. Imagine that you meet someone with the money to produce a game for her Web site, but she doesn't know what kind of game she wants to make. However, she will know some things: She'll know the demographics for the target audience. She'll know about any restrictions on content, and she'll have a sense of the sort of games she thinks her audience likes. Give her enough information in this portion of the treatment to give you a "yes," "no," or "maybe" based solely on the overview.

▼

It is possible to do the following in the *n-Virae* game space: compete, explore, chronicle, procreate, band together in teams, communicate, eat, get sick, get well, spread diseases, transcend your immediate level of existence, discover archeological artifacts, create enhanced or false lore, and commit crimes.

This is a never-ending game, because the *n-Virae* environment will evolve with use. Users who transcend several levels will eventually earn the right to design new characters and press them on the newborns (users just entering the game). Along the way, users will have the opportunity to chronicle their experiences in story stones, thus adding their own adventures to the mythical backbone of this place.

Platforms

Target platforms for *n-Virae* are Windows 9*x*, NT, and 2000 as well as Mac OS 8.1+. The basic engine for the game will be developed in Macromedia Director 8.5. The Macromedia Director Multiuser Server version 3.0 creates the connections between players across the Internet. We will modify various aspects of the display depending on the playback capacities of the systems that attempt to play the game. Players will be given the option to customize their interface for speed or to allow the computer to do the customization for them. They will be warned if their custom settings will likely result in performance issues. Multiuser communications will be transmitted through a central host over IP and UDP, depending on the potential for error checking for the specific action. It is possible that we may try to port the game to Shockwave.

Players

n-Virae is a multiplayer experience. As such, players inside the game environment may interact with one another and the environment in a variety of ways. The short-term goals of the game are survival and growth, although players may choose varied goals depending on their own interests. Fifty players may exist in each *n-Virae* space at any given time. Users may join sessions that are public as well as generate private password-protected sessions. Users play the game over the Internet.

OVERVIEWS
CONTINUED

PLATFORM INFORMATION

Planning the delivery platforms for your game is a major decision. Don't take it lightly. Regardless of how interchangeable your game is supposed to be among the major platforms, there will be operating system–specific problems if you plan to support your game for more than one operating system. Don't kid yourself. Every version of the Mac OS and Windows requires independent testing. Add the problems created by various support strategies for 3D, and you will soon realize you are headed for a tech-support nightmare if you don't make some hard decisions right up front. This is the place to announce your intentions—to yourself and to your team. It's also a good place to include strategies for overcoming inherent problems with multiple operating systems and multiple 3D hardware and 3D software support.

PLAYERS

It is important to identify the maximum number of players that will be able to play the game at once. If there is more than one player in the game space at a time, talk about the special circumstances that must be addressed in order to facilitate this phenomenon.

Interface and Chrome

The primary screen will be a 3D view of the *n-Virae*. The animations are well developed, and the multiuser interactions will provide the added benefit of interpersonal communication among players. The art style is based primarily on Friedensreich Hundertwasser and Leon Bakst, the architecture of Gaudi, and the style of the Art Nouveau period. Characters will be 3D sprites, presenting their communications as text in the interface bar beneath the 3D portal. A major goal of the project is to allow this bar to become as minimal an influence as possible.

A small translucent control pad will give players access to their journal, their map, and an overview of their character's health, hunger, and disposition. This pad will float over the 2D portion of the interface. The 3D area must be protected from any crossover to 2D rendering at all costs. The onscreen character will respond to the player's requests to move via mouse and keyboard commands.

We will take advantage of the often severe lighting of the 3D environment and the universally fauvist color palette to create a 2D background that provides an elegant transition to the 3D world.

Startup

The game plops users in random locations on the first level. By default, it tries to place them in empty areas so that a first-time player is not faced with a crazy person within his or her first few seconds of play. Players are given no information and are left to fend for themselves, although a first-time player who is rapidly starving or dying of sickness may encounter a sentient game element that points out these problems and suggests remedies. However, a first-time player is almost equally as likely to encounter a twisted game entity that suggests flawed solutions or demands things in exchange for the information.

INTERFACE

Briefly describe the interface you imagine for your proposed project. I find that it helps to compare the aesthetic of the interface to artists or design images that strike a chord for me. Sometimes I compare the interface to other games that have similar formats. I find it very helpful to look to other examples in order to avoid the problems they have encountered.

STARTUP OR WALKTHROUGH

Depending on the nature of the game, you will want to either describe a typical walkthrough of the game or describe the first few moments of gameplay. If you go the startup route, as shown here, you will want to talk about the various aspects of the game that a player might encounter while playing the game as well as the sorts of things the character might try to do. If you use the walkthrough model, just describe a typical game from the viewpoint of the central character and/or player.

Objectives

The object of the game varies according to the desires of the player. Generally speaking, the objectives within the game are survive, procreate, form friendships, transcend levels of existence, uncover the past, act bravely (in order to be added to the mythology of the environment), and create your own lore.

Entities

Here are the entities in the game:

- World objects
- Characters
- *n-Virae* sentient beings
- Environmental influences

Features

Backdrop and overlay properties include the following:

Feature	Description
Speak and listen	Text-based computer-enhanced/altered chat.
Move character	Mouse and keyboard control of onscreen character movements.
Read journal	Read the things that the system has written about the player's journey thus far and read their own comments.
Write in journal	Write in their journal.
Read guidebook	If the player finds a guidebook, they may use it as a map to portions of the landscape.

OBJECT OF THE GAME

This element is critical. If you don't know what the object of the game is, how on earth will the players know? Even if you want to give the players tons of freedom, don't forget that they signed on for a game. Clearly define the objectives that the players may seek during gameplay.

ENTITIES OR SPRITES

List and define all the sprites (whether they're characters, props, architecture, or other) that you plan to see in the game. You may want to divide these into groups, as I have done here. Some will require more explanation than others. I've reduced this section substantially for this discussion. If you'd like to see the entire treatment and scenario, it is available in Appendix A.

FEATURES

Now we are starting to think more technically. This section could either appear in your treatment or in your spec (technical specification). Prepare a list of all the things that may be done in the game and begin to visualize it as a programming problem rather than a part of the story. Describe each proposed feature as a technical element.

This is the core of the biggest problem you face as a developer. If you start to think logically too soon, you'll make an ugly, kludgy, unplayable game. Believe me, I've made lots of them. If you start too late, or never, you'll make a perfectly lovely bit of unusable goop. These elements must be balanced.

▼

| Read myth from story stones | The player can learn the mythology of any level from it's story stones. |
| Add myth to story stones | The player can add to the mythology of any level by writing new legends in the stones, but they must be careful—the stones don't like liars. |

3D Resources

The game will require a large assortment of low-polygon three-dimensional models. In order to ease translation, all models should be created in 3D Studio Max and exported as W3D files or merged into a central Max file. Here's a list of the required 3D resources:

- Character models
- World sentient beings
- Tokens
- The environment

Data Structure

The Network Services object handles all access to the server and all communications between clients. It's functions include connecting, reading and writing data, listening for incoming network operations, and parsing incoming connections for commands.

The 3D World Services object takes care of the functions needed in order to make the 3D objects move and interact with each other. These include camera manipulation, lighting, model animation, model transformation, and loading/unloading of 3D models and worlds.

The Intelligence Services object handles the gameplay elements of the experience. Included is the analysis of user actions in order to determine the degree of success or failure of various actions, the analysis of user health/intelligence/strength and hunger properties, storage and retrieval of narratives, and creature/user interaction.

FEATURES
CONTINUED

RESOURCES

This section could either appear in your treatment or in your spec. In the next step, you should list the resources you will need in order to create the game. Think of this as a media list. I like to use this list to prepare the schedule of media generation once the project is underway. Be certain to list multiple states of an object if you will need to create media for more than one state. This includes things such as multiple button states as well as 3D bone and keyframe animations.

DATA STRUCTURE

The way you organize your program conceptually will play a big part in the speed and responsiveness of the game. Most games have underlying structures. It is best to look for sets of similar functions and then organize the data in groups aligned to these conceptual objects.

At the very least, separate your game's screen-drawing widgets from your game's data-storage and data-manipulation widgets. You will probably find you can break your game into an organizational structure of three to five parts.

NOTE

Collision detection and AI are part of every game, even if their roles are so minimal that you don't call them that anymore. You usually find that you need an independent object to handle collision, and in some cases you need an AI object to deal with the game logic and logic of in-game adversaries. In this case, collision detection and AI are going to be handled by objects that are local to the individual characters rather than by a global object. You may want your collision and AI handled centrally as well. Time management may also be handled in this manner.

Rules

The rules governing actions in the game are based on behaviors assigned to objects that will poll the properties of all the objects involved in the proposed action. The environment will then enable, enhance, or disable actions based on the rule sets of the environment. In this sense, the environment is the gatekeeper of all actions.

Object interaction will happen as follows:

- The game alerts environment sentient beings of the location of the player's character. For example, the narrative manager tells a story stone that a player has just come close enough for the stone to check to see whether it holds a grudge against the character. If the stone does have an axe to grind, it may choose to attack the player.

- The game searches for world objects/characters in the player's field of view and displays them to the player. A player may have dropped some food or a weapon on a specific spot. The game engine checks the grid and finds the object. It places the object when the player reaches this area.

- The game records and broadcasts the player's location. It is important to realize that the game has to share information about the actions of many players on different machines. The current actions and position of the character are broadcast to other people playing on other machines so that they can observe the behavior of everyone who is playing the game.

- Environmental sentient beings check their history with the player and run modified routines when appropriate. A history of kindness with the player might trigger a normally hostile sentient being to be kind to the player and share some magic token.

- Environmental sentient beings check their proximity rules for handlers and run them if they are triggered by the location of the player. Just as you might see or hear a person passing by, the sentient beings might be stimulated by the actions of a nearby player. The player's speech might trigger a hearing handler in one of the beings.

TECHNICAL RULES

This section could either appear in your treatment or in your spec, although it will make the most sense to put it into the spec. Every game has rules. It is always shocking to me that the bulk of the programming I do is designed to prohibit cheating in a game. Game players have rapidly come to expect the game to serve as the monitor of poor sportsmanship. As you design your game, start thinking like a player. Ask yourself how you could cheat at this game. You will need to anticipate as much of this as possible in order to avoid problems later in the development process.

This is also a good place to begin documenting your plans for the mechanics of intelligent agents and objects within your game. Start thinking about a model for analyzing information and issuing commands that will centralize the logic in the game. Things get fuzzier as your game gets more dynamic. Centralizing commands can help reduce errors and smoothly blend actions.

Methods and Properties

Here is an abridged list of methods and properties:

Name	Description

`mCameraTrackModel(<"modelName">,`
`<VectorDistToModel>,`
`<booleanLockModelToModelRotation>,`
`<percentDegreeOfMotionTolerance>,`
`<integerTimeSteps>)`
This behavior must be attached to the active 3D world sprite. Calls to the functions of the behavior should reference the sprite—for example, `sprite(1).mCameraTrackModel("arg", arg2)`. If there are fewer than five arguments, the handler will assume the omissions are from the end of the list.
	Spawns a behavior dialog when attached that allows us to choose which model we want the camera to follow and what the vector to the camera from the model should be. It also provides a check box to enable rotation matching, a slider to set the degree of wiggle room given to the model before the camera starts to match the movement, and another slider to allow us to choose the number of frames used by the behavior to get to the new camera position when the model moves quickly. The behavior accepts the following arguments:
	
	`<"modelName">`—Accepts a string or an integer representing the model within the active 3D member that should be tracked. The value is stored in a property called `pCameraTarget`.
	
	`<VectorDistToModel>`—Accepts an integer in default world units representing the distance/vector of the camera to the model. The value is stored in a property called `pCameraDistanceToTarget`.
	
	`<booleanLockModelToRotation>`—Either `True` or `False`, this property determines whether the camera will be locked to the rotation of the model being tracked. If this

METHODS AND PROPERTIES

This portion of the document is what most people think of when they imagine a spec. Describe each method you imagine you will need in the proposed game. You should separate these by objects or global scripts that fit the categories you defined in your discussion of data structures.

Regardless of your organizational strategy, you should try to list all the methods and the properties they will use. It is important to document these well because in an ideal world, you may not have to do them all by yourself. The list you see here is a condensed example, but it should give you a good idea about how you might plan the methods that will support each feature you have proposed for your game. I like to work down the feature list and create at least one overall handler for each feature. In some cases, you will want to roll multiple functions into a single handler.

▼

property is `True`, the camera will always return to the same rotational relationship with the model. If this property is `False`, the camera will maintain the distance vector from the object, but it will not orbit the model when the model turns. The value is stored in a property called `pCameraLockRotation`.

`<percentDegreeOfMotionTolerance>`—A rating from 1 to 100, this property determines the amount of wiggle room the model is given before the camera takes action. The value is stored in a property called `pCameraTolerance`.

`<integerTimeSteps>`—Determines the number of frames over which the camera-realignment procedure will occur. The smaller the number, the more radical the camera movement. The value is stored in a property called `pCameraReactionTime`.

pCameraTarget	access = get/set
	sprite(a).pCameraTarget = modelRef
	default = member(x).model[1]
pCameraDistanceToTarget	access = get/set
	sprite(a).pCameraDistanceToTarget= vector(x,y,z)
	DefaultVector = vector(250,250,100)
pCameraLockRotation	access = get/set
	sprite(a).pCameraLockRotation = 1
	default = 0

**METHODS AND
PROPERTIES**
CONTINUED

▼

`pCameraTolerance`	`access = get/set`
	
	`sprite(a).pCameraTolerance = 50`
	
	`default = 0`

`pCameraReactionTime`	`access = get/set`
	
	`sprite(a).pCameraReactionTime = 20`
	
	`default = 10`

`mMoveCharacter(<whichCharacter>,` `<whichMotionName>,<vectorDirection>)` This behavior must be attached to the active 3D world sprite. Calls to the functions of the behavior should reference the sprite—for example, sprite(a). mMoveCharacter ("arg", arg2). If there are fewer than three arguments, the handler will assume that the

This behavior does not use a dialog when added to the object. When called during playback, the behavior accepts the following arguments: `<whichCharacter>`—A reference to the model within the active 3D world that will be moved. This value is stored in the property `pActiveCharacter`. `<whichMotionName>`—A reference to the omissions are from the end of the list. animation cycle that will be used for the movement. This value is stored in the property `pActiveMotionCharacter`.

`<vectorDirection>`—The direction that the model should be pointing for the movement. This value is stored in the property `pActiveMotionDirection`.

It is important to note that this behavior needs to be able to stack these motions into the bonesplayer modifier playlist.

We'll use another behavior to abort such movements if the stack is too deep and therein keep control over the immediate motion. This could, however, get tricky, especially with the need to rotate the models in order to get the bipeds moving in the intended directions.

METHODS AND PROPERTIES
CONTINUED

This should give you a fairly clear sense of the basic elements you can find in a treatment and spec. Don't be fooled by the simplicity of the description of entities and other resources or by the limited nature of the handlers described in the spec—yours will be much more extensive. If you want to look at some more complete versions of game treatments and specs, consult Appendix A. While you are there, notice that the descriptions of media and the list of proposed handlers are extensive. You should plan your project carefully. The time you spend here will be well worth the extra effort.

Writing Your Own Game Treatment

Now it's your turn. Oh sure, I know, you don't really think that this treatment and spec stuff is really worth all the effort. I used to be a cynic, too. Indulge me for a moment. If you have an hour to spend on a project, spend 20 minutes planning. If you have 10 hours to spend on a project, spend 3 hours and 20 minutes planning. Whatever amount of time you have, spend one-third of that time planning your project.

The plan is everything. We hardly ever plan any project adequately. If you don't plan adequately, you'll end up reworking every single aspect of the project and rewriting every line of code at least once—perhaps even more.

I didn't believe this rule when a good man tried to feed it to me. So, I don't imagine you are sold on it yet, either. Indulge us both and try this method on something small first. A day's work would be a good test. Instead of spending the first hour with that nervous confused feeling in the pit of your stomach, cleaning your desk, or whatever else you can think of to avoid beginning the project, try planning for 2 hours. (I figure you got in late and you'll finish within 6 hours because this will be much more efficient that the average person's day of work.)

Think the project through carefully and try to imagine several different approaches. Take notes on the ideas you think will work. Pretend that you are stuck in an elevator without a laptop. Write down descriptions of the handlers you imagine you will need and draw diagrams of the navigation and tool systems.

I was shocked when I found how effective this strategy is. It's absolutely amazing. It reduces headaches, calms your fears, and makes your projects flow much more smoothly. Try it. You'll love it.

One way to approach this planning time is to write a treatment, like the one you just looked at for *n-Virae*. Note that the last bit of the example is the spec (technical specification), and the first section is the treatment. You may find yourself thinking, "Now hold on, Al. Those notes were a little soft on which item goes where. I'm not sure I know the difference between a treatment and a spec."

There really is no universal standard to state which items belong in which document. There is a general understanding that creativity and art belong in the treatment, and technical information belongs in the spec. They have different purposes. The treatment is a proposal generally intended to build support for a project, just as it would be in film. The spec is a technical document, used to organize, plan, and facilitate progress.

Exercise 2.1: Write Your Own Game Treatment

Try writing a treatment for your ideal game. Use the format I've outlined in the preceding section. Here's a list of the categories to speed you along in your writing. Just work through each numbered task, answering each question carefully. Use the *n-Virae* example from Appendix A to get ideas about the format. Feel free to sketch as you go along and don't forget to grab your story web from the last chapter to get your imagination going.

- **Overview.** What style of game is this? To what audience will it appeal? What other games could be compared to this one? What are the differences between the proposed game and the others?

- **Platforms.** On which computer platforms will your game run? Give specific operating systems and versions. Realize that the broader your support, the more time this will cost you.

- **Players.** How many people will be able to play your game at one time? If more than one, is this an online game? Will it be networked?

- **Interface.** How will the player give and get information from the application? What mechanisms will you use to help the user know what is happening and make play more fun and less work?

- **Startup and/or walkthrough.** Describe the manner in which the game will be introduced to the player. Will there be backstory or cinematic elements? Will there be credits or instructions? Will the user be given the opportunity to adjust any preferences? What will a typical game be like?

- **Objectives**. List and explain the objectives a typical player would have while playing the game. What sort of things will the user try to do? What will/should he or she want?

- **Entities/sprites.** Who or what are the characters in this game? Is there anything unusual about them?

- **Chrome.** Describe the overall aesthetic style of the game. Does it have a look? Does its appearance refer to a location, historical period, or artistic style? What is the color palette? Are there any patterns, shapes, forms, or textures that are prevalent or repeat in the chrome?

- **Rules.** What are the rules/laws of the game space you envision? How do they affect the game and specifically the choices the player will be able to make?

- **Resources.** What kinds of media do you need for the game? How much media do you need and what does it represent?

Planning the Interface: Not Too Pretty, Not Too Ugly

The interface is the communication channel you will use to help the players understand their goals in the game space. It will guide the players to the solutions by which they might achieve those goals. It will echo your story. The tone you establish from the onset of the game will guide the players' choices and help them enjoy the experience.

An interface does not need to be pretty, but it doesn't have to be ugly. It needs to be appropriate. It should grow from the narrative backbone of the game. This is true even when the game isn't the sort of thing you would normally associate with stories.

Even a simple arcade game is dependent to some degree on storytelling concepts. If you didn't know that the complex polygonal forms in Lyle Rains and Ed Logg's *Asteroids* (Atari, 1979) are big rocks and that the triangle is a ship, you will not be likely to spin and shoot. Even the concepts of spinning and shooting are fundamentally narrative.

The interface can be a substantial contributor to any narrative. It will help guide the players if you have done your homework and planned ahead carefully. If you refuse to consider the impact your interface has on the game, it is more likely to irritate the players and mask the story you have worked so hard to create.

In this section, I'm going to let you watch over my shoulder as I work on the interface of a cool little game called *Word Wacky*.

Blending Chrome, Story, and Interaction

I started designing *Word Wacky* a couple of years ago. I've always loved word games, and I wanted to create one that would allow the player to roll lettered dice and make words from them. Consider the unsuccessful initial interface shown in Figure 2.1 (but try not to laugh out loud). The game has some similarities to a very old word game called *Perquackey* (1956, Hollingsworth Brothers). Although that game is fundamentally different in several ways, I wanted to combine my memories of word games into a universal word game, and *Word Wacky* was the natural result.

FIGURE 2.1

An early interface for Word Wacky illustrates serious design problems. Don't do anything like this.

There is so much wrong with this early version that I hardly know where to start. As you load the game, you are treated to a hideous image with hovering text. As a general rule, when designing games for the Internet, it is never a good idea to force the download of enormous graphics just for the sake of the graphic. No one wants to see it.

Creating a complex interface just because you can is a bad idea. You are not trying to make an interface in order to impress folks with it; you are trying to make an interface that helps the user understand the inherent drama of the game. Even *Word Wacky* has a story, and it's a simple one. The player has to think up words and enter them quickly so he'll get a big bang out of his own brilliance, but the game has a nasty clock and limits the player's choice of letters, so he tries over and over until finally he reaches a high enough score to satisfy his ego.

The challenge of the game is creating words with the appropriate letters. The clock adds the excitement. The reward is, at this point, intrinsic. When a player creates words, she is rewarded with points and a sense of self-satisfaction. The challenge/reward model is in place already. One thing to notice at this stage is that it doesn't have much of a staircase of complication.

The second screen, shown in Figure 2.2, is even more embarrassing than the splash screen. It shames me, but you will learn from my mistakes. Therefore, have a gander at the pathetic second screen of this initial version of the game.

FIGURE 2.2

An unsolicited help screen with way too much information.

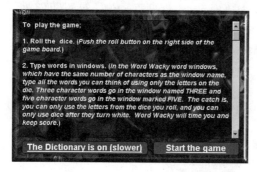

What on earth is that? Imagine the prospective player's response: "I'm here to play a game, not read a novel!"

In the first place, nobody asked the game for this information, and in the second place, you would need to be really, really dumb to require this much information before playing the game. I should have kept it simple and taken the player immediately to the playing area of the game.

Your description of a rule or concept in the game does not need to be exhaustive. If you think the user might require additional information about the interface, put the overflow in a help file, screen, or database that may be called on command and not forced upon unsuspecting game players.

Moving on to the playing board itself, shown in Figure 2.3, you'll see even more crimes against civilized design. The first and most substantial problem is that the interface does nothing to help the user understand how to play the game. Who wants to study the interface for half an hour in an attempt to decipher the purpose of each widget?

FIGURE 2.3

The playing area is cluttered and lacks focus.

There is no focus in the interface. When designing the interface for your game, you want to keep in mind the fundamental elements and principles of design. You should use the elements according to the rules laid out in the principles to achieve a cohesive composition that helps the users figure out what the heck to do, what this game is about, and where they are headed next.

NOTE

Appendix B, "Composition Basics," provides a quick overview of the fundamentals of composition.

Each element is a similar size, the buttons recede, and the text printed beneath the words is difficult to read. The whole monstrosity seems to pull your eye up to the upper-left corner of the interface as if to say, "Go back where you came from." This is an interface in serious need of repair.

If you haven't already done so, open the file marked WordWackyBad.html on your companion CD-ROM. Assuming that you stay and play a round in this nasty interface, you'll soon see an equally nasty display area that slowly trudges through each word, checking an online dictionary to see whether you have selected legal words.

Boy, this game has it all: It is slow, it is dull, and it is ugly. Now open the file WordWacky2.dir on your companion CD-ROM and click Play. I've made some changes. The opening screen is still present, but it has been simplified and fades in elegantly. The user must click to continue, but notice that I've taken the time to change the cursor from a standard pointer to a finger when you roll over the title in order to help the online user realize that a click is in order.

Once you click the splash screen, you'll notice that the second screen fades in as well. The second screen in the original game was a novella of instructions. The splash screens from both versions are compared in Figure 2.4. In the improved version, you may notice that the color palette has been vastly improved—there is visual focus and the display is in motion. The Roll button flashes quietly in the lower-left corner. It won't take a rocket scientist to figure out how to start the game. I've added large numerals to indicate to the player that the given number of characters is the limit for words typed in the correlating field.

FIGURE 2.4

The text-heavy original Word Wacky splash screen beside the improved, ready-to-play splash screen.

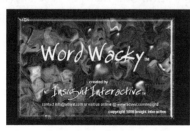

If the player still feels confused or wants more information, he can click a simple button that leads to the rules. Click it now. If you compare this new rules screen to the original (see Figure 2.5), you will immediately see the difference.

FIGURE 2.5

Compare the original rules screen to the Word Wacky II rules.

Notice as the words page fades in that I'm using typography as art throughout the new interface. Ask yourself, what is the style or genre of this game? It is a word game. It is only logical to take advantage of characters, fonts, and words in a game of this genre. It is making lemonade from lemons as my Dad used to say. This is a game about words. Embrace it. Love it. No matter what your game is about, point big fat arrows toward it. If you embrace your game's inherent style, meaning, and genre, you will find that the graphics fall more easily into place.

Comparing the old and new versions of the help screen is bizarre. I've eliminated the online dictionary in favor of an onboard dictionary (because it is much faster) and simplified the Start the Game button into a less-verbose Play button. I looked at the rules and realized that I could say everything important in just two rules and two bits of information. I separated the rules from the information in order to maximize clarity.

If you click the Quit button, you will notice a similar simplification. (The quit screens from both versions are shown in Figure 2.6.) Here, I added some text in order to marry the help screen to the quit screen visually. I simplified the buttons to avoid further embarrassment.

FIGURE 2.6

Word Wacky quit screen and Word Wacky II quit screen.

Move back to the main gameplay screen. This screen is shown in Figure 2.7. Go ahead and roll the dice. You should notice immediately that I've made a change to the dice. In the original, the dice immediately change to their new position, but in the newer version, the dice animate in order to suggest motion. After a bit of motion, each die sticks on a letter. The curser flashes in the first position of the field labeled "Three" as if to say, "Type, you idiot." The players may also click the dice, and the characters they click will appear in the field below.

FIGURE 2.7

Word Wacky play screen and Word Wacky II play screen.

Once the clock has run its course, the program moves to the verification screen. This was the epitome of dull in the previous version, but in this version, I've changed a few things. An onboard dictionary accelerates error checking exponentially. While you wait, the system teases you with all the words you could have used if you were really clever. The average checking time in the new interface is about 5 seconds; it was about 60 seconds in the original.

These are strong improvements, and the new version is nothing to be ashamed of—but it could be better. In fact, using only the concepts we've discussed thus far, we could take this game out of grandma's closet and into the pop-culture mainstream.

In Chapter 1, "The Story: How Much Is Too Much?" we talked about using a staircase of events. Each step in the staircase leaves the user feeling challenged to continue as well as rewarded for a job well done. If we were to consider this challenge/reward model and think of the game as even more fundamentally a story about the brilliance of the player, we could maximize the excitement of gameplay, speed the user's comprehension of the interface, and tell a riveting story to just about anyone.

Word Wacky 3D: An Interface Exploration

Even though I've already made this game (twice), I'm going to start my plans with a treatment and spec. I'll open this up to you here because it gives you a slightly different example and because I think it will help you to follow my thought pattern as I develop ideas for the pop-culture version of *Word Wacky*, called *Word Wacky 3D*. Open the file WordWacky3D.dir on the CD-ROM. Go ahead and play for a while before reading on. Just click, rewind, and play to amuse yourself.

In order to remain focused on the ideas behind the project, the treatment/ spec has been substantially edited here. The entire document appears in Appendix A.

Overview

Word Wacky is a wild-paced, scream-at-the-monitor-with-your-friends, roll-the-dice-and-make-a-word game. Simple to use, this game gets faster and wilder the longer you play it. In an effort to shift the demographic of the game to pop-culture teens and twenty-somethings, it will have a retro-70s aesthetic.

The game punishes your mistakes heartlessly and rewards your successes generously. The better you perform, the more time and rounds you are awarded with. If you perform badly, you will lose both time and opportunities. The challenge is to at least beat the clock and to pummel the clock if you want to go far. The faster you play, the more points you'll earn. Earn enough, and you'll be granted longer clocks and additional rounds. *Word Wacky 3D* is a digital house of cards. Players need intellect, skill, concentration, speed, and luck to defeat the ever-racing timer and master the wheel of words.

One player at a time may play the game. It has that gather-around flavor, encouraging others to watch, taunt, and shout out genuine as well as misleading answers.

Interface

I want the game to have an edgy, techno-organic feel. It should be strange and slightly retro-70s. It should feature a color palette of deep purples and analogous colors with complementary lights and glowing alarms. The interface is illustrated in Figure 2.8.

MATCHING THE DEMOGRAPHIC

One of my major goals with *Word Wacky* 3D is to use the interface, particularly the aesthetic of the interface, to create a strong appeal for people in their teens and twenties. At this point, the audience desired has a strong interest in retro-70s and 80s fashion and visual images.

The logical approach to the problem is to build on the retro fever in order to create a game that appeals to the relevant demographic.

TAPPING INTO COMMON EXPERIENCE

Most people have been to a circus or a carnival. The flashing race lights of a carnival midway are part of common cultural knowledge for virtually anyone who might be playing this game.

As I began to sketch the retro-style interface, I also knew that I wanted to tap into a player's prior experiences to suggest that the game was wild and crazy.

A carnival seemed a solid starting point. It seemed to me from the onset that the game could mimic midway rides. A Ferris wheel seemed like a good leaping-off point.

As I sorted the interface elements, I began to imagine these widgets in a retro-carnival atmosphere. I tried to keep usability in mind as I visualized an interface that set the stage for excitement.

▼

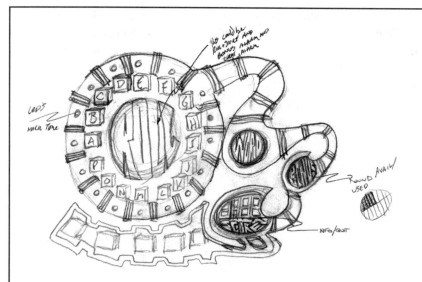

Figure 2.8   *Word Wacky 3D* interface sketch.

There are several aspects of gameplay that must be reflected in the interface. I've listed them, separating them into informational and input elements.

Information elements:

- A visibly running timer. Players lose led lights every 2 seconds in the normal mode, but lose lights faster if things are going badly.

- A visibly reducing round counter (limits total rounds).

- The current state of the dice.

- The current score (replaces the Roll button after a round begins).

- Bonus notification (flashes in the Roll/Score position for 2 seconds when a bonus is achieved).

- Illegal submission alarm(s) or score reduction. Flashes in the Roll/Score position when an illegal action is detected.

- Possible correct answers taunting the player. (Note: Move this feature to the round summary.)

**TAPPING INTO
COMMON
EXPERIENCE**
CONTINUED

▼

- Round summary screen, showing successful and failed answers with complete points breakdown, round by round. (This is an optional feature.)

Interface elements:

- Roll button.
- Information button. How to play as well as copyright and creation information.
- Quit button.
- Keyboard and mouse input alphabetical characters.
- Sum button (appears in the Word button position at the end of any given round and stays until the Roll button is clicked). This button leads to a text-only screen summarizing the actions and results for each round. (This is an optional feature.)

Startup

After the splash screen, the game launches directly to the playing screen. The clocks are stopped, but the dice are dancing. The Information button and Quit button are always enabled. The keyboard input is disabled. There are 3D dice spinning on their own axes, spread in a circle around the central display. It all looks like a Ferris wheel with chaser lights.

**TAPPING INTO
COMMON
EXPERIENCE**
CONTINUED

WHY 3D?

I made the decision to move the game's dice into a 3D world because I wanted to tap into the players' sense that the dice were actually spinning and I wanted the players to feel like they could just click and drag them from one position to the next.

I think that games are more immersive if you can sort of think to yourself, "Grab that T and move it over here...now move the L." That's the way we'd do it if the dice were on the table, so adding that kind of immersive interactivity to the rack seemed the right approach.

Objectives

The player clicks the Play button to stop the dice and begin a round. Once the dice have landed, the player must create words, three to six letters long, using only the letters on the face of the dice. After each visible die is clicked, the dice move into the display position on the bottom of the interface in the next available slot. If the player clicks the Word button and the word is valid, the score is increased and the dice are reset. Normal rounds last 60 seconds. All players are given five rounds at the beginning of the game. Players may earn additional rounds if they earn high-enough scores during any given round. Rounds are lost when a player earns too few points during a given round.

Resources/Entities

We'll need one die (cube) with each of its six sides mapped as a single mesh. There will be no mesh deformation, so this will be a 12-polygon model. The interface will be drawn onto a backdrop. The lights will be 3D objects floating in front of the backdrop. The buttons will be 2D sprites above the 3D world.

This should not be a substantial performance problem because there is very little work for the 3D renderer to do. I'll change the appearance of the buttons and so on by swapping the textures on-the-fly. The remaining entities are graphics created in Photoshop and audio files.

CHOOSING THE FONT

During your earlier interaction with the game, you probably noticed that the font in the finished game is not the font in my initial sketch.

It really is never a good idea to deliver excess baggage via the Web. Although this game will likely be delivered both as an independent executable and as a Shockwave game, it would be crazy to ship custom labels for all those buttons. Not only would this be seriously bandwidth heavy, but the resulting buttons and labels would be harder to read than their low-bandwidth variants.

As I worked on the interface, I chastised myself for having drawn the excessive one in the first place and then considered my options. "This is still a word game," I thought. I began to consider the possibility of using a Times or Book Antiqua font. I imagined bold versions of one of these, because it is the style that words are presented in on various children's television programs.

It is an iconic way to present text (in the sense that the individual letters contain symbolism beyond their mere meaning as letters). The font draws attention to the text as text and triggers a memory in most people of assembling words, especially when the characters are all lowercase.

PLANNING THE MEDIA

Using 2D sprites on top of 3D sprites has one substantial limitation. If you disable a 3D sprite's Direct to Stage (DTS) property, you will substantially slow down the rendering engine. You cannot put anything on top of a 3D sprite unless you do this, so it presents a good first challenge for the interface.

Another, equally viable way to approach this problem would be to use imaging Lingo and textures to change the appearance of the backdrop in the 3D world and leave the DTS property on.

If there were thousands of polygons in the 3D world member or the animation needed to be considerably more complex, I would have needed to go this second route.

I chose the first, because it will save time. It won't kill the animation too badly on most machines, and it is simpler.

Functions, Handlers, and Properties

It is reasonable to divide the proposed program into five basic subsections based on function.

The first group, data management, will contain information that we need to check in order to keep the game on track. As the game is played, we'll store and retrieve information from the data management object.

The second group, game logic, is the largest. It contains six subsections of its own. This object will handle all of the game's rules of play and respond to user inputs. It is organized into subsections that further specialize the jobs that it must do during gameplay.

The third and fourth groups will handle the display elements of the game. They will work in conjunction with the data management object and the game logic object to change the appearance of the screen. The game logic object receives user input and sends requests to the data management object.

The final section is devoted to audio. Because Director's built-in audio systems are able to do everything we need, we'll just use those.

This tells me we need to build four objects for this game. They will probably have the public methods specified in the following table of data-management methods and properties:

Figure 2.9   *Word Wacky 3D* interface.

HALF THE BATTLE

The aesthetics of the interface are really only half the battle. The other major consideration is the interactivity itself. A big part of the storytelling lies in the way the player uses the widgets on the screen.

Whenever these uses conflict with the underlying narrative, the players will be thrown out of the world of the game and into their own reality.

The player's immersion in the narrative is dependent on a concept that dramatists call "willing suspension of disbelief." Essentially, this means that the player enters into an unspoken agreement with the game. The agreement is simple. The player agrees to pretend that the illusions in the game (or on the stage) are real. In return, the game (or the play) doesn't change the rules or distract the player (or audience) from the core of the story along the way.

As you design the interaction, look for ways to increase immersion. If you really try, you will find great ways to enable the users to input information without throwing them out of the game.

Methods and Properties

Name	Description
mInitGame()	Clears global variables; sets all media to the default values. Builds the array of dice and places faces on each one.
mRollDice()	Rotates the dice models on two axes. Stops the rotation in a position that leaves the dice aligned appropriately to the camera. Records the active faces into a list that is accessible to validation handlers.
mResetGame()	Resets the game to its default state. Erases score information, action-tracking information, and dice roll data.
mValidateWord()	Tests a submitted word against (a) the dictionary, (b) the valid characters, and (c) duplicate words this round.

EXECUTING THE SPEC

It is a good idea to start building your game with your spec in hand. I paste the names and descriptions of the handlers directly into a text cast member and start from there.

Keep in mind, however, that you will probably not end up with handlers that match your initial proposal exactly. Few people can think every conceivable issue through carefully enough in order to solve every problem.

Remain flexible, but work from the spec. You did the planning for a reason. Build a schedule from it and come back to it as you work in order to make certain you are not drifting away from your original intentions.

NOTE

Remember that this is only a partial spec. The full spec can be found in Appendix A.

The major objective of this revision is to blend the appearance of the interface with the game's narrative. My goal was to create a fast-paced and exciting variant of the game that retained some of the challenge/reward model from prior versions—and added to it. I wanted to add complications to the game's story in order to allow players to feel that staircase of unresolved tension laced with a constant enticement to continue.

By adding complications to the scoring and timing routines, using sound effects to reward and rebuke the players, and increasing the clarity and visual appeal of the game, these goals have been met. Along the way, we cleaned up the rules of interaction and made the game more easily usable.

I have given you the source code for the second and third variants of *Word Wacky*, so feel free to poke around and see how everything works. The code is reasonably commented, and I have named most items in a verbose enough fashion to indicate their functions. You will find the code on the CD-ROM within the file named `wordWacky3D.dir`.

A cursory glance at the code for *Word Wacky 3D* should get you warmed up. In the next chapter, we'll start moving away from fixed-screen games and into immersive real-time games.

CHAPTER 3

Managing Your Story On-the-Fly

Now we're ready to say goodbye to traditional flat-screen interfaces and start looking at immersive real-time 3D games. The instant that we drop an interactive camera into a real-time 3D world, the rules change. Many of the conventions of branched narratives and 2D input that we have become accustomed to are immediately discarded when working in a 3D universe.

Adding 2D navigational tools inside this sort of universe can be an acceptable and even successful part of the narrative. However, it is not the most intuitive solution in most cases because 3D worlds seem a lot like the world in which we live. It is logical to approach interaction in a manner that is more consistent with the manner in which we might interact with actual objects in our own world.

One of the most fundamental elements of life in our 3D universe is that it is *dynamic*. Things change over time. Now you can either look at this as a terrifying limitation, or you can see it as an awesome and liberating opportunity. I choose to see it as an opportunity.

After reading and understanding the chapter, you should

- Know how to create characters that choose their own responses dynamically
- Know how to randomize responses
- Understand what actors and playwrights do about conflict and stories
- Understand how to encourage actions that lead to conflict

In this chapter, you'll see concrete examples of several game elements, learn how to use object-oriented design to craft dynamic game spaces, and learn ways to make your characters and objects exchange information.

I'll talk about the pitfalls of exposition (the most common reason that stories and games don't get along), and then we'll examine conflict. Conflict is the glue that bonds games and stories together. You'll have a chance to get your Director 3D feet wet as we walk through the creation of *Battle Ball*. You'll see some simple examples of these concepts in action.

I'll discuss the importance of conflict, even in game moments that feature friendly communication. Every character needs something, and it should always cost your player something to advance his or her own cause. Finally, I'll talk about the importance of reducing predictability in your games by randomizing responses.

Creating Dynamic Plots

You may remember my introduction to plots from Chapter 1, "The Story: How Much Is Too Much?" Think back a second to the description of plot as a series of events, each unresolved and each more tense than the preceding moment. In a static plot, these events are always the same. They generally occur in the same order, and their content remains fixed. The manner in which characters interact remains constant. The strategies that led to success the first time you encountered the plot lead to success the second, and the strategies that led to failure the first time always lead to failure.

In a dynamic plot, the events are flexible. The manner in which the characters interact does not remain constant. It is deliberately variable. The effects of an action are unpredictable, just as they are in everyday life.

In a static plot, the princess always awakens when kissed by Prince Charming. In a dynamic plot, you can't be so certain. The princess may only be able to find true love with the dragon during this incarnation, at this moment of game play. Moments later she may shift her affections to the villain or an ogre. Characters are dynamic, ever changing, and full of surprises in a dynamic plot. (We'll likely place a few limits on that dynamism in order to prevent total insanity.)

Change is a central part of a dynamic plot. The characters, environment, and objects within the game are all subject to change without notice.

Although dynamic plots are a more logical approach to building real-time 3D immersive games, using dynamic plots versus static plots creates some new problems for the developer.

In some ways, dynamic plots are considerably more difficult than static plots to wrap your head around. In another sense—that they more closely mirror the personal experiences of people—dynamic plots can be much less cumbersome.

Spatial, Psychological, and Narrative Spheres of Influence

The concept of spheres of influence was introduced in Chapter 1. The simple game/proof we will create later in this chapter relies heavily on spheres of influence. We will use model-based spheres of influence to detect collision and interpenetration of spheres due to relative proximity. Think of this type of event as a spatial use of spheres.

Spatial spheres of influence are simulated physical areas surrounding 3D nodes that register and alert the system to collision events between nodes within the 3D world. They are spatial, because they use the distances and coordinate systems within the 3D world in order to work. The ball bouncing off trees in the forest in Chapter 1 uses this type of sphere of influence. The ball sees the tree, reads the angle of impact, and bounces off the tree in a semiplausible direction.

Although we haven't seen any other types of sphere of influence yet, they do exist. Psychological spheres of influence may be modeled in a similar fashion. Obviously these would not depend on the coordinate systems of the 3D world or on simulated physical proximity. Psychological spheres of influence are scanning for a different type of violation. These may include emotional violation, intellectual violation, and spiritual violation.

Remember, any interaction between two objects is an act of violence. Given that understanding, you can begin to access the degree of violation and compare it to the level of desirable violation (yes, there is such a thing).

There are simple parallels to this concept in everyday human behavior. Have you ever met a person who stood way too close while he talked to you? Of course you have. This is an undesirable violation of your personal space.

Have you ever wanted someone to get closer than that for a hug? Of course you have. This is a desirable violation of your personal proximity limits. A hug from an enemy during a fight will meet with a different response than a hug from a loved one.

In the same sense, communication between people is rooted in this fundamental concept of levels of desirable and undesirable violation. Speaking is a violation of silence. Emotional expression is a violation of emotional tranquility. Intellectual curiosity is a violation of memory.

Substitute the word *event* for the word *violation* and this concept is both easier to accept and easier to translate into code. Any object, physical or conceptual, that has a rest state and an excited state may model dynamic states this way.

The last sphere of influence we'll talk about is an overarching story sphere. It has a default resting routine and is capable of being violated. This resting (or *stasis*) routine consists of the behaviors that the story sphere object performs in order to remain balanced and stable. It is not that hard to see that we'll be able to give our narrative sphere of influence a set of desired violations. The resulting narrative sphere object will work diligently to encourage the sorts of events it wishes would occur.

Exposition That Engages

One of the most common reasons that dramatic writing (play, screenplay, and game) fails to entertain an audience is the lack of active, well-integrated exposition. People get really hacked off when you feed them too much passive exposition. Exposition should be revealed as the result of conflicts. Exposition that is not evoked by conflict is passive.

Imagine a couple getting ready for a date. Now let's start a fight between them when she finds another woman's clothing in the sheets of the bed. It is not difficult to see that they will argue. Now is the time she (as your messenger) should introduce the exposition that reveals that he is a real dog. If it were done before this, it would seem contrived and forced, but as a product of genuine and relevant action, it works.

The same concept applies to a game. Don't tell us that the princess turns into a swan via lame text screens that we don't care to read. Let us work to find the princess, meet her, and experience traveling with her as she struggles to avoid revealing this truth to us. Eventually we'll learn about the amazing transformation either by witnessing it or by forcing it out of her through some marginally related confrontation. Either way, the results heighten the reaction and increase the plausibility.

When you add to all of this our desire to deliver dynamic rather than static exposition, you quickly identify a need for a fundamentally object-oriented approach to this problem. If we see the objects as the characters and intelligent agents within our environment, we can begin to form a model for the game.

One good way to visualize an object-oriented approach to dynamic narratives driven by the actions of intelligent agents uses a good deal of toilet paper. That's right—toilet paper.

I'm thinking of a Mummenschanz Mask Theatre performance that was insanely popular when I was a kid. Essentially, a giant head formed only of rolls and bits of toilet paper entertained us for a few minutes (see Figure 3.1). I suppose that we, as a culture, were easier to entertain in the late 70s.

FIGURE 3.1

The Mummenschanz Mask Theatre performance of the toilet paper face.

The comparison here is simple. Within this toilet tissue metaphor, the rolls of toilet paper that construct the mouth and eyes of a Mummenschanz puppet are networked dynamic objects with variable properties—networked in the sense that a central intelligence object (the performer) knows the state of each roll of toilet paper. When the mouth roll is unraveled, we (the audience) perceive an extended tongue. These qualities are remembered by that central intelligence and every imaginable variant is attempted by the performer in order to explore the potential for response.

Now let's pretend that a computer-driven simulated intelligence controls the rolls of toilet paper. Our software dynamic object could do the same things. It can unravel and re-roll the toilet paper. It can try lots of variations and record responses to different combinations. It is even possible for the dynamic object to learn the effects of its self-modification on the environment. When the Mummenschanz puppet's tongue goes out, people laugh. The manner in which the tongue goes out affects how much people laugh. In this example, the rolls of tissue are not intelligent; human performers lend them intelligence.

Encouraging Actions That Lead to Conflict

In Chapter 1, I briefly outlined Edwin Guthrie's psychological theory of motivation. Guthrie's theory breaks the process of object stimulation and subsequent resolution into the following steps:

- A stimulus event upsets or excites the object, which is then driven to restore stasis.

- The proposed response is compared with those that the object remembers using in similar circumstances.

- Repetition of like responses leads to habit.

- The initial event creates both direct excitement and secondary stimuli in the object.

- All responses are motivated by the desire to remove the initial stimulus and return to stasis.

- Sooner or later, something succeeds in removing the stimulus and the object returns to stasis.

NOTE

It would be awfully narrow-minded to stop any investigation of the motivation of human action at behaviorism. We aren't really trying to make intelligent objects for our games; we are just trying to create reasonable simulations. For this, Guthrie's theory is a more than adequate launch pad. Although this list is based on Guthrie's, I have freely deviated from the original.

Inciting the Intelligent Agents

You could consider Guthrie's model an accidentally prepared roadmap for designing intelligent agents. That wasn't his objective, but it amuses me. It certainly falls outside the original intention of the theory of motivation, but because our work with plot is entirely dependent on simulating the actions of characters, this theory can help us to design agents that make choices that are logically motivated.

The object in Guthrie's model begins in a state of relaxation and contentment. The object is balanced. It is in stasis. Stasis is a trick of perception—the time interval before an audience is aware of actions and reactions. Stasis is the idling state of the object. It is a rest state where all motivations have been adequately addressed. Stasis is the habit phase, where behaviors are executed in order to prevent the stimulus from occurring.

The first event for the model can be compared to a theatrical and literary concept called the *inciting incident*. During an inciting incident, some event—either the product of internal motivations or the result of external stimuli—causes sufficient interruption to evoke a reaction from an intelligent agent. In order to irritate the intelligence, the stimuli must conflict with its motivational drives. The object will not regard all stimuli as negative influences. Some will be found desirable by the object.

In the next phase of our model, motivation combines with memory in the selection of action/reaction. Our virtual intelligence evaluates the event and searches for similar past experiences to plan a reaction. Once a similar or matching event-response is located, the intelligence reacts in the manner that is most likely to produce the desired outcome. If the attempt removes the irritant, the intelligence logs the success in memory and returns to stasis. If the attempt fails to remove the stimulus, the intelligence logs the failure and makes another selection. The object makes its choice of reaction based on prediction via pattern matching.

NOTE

We won't be implementing memory in our game. I've simplified the paradigm in order to focus on the most substantial elements.

Actions that yield expected results are more likely to be selected in future cycles and may even be applied as a form of prevention or protection by adding them to the stasis routines. You could describe stasis routines as "habits" that the intelligence executes while idling.

Motivations drive all action and reactions. Without motive there is no action. Motivations can even generate actions and events within an individual intelligence and lead to conflict within that individual entity.

The actions of one intelligence appear as events to another intelligence. Actions from any intelligence lead to reactions from the other intelligences that come into contact with the original intelligence. This occurs both when the motivations of the two intelligences are in conflict with one another and when the violations occur between two objects whose motivations are cooperative.

In a sense, we might say that the behaviors of conflicting intelligences engage in negotiation with one another. For each intelligent agent the ultimate goal is to return to stasis.

The Art of Negotiation

Negotiation is the heart and soul of what we call conflict. There are infinite methods of negotiation. The most logical form of negotiation is almost never the most dramatic. Likewise, it is almost never the method chosen by individual intelligences as their preferred strategy.

In other words, it is logical for the entities to exchange a list of needs and desires and to negotiate in a manner that leads to consensus approval of the solution. Most often, however, the entities will abstract the needs and desires and negotiate in various methods, many of which are nonproductive in order to try to "win."

It is this desire to win the negotiation that prevents simple logic from serving its purpose. The desire to win must be factored in to the potential intelligence.

The intelligence logs the release of the incited stimuli and remembers negatively those actions that failed to resolve the conflict and positively those actions that succeeded. This is, of course, a generalization. The log is relative. An entity might log a value of positivity or, even better, a positive-to-negative ratio for the strategy. The more complex and comprehensive the memory, the more accurate the predictions will be when patterns are associated during the comparative phase of new events.

Conflict Resolution Strategies

Strategies are reusable behaviors with dynamic arguments. In other words, an entity may use the same strategy in many different situations while substituting any of the properties of the behavior, the objects that are influenced, and the concepts under negotiation.

In accordance with Abraham Maslow's hierarchy of human needs, the motivations essentially fall under the following classifications: physical safety, food and shelter, love and belonging, self-awareness and acceptance, and self-actualization. Intelligences tend to abstract these motivations. This action seems to deter awareness of the underlying motivations

Maslow suggests that intelligences are limited by a foundational relationship between these objectives. The objectives on the base layer of this hierarchy must be satisfied before the intelligence will seek any of the higher levels. In a related way, the intelligence will forfeit the upper levels if any lower level is threatened or removed. Our virtual intelligences then, should be guided by these motivations in this order (although if asked about the motivations behind an action, they would probably give a deceptive response or abstract the motivation in some way).

Example: *Battle Ball*

I think that the best way to really wrap your head around these ideas is to start messing around with a game example that puts the ideas to work.

Battle Ball is a weird little game proof I created to demonstrate the concepts of dynamic objects within a game. I've included the media for the game on the companion CD-ROM, along with the finished game. Over the next several pages, I'll introduce you to *Battle Ball* and describe the code I used to create the characters and effects.

Before we begin, open the file labeled `BattleBall.dir` found on the CD-ROM. Rewind and press Play.

After the splash screen, the primary game screen, shown in Figure 3.2, appears.

FIGURE 3.2

The primary game screen for Battle Ball.

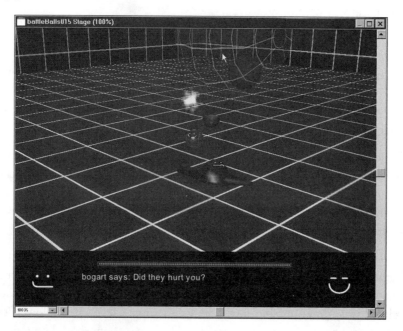

The Game Screen

The game screen is divided into six elements:

- The large central area is occupied by a 3D sprite.

- Directly below this is a green power bar that will indicate the player's life force.

- Below the life force indicator are two rich-text sprites. The top one, named "display," will display the messages that the player's character hears and says during the game.

- The bottom sprite, named "battle," will display text that describes attacks and other nonverbal events that occur in the space.

  These text areas serve to supplement the information that the user might otherwise glean from the 3D environment alone. In some cases, this has been done to optimize the movie; in other cases, it has simply been done to simplify the game.

- To the left of the text areas is another text sprite that displays the facial reaction of the character that is speaking.

- On the right side, the player's face is displayed. This provides visual cues for the player during game play.

The player's objective is simple: Free the trapped battle ball. Unfortunately, the deck seems stacked against him. Not only do the red battle balls pose an escalating threat, the blue battle balls are reticent to assist. Enough coaxing will eventually secure some help, in the form of magic, from several of the player's teammates.

Now stop the game and open the cast window using the thumbnail view. If you make your cast window 10 cells wide, you will get a peek at the overall structure of the media and code for the game (see Figure 3.3).

The Cast

The cast is easily divided into six categories: 3D media, scripts, text members, shapes, fonts, and sounds. Let's start with those at the end of the list, because you are probably already familiar with members of these types.

The sound files in the bottom row are used to create the background music and an occasional mouse response. If you played the game already, you may be wondering about this. The background music clearly changes tempo as the game advances levels. This is done with only one sound file, thanks to the new #rateshift property of Director's sound command. In the message window, type the following:

```
sound(8).play(member("bkLoop"))
```

Press the Return key when you are finished typing. This starts the music. There is nothing out of the ordinary here. Now type the following command into the message window and press the Return key:

```
sound(8).play([#member: member("bkLoop"), #rateshift:12])
```

This may be amusing, even exciting at first, but you'd be ready to slug me if I didn't mention here that you can stop this or any such sound simply by clicking the Stop button on the control pad in the toolbar. Stop, even when the movie isn't playing? Yes.

FIGURE 3.3

The cast for Battle Ball.

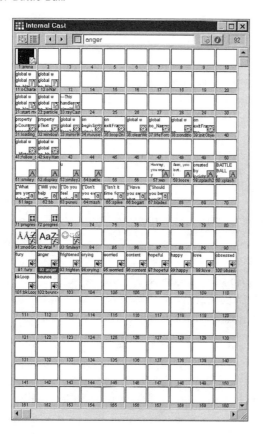

Moving on up the cast, sounds in the next row are named to match the emotional states—such as anger, crying, worried, hopeful, and happy— of the characters in the game. In other words, the names of the emotions that the characters express are the same as the names of these sounds. In this case, the characters share these sounds. You might like to modify these ideas and enhance your characters by giving them individual voices.

Above the sounds you will find the fonts used in the movie. I embed the fonts in order to ensure the player sees the same thing I do, regardless of the fonts available on her system.

The next row contains the shapes used to make the loading bar and life-status bar. Using shapes is much less expensive, in terms of download bandwidth, than using bitmaps. Here, I've taken advantage of one of the built-in textures to give my progress bar a more finished look.

The next two rows contain field and rich-text cast members. The fields store the data that the characters use to speak. The rich text is used to display this information to the player.

Moving up the cast, the next four rows contain scripts. Most of these scripts just handle routine business, such as looping on the frame or moving to a new frame when a mouseUp event is received.

We will focus most of our attention on the parent scripts (second row from the top). These scripts generate the characters' intelligence in the game as well as the narrative management object. The character object scripts handle the bulk of the spatial sphere of influence and psychological sphere of influence, whereas the narrative object script handles the narrative sphere of influence.

The last item (the top row) in the cast is a 3D cast member.

The 3D Cast Member

Inside the 3D world are 21 models: five planes that comprise the floor and walls of the arena, seven spheres and seven small planes that compose the battle balls, one spheroid cage hanging above the center of the battlefield, and the trapped battle ball inside the cage. During game play, we will add and remove a pair of particle fountains that represent the level of experience or magic that the player has attained.

The 3D cast member takes advantage of the userData property of models in order to assign properties to models at design time. This little-known feature allows developers to enter property and value pairs in the user-defined properties field from within a 3D modeling package and then access those properties from Lingo.

Think of it as a way to attach information about a character to the character without having to devise some complex scheme in Director. From within 3D Studio Max, simply right-click a model and choose Properties. The Properties dialog appears. Click the User Defined tab (see Figure 3.4).

FIGURE 3.4

The User Defined tab of the Properties dialog in 3D Studio Max.

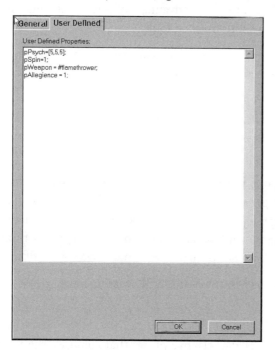

In the dialog, type the property-value pairs you want to define. Once the file is exported from Max and then imported into Director, you may access the properties via the userData property of the appropriate 3D model. Try this in the message window:

```
put member(1).model[2].userData

-- [#pPsych: "[5,5,5]", #pSpin: "1", #pWeapon: \

" #flamethrower", #pAllegience: " 1"]
```

This feature alone would be great, but the userData property supports both get and the set access. Type the following in the message window:

```
member(1).model[2].userData.pWeapon =3 #hamsterCage

-- [#pPsych: "[5,5,5]", #pSpin: "1", #pWeapon: \

#hamsterCage, #pAllegience: " 1"]
```

While you are thinking about it, notice that all the values have been converted to strings within Lingo. Later you'll see me restore integers and lists to their correct data types by using the value() command. It will save you some frustration if you lock this trivia into your brain now. I've included the 3D Studio Max file on the CD-ROM as well, so if you have Max, feel free to open it up and putter around (bbArena.max). Even if you don't have 3D Studio Max or another authoring program, you may still use the model's userData property.

The model[2] referenced in the previous command is bb, the player's 3D personae. Each of the character models has four properties defined within the userData property: pPsych, pSpin, pWeapon, and pAllegience. These properties store information about the individual that helps the game engine to make decisions at runtime. The most important and least immediately apparent of these is the character's initial psychological state. I created a mathematical model designed to represent the emotional states of the characters in the game. This is most easily explained with the assistance of Figure 3.5.

FIGURE 3.5

This diagram illustrates the conversion of discreet psychological states into a numerical index.

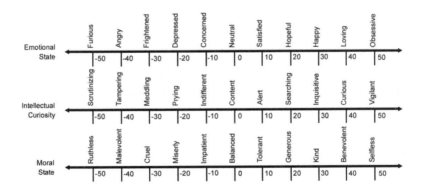

A simple model of psychological motivations

The pPsych **States**

It would be silly to try to develop too extensive a model for such a simple game, so I kept things very basic. The numeric model of the psychological state of any given character is essentially broken into three integers used to represent the emotional, intellectual, and moral states of the character at any given moment.

It was essential that these elements be reduced to numbers in order that we could evaluate the effects of one character on the next.

The emotional state is the most important of these, and the only one that I was worried about expressing, although the other elements certainly contribute to the model.

Each state is expressed as a number between −50 and 50. The farther an intelligent object's composite state moves away from zero, the more agitated that object becomes. Negative numbers are used to express negative emotions, curiosity, and moral states, with escalating degrees of irritation. Positive numbers are used to express positive emotions, curiosity, and moral states, with escalating degrees of stimulation. These values are then averaged in order to obtain an overall psychological index that may be expressed by the object.

The manifestation of these emotional outbursts includes changes to the facial expression, shader coloring, opacity, and size of the character models within the space. Strong negative emotions can cause a character to attack, regardless of its affiliation. Strong positive emotions can lead to love, obsession, and an absurd need to follow the player's onscreen representative wherever it goes.

How the Game Lingo Handles Emotions

The Lingo that handles these emotional shifts is broken into two parts. First, a series of mathematical expressions averages the values of each model's three psychological indicators and then pulls each model's indicator values out to the more stimulated zone or back toward the less stimulated zone, depending on whether the model was a friend or an enemy. The easiest way to accomplish this mathematically is to convert the list of three numbers into a Lingo vector. This way, I can perform vector math functions on items from more than one list.

The second part of the handler is an enormous case statement. The case statement converts the character's overall psychological index (the averaged value of all three psychological components) into action. In this design, psychological states are converted into action without regard for history, prediction, or motivation. It is not difficult to see that these elements could be added to a structure like this in order to compound the dynamism of the character and increase the sophistication of its choices. A portion of this statement is found in Listing 3.1. It's the section that handles the reaction to friendly characters (the blue battle balls).

LISTING 3.1   A Section of the *evaluateStimulus* Handler

```
 1:    ----------------------------------------------FRIEND REACTION LOGIC
 2:          1:
 3:            -- this is a friend
 4:            case TRUE of
 5:              ----------------------------------------NEGATIVE STIMULI
 6:              (tMyAgitation > -51 AND tMyAgitation < -41):
 7:                --- the character is furious, ruthless and scrutinizing
 8:                me.mEmote(#fury) -- emote fury
 9:                me.mAttack(whichModel, #nonLethal, \
                    ((tMyAgitation) * -1), tMyWeapon)
10:                --- attack the other character without causing serious harm
11:                --- set the intensity of the attack \
                    based on the level of agitation
12:                me.mChangeColor(rgb(255,0,0))-- change color of the shader
13:                me.mHide(100)--set the opacity to full
14:                me.mspeak(whichModel, tMyAgitation)--talk to the model you hit
15:                me.mAttract(whichModel, 10)--move toward the model that you hit
16:              (tMyAgitation > -42 AND tMyAgitation < -33):
17:                --- the character is malevolent, angry and tampering
18:                me.mAttack(whichModel, #gestural, \
                    ((tMyAgitation) * -1), tMyWeapon)
19:                me.mEmote(#anger)
20:                me.mChangeColor(rgb(205,90,90))
21:                me.mHide(100)
22:                me.mAttract(whichModel, 10)
23:                me.mspeak(whichModel, tMyAgitation)
24:              (tMyAgitation > -34 AND tMyAgitation < -25):
25:                --- the character is cruel, frightened, and meddling
26:                me.mAttack(whichModel, #gestural, \
                    ((tMyAgitation) * -1), tMyWeapon)
27:                me.mEmote(#frightened)
28:                me.mHide(40)--set the opacity to 40%
29:                me.mAvoid(whichModel, 15)--run away \
                    from the model that you hit
30:                me.mChangeColor(rgb(50,125,50))
31:                me.mspeak(whichModel, tMyAgitation)
32:              (tMyAgitation > -26 AND tMyAgitation < -17):
33:                --- the character is miserly, depressed and prying
34:                me.mEmote(#crying)
35:                me.mHide(100)
36:                me.mChangeColor(rgb(0,0,255))
37:                me.mAvoid(whichModel, 5)
38:                me.mspeak(whichModel, tMyAgitation)
39:              (tMyAgitation > -18 AND tMyAgitation < -9):
40:                --- the character is impatient, concerned and indifferent
41:                me.mEmote(#worried)
```

LISTING 3.1   Continued

```
42:                 me.mChangeColor(rgb(125,125,125))
43:                 me.mHide(100)
44:                 me.mAttract(whichModel, 10)
45:                 me.mspeak(whichModel, tMyAgitation)
46:                 -------------------------------------------STASIS
47:             (tMyAgitation > -10 AND tMyAgitation < 10):
48:                 --- the character is balanced, neutral and content
49:                 me.mHide(100)
50:                 me.mChangeColor(rgb(55,225,225))
51:                 me.mspeak(whichModel, tMyAgitation)
52:                 me.mAttract(whichModel, 10)
53:                 ---------------------------------------POSITIVE STIMULI
54:             (tMyAgitation > 9 AND tMyAgitation < 18):
55:                 --- the character is tolerant, satisfied and alert
56:                 me.mEmote(#content)
57:                 me.mHide(100)
58:                 me.mChangeColor(rgb(55,225,225))
59:                 me.mspeak(whichModel, tMyAgitation)
60:                 me.mAttract(whichModel, 10)
61:             (tMyAgitation > 17 AND tMyAgitation < 26):
62:                 --- the character is generous, hopeful and searching
63:                 me.mEmote(#hopeful)
64:                 me.mHide(100)
65:                 me.mChangeColor(rgb(155,0,225))
66:                 me.mspeak(whichModel, tMyAgitation)
67:                 me.mAttract(whichModel, 10)
68:             (tMyAgitation > 25 AND tMyAgitation < 34):
69:                 --- the character is kind, happy and inquisitive
70:                 me.mEmote(#happy)
71:                 me.mHide(100)
72:                 me.mChangeColor(rgb(225,225,0))
73:                 me.mspeak(whichModel, tMyAgitation)
74:                 me.mAttract(whichModel, 10)
75:             (tMyAgitation > 33 AND tMyAgitation < 42):
76:                 --- the character is benevolent, loving and curious
77:                 me.mEmote(#love)
78:                 me.mHide(100)
79:                 me.mChangeColor(rgb(200,0,200))
80:                 me.mspeak(whichModel, tMyAgitation)
81:                 me.mAttract(whichModel, 30)
82:             (tMyAgitation > 41 AND tMyAgitation < 51):
83:                 --- the character is selfless, obsessive and vigilant
84:                 me.mEmote(#obsessed)
85:                 me.mHide(100)
86:                 me.mChangeColor(rgb(100,0,100))
```

LISTING 3.1 Continued

```
87:                 me.mAttract(whichModel, 100)
88:                 me.mspeak(whichModel, tMyAgitation)
89:            end case
90:            --------------------------END FRIEND REACTION LOGIC
```

There is a similar `case` statement in the parent script of the characters that handles enemies. It is a bit more violent, featuring `#lethal` attacks and more aggressive attraction.

Each character also has an `mRelax()` method designed to return it to its natural state. This ensures that characters don't get more stimulated than they should. It also prevents a world full of satisfied and content little critters.

Characters are able to receive stimuli, because they see, hear, and feel. Well, not *really*, but they do have methods that support these concepts logically. If a character speaks to another character, the receiving character is sent an `mHear()` command. If someone attacks another character, the victim is sent an `mFeel()` command, and if a character spots another character, an `mSee()` command is sent.

There are no methods for smelling or tasting, because there is nothing in this game to eat or smell. However, I don't think such methods would be out of the question, especially if you wanted to simulate a fairly complex world.

The Score

Now that you have a sense of the pieces that make up the cast of this game, let's take a look at the score. Open the score (see Figure 3.6) of the movie in Director and rewind.

Before we go any further, I want you to notice the sprite in channel 10. It's a copy of the 3D world that has been moved offstage. Now before you assume that I've lost my faculties, let me explain. The behavior of the 3D member can be less than 100-percent reliable if the member hasn't fully downloaded and settled into memory before the movie starts to play. It is always a good idea to use the 3D preloader provided via the Publish dialog to prevent this sort of unreliability, but this alternative is a good safety net in the event that you are less certain about the manner in which your movie will be viewed.

FIGURE 3.6

The score of Battle Ball.

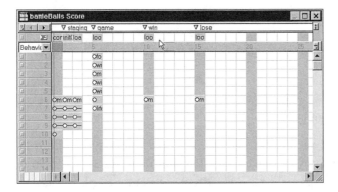

Director loads cast members in order of use, unless you specifically change the cast preload property. Director loads cast members in order of use (unless you specifically change the cast preload property), which encourages the Shockwave player to become aware of our 3D world and lets me rest a bit easier.

There are four markers in the movie. The first marker is used to identify the staging area, where the movie verifies the state of the w3D member and initializes the objects. The second marker defines the game space. The game loops on a single frame until the player either wins or loses. If the player wins, the playback head advances to the third (win) marker; otherwise, it advances to the fourth (lose) marker.

The first frame script, called `conditionalLoop`, simply waits for the w3D member to reach its fully loaded state and then moves the playback head into the staging frame. The movie is only there for an instant, just long enough run the `initObjects()` handler, initializing the character and narrative objects. Afterward, the playback head moves on to the third frame. Then the system waits for the w3D member to reach the fully loaded state and give the user a visual signal that the program is working behind the scenes to prepare the game.

In this case, the progress bar is essentially decorative. Its only real purpose is to delay the user for a second, in case something has gone awry with the 3D model.

From here the playback head jumps to the fifth frame. This is the game screen. Its frame script contains a simple looping command, which is shared by the win and lose frames.

The only remaining behavior script that is not tied to the game play section of the movie is a simple mouseUp script that is shared by the splash, win, and lose sprites. It sets the cursor to a finger and moves the playback to the game zone if the w3D member is ready.

Most of the sprites used in the game play section of the score have simple behaviors that assist them in communicating with the objects in the movie and the models in the w3D cast member.

Several of the text members use the windowWasher behavior to clean their members after enough time has passed for the player to read the text.

The progress bar uses the lifeForce behavior to find and translate the narrative-management object's record of the player's health into a real-time display of diminishing life.

The w3D sprite hosts two behaviors. The first one is a simple camera behavior that follows a model. The second behavior checks the keyboard input and moves the player's onscreen model as directed by her keyboard commands.

The initObjects script does several important jobs that get our 3D world rolling. I've placed it here for your convenience. The code begins with the declaration of global variables that will be used to provide access to the 3D models and the narrative-management object:

```
 1: global w
 2: global co_blades
 3: global co_bogart
 4: global co_spike
 5: global co_mash
 6: global co_punwu
 7: global co_bb
 8: global co_lags
 9: global no_nar
10: global faceTextureList
```

The global w is a reference to the 3D member. The 3D member is itself an object, and as we go along you may notice that working with it is a lot like working with our other objects. Each of the globals preceded by the letters "co" will hold a character object. The no_Nar global is a reference to the narrative-management object, and faceTextureList will hold a property list describing the keyboard equivalents of each emotional state.

When the movie begins, I clear the globals for good measure and assign member(1) to the global w:

```
12: on startMovie()
13:   clearGlobals()
14:   w = member(1)
15: end
```

Once the playback head leaves the second frame, an initObjects command is issued. Because this is a Movie script, it finds a handler here and things really get moving. First, objects are created for each character. The parameter passed after the script name is the index number of the model in the 3D world. The object will use this reference to maintain a hook on its representative model. Here's the code:

```
17: on initObjects()
18:   co_blades = new(script "oCharacter", 7)
19:   co_bogart = new(script "oCharacter", 6)
20:   co_spike = new(script "oCharacter", 5)
21:   co_mash = new(script "oCharacter", 4)
22:   co_punwu = new(script "oCharacter", 3)
23:   co_bb = new(script "oCharacter", 2)
24:   co_lags = new(script "oCharacter", 1)
25:   no_nar = new(script "oNar")
```

After the objects are born, I add each one to the actorList. This is because objects on the actorList receive a stepFrame event, telling them that the playback head has moved a frame. Here's the code:

```
26:   add(the actorlist, co_blades)
27:   add(the actorlist, co_bogart)
28:   add(the actorlist, co_spike)
29:   add(the actorlist, co_mash)
30:   add(the actorlist, co_punwu)
31:   add(the actorlist, co_bb)
32:   add(the actorlist, co_lags)
33:   add(the actorlist, no_nar)
```

NOTE

The `stepFrame` event is a special event that is only sent to objects that reside in the `actorList`. Every time the playback head advances a frame or an `updateStage()` command is issued, the objects in the list receive an event. This means you can disable the update messages for an object simply by removing the object from the `actorlist`.

Now I set the `faceTextureList` and update the faces of all the models using the images I generate via imaging Lingo. All the possible emotional states are generated here as textures, and then the models may use whichever one they need without influencing the textures used by the other models. Here's the code:

```
34:   faceTextureList = [#obsessed:"y", #love: "s", \
      #happy: "a", #hopeful: "d", #content: "u", #worried: "g",\
      #crying: "l", #frightened: "o", #anger:"q", #fury: "r"]
35:   repeat with iterTextures = 1 to count(faceTextureList)
```

Adding the textures to the world is a fairly simple matter. First, I set the text of a rich-text cast member to the value of the *n*th item in the `faceTextureList`. Then I create a Lingo image object simply by assigning the `image` property of the text member to the variable `ImageObject`.

Once the image is ready, the texture is created using the `newTexture` command. The command requires three parameters: a string representing the name of the new texture; a symbol, either `#fromCastmember` or `#fromImageObject`, telling the command what type of resource you plan to use; and either a Lingo image object or a cast member reference, depending on which type you specified. You are commanding the 3D member (remember, it is an object) to create this new texture for you, so the dot syntax approach says that you should reference the world `w` and then issue a command, like so:

```
w.command()
```

Note that there are parentheses around the parameters for the command. If you think about it, the only difference between a standard command and the object command is that you reference the object followed by a dot and then issue the command:

```
36:     member("smiley").text = faceTextureList[iterTextures]
37:     ImageObject = member("smiley").image
38:     w.newTexture(string(getPropAt(faceTextureList, \
iterTextures)), #fromImageObject, imageObject)
39:   end repeat
```

Once the handler has done this for all 10 items in the list, it resets the text member to a blank display, because we're going to use it for another purpose now that this chore is done. We created textures, but they are just little texture objects without homes at this point. They are also not visible, because textures need to be assigned to shaders in order to be seen. Wrap your head around it this way: A `modelResource` needs a model; a model needs a shader; a shader can have a texture. So, let's work on those shaders. First, we know that we want to change the hue of our battle ball models during the game. You can't change the hue of a texture, but you can blend the diffuse shader color with the texture if you turn on the model's `useDiffuseWithTexture` property.

In this next bit of code, I turn that `useDiffuseWithTexture` switch on and then move on to the faces of each character that are called by the same names, but with the addition of the word `Face`. Under this system, `bb` has a face model called `bbFace`. Using naming conventions like this helps me to reference models with `repeat` loops rather than working through individual statements or checking all the models for the one I need.

Finally, I want to be able to see that face regardless of whether I'm in front of the model or in back, so I switch the visibility of each face model from the default, `#front`, to `#both`. Here's the code:

```
40:  member("smiley").text =""
41:  repeat with iterModel = 1 to 7
42:    w.model[iterModel].shader.useDiffuseWithTexture = 1
43:    myFace = w.model[iterModel].name&"face"
44:    w.model(myFace).visibility = #both
```

Now this may be a bit strange to imagine if you haven't got a copy of 3D Studio Max, but parts of the animation that you see in the game are prerecorded keyframe animations, and parts of the animation are controlled via Lingo. Because the local coordinate systems of the spheres vary, and their direction is dynamic due to the spin, I wanted to take advantage of the relative stability of the faces to handle the bulk of the model's motion. You might want to visualize this as models that are dragged around by the face.

In this next section, I attach the character models to their faces as children of the faces. This has some cool side effects. If I move the face via code, the body will come along for the ride. In fact, it will go wherever I take the face and match the face's rotation as well, regardless of the orientation of the child (character body) as it spins.

Because I have a natural aversion to math, I liked this solution: The `addChild()` command is supported by model objects. This is not a slip of the tongue. I don't mean the character objects that we created moments ago. I mean the model objects that are inherent in the 3D member object. This should be starting to echo in your head. Most properties of the 3D member are really objects. Just as the 3D member has methods, these child objects masquerading as properties have methods that they support. Some of their properties are, in turn, objects as well.

Therefore, the `addChild()` method is a method of 3D models. Because the model is a child of the world, you need to reference first the world and then the model. The dot syntax approach looks like `w.model[x].addChild()` or `w.model("ModelName").addChild()`. This method requires only one parameter, but it will accept a second. The first parameter, which must be included, is a reference to the child model.

To reference that model, you'll need to start with the world and work down to the model. The second argument is a symbol that instructs the function to preserve the world-relative position of the model—or preserve the parent-relative coordinates of the model. I know that's hard to visualize, so bear with me as we look at an example.

A room has a stand, a lamp, and a couch. The couch is near the south wall, the stand is near the west wall, and the lamp is on top of the stand. Each of the models is a child of the world. If I want the lamp to remain with the stand no matter where the stand is moved, it would make sense to make the lamp the child of the stand. I would be in good shape if I used `#preserveWorld` as my argument, because the lamp would not move when the child is added to the stand.

If I used the `#preserveParent` argument, on the other hand, the lamp would move west by the exact distance that the stand is from the center of the room. Were there any gravity in the room, the lamp would crash to the floor and break. If the lamp's original `transform.position` was `vector(0,0,30)`, its new `transform.position` would still be `vector(0,0,30)`. The difference is that the measurement of the vector doesn't originate at the center of the world. Now it would originate at the stand.

Next, I set things off on the right foot by aiming the models at the player using the `interpolateTo` command. Finally, I apply the `"content"` texture to each model's shader:

```
45:     w.model(myFace).addChild(w.model[iterModel], #preserveWorld)
46:     if w.model[iterModel].name <> "bbFace" then
47:       w.model(w.model[iterModel].name&"Face").\
        transform.interpolateTo(w.model("bbFace").transform, 20)
48:     end if
50:     w.model(myFace).shader.texture = w.texture("content")
51:   end repeat
```

I start the background sound and tweak the volume. Then I fine-tune the shaders on the cage and on our primary character model:

```
52:   sound(8).play(member("bkLoop"))
53:   sound(8).volume = 125
54:   w.model("Sphere01").shader.emissive = rgb(255,255,255)
55:   w.model[2].shader.emissive = rgb(255,255,255)
56: end
```

The last element of the startup scripts is the stopMovie handler. I like to reset the world with the resetWorld command on the stopMovie event. This prevents you from getting thousands of errors as you work in the development of your game and keeps you from deluding yourself about saving any of the changes that you make to the w3D world via Lingo. Next, I reset the actorList and then clear the globals:

```
58: on stopMovie
59:   w.resetWorld()
60:   the actorList = []
61:   clearGlobals()
62: end
```

This script works to set up the space so that the object's scripts may gain full control over the activity within the 3D world. With relatively little effort, we've got characters that are able to move, change appearance, attack, avoid, chase, speak, think, relax, and express emotions. Each one can communicate with the player's character and have conflicts with one another and the player's character.

Perhaps most importantly, the conflict experienced is the source of the communication and the only channel for narrative exposition. The characters negotiate with one another through emotional exchange and through attacks of varying intensities. You should be able to see the framework here for more extensive implementations of these concepts.

The other parent script in *Battle Ball* is the parent for the narrative-management object. Unlike the character objects, the narrative-management object has no physical representation. Only one object is created from this script.

The narrative-management object handles the special events and properties that control the complexity of the game. In this challenge/reward plot model, we want the game to become more difficult as the player experiences more elements.

If the player succeeds in coaxing magic out of one of the other characters, the narrative-management object alters the level (#pLevel) of the game. The background music accelerates, and the characters are allowed to move faster. The attacks grow more punishing and the degree of attraction and repulsion characters "feel" for one another grows more severe.

Think about these factors in terms of our staircase of plot. There is an event, born of conflict (the player negotiates emotionally with the character), in order to get the magic. The instant that the challenge is met, the stakes are raised. The player can see the cage lower toward the floor, indicating that he has moved closer to freeing his trapped comrade, and clues from his journey have probably prompted him to realize that this is his overarching goal.

Each time the player obtains more magic, the cage moves lower and the magic particle fountains change color. The pitch of the background music accelerates, and the player is left with a sense of both reward and urgent renewal of the challenge.

Characters are based on people. Even characters that aren't human are generally anthropomorphic (assigned human characteristics). People want things— things such as safety, shelter, love, group membership, and self-confidence— and rarely more purely noble things.

The way that these things appear in life is in pursuit of abstract things that are rooted in these fundamental needs. In order for characters to really interest a player, they should demand something from the player.

Conflict and negotiation are more interesting than passive exposition and finger twitching. We don't know what the outcome of a negotiation will be. The more strategy options the player controls, the more engaged she will become in the narrative of the game. Even during cooperation, characters need to negotiate. Aggressively opposite characters will make this journey toward conflict an easier one to take.

In the next chapter, we begin to look at the many ways we can integrate dynamic control into the various 3D elements within a game. We'll explore cameras, lights, sounds, and even shaders that are meant to dynamically self-modify in order to enhance game play and the overall entertainment experience.

CHAPTER 4

Revealing the World Dynamically

Game designers have a rich heritage from which to draw in the representation of stories through visual imagery. The cinema has been creating conventions for communicating narrative concepts (storytelling) for more than a century. In addition, we can draw on the tactics of live television broadcasters. In fact, live-broadcast sporting events provide a fantastic paradigm upon which we might build because the underlying problems and objectives are very similar. Sports are games, and most bear some substantial relationship to electronic games. Both are dynamic, and the outcome of each is unknown. Both provide challenges and rewards with ever-escalating levels of tension, as the outcome of the event grows nearer.

Over the last 50 years, live broadcasts have grown more and more sophisticated and have incorporated many of the "tricks" of conventional theatre and film in order to enhance the emotional effect of the event. A superb example of this may be seen in broadcasts of the Olympic games. Virtually all material that can be altered for emotional enhancement is altered—video effects, lighting tricks, background music, and even enhanced audio sound effects that accentuate the labor, suffering, or triumph of each athlete.

After reading and understanding the chapter, you should

- Know how to use 3D information to control sound dynamically
- Know how to use 3D information to control the cameras dynamically
- Know how to maintain a consistent visual palette
- Understand the relationship between visual elements and the player's emotional and psychological response

- Understand the relationship between the aural elements and the player's emotional and psychological response

- Have experimented with dynamic cameras, lights, sounds, and shaders

In this chapter, we let the traditions of theatre, film, and television guide us to some tricks that will allow the environments in our games to self-modify in the interest of presenting a more appropriate mood. We'll adjust the sound, lights, shaders, and cameras in order to create visually appealing and emotionally evocative game spaces.

We will explore the look, feel, and sound of our 3D world. I'll talk about adapting these elements dynamically in order to add tension and visual appeal to our games. Then you'll have a chance to play with the various elements that make up the visual and aural experience for the player. I'll give you some tips about using these devises to encourage the emotional and psychological response you'd like your game-story to have.

Along the way we'll examine the influence of the interface on the entertainment experience. Then I'll describe the process of generating simulated environments that are likely to enable conflict (in the dramatic sense) to emerge and build. You'll learn about the importance of color and shapes for establishing visual appeal and maintaining unity. Finally, I'll give you some ideas about using visual themes and styles to create quick, consistent chrome for your project.

Smart Sounds

One of the things that generally separates cinema from electronic games is the incredible breadth of camera angles, lighting effects, and sound effects/scores we find in a film. Games do not generally feature this sort of variety. This lack of variety was inevitable when we were working with flat 2D graphics, but in a 3D universe, we have considerably more fluid control over the image and the relationship of sound to that image.

One of the ways that we can breathe extra life into our games is by augmenting them with sound effects. In prior chapters, you've seen me begin to address this by altering the tempo of a given background loop. If we take full advantage of the combined power of 3D worlds and Director's sound engine, we can create extremely dynamic sound effects and atmospheres within our 3D worlds.

There is a substantial reason to place this emphasis on the audio effects that enhance your game. Great sounds make the visual elements within your game seem more professional. Unfortunately, the inverse is also true. Crappy sounds can make even the most beautifully illustrated game look bad. People actually regard the visual effects with more esteem if the audio track is well implemented.

The flip side of this desire for rich, full, dynamic sounds is the substantial size that sound files add to a project. In most cases, sound files take up more space in a project than any other element. The only common exception is full-motion video.

The good news is that we can take advantage of the dynamic playback of sounds to fool the player into believing that there is substantially more variation in the audio track than there actually is. The ideal solution is to combine small audio files with extensively dynamic playback solutions in order to create a world that seems unpredictable, alive, and immediate.

Another way to enhance the dynamism of our games is to alter the lighting, special effects, and camera angles/effects on-the-fly. It is no secret that the angle from which a camera views a scene and the intensity and hue of the lighting have a dramatic effect on the 3D scene.

We have the capability to change those appearances dynamically with Shockwave 3D, and it can be a powerful tool in our continued effort to tell stories dynamically.

Imagine, for example, a simple over-the-shoulder game with a biped figure walking across a generic landscape. If we slowly, over 2 or 3 minutes, ramp down the lighting and introduce fog, we can move the character from a day-light scene to a dusk scene. Along the way we could add initially distant, then exponentially louder sounds of woodland creatures. The further we move into the creepy look, the more intermittent spooky sounds we could add. Just as the ever-escalating pace of the ticky drumming noise made you feel anxious when you played *Word Wacky 3D*, these effects make players feel edgy and anxious. If we do a really nice job, our effects may even make them jump or give them that "heebie-jeebie" feeling.

Now imagine this experience for a moment from the player's perspective. As you play the game, the camera suddenly cuts to a different shot. You are still in control of the game; this isn't *cinematic*. You might wonder what has happened, confused because you weren't in any obvious peril at that moment.

This second shot looks familiar. You recognize the landscape. It is not far from here, but something about this shot is wrong. It is discolored and seems strangely blurred.

Now hundreds of spiders rush into the shot, and you realize that this second shot is a point-of-view angle from one of the spiders. The sound grows to almost overwhelming levels as the spiders claw and fight to get to the head of the pack.

The camera cuts back to an over-the-shoulder view of the hero as the sound of the approaching swarm returns to a distant squeal. After a moment, you realize that the sound of the spider swarm is swelling. You detect that the sound is coming from the right so, like any good player, you start running left as fast as you are able.

The scene's drama is heavily reliant on camera angle, lens effects, lighting, and sound to tell the story and move the player to experience the emotional intensity of the moment. That's the rush we want people to have when they play a game. The emotional response doesn't have to be fear; it may be anything—amusement, excitement, a sense of achievement or accomplishment, or elation, for example. The key is that there is some response.

The computer, through the use of dynamic narrative management tools, can produce any of these effects easily.

Making the Place Sound Right for the Moment

In order to solve the challenge of assigning sounds to the game dynamically, you first break the task down into its component parts. The job of creating sound for your game is really a multifaceted project.

Feedback

Games need sounds that reinforce the users' actions—feedback. These sounds don't need to have anything to do with the story, and they usually don't meld too perfectly into the game space. It is preferable to keep this sort of sound consistent throughout the game rather than to change it during gameplay. This is because players regard such changes with suspicion—they assume that a different reinforcement sound indicates that the action now triggers a different response than it did the last time they used it.

Underscore

The underscore of a game—the music track, generally instrumental, that plays in a loop beneath the other action—can be its biggest asset or its biggest pitfall. The underscore is the musical accompaniment for the game. It is generally created with a series of short musical phrases that have similar melodies and that may be tied together in various combinations in order to create a varied musical background. It is similar to the soundtrack of a movie.

Underscoring may be used quite effectively to enhance a mood or tone in a scene. As events in the game change, the underscoring changes to suggest the mood or emotional state of the heroic figure or player.

Because underscoring is generally found throughout a game, it can get horribly monotonous if you don't do all that you can to vary the music. Think about the first time you ever played *Mario Brothers*. Do you remember that awful music looping over and over, eventually creating a sort of aural retinal burn—the audio equivalent of staring into the sun?

A good approach to underscoring a lengthy immersive game is to make certain that you have at least five tracks of loopable audio that will blend together effectively regardless of the order in which they are blended. You should have five such tracks for *each* audio tone or mood you want to represent.

By combining these sounds in varied sequences, adjusting the playback speed, and varying the volume, you should be able to create an interesting enough variety of sounds so that the players won't feel that they've been listening to the same exact 12 bars of music for the past 2 hours.

TIP

> Keep in mind that each loop must contain at least one complete musical phrase. Short phrases of only one or two bars would lead to the same sort of painful droning that an insufficient supply of loops creates. Try to make the loops at least 8 seconds long. If you can afford the file sizes, they may be considerably longer.

Background Noise

The sound effects that players really don't hear—but do notice when they aren't present—are background noises. These sounds can be a major boon to immersive 3D games. They add depth and richness to the soundscape, and they can aid in setting the overall scene.

Background noises include nonmusical sounds, such as people talking in the distance, dogs barking, crickets chirping, or any sound that suggests a place. These are general sounds that the players might hear if they were in the location suggested by the 3D scene.

These sounds should change dynamically as well. Unlike the underscoring, these changes should be motivated by the spatial environment in which the game is played. Although these sounds certainly do contribute to the overall ambiance of the game, their primary mission is tied to the story. They are there to help set the scene.

Motion Enhancement Sound Effects

One great way to help demonstrate physical violations, disruptions, and other physical events within the 3D space is to trigger motion-enhancing sound effects during gameplay. If a 3D model bounces off a wall, players observe the change in direction with minimal interest. If players witness the bounce accompanied by an appropriate sound effect, their response is substantially greater. They will be more aware of the event and more able to assess the relevance of the event.

If that same event occurs and the model complains or creates a sound that suggests pain, or even pleasure, players feel more aware of the nature of the character.

This category includes simple tracking effects, such as the sounds of breathing, running, galloping, and footsteps. It also includes event sounds, such as bombs, magic sparkles, and rainstorms.

Vocals

Characters often speak in the games we create. These are some of the hardest sounds to deal with, and the potential for plausible dynamic response is stifled significantly by the need to either prerecord responses or rely on text-to-voice translation software.

Sometimes these are limited to an occasional verbal expression. Sometimes they include lengthy prerecorded lines that the game characters use to inform the player about the environment or to challenge the player to perform a given task.

These may be as simple as the sound of a character screaming "Yeah!" every time a given event occurs or as complex as multithreaded dialog that is triggered by the cumulative actions and interactions of the character. In *Starship Titanic*, the dialog is determined dynamically based on a sophisticated text parser and the game's internal artificial intelligence calculations.

Generally these sounds are prerecorded sound files that are played back by the system when a given event occurs. There is no hard rule about creating or delivering such vocals. However, there is one simple guideline I can give you: Dialog and vocals should always be louder than overlays, background noise, and motion-enhancing sound effects. This is because the player will want to hear these moments clearly. It is more difficult to listen to the words of the character while playing the game than it is to respond to the other aural elements. It requires that the player think specifically about the meaning of the dialog and then translate those words into action.

Obviously the most likely candidates for dynamic sound manipulation are the underscore, background noise, and motion enhancement. These may really be divided into two separate classes. The underscore may be used to create dynamic changes in the overall tone, aesthetic quality, and mood of the moment, whereas the other two categories (background noise and motion enhancement) may be dynamically adjusted in order to bring special emphasis to moments, actions, or events within the story.

Classifying Sounds

In theatrical design, we distinguish choices that are attributed to environmental and spatial influences from those that are attributed to emotional motives. Environmentally motivated design choices are called *motivated*, and emotionally motivated design choices are called *motivational*. It makes sense to adopt these classifications in our discussion of both dynamic sounds and images.

For the most part, motivational changes (changes to the underscore) are the result of adjustments in the following areas:

- The sequence of a group or collection of sound loops.
- The rateshift of a sound loop or group of sound loops.
- The volume of a sound loop or group of sound loops.

- The frequency of playback for each sound loop in the group of sound loops that echoes the desired emotional representation.

- The emotional tone of the game. The group of sound loops is changed in order to reflect this.

Motivated changes (changes to the background noise and motion-enhancement sound effects) are generally created through the following actions:

- The sequence of a group of sounds changes.

- The volume of a sound or group of sounds varies as proximity to the camera changes.

- The left-to-right pan of a sound or group of sounds varies as the directional relationship to the camera changes.

- The narrative function of the sound triggers changes in the frequency of playback, alterations of the representative sound, and variation in the rateshift property.

A quick examination of both lists reveals a couple of important things. First, there is a little crossover, so some of the handlers we write will be useful for both purposes. Second, only the motivated sounds need to know about the state of objects in the 3D world. These are the only objects that appear to react to events within the 3D world, so they are the only ones that really need much awareness of it.

One of the neatest things about motion enhancement in a 3D game is the potential to simulate 3D soundscapes to match the 3D environment. We can dynamically adjust the relative pan and volume of an audio effect in response to the spatial relationship of the sound's source. In other words, the sound of birds to the left can be assigned to the left speaker, and the volume of the sound effect can increase as the birds approach the camera.

The underscore has two major purposes. One, it is simply working to fool the players into believing that the score is more complex than it really is. And two, it is used to evoke emotional responses in the players. If we are using a narrative-management agent to monitor the players' actions and to play the sounds, the agent can choose sounds that are compatible with the emotional states that we have identified as appropriate for the players at their current levels of experience.

Smart Spaces

The elements of the 3D member that contribute to the overall visual appearance of the 3D game are also an important tool in our storytelling and game-making arsenal. Controlling these visual elements is equally as powerful, and it is a trick that should not be overlooked.

For many years now, one of the largest single deterrents to delivering rich, multiperspective, dynamic graphical images to players via the Internet has been the extraordinary bottleneck you face in asking them to download enormous movie files. Now you can create many of the same effects—in some cases, the exact same effects—without the download issues. One view of the model is equal to 10,000 views of the model as far as download time is concerned, so why not go a little crazy with this new found universal perspective.

Visuals in the Gamespace

The problem of creating dynamic visual representations of your game space may be broken down into subsets based on the purpose of the manipulation. Here are the major purposes:

- *To aid the user in working with the interface.* This category is very similar to its counterpart in dynamic sound. As such, similar precepts cross over between the sound elements and the dynamic visual elements. Players do not react well to arbitrary dynamic changes in the visual appearance of the interface elements. They want to know that the look of the button, readout, or widget is constant. This allows them to keep their mind in the game and off the control devices.

- *To tell the story.* Choices that are made that assist in the retelling of the story may be assigned dynamically. These are generally visual elements, such as evidence of a struggle or battle that clues the user in on a recent conflict in the space. A player might walk into a cabin to find the table set and porridge cooking on the stovetop.

- *To suggest the environment.* Enhancing the environment may be absolutely dynamic. This could include changes that suggest alternative times of day or the influences of 3D models, such as candles or lamps, on the appearance of the environment.

- *To trigger emotional responses in the player.* This is the most dynamic of the four purposes. Changes of this type may influence any aspect of the visual appearance of the model. They are considerably more flexible than changes to sounds that enhance the story, because these changes are rooted in the emotions. The impending attack of the spiders described earlier in this chapter exemplifies this method of dynamic visual manipulation.

Those elements that may be adjusted dynamically without frustrating the user can essentially be broken into two categories: emotional stimulus and environmental/narrative enhancement. You may notice that these directly parallel the motivated and motivational classifications used to define the dynamic sounds.

Motivational changes to the visual elements (changes that are designed to stimulate an emotional response in the player) generally require changes in the following areas:

- The color of light in a scene.
- The intensity of light in a scene
- The direction/angle of light in a scene
- The angle/orientation of the camera
- The depth of field of the camera
- The properties of the shaders attached to key models in a scene
- Special effects in a scene

Motivated changes (changes to the visual elements that are designed to reflect changes in the environment of the game or changes to lead the player to a clearer understanding of the story behind the game) generally require the following:

- Changes in the position of the camera.
- Less extreme changes to the color of light.
- Less extreme changes to the intensity of light.
- The direction/angle of lights and the camera to be motivated by logical onscreen sources of light and sources of image.

Keep in mind that you shouldn't think of either of these lists as prohibitive, but they might prove very useful if you want to change something to alter the mood or the time of day and you aren't certain where to begin.

Exercise 4.1:   Evocative Sounds, Cameras, Lights, and Shaders

Now let's try some tinkering to see what sort of things we can accomplish with lights, cameras, sounds, and shaders. Open the movie named 04Evoc01.dir on the companion CD-ROM.

This is the completed version of the exercise. Go ahead and click the Rewind and Play buttons and watch the movie play for a few minutes. Figure 4.1 shows the state of the lights after a few seconds of play. Watch the tabs below the 3D world to track the changes in the lighting as you experiment with mouse movement.

FIGURE 4.1

The exercise movie features dynamic sound and lights.

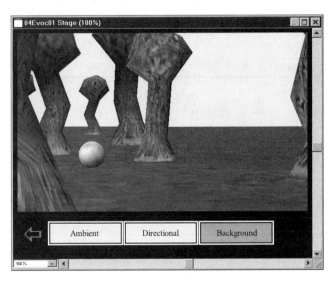

Immediately you should notice that the mouse is attached to the ball. I've attached the mouse motion to the motion of the 3D sphere and then made some other adjustments to the sound in the 3D space based on the distance between the mouse and the camera. I've also made some adjustments to the sound based on the direction that the ball moves away from the camera.

Finally, I've made some time-based adjustments that basically change the nature of the light and background over a period of time. You'll need to watch the program run for at least two or three minutes to see all the effects.

If your computer doesn't support left and right speaker separation, you may not realize that the pan is being adjusted dynamically as well. The effect should suggest that the ball is somehow the source of the sound. When the ball moves farther away, the sound diminishes. When the ball moves closer, the sound grows louder. When the ball moves off the screen to the left, the sound pans to the left speaker channel, and as the ball moves to the right, the pan mirrors that motion as well. I included a couple of arrows to mimic the effect for those who don't have speaker systems that support panning.

Now that you've got a reasonable sense of what this little project can do, it's your turn to dig around under the hood and make your own version.

Find the `04Evoc02.dir` file on the companion CD-ROM and open it in Director now. This is essentially the same movie, except for the absence of the script that handles the dynamic lights and sound. The complete script is shown in Listing 4.1. You may use it as you work through the steps to replicate this movie.

LISTING 4.1   The Tracker Behavior

```
1: global w
2:
3: property pCenterPoint
4: property pClock
5:
6: on beginSprite(me)
7:   cursor 200
8:   w = member(1)
9:   pCenterH = (sprite(1).rect.width / 2)
10:   pCenterV = (sprite(1).rect.height / 2)
11:   pCenterPoint = [pCenterH, pCenterV]
12:   w.bgColor = rgb( 166, 202, 240 )
13:   w.ambientColor = rgb(255,255,255)
14:   w.directionalColor = rgb(255,255,255)
15:   sound(8).play(member("freakyghost"))
16:   sound(8).volume = 100
17:   pClock = the ticks
18: end
```

LISTING 4.1   Continued

```
19:
20: on exitFrame(me)
21:  if the ticks - pClock > 30 then
22:    w.ambientColor = w.ambientColor - 1
23:    w.directionalColor = w.directionalColor -1
24:    w.bgColor = w.bgColor - 1
25:    pClock = the Ticks
26:  end if
27:  tTran = w.model("GeoSphere01").transform
28:  tTran.position.x = ((pCenterPoint[1] - the mouseH )) * 4
29:  tTran.position.y = (the mouseV - pCenterPoint[2]) * 10
30:  w.model("GeoSphere01").transform.interpolateTo(tTran, 2)
31:  tDist = w.model("GeoSphere01").transform.position.distanceTo\
32:  (sprite(1).camera.transform.position)
33:  tDist = tDist / 1000.000
34:  tDist = (10.000 - tDist)/10.000
35:  tVol = 255 * tDist
36:  if tTran.position.x < 0 then
37:   sound(8).pan = 100 * tDist
38: else
39:    sound (8).pan = ((100 * tDist )* -1)
40:  end if
41:  if sound(8).volume <> tVol then
42:    sound(8).volume = tVol
43:  end if
44: end
```

To replicate the exercise movie, follow these steps:

1. Create a new behavior cast member and name it **tracker**.

2. Let this script and a few others know that "w" is a global variable. To do this simply, type **global w** as it appears in the figure. (We'll use it to refer to the 3D world as we have in previous examples.)

3. Declare two properties, pClock and pCenterPoint. At this point, your script should look like the one shown in Figure 4.2.

4. Enter the beginSprite handler as it appears in lines 6–19 of Listing 4.1. Each of these commands needs to be executed only once in order to prepare the movie. You may already be familiar with the first command, cursor 200. This line simply changes the cursor to an invisible one, getting it out of our hair so that we can remain focused on the world and the ball. We don't really need it because there isn't anything to click.

FIGURE 4.2

First declare your global and properties.

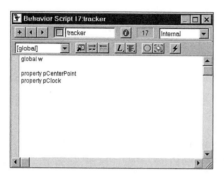

Lines 9–11 figure out where the center of the stage is and make a note of this location in the property pCenterPoint. This value is stored along with the behavior so that we can access it quickly when we need it.

Next comes a command with which you may not be familiar: w.bgColor = rgb(166, 202, 240). It tells the 3D cast member (referenced by the variable w) to change its background color to a pale blue. I want to start with that color, but you can start with any value that amuses you.

Lines 13 and 14 set the default lights of the 3D world to display using a white-colored light. You probably noticed that the environment slowly fades from daylight to a very dark night scene. These two lights do the bulk of that work.

In lines 15 and 16, we turn on the sound and set the level, playing a file named rundle_a. You could just as easily use one of your own sounds—just import it and change the name here to reflect the name of your sound file. If you do use a new one, make sure that it is set up to loop.

The last line makes a note of the time when we started playing the movie. In order to make gradual changes without sacrificing the playback rate, we'll track changes in the ticks against this record of time. Your script should now look similar the one shown in Figure 4.3.

5. The last handler is the exitFrame handler. For convenience, I'll break it down into three parts. First, type in lines 20–26. This section of the code will only execute twice a second, which is fairly slow compared to the execution of animation, but it can run much slower. If you raise the integer 30 to 600 or more, changes will become subtle enough that a player is unlikely to notice the dimming effect until the effect has reached a fairly

dramatic level. The effect shifts the value of three elements. The W3D member's ambient color property is an rgb color object, which represents the color value of ambient (reflected) light within the environment. By slowly subtracting an equal amount from each hue, we'll get a gentle glide to a darker value variant of the same color we began with (w.ambientColor = w.ambientColor - 1).

FIGURE 4.3

The beginSprite *handler gets everything ready for business.*

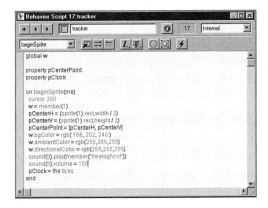

```
Behavior Script 17:tracker

+  ◀  ▶   □ tracker                    ❶   17   Internal        ▾

beginSprite        ▾   🔊 ≕ ⊟  L 𝑬  ○▦  ⌁

  global w

  property pCenterPoint
  property pClock

  on beginSprite(me)
    cursor 200
    w = member(1)
    pCenterH = (sprite(1).rect.width / 2)
    pCenterV = (sprite(1).rect.height / 2)
    pCenterPoint = [pCenterH, pCenterV]
    w.bgColor = rgb(168, 202, 240 )
    w.ambientColor = rgb(255,255,255)
    w.directionalColor = rgb(255,255,255)
    sound(6).play(member("freakyghost"))
    sound(6).volume = 100
    pClock = the ticks
  end
```

Second, the directional color applies because I added a directional light by selecting one from the drop-down menu in the Property Inspector for the W3D cast member. This world uses a #bottomRight directional light. The trick with the ramping is handled the same way it was for the ambientColor property (w.directionalColor = w.directionalColor - 1).

Finally, the background color of the 3D world is changed in the same manner (w.bgColor = w.bgColor - 1). At this point, the pClock property is reset so that it will be triggered again in one half of a second (pClock = the Ticks).

6. Now enter lines 27 through 35. The overall purpose of these lines is to calculate the level to which the sound should be set. With the line tTran = w.model("GeoSphere01").transform, I get a copy of the transform of the ball. I want to avoid working directly on the ball's transform. Once there is a copy, I can set the x- and y- axes of the transform's position to reflect the movements of the mouse.

Now in order to understand this, you need to remember that this is a 3D Studio Max–generated world. That means that z is the up-and-down axis. We know that the goal is to move the ball along the ground, either on the x-axis or the y-axis. If we simply match the players' left-to-right motions to the x-axis and their top-to-bottom motions to the y-axis, we'll get the ball to move along the ground plane.

The last trick in this ball animation sequence involves the command that actually moves the model: `w.model("GeoSphere01").transform.interpolateTo(tTran, 2)`. It uses `interpolateTo()` in order to move the ball part of the way to the goal, and it has the net effect of dampening the motion as the mouse stops.

Next, we have to determine how far the ball is from the camera in order to calculate the volume at which the sound should play. This is done with the `distanceTo()` command. Use this command on a vector in order to calculate the distance in standard world units between two vectors.

We then do a bit of math to convert the resulting distance into a number that can be translated into values between 0 and 255, the range of the sound volume. The net effect is a distance-sensitive volume system. I implemented this method in this form so you could see that the model wouldn't need to be attached to anything in order for us to change its volume based on distance from the camera. It could just as easily be wandering around independently.

7. The last section of the `exitFrame` handler attaches the pan of the sound to the direction of the sound source from the camera. Director allows you to set the left-to-right pan of an audio signal using a range from –100 (totally left) to 100 (totally right). Go ahead and type in lines 36–44 now. You may check your work against the script shown in Figure 4.4.

8. Finally, click the lightening bolt to compile your script. Assuming that you receive no alerts, save your movie. Drag the `tracker` behavior over to the W3D sprite and drop it. Rewind and play to admire your work.

9. You might want to play with the rateshift property of the sound member you are working on. See if you can adjust the rateshift of the sound dynamically.

FIGURE 4.4

The finished script.

```
Behavior Script 17:tracker
tracker                         17  Internal
[global]

on exitFrame(me)
  if the ticks - pClock > 30 then
    w.ambientColor = w.ambientColor - 1
    w.directionalColor = w.directionalColor - 1
    w.bgColor = w.bgColor - 1
    pClock = the Ticks
  end if
  tTran = w.model("GeoSphere01").transform
  tTran.position.x = ((pCenterPoint[1] - the mouseH )) * 4
  tTran.position.y = (the mouseV - pCenterPoint[2]) * 10
  w.model("GeoSphere01").transform.interpolateTo(tTran, 2)
  tDist = w.model("GeoSphere01").transform.position.distanceTo\
  (sprite(1).camera.transform.position)
  tDist = tDist / 1000.000
  tDist = (10.000 - tDist)/10.000
  tVol = 255 * tDist
  if tTran.position.x < 0 then
    sound(8).pan = 100 * tDist
  else
    sound (8).pan = ((100 * tDist)* -1)
  end if
  if sound(8).volume <> tVol then
    sound(8).volume = tVol
  end if
end
```

Making Everything Match

One of the many things that can go wrong as you begin to develop more dynamic games is a slow drifting toward chaos. This usually erupts initially in the form of visual chaos, and it is identifiable by almost any witness other than the game's developer.

It is one of the sad realities of game design and development that developers are notoriously bad at evaluating their own games. This is especially painful and true when it comes to interfaces. There are some clues that you may use as you work to prevent this visual confusion. Many of them are rooted in the fundamental elements and principles of design. (If you need a refresher on these principles, you will find a brief summary in Appendix B, "Composition Basics.") It is imperative that you recognize the elevated state of importance that people give to every single aesthetic, aural, and logical choice you make in the design and development of your games.

If you put that penguin there, it must be for some terribly important reason. After all, no one could be insane enough to put a penguin in the middle of a bloody first-person shooter staged in the Nevada desert without having a really, really good reason.

Sooner or later you will be guilty of dropping penguins in the desert, and when you do, remember your Aristotle.

Probability and Plausibility

That's right, I said Aristotle. That crazy old philosopher and teacher had a few really helpful hints to offer about the creation of dramatic events. One of the most universal of these is something commonly called *Aristotle's Law of Probability*.

This precept essentially says that anything you demonstrate that could actually happen in your story/game space will be okay with the audience, but anything that you suggest (via context) that isn't likely to occur in your world will irritate your audience.

In short, if you set your game in the desert, and there's no way that there would be penguins out there, the audience is going to assume that the presence of the penguin is either the biggest mistake in game design history or a huge and significant clue about the eventual solution to the game.

You can and should use this convention to your favor, but remember as you work that it holds true for all kinds of things within the world. It even applies to items as simple as the color of a character's coat.

Using Palettes and Shapes to Bring the World Together

One way you can actively work to tie the various elements of your 3D world together is through the use of analogous shape and color schemes.

Color palettes can be a really huge issue when you are first beginning to design games. It's easy to forget that all the hundreds, sometimes thousands of individual media elements will eventually exist within the same tiny little space, separated by only a few pixels on the screen.

You can avoid an ugly game if you make decisions about the exact nature of the colors before you begin the process. By doing so, you will also avoid the huge and painful process of reworking various images in the interest of blending back down to a more analogous palette.

This element of planning is even more important in the development of real-time 3D games than it is in the creation of 2D games, because the palette for the models and their textures is heavily influenced by the palette of the lighting and any camera effects that are applied. As you saw in Exercise 4.1, the color of every object in the space can be completely altered just by adjusting the lights.

The other major element that has the potential to blend the world into a unified whole is the overall geometric shape of the objects. The repetition of similar forms and shapes unifies the overall visual appearance of your game.

If you echo the quality or style of your game with the quality of lines and shapes found in the images, the game will feel more inherently right. Use sharp angular lines with dramatic contrast in dark and light coloration to create an edgy, harsh, menacing world. Use soft angles, dull colors, and suggestive shapes to create a sense of mystery and suspense. If you use round, light-colored, spiraling shapes, your game will have a fun, comical appeal.

You can, of course, mix these lines, shapes, and forms. If you do, realize that it may eventually lead to a problem in the overall appearance of the game. You could easily end up with so many dissimilar colors and shapes in the 3D space that the player feels uncertain about everything from navigation to the goal of the game.

A minimal use of either one of these unifying elements in total discord with the others can be a major tool for you. A red rose in a black and white world immediately lends focus and significance to the rose. If the rose is a critical element of the plot or the next major token that craves acquisition, then you're cooking with gas, baby.

Tapping into Visual Themes for Inspiration

One of my favorite methods for discovering the visual flavor of the 3D world is by looking to visual art and film for inspiration. I have often found that the palette of a given painting, once analyzed, can open the door for a team of people to visualize colors that may suit their current project well.

In a similar sense, the lines, shapes, and forms found in paintings can serve as guideposts to help you understand how the shapes, lines, and forms you choose to display in your game will suggest various moods to your audience.

You can find visual themes in all sorts of places. I once worked for a couple of producers who loved to eat. Every time we had a meeting, I would be dragged to yet another restaurant. At first, I couldn't figure out why my color ideas were constantly being rejected. Finally, I realized that the only color ideas that ever appealed to these two were color descriptions based in food. The colors tan, pale yellow, and red-violet were certainly not acceptable to them, but the colors toast, butter, and raspberry jam were!

There are visual themes everywhere—in nature and in our more civilized spaces. Look around you and ask yourself, "Why do I like the look of those things together, but I don't like this with them?" If you do this, you'll be well on your way to choosing great looks for your games.

Exercise 4.2:   Dynamic Sound, Light, and Cameras.

I've prepared a sample movie—04Studio02.dir on the companion CD-ROM— to give you the opportunity to spend some time exploring many of the concepts I've talked about in this chapter.

I've labeled a screen capture of the interface in Figure 4.5. You may find it helpful to consult this figure before you begin experimenting with the movie.

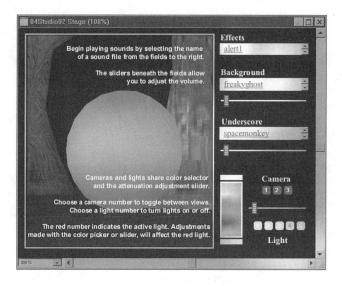

FIGURE 4.5

The labeled interface.

Rewind and click Play to begin working with the studio. All the interface elements are on the right side of the screen. Working from top to bottom, you will find a scrolling list of sound effects, typical of the sounds that are used to enhance motion events.

The mechanics of these elements are fairly straightforward. A rich-text member lists the names of sound cast members. Each name is hyperlinked to an empty reference. If you click the name of an effect, a message is sent to the sprite instructing it to play the sound.

The point is to give you the opportunity to look at 3D images, manipulate their appearance, and mix sound effects, backgrounds, and underscoring simultaneously.

Choose a background sound from the Background list. You can adjust the volume of the sound by using the slider just below the field. (The Effects channel volume is not accessible.) Once you have the background level comfortably set, start one of the underscore sounds and adjust its volume.

Listening to the combinations that can occur when you blend these sounds at various levels can be very educational and often surprising. Try starting the background called `cartoonelec` and the underscore labeled `arcademusic`. It shouldn't take you long to figure out what sort of effect you can achieve with these sounds.

It is always surprising to me that simple changes to the overall sound scheme can totally alter its nature. With `arcademusic` still looping, switch your background to `boogieman`. Drop the volume on `arcademusic` to about 25 percent. Wow, what a difference!

There is also a clue here about the manner in which you should organize your sounds. Separate the sounds that you will be using into tracks. Dedicate each track to a certain type of sound in order to ensure that you can play back more than one sound at a time.

Below the sound widgets you'll find camera and lighting controls. The camera buttons enable you to select any of the three cameras I have placed in the environment. The white bar launches the color selector. Click the white bar adjacent to the camera label and you can add a colored filter to the lens of the camera. You can use the slider bar below the camera buttons to adjust the opacity of the color filter in front of the camera's lens.

The slider only affects the camera color filter when the last color chip selected was the camera's color chip. If the last color adjustment you made was an adjustment to a light's color filter, the slider bar will adjust the intensity (attenuation) of the light that is currently highlighted.

Clicking any of the yellow light toggles switches the corresponding light off. A second click turns that light on and selects it as the current light. Once a light is the current selection (has a red number), you can adjust its color filter by using the lighting color chip. You may also adjust the intensity of the spotlights (1, 2, and 3).

This movie provides you with a good playground for experimenting with various visual effects and aural combinations. You might also try using the Property Inspector for the 3D member to adjust the properties of the lights in the scene.

The dynamic manipulation of the various elements that form the 3D scene is clearly a potent tool in game creation. In the next part of the book, I'll introduce you to Director's new 3D features. I'll give you examples and exercises to test your skills and understanding of the many new features that are now supported.

PART II

Building Blocks of Shockwave 3D Games

Master the tools and rules of 3D Lingo as I walk you through examples, demos, exercises, and explanations of hundreds of Director's newest features.

CHAPTER 5

An Introduction to Director 3D

There are some basic differences between the way Director works with 3D scene cast members and the way it works with most other media types. Getting familiar with the new elements of the interface is important if you plan to be working with Director's new 3D features. It is also important to recognize the fundamental differences in structure of the new 3D media type. Learning how to work with this new type of data conceptually will save you tons of frustration.

After reading the chapter you should

- Know how to use the Property Inspector for 3D sprites and cast members
- Know how you can manipulate and change your 3D model within Director
- Understand how a model's orientation affects its movement
- Understand the basic principles of 3D Lingo
- Have created some models from scratch
- Know how to animate models with Lingo
- Know the properties of a 3D model in Director
- Know the commands supported by 3D models in Director
- Know how to manipulate the position and rotation of models in the 3D world via Lingo
- Understand the process of controlling a 3D model
- Understand how to relate user input to animation within the 3D world

In this chapter, I discuss the interface controls that enable users to manipulate 3D cast members directly within Director. I explain the way that the Property Inspector allows you to control your 3D cast member, and I give you some sense of the limitations it holds. I also talk about Cartesian coordinate systems used for orienting each object in your 3D world, and you learn how to compensate for the varying coordinate systems used in some of the 3D authoring packages that export media into Director. We'll take a look at the 3D viewer found inside Director, and I'll explain how to use it.

After that, I explain the structure of Director's 3D media type and the importance of understanding it as an object. Although you may have been able to slip by with little to no understanding of object-oriented structures in the past, Director's 3D media type relies so heavily on the object-oriented model that you'll find it necessary to embrace the form. Next, I introduce you to some of the fundamental Lingo concepts used to manipulate 3D media within Director. Together we'll create some 3D magic entirely in Lingo. I walk you through each step of creating models, lights, and a camera in order to animate some simple spheres.

In the second half of this chapter, I give you a substantial guide to use when working with models in your Director games. You get an overview of a model's properties, and then we'll move on to the commands supported for 3D models. Finally, we'll use these properties and commands to complete our first complex animation. I show you how to create an intricate model of an airplane, and then we animate each of its parts separately. By the end of this chapter, we make it possible for a user to steer our flying machine.

NOTE

If you are unfamiliar with properties and commands in Lingo, you might want to do some additional reading in general Lingo use before pressing on. There are several good books available that introduce Lingo fundamentals; you can find good lists of the latest books online at http://www.director-online.com. You will also find a host of good articles on the site that can help you gain a better understanding of traditional programming in Director.

3D Interface Elements

If you are not already familiar with the Macromedia Director interface, I encourage you to do some investigation before you go much further. A number of good resources are already available that discuss these elements, and Director is sold with substantial documentation.

The interface elements related to 3D in Director are fairly few and remarkably simple at this point. In Director 8.5, two new tabs (the 3D Model tab and the 3D Text tab) appear on the Property Inspector, which you can see when viewing either a 3D member or text as a 3D member. The 3D Model tab (see Figure 5.1) allows you to control various aspects of the 3D cast member. The 3D text tab gives you access to the properties of rich text members that are displayed as 3D text.

FIGURE 5.1

3D cast member properties dialog.

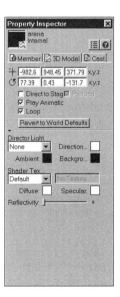

Director's Property Inspector changes its display dynamically in order to give you information about the object that is currently selected within the interface. Let's take a closer look at the Model tab first. To display this tab, select a 3D cast member.

The Property Inspector's 3D Member Tab

If you are familiar with Director 8, you will recognize the Property Inspector. This interface element changes dynamically in order to provide you with relevant information about the item currently selected. The Property Inspector, like the cast, may be toggled between a list display and a graphical display. The List View toggle button is next to the blue Help icon in the upper-right section of the Property Inspector. Figures shown here use the graphical display.

The Member tab allows easy access to several crucial properties. To view the properties of a W3D cast member, simply select a W3D cast member in your cast and open the Property Inspector (Window, Inspectors, Property Inspector).

TIP

> You can always use the shortcut Ctrl+Alt+S (Cmd+Alt+S on the Mac) to display the Property Inspector.

In order to access the 3D properties, you'll need to click the 3D Model tab within the Property Inspector. Beginning at the top of the Model tab, the first item is the three-dimensional location (or worldTransform) of the default camera used to view the world. These three fields represent the X, Y, and Z positions of the camera in the three-dimensional world.

NOTE

> It is a bit of an untruth to say that the fields represent a position in three-dimensional space. Each of the elements we discuss in this section is represented by a vector. A vector is more than 3D position data. A vector represents a line in a given direction and of a certain length. If a vector's origination point is the center of the 3D world, its units correlate to its position relative to the world, but it doesn't have to be this way. It is simpler to think of vectors as points in space, but this misses the mark, so be careful to remember that the vector is much more.

Directly below this element is a display of the X, Y, and Z rotation of the camera. This vector represents the degrees of rotation around a given axis for the camera object. I'll talk more about rotation and translation later in this chapter.

Next, there's a set of four check boxes, giving you easy access to several properties of the member that you may recognize from previous exposure to Director:

- *Direct to Stage*. Allows you to enable or disable Direct to Stage playback. Enabled by default, Direct to Stage playback gives the 3D rendering system direct access to the *rect* (the rectangular area of the display screen) assigned to the 3D member.

  If you are not planning on putting any other media on top of your 3D member, or changing the background ink of your member, then this is definitely the best option. If Direct to Stage is disabled, your playback performance will be slower—how much slower depends on a slew of variables, but it will always be somewhat slower.

  If you want to display any other media over the top of your 3D sprite or to use a different kind of ink on the sprite, you'll need to uncheck this box in order to disable Direct to Stage.

- *Play Animation*. Allows you to enable or disable any internal animation. Because you can control animation from Lingo, you may want to initially disable any animation embedded in your 3D cast member. This box will grant you quick access. It is enabled by default.

- *Loop*. Enabled by default, Loop tells Director to repeat your animation cycle when the animation keyframes reach their end. With the Loop option enabled, your animation cycle repeats over and over again as long as the Director movie is playing.

- *Preload*. Controls the Preload property. This property is off by default. Preload is used for externally linked W3D cast members only. Director will disable this feature for internal cast members. If it is enabled, the external cast member is completely loaded into RAM before it is drawn to the screen; otherwise, the member will stream in while the animation begins to play.

  The advantage to preloading the media is that the detail may be drawn more fully and playback performance will be smoother. The advantage to streaming the media is that the playback happens almost immediately.

Below these check boxes is the Revert to World Defaults button. Clicking this button causes all the properties displayed on the tab—with the exception of the check boxes—to reset to the state that they were in when Director first imported the movie. This is the same as running the `revertToWorldDefaults` Lingo command.

Now, if your Property Inspector seems to stop just below the Revert to World Defaults button, you need to toggle down the extended display by clicking the small black triangle on the left. This button allows you to display or hide the extended properties of any given object. For our purposes, the extended display is best.

The properties listed in the extended display allow you to manipulate the default light and material objects. Each world is assigned a default camera, a default light source, and a default material (composed of a shader and its texture).

The first element, Director Light, allows you to select a direction for your default light. Simply press and hold down the left mouse button on the triangle at the right side of the drop-down menu. While still holding the mouse button down, select a direction for your light from those listed in the menu.

The second element, Ambient, controls the ambient color of light in your 3D world. It works like any other color chip in Director. It is important to remember that color filters applied to light react quite differently from colors applied to materials.

NOTE

If you are unfamiliar with the differences between lighting color theory and color theory for pigments, you may want to do some additional reading about additive and subtractive color mixing. There are some good general resources on color theory online (`http://www.arce.ukans.edu/book/color/theory.htm`), or you might prefer to read about more traditional aspects of lighting by curling up with a copy of Stanley McCandless' books on stage lighting: *A Method of Lighting the Stage* (1958) and *A Syllabus of Stage Lighting* (1964).

The Directional color chip allows you to set the color of the default directional light within the scene. A directional light is an infinitely wide beam of light that illuminates models from a given direction with light of the color specified either via this color chip or through Lingo. Use this chip the same as the one for ambient light.

The Background chip enables you to choose a background color in much the same way. The background color does not reflect any actual object in the 3D world; it simply determines the color displayed if there are no models in the display area.

NOTE

If you disable Direct to Stage and select Background Transparent ink for your 3D member's sprite, you accomplish the same sort of background mask clipping that you do with other image media in Director. In other words, it is possible to have 3D objects in a transparent 3D environment. The major difference is that the background of the 3D member will clip away regardless of the color you've assigned to the background color of the sprite. Background Transparent and Copy are the only two inks supported by the W3D member. Only Copy ink is supported when the W3D member is drawing direct to stage.

The final section of the Property Inspector's extended display contains manipulators to help you adjust the shaders assigned to objects by default. If you create a model and do not assign a shader to that model, the default shader represented here is assigned.

If you haven't worked much with 3D before, this material/shader/texture concept can be a mystery. Essentially, *material* is the common name for a data object that contains information about the way to treat the surface of a 3D model.

A material is composed of two separate parts: a shader and its texture. A model must have a shader in order to be visible, but it does not need to have a texture. The texture, although an object by itself, is a child of the shader.

The first of the material tools is a drop-down menu for Shader Texture assignment. This menu has three options:

- *None.* If you choose None, default models are rendered without any texture.

- *Default.* If you select Default, Director assigns a pink and white, checkered texture to the default objects.

- *Castmember.* If you pick Castmember, the text entry field next to the drop-down menu (in Figure 5.1, this is the grayed-out No Texture box) becomes enabled. Type the name of a bitmap cast member in the enabled text field, and the cast member's bitmap becomes the default texture applied to objects that have not been assigned a shader.

The last three items on the extended display are elements that allow you to adjust the qualities of the default shader. The Diffuse color chip allows you to assign a color to describe the model surface's reaction to diffuse light. Use the Specular color chip to assign a color to the model's specular highlight (the part of the object that is completely highlighted—imagine the sheen on an apple or the glint in someone's eye). The Reflectivity slider allows you to set the amount of surface area dedicated to reflected light.

Creating a 3D Text Member

Creating a 3D text member is considerably easier than you might imagine. Create a rich text cast member by opening up the Rich Text Editor and typing characters into it.

TIP

You can access the Rich Text Editor by pressing the keyboard combination shortcut Ctrl+6 (Cmd+6 on the Macintosh).

You'll want to increase the size of the text to at least 36 points so that you can see what you are doing. Close the text editor and select the newly created text member in the cast window. With the text member still selected, open the Property Inspector (see Figure 5.2). The Text tab looks almost exactly as it did in Director 8, except for the addition of a display mode selection menu. Select the Display drop-down menu and choose 3D Mode. Now just drag the member onto the stage exactly as you would in the case of any other text member. Choosing 3D Mode eliminates many of the properties that may be accessed via Lingo or set in the Property Inspector.

A few additional properties and commands are available related to the generation of 3D text. I'll discuss them in more detail later.

FIGURE 5.2

The Property Inspector's Display drop-down menu.

Modifying 3D Text Member Properties

The 3D Extruder tab appears just to the right of the Rich Text tab once a rich-text member has been converted to 3D text. This specialty tab on the Property Inspector (shown in Figure 5.3) will look familiar now that you've spent some time learning about the 3D Model tab. The first two items on the 3D Extruder member tab of the Property Inspector are identical to those listed on the Model tab. They function in the same way. Below these vectors are three check boxes that are specific to 3D text:

- *Front Face.* If you disable (uncheck) Front Face, the front face of the text will not display. The text will appear as hollowed-out shapes if the Tunnel property is enabled. It is possible to disable all of the faces, or faces in any combination.

- *Back Face.* If you turn off Back Face as well, only the sides of the 3D letters will be drawn. You could turn Front Face back on and then only the front and sides would be drawn. You might also want to try disabling the Tunnel property and leaving front and back faces visible.

- *Tunnel.* This option allows you to enable or disable the sides (or *tunnels*) of the 3D letters as well.

FIGURE 5.3

The 3D Extruder tab of the Property Inspector.

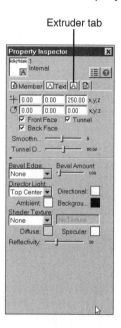

The Smoothness slider allows you to increase or decrease the amount of detail that is used to draw the text. The higher the number, the more precisely the text is drawn.

You can adjust the depth of the letters by using the Tunnel Depth slider. Figure 5.4 shows a 3D text member with front, back, and side (tunnel) faces displayed and a depth of 4.05 units.

The next set of interface elements is for the bevel type and depth settings. The Bevel Edge drop-down menu has three options for bevel type: None, Miter, and Round. The image in Figure 5.4 shows the miter bevel, which scores a straight cut off the outer edges of the letters. The Round option makes the same cut but with a rounded edge.

The bevel amount in the Property Inspector is limited to 10 units, but the bevel can be adjusted via Lingo to reach a depth of up to 100 units. To use either of these bevel-adjustment devices, simply move the Bevel Amount slider to the desired setting.

FIGURE 5.4

The stage with a single 3D text member sprite.

The final two sets of items are the same as those found on the Property Inspector's Member tab: Director Light and Shader Texture, which were discussed earlier in this chapter.

Getting Oriented

If you are unaccustomed to working with three-dimensional representations, the leap from 2D to 3D can be a substantial hurdle. As illustrated in Figure 5.5, Director finds points in three-dimensional space by identifying the relative location of an object along three planes.

NOTE

Remember that every vector is relative. It is a line after all, and as such must have a beginning point and an endpoint. When I say this vector is relative to its parent, I am saying that the tail of the vector line starts at the parent's transform. Likewise, the parent's `transform.position` is a vector representing a line from its parent to its current position.

These planes are known as X, Y, and Z. The location of any object is generally measured based on its relative distance from the center (0,0,0) point of the 3D world. It is possible to measure positions relative to other models, cameras, and lights.

FIGURE 5.5

Locating an object's position in three-dimensional space.

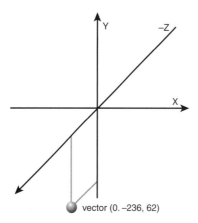

vector (0. –236, 62)

These three-element objects are known as vectors and are expressed in Lingo like this:

```
vector(5, -10, 9)
```

In Shockwave 3D format, the default world coordinate system is oriented with the x-axis running left to right, the y-axis running up and down, and the z-axis moving from back to front. Each of these axes has a positive and a negative side, converging at the center of the 3D world.

The x-axis is positive on the right and negative on the left. The y-axis is positive moving up and negative moving down. The z-axis is negative moving back into the depths of the screen and positive as moving toward the viewer.

It is entirely possible to import W3D members that do not use this coordinate system. In fact, if you are using 3D Studio Max, you will always be importing 3D worlds that do not conform to these coordinates.

The worldTransform position of the default camera in Director 3D is zero units on the x-axis (that is, the center of the x-axis), 0 units down the y-axis, and 250 units in the positive direction along the z-axis. This determines only the physical location of the camera and has no effect on the direction that it is pointing or on the degree to which it is rotated.

You'll recall that the second vector in both the Model and the Extruder tabs of the Property Inspector dialog represents the rotation vector of the default camera. To understand how that rotation will be applied, imagine a pipe penetrating your object (in this case, the camera in the same direction as the axis). The pipe intersects with the object at the pivot point (see Figure 5.6).

FIGURE 5.6

X, Y, and Z rotation is seen as heading, pitch, and bank motions.

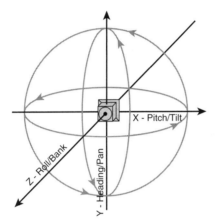

If you rotate your camera two degrees at a time along the z-axis—by changing the rotation Z to the rotation Z + 2—you'll see the camera roll over about 180 degrees, and you'll view your world upside down.

NOTE

You can alter the rotation of the camera by adding 2 to the value in the Z field of the camera's rotation setting in the Model tab of the Properties Inspector. You won't see much rotation if you aren't looking at a member with models in it. Try importing one of the W3D files from the CD-ROM to use as a test base.

Imagine a pole penetrating the camera object through the z-axis (the lens and back of the camera). The camera would only be free to rotate one way, like a pig on a barbecue spit. That rotation is known as a *bank* or *roll*. If you try the same experiment with the y-axis, you'll see the camera rotate toward the right in a complete circle, until returning to the origin 360 degrees later. This panning motion is known as *heading*.

NOTE

If you start trying these things and the results seem inconsistent with those listed here, you probably are working with a W3D file that is using a different default coordinate system. The most likely difference will simply be that the y-axis will be horizontal and the z-axis will be vertical. Just substitute the Z rotations with Y rotations, and you should be fine.

The tilting motion of the x-axis rotation is called *pitch*. I find it easier just to think of the three elements of rotation as tilt, pan, and roll rather than X, Y, and Z. However, some applications do call these maneuvers pitch, heading, and bank.

The 3D Viewer

The final interface element used in manipulating 3D models inside Director is the 3D viewer. Director's native editors and viewers have never been very powerful. The logic behind this is that the developer is most likely to use an external editor to do any serious work in the medium.

You can create 3D files in 3D Studio Max, Maya, SoftImage, Lightwave, Cinema4D, and many other 3D modeling packages. In most cases, you simply create an appropriate file in the external editor and then select Export from either the File menu or the Plugins menu. In Chapter 8, "Low Polygon Modeling and Third-Party Exporters," I'll walk you through the export procedures for 3D Studio Max, Maya, and Lightwave.

You can export any mesh models, keyframe animation, and Inverse Kinematics animation as well as most lights, cameras, and materials. If you use 3D Max to author your 3D files, you may use the physique and biped modifiers to create exportable bones and bone-based animations.

In addition, Havok makes a plug-in and Xtra combination that allows you to create custom physics effects in Max and then export them into Director. The Havok Xtra is Shockwave safe, and you'll see me make good use of it later in this text.

To open the 3D Viewer, simply select Windows, 3D Shockwave from the drop-down menu at the top of the Director interface. You may also click the 3D Viewer button on the toolbar (see Figure 5.7).

FIGURE 5.7.

The 3D Viewer button is to the right of the Rich Text Editor button on the Director 8.5 toolbar.

The Director 3D Viewer allows you to view and, to a small extent, to manipulate the models you have imported into each 3D cast member (see Figure 5.8). The 3D Viewer will display the view into the 3D cast member's world via the default camera.

On the top row of the Viewer's 3D interface is a toolbar that is similar to those found in most of Director's media editors. Clicking the plus symbol (+) on the far left of this top row creates a new empty 3D cast member. You can have as many 3D members as your computer's RAM allows.

FIGURE 5.8.

Use the 3D Viewer to visualize the state of a 3D member from within the authoring environment.

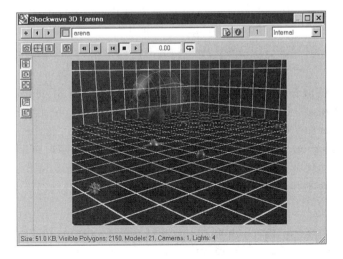

The left and right arrows to the right of the plus symbol (+) change the active 3D member to higher- and lower-indexed 3D members in the active cast. The square in the depressed button to the right of the arrows is a drag tool. If you have the editor open and you don't want to move to the cast window to drag this member onto the stage, you may simply grab this small square and drag it to the stage—when you release your mouse, the cast member will be placed on the stage.

The text window on the top row of this editor is used for the name of the asset. Type the name you want to use to describe the member. You may find that it is more useful to include classifications in your member names.

Moving to the right on the toolbar, you'll find the same Cast Member Script and Script Information buttons that you would on any member editor. The cast member number is displayed to the right of these buttons, and the final element on the top row allows you to toggle between the available casts.

The second row of buttons may seem much less familiar. The first of these buttons, Reset Camera Transform, controls the default camera. Clicking this button resets the default camera either to the position it was in either when the world was first loaded or to the default position declared by using the next button, Set Camera Transform.

The second button to the right is the Set Camera Transform button. Clicking this button locks the default view of the default camera into the active position. It is important to note that this does not mean that your new default camera position and angle erase the file's original default position and rotation information. If you want to revert to the saved state of an imported W3D member, you may use the `revertToWorldDefaults` command.

The third element on the second row of the toolbar for the 3D editor is the Rootlock button. Rootlock is used with keyframe and bone-based animations to prevent an active animation from wandering out of range. If the Rootlock button is toggled on, the root model or bone is locked in place, whereas the rest of the animation is allowed to continue unimpeded. This button is disabled if there is no animation in the 3D world.

The next button—a globe icon—is the Reset World button. At first it may seem to have the same function as the Reset Camera button. The crucial difference is that the Reset World button also moves all the models, cameras, lights, and animations back to their original positions. These differences are reflected in the corresponding Lingo commands.

The `resetWorld()` command (which corresponds to the Reset World button) and `revertToWorldDefaults()` command (which does not correspond to any button), although similar, do not behave in the same manner. The `resetWorld()` command kills all the new nodes that have been created but doesn't mess with the camera orientation or position. The `revertToWorldDefaults()` command puts everything back just as it was on import.

3D members measure time in milliseconds. If you are used to Director's frames-per-second model, you may find this odd. It is an important part of the transition to calculating things in the 3D world. You'll see evidence of the millisecond shift in the animation playback controls found on the 3D viewer's second row of tools. The animation tools can be seen in Figure 5.8, which is showing the 3D viewer. The first two animation tools allow you to shuttle an animation back and forth; the next three buttons are used to rewind, stop, and play the animation.

The text field displays the current playback time in milliseconds, and the Loop button (the last tool on this row) toggles the loop of animation on and off. If the button is down, the animation in the member returns to the beginning of the cycle every time it reaches the end. If the Loop button is up, the animation stops after the keyframes have played through one time.

On the left side of the 3D Viewer are five buttons stacked vertically. These buttons control the dolly, rotation, pan, and tilt of the default camera. Choosing one of the first three buttons deselects the other two. The active button appears in the down state, and the other two are raised.

The top button is the Dolly Camera button. If you move your cursor over the image of the 3D member in the editor while the Dolly button is selected, the cursor changes into a dolly cursor. Hold down the left mouse button and move your mouse upward over the 3D viewing area in order to dolly the camera forward. Try opening the Property Inspector to the 3D Member tab while you work and then click the Set Camera Transform button (the crosshairs) to verify that you are moving the camera and not just zooming in and out.

The second camera control, the Rotate Camera button, controls the default camera's rotation. You can rotate the default camera by clicking this button and then holding down and dragging the mouse. (The fourth and fifth buttons are modifiers to help you rotate more successfully.)

The last of the top three buttons is the Pan Camera button. Click this button to move the camera up, down, left, or right.

At the bottom of the Viewer you'll find information about the current member. The number of polygons, models, lights, and cameras follows the size of the file.

3D Object Structures and Lingo Concepts

If you are already familiar with Director, you know that a sprite is an instance of a cast member on stage. This is not exactly the case with a sprite that uses a 3D member as its resource. When you're using 3D members in Director, a sprite is a view port into that 3D member's world.

The entire 3D world is stored in the member. If you have more than one camera in the 3D world, you can create multiple views into the world. You may also assign camera views to each sprite dynamically. In other words, you may cut from camera A to camera B by changing the sprite's active camera property.

Because of this fundamental difference in the cast/sprite paradigm, many of the properties you might instinctively associate with the sprite in other media types are actually properties of the member in Director 3D. All the models, lights, cameras, and so forth are child objects of the member. It is important to note that whichever camera is actively being projected onto the screen is a sprite property.

3D Object Structures

To really get the most out of Macromedia Director's 3D capabilities, you'll need to use the 3D Lingo to gain access and manipulate the properties of your 3D objects. There are a couple of very basic concepts you'll need to understand in order to go much further.

The first is the concept of an object in programming. An *object* in Director is an instance of a script. But if you are new to objects, it may be easier for you to think of them as smart little widgets. Try starting with what you already understand about the concept of an object.

The cup you drink from is an example of an object. It has a color, such as black or brown, and it has a size. Now extend that definition to include objects that may have no apparent physical properties. You could call wind an object. It has properties such as speed and temperature.

Many of Director's 3D objects have physical appearances. Some do not. It's perhaps easiest to think of an object as, say, the ball or ground plane you see on the screen, but it is important to remember that at its root, the concept of an object is simply a way of organizing information within the program.

The second concept is that objects have properties. A ball, for example, has a color property. It may be red, yellow, blue…whatever. The color property, which we might arbitrarily call pColor, has some value. It could be different in any number of objects; even if all the objects have the same basic properties— pColor, pRadius, pWeight—the value of pColor, or any of these properties, is variable.

Any property, then, may be thought of as a two-part entity composed of a variable name and the value of that variable. We might write one like this: [#pColor:"red"]. Alternatively, if a few properties were assigned to that object, we might write it like this: [#pColor:"red", #pRadius:5, #pWeight:15].

Your 3D world can be created and manipulated within a cast member, just as you might import and manipulate a bitmap using imaging Lingo. There will be no camera to look into your world, however, until you place the member on the stage and create a sprite. It would perhaps be more accurate to say that the camera is useless until you drop the member on the stage and therein form a sprite. As a result, camera commands are generally given to sprites, and world modifications (animating models and transforming lights, for example) are given to the 3D member.

There are several types of objects in a 3D Director cast member: models, shaders, textures, lights, bones, animations, model resources and cameras. I talk about each of these object types in detail in later chapters.

Exercise 5.1:   3D Lingo Concepts

This is a great point to stop reading and try a little experiment. In this exercise, we'll make a couple spheres and a ground plane entirely in Lingo. Before you begin this exercise, create a new 3D cast member and drag it onto the stage. Make certain that the cast member is in the first member position and that the sprite is in the first channel. Save your movie, giving it a useful name. Open a script window—it should default to a movie type script.

The first handler in the movie script responds to the startMovie event. It simply calls our scene-generation handler called makeOne():

```
on startMovie
  makeOne()
end
```

The `makeOne()` handler starts by assigning a variable name, `w`, to the 3D world. In this case, the 3D world is stored in member 1, so the variable name `w` is assigned to hold the member of `sprite(1)`:

```
on makeOne
  w = member(1)
  -- make a variable which holds the member of sprite(1)
  -- our 3D member. This will serve as shorthand for
  -- member(x).
```

The next section of code creates a model resource for a flat plane in the 3D member. It is important to note that a model resource is not the model itself. It is one of those invisible objects and, in this case, is one that is needed in order to generate the visible manifestation of the ground plane. The width and length of the model resource are set at 200 units each, and then a new model object, called `Ground`, is created. Finally, the model resource is assigned to the `Ground` object and the visible model is born:

```
  -- This next bit makes a ground plane
  tGroundRsc = w.newModelResource("Aplane", #plane)
  -- Use the syntax member(x).newModelResource("name",
  -- #type) to create the model resource first.
  -- Nothing will appear on screen, but the model needs
  -- a resource in order to be generated.
  tGroundRsc.width=200
  tGroundRsc.length=200
  -- Use the syntax member(x).newModel("modelName") to
  -- create the new model.
  tGround = w.newModel("Ground", tGroundRsc)
  -- Declare the model and assign it a resource
```

Once the model of the ground plane has been generated, it is time to move it into the position you desire. You may notice that I sneaked in another object. The transform object contains a list of the world-relative position, rotation, direction, and scale of the given object. As a result, you can access the position of a model, light, or camera with the syntax `model[x].transform.position`.

Light is the next feature added to our small scene. The command for creating a new light resource is newLight(). It requires two arguments: the name of the light and the type of the light. The name can be any text string, but the types are limited to #point, #spot, #ambient, and #directional. Before we add those lights, I'll just rotate the ground plane so that it is properly oriented:

```
tGround.rotate(90,0,0)
member(x).camera.transform.position = (0,60,250)
--This next bit makes some new lights for the space.
tLight1 = w.newLight("light", #point)
-- Create a new light object using the syntax
-- member(x).newLight("lightName", #type)
tLight1.transform.position=vector(0,40,0)
-- Now just make adjustments as desired using syntax like
-- member(x).transform.position = vector(x,y,z)
-- member(x).transform.rotate = vector(x, y, z)
-- member(x).light[1].color = rgb(r,g,b)
-- member(x).wPosition = vector(x,y,z) ...etc.
tLight2 = w.newLight("light2", #point)
tLight2.transform.position=vector(0,-40,0)
tLight3 = w.newLight("light3", #point)
tLight3.transform.position=\
vector(-100,-40.5,-40)
```

We've written all this code and, finally, we have created something visible in the 3D world. If you are making your own version as we go, go ahead and call the makeOne() handler from the message window while the playback is running. You should now see your ground plane appear on the stage. One last element must be added in order to see our 3D plane in all its glory: the models.

Models are assigned a default texture in Shockwave 3D unless they have a specific shader assigned to them. The default shader features a pink-and-white checkerboard pattern. In the next bit of code, we'll create a new shader object and then assign it to the model. Because shaders are independent objects, you may use a shader on more than one model. It is important to understand, however, that this independence also means that any changes you make to a shader affect the display of every model that uses this shader. Here's the code:

```
tShader1 = w.newShader("Shader1", #standard)
--Declare the new shader for this model
-- Use the syntax variableName = \
   member(x).newShader("shaderName", #shaderType)
tGround.shader=tShader1
--set your new model to use this new shader.
```

The next step is to create a new texture object and assign it to the shader. Even though textures are independent objects themselves, they must be assigned to shaders in order to appear on the surface material for a model.

Think of it this way, a model without a shader will not be visible. So models generally need to have shaders. A shader without a texture still appears on screen, so a model's surface doesn't need a texture to be visible. If a texture is going to be added to a model, it must be added to a shader that is attached to that model. Now here's the code to create the new texture object:

```
txtur=w.NewTexture("blueBerry", #fromCastmember, member("blueberry"))
-- create a new texture object called "blueBerry"
-- Use the syntax member(x).newTexture("textureName",\
   #fromCastOrImage, #memberOrImageObject)
w.model("Ground").shader.texture=w.texture("blueBerry")
-- Finally set the texture of the shader to the new texture object.
```

This last bit creates a couple of balls to put into the space. It also adds shaders and a texture to one of the balls and places them into their beginning positions. Just as we did with the ground plane, we must first create a model resource object, and then we'll create the ball model. The resource is then assigned to the model and, once a shader is assigned, the ball has a visible form:

```
tball=w.newModelResource("sphere", #sphere)
tball.radius=4.5
-- The radius of the sphere in w units
w.newModel("ball")
w.model("ball").resource=\
w.modelResource("sphere")
sh=w.newShader("myshader", #standard)
w.model("ball").shader=sh
txt = w.newTexture("tangerine", #fromCastMember,\
member("tangerine"))
w.model("ball").shader.texture =\
w.texture("tangerine")
w.model("ball").transform.position=vector(-25,4.5,0)
tball2=w.newModelResource("sphere2", #sphere)
tball2.radius=4.5
w.newModel("ball2")
w.model("ball2").resource=\
w.modelResource("sphere2")
sh=w.newShader("myshader2", #standard)
txt = w.newTexture("lemon", #fromCastMember,\
member("lemon"))
```

```
sh.texture = w.texture("lemon")
w.model("ball2").shader=sh
w.model("ball2").transform.position=vector(25,4.5,0)
```

The final step in this process is to aim the default camera toward the models. In order to ensure that the camera is pointing in the proper direction, set the transform to transform(). This returns the camera to its default orientation and positions it at the center of the world. Next, move the camera into a position above and in front of the models. Finally, rotate the camera slightly in order to provide the best view of the scene. Here's the code that does this:

```
-- reset the camera to vector(0,0,0)
sprite(1).camera.transform=transform()
-- move the camera to the desired height and distance away from our models
sprite(1).camera.transform.position=vector(0,15,75)
-- tilt down a bit for that hovering above and front of look.
sprite(1).camera.transform.rotation=vector(-10,0,0)
end
```

Finally, when we stop the movie, we reset the world so that we don't get errors the next time we try to create the models:

```
on stopMovie
  member(1).resetWorld()
end
```

The bulk of your work with 3D objects and worlds in Director Shockwave Studio is through Lingo commands. This is one of the first things that game developers realize even when they are working with two-dimensional media. Creating fast-paced interactive games requires some programming.

Working with Models

The basic unit of 3D graphics is the model. A model is any object in the 3D environment that has discernable visual properties. In the case of Shockwave 3D, a model is generally composed of polygons grouped together to form one or more meshes. The areas defined by these polygons are shaded, and sometimes textures are applied to those shaded surfaces. The spheres we made in the first chapter are a good example of models. Each mesh on a model may be assigned an independent shader/texture.

It is possible to control and modify virtually any of the properties of models in the 3D world by using Lingo. In this section, I'm going to introduce you to the properties of Shockwave 3D models and the commands used to work with these models. In later chapters, I'll take this control even further with model modifiers that expand the options available for manipulating your models.

In order to comprehend the way that information such as the relative position of a model in your 3D world is stored in Director, you need to understand the scene hierarchy. This is the way that objects in the 3D member relate to each other and the degree to which they are dependent on one another.

If you have worked with object-oriented programming before, the concept of parent-child relationships will not seem new. In fact, it should not seem all that threatening even if you have only been exposed to the object-oriented paradigms presented thus far in this book. In Director's 3D cast members, every object is a child of a single parent called world, or they are children of one of world's descendants. In other words, your world may contain a model called biplane, and that model is a child of world.

Changes that you make to biplane do not affect world, but changes that you make to world do affect biplane. If you really want that biplane to look real, however, you need a propeller. Now you are going to want that propeller to spin, but you don't want biplane to spin. You want the propeller to move around world's space with the plane. If propeller is a child of biplane, it can fly around with biplane and still be free to spin without affecting the plane.

These hierarchical relationships are crucial to creating interactive 3D animations. It is imperative that you keep the relationships of objects in the 3D world in mind as you begin to consider the way you will manipulate your models.

If you modify the transform of a parent, all the children move in the same way that the parent moves. This applies to both the model's position and its rotation, because a model's transform property is that model's position and rotation relative to the parent. If the parent is not world, the two models appear to move around in the world as if they were attached to one another.

These relationships can seem peculiar if you are moving from Director's traditional 2D environment to its new 3D capabilities. In the 2D display method, there are absolute positions relative to the screen. In a sense, the camera into a 2D scene is fixed and immobile. This is not the case in 3D models.

The camera may be moved around the space in any direction, and it may be rotated in any direction. Likewise, the models may be moved to any position relative to the 3D world, relative to a parent model, or relative to their own orientation.

The commands to move objects around according to various orientations in the space are `translate()` and `rotate()`. Using our biplane example, you would move the plane forward by sending the command `world.model("biplane").translate(5,0,0, #self)`.

It doesn't matter what direction the plane is flying in this situation, because the forward motion calculation will be applied relative to the current position and direction of the plane model. This also brings immediately to light the inherent problems with creating your models and then getting them into the Shockwave environment. You need to be sure that you really did orient the model with the nose pointing down the positive x-axis in the authoring environment if you want it to respond to your flight commands appropriately.

To rotate the plane using the self-relative method, use the command `world.model("biplane").rotate(-10, -10,0, #self)`. This causes the plane to bank to the left. Of course, we want the plane's propeller to spin while the plane moves forward and banks left or performs any other maneuver. There really isn't any need to handle it any differently. We could write `world.model("propeller").rotate(3,0,0, #self)`.

If you repeat this command each frame, you'd see a spinning propeller. The propeller automatically receives the movements of the biplane, its parent, but the `rotate` command with the `#self` option adds this rotation to the active rotation passed down from the parent. As a result, the propeller stays attached but spins independently.

Now if we want our plane to be able to land, we need to give it some landing gear. Imagine that we've upgraded to a jet or some similar aircraft that includes hydraulic landing gear. Now the position of the wheels is not constant. We generally want the wheels to follow the plane, but there will be times when we want the wheels to translate separately from the parent, but relative to the position of the parent model. In this case, you might try using syntax such as `world.model("jet").child("wheel").translate(0,-3,0, #parent)`.

You might, however, decide that your wheels should come down from the undercarriage of the plane on an arc as if they were attached to some sort of mount. You could create a small model at the center of the desired rotation and use it as the parent for your wheels. Now using the parent origin method of model rotation, you could pass the command

```
world.model("spinHub").child("wheel").rotate(0,-3,0, #parent).
```

Now if we want to simply move our plane around the virtual skies of our 3D environment, we simply call the `translate()` and `rotate()` commands using `#world` as the `#type` argument. The resulting motion appears to occur relative to the 3D space. The syntax would look like this:

```
world.model("plane").translate(10,20,0, #world).
```

The important part to remember here is that the motion occurs according to the relatively fixed position of the 3D world. This is a fundamentally different kind of motion than the kind you get when you are manipulating the object relative to itself or to its parent.

The last and perhaps most exciting of these motion `#type` arguments is not a type at all. Director's `translate()` and `rotate()` commands allow you to use another object as the reference for relative motion. This means you can use these commands with a camera (the active camera, for example) as the `relativeTo`/`#type` argument. Perhaps you want to have that plane move in directions that are relative to the view the user is seeing on the display monitor. If you used the syntax `world.model("plane").translate(vector(-3,2,0),` `sprite(1).camera)`, the plane would roll right and move toward the right side of the screen. If you wanted to set up a 360-degree spinning dolly shot, the kind made popular in *The Matrix,* you could use this syntax:

```
sprite(1).camera.rotate((vector(0,0,0), vector(0,0,-1), 10,
member(1).model[1])
```

In this example, the camera is the object being rotated:

```
(sprite(1).camera.rotate)
```

The next bit, `(vector(0,0,0))`, is the center point of the spin. Then a directional vector is given to determine the plane along which the rotation will occur.

The same tilt, pan, and roll qualities apply here as they do in any other rotation. The elements within a direction vector are easily expressed as 1, 0, or -1 along the X, Y, and Z planes. The 10 in our example represents the degree of rotation, and the last element—(member(1).model[1])—is the relative object upon which all comparisons must be based.

NOTE

Direction vectors are actually just vectors known as *unit vectors* that because of their nature don't exceed a size of 1.0 for any of their components. We'll talk more about them in the next chapter.

The model is at the core of 3D graphics. You will be able to work with the models in your worlds to create narratives and games using the Lingo that gives you access to each of the properties and commands of these models. Now let's investigate these properties and commands.

Properties

Following are the basic properties of the 3D model. You will find that each of these properties obeys the rules of syntax used throughout Lingo.

boundingSphere

The boundingSphere property contains a two-item list. The first item is the transform.position of the model in the 3D world. This is the world-relative x, y, z position of the center point of the model. The second item is the radius of a sphere that is exactly as large as is necessary to encompass the entire model. Imagine wrapping a model inside an ball that is perfectly sized to the model.

In order to gain access to the boundingSphere of a model, either use the verbose syntax—the boundingSphere of member ("whichMember").model[whichIndexNumber] —or the dot syntax equivalent— member ("whichMember").model [whichIndexNumber].boundingSphere. You can get a model's bounding sphere, but you cannot set it.

debug

The `debug` property is a Boolean toggle switch that allows you to change the display mode of the model. If you set the `debug` property to 1 or `TRUE`, you will see the model along with a wireframe display of the bounding sphere and a colorized display of the coordinate system vectors for the model. The red line points toward the positive X vector, the green line is positive Y, and the blue line represents the positive Z.

You can set or get the `debug` property of any model using either the dot syntax `member("whichMember").model[whichIndexNumber].debug = 1` or the verbose syntax equivalent: `the debug of member ("whichMember").model[whichIndexNumber] = TRUE`. Turn the debug display property off by setting the property to `FALSE` or `0`.

modifier

The `modifier` property contains a blank list by default. If you add a modifier to your model, that modifier's name is added to this list. The list can contain as many modifiers as you add, and the modifiers are sorted in alphabetical order. You access a modifier either by a reference to the list—`member(whichMember).model[whichIndexNumber].modifier`—or a reference to the index position in the modifier list. Verbose and dot syntax options are both available here as well. Note that the `model[x].modifier[y]` option allows you to either search for the *n*th position item in the list or to match the name of the modifier as a text string.

NOTE

Modifiers are discussed at length in Chapters 7, 9, 10, and 11.

Use the syntax `"member(whichMember).model[whichIndex].name"` to poll the system for the name of any given model. It will be returned as a string. You normally set the name of a model using the Model Properties dialog of the 3D Scene Creation Utility, which you used to create that model. You may set the name of a model that uses Lingo as well.

parent **and** child

Models also have `parent` and `child` properties. As I discussed earlier, relationships may exist between the virtual objects in the 3D world. The parent of a model affects its child. Move the parent, and the child will move the same amount, along the same vector, and so forth. A child does not have this sort of impact on its parent. One way to create a parent or child relationship via Lingo is to simply set the parent or child of the model to any other model. You might write `member(whichMember).model[whichIndex].parent = member(whichMember).model[whichModel]` in order to assign the first model as the parent of the second. The `addChild` command is more robust, and you will probably find it a better method of handling parent-child relationships. The `addChild` command is discussed in the "Commands" section later in this chapter.

pointAtOrientation

The `pointAtOrientation` property supports get and set access. It contains a list with two vectors. The first is the object-relative direction vector for the model, and the second is the up vector for the model.

We worked with model resources in the Exercise 5.1. The `modelResource` property actually contains a pointer to the geometric resource object that was used to generate this model. You can get and set the model resource of a model using the syntax learned in the first exercise.

shaderlist

You may recall from Exercise 5.1 that you can access the shader of any model via its `shader` property. It is possible to assign more than one shader to a model. To gain access to the list of the model's shaders, use the `shaderlist` property.

You can poll the `shaderlist` property of an object using the syntax `member(whichMember).model[whichIndex].shaderlist`. The system returns a list of pointers to the `shader` objects used by the model. As is the case with any such list, you may also poll it for the shader at index position *n* or the shader named `shaderName`.

transform

The `transform` property of a model contains a reference to the model's transform object. Lingo uses 4×4 matrices to accelerate the 3D calculations and speed up the program. I am committed to avoiding any brain damage to the readers of this text, so suffice it to say that the matrix math makes your head hurt. The only really relevant information for most applications is that the lists generated to represent the model's position, rotation, and direction are vectors with a fourth element, rather than the three-element vectors we've been working with thus far. It's the fourth element in the list that allows the magic matrix math to function properly.

I tell you this only because it helps to explain why a transform looks the way it does. If I ask the system to put the transform of a given model, using syntax such as `put member(whichMember).model[whichIndex].transform`, I'll get a list like this: `--transform(1.0000,0.0000,0.0000,0.0000,` `0.0000,1.0000,0.0000,0.0000,  0.0000,0.0000,1.0000,0.0000,` `10.0000,12.1364,30.8706,1.0000)`. Remember the term 4×4 matrix? Look at the list again, only breaking it into groups of four, as shown in Table 5.1.

TABLE 5.1   Visualizing a 4×4 3D Matrix

1.0000	0.0000	0.0000	0.0000
0.0000	1.0000	0.0000	0.0000
0.0000	0.0000	1.0000	0.0000
10.0000	12.1364	30.8706	1.0000

If you are into the math, you certainly don't need me offering tips, and if you are not, it really doesn't matter. Just remember that somehow this mystical list of numbers is able to tell you the information you need about the model, and it stores it all in a surprisingly compact form.

userData

The `userData` property holds a blank property list by default. You may either enter variable/value combinations into the `userData` field in your authoring package or add variable/value pairs to the list by using Lingo. Obviously you may update the value of any `userData.property` by using Lingo. You would use syntax such as `member(whichMember).` `model[whichModel].userData.propertyName`.

visibility

The `visibility` property contains a symbol that represents the sides of the object that are rendered. Your choices are `#none`, `#front`, `#back`, and `#both`. They each do what you would expect. If you select `#none`, no surfaces of the mesh are rendered. Your object vanishes.

If you select `#back`, only the back or inside surfaces of the object are projected onto the screen. This is obviously the ideal choice for drawing the inside of objects. When `#front` is used, the backs of objects are not drawn. This can be a problem in some cases, so `#both` (front and back faces) may also be used.

worldTransform

The `worldTransform` property gives the 4×4 transform of the model relative to the center of the world. All objects begin their existence as children of `world`. Their initial transforms are therefore relative to the center of the 3D world.

If an object is parented to any object other than `world`, it displays a transform relative to the parent object. Use `worldTransform` if you want to get the world-relative position of an object that has a parent.

These are the basic properties of the 3D model. They are fairly simple to get and set. The syntax for each is basically the same. You may find that it is much easier to work with such objects if you first set a variable or property to the model you want to work with. You might write `pSphere = member(1).model[1]` and then simply refer to the dot properties of `pSphere` from that point forward.

Commands

While getting and setting the properties of models gets you started, you will want to learn the commands supported by the model object as well in order to fully take advantage of Director's powerful 3D Lingo.

addChild

If you want to add a child to a model's list of children, use the `addChild` command. You would use the syntax
`member(whichMember).model[whichIndex].addChild(whichChildModel, whichPreserve)`. If you use the optional `whichPreserve` argument, you may set

the child to either a world-relative or a parent-relative transform. To set the model to world relative, use the argument `#preserveWorld`. To make the child object transform relative to the parent, use the argument `#preserveParent`.

The advantage to using this command over simply setting the `parent` property of a child object is that you may pass the relative argument. It gives you a bit more flexibility.

addModifier

The `addModifier` command allows you to add modifiers to the stack of resources available to your model. The modifiers available to you are dependant on the modifiers present in the renderer services object. By default, you have access to the `#collision`, `#bonesPlayer`, `#keyframePlayer`, `#toon`, `#lod`, `#meshDeform`, `#sds`, and `#inker` modifiers. You call `member(whichMember).model[whichIndex].addModifier(whichModifier)` in order to add the collision modifier to a model. This makes it possible to apply various forces to the model and detect and resolve collisions.

child

The `child` command returns either the *n*th indexed child or the named child of a model. It returns `void` if there are no children or if `index` is greater than the maximum number of children.

clone **and** cloneDeep

The `clone` and `cloneDeep` commands allow you to make copies of a given model. In the case of `clone`, a copy of the original model and copies of each of the original model's children will be created. If you use a blank string (`""`) as the `name` argument, the copy will simply exist as a data object—it will not be added to the world, and it will not have any children. The advantage to this is that you can rapidly create temporary instances of a model.

If you name the clone, a copy is made that refers to the original model's resource and shader. Changes to either of these are reflected on both the clone and the original. The clone does get its own children and unique transform and modifier properties. This means that it appears in the world, it copies the original model and any children that were attached when the handler was called, and you are able to control its location, rotation, and other basic properties separately.

The `cloneDeep` command, on the other hand, takes the copying one step further. Instead of creating a reference to the model's original shader and model resource, `cloneDeep` creates a new model resource and shader. This way, you can modify the resource or shader without affecting the original model's resource or shader.

getWorldTransform

If you want to find out the world-relative position of a model that is parented to some other object in your 3D world, one way to do so is to use the `getWorldTransform` command. This command returns the world-relative position of a model regardless of the default relative orientation of the original model.

isInWorld

The `isInWorld` command returns a Boolean TRUE or FALSE result. The result of the `isInWorld` function is TRUE if the model passed in the argument is present in the world; it returns FALSE if it is not. As you saw in `clone`, it is possible to create a model that is not in the world.

loadModel

The `loadModel` command is used to load the contents of a W3D cast member into the active W3D cast member. This is essentially the same thing as calling the `loadMember` function, except that all the objects within the W3D file that is called are be loaded as children of the model that calls the `loadModel` function. You won't find this command in the Lingo dictionary. Use it like this:

```
loadFile(fileName, booleanOverwriteOriginals, \
booleanGenerateUniqueNamesForDuplicates)
```

pointAt

The `pointAt` command expects at least one argument—a world position expressed as a vector. It also accepts a world up vector. If you call the `pointAt` command, the model will rotate to face the direction you pass in as an argument. The model's understanding of what is facing forward is determined by the setting of the model's `pointAtDirection` property.

registerScript

The `registerScript` command registers a handler (you choose the name) whenever the event passed in the `eventName` argument happens to this model. Essentially you pass events to the model's script, and then it will call the handler listed in this command's argument.

removeFromWorld **and** removeModifier

The `removeFromWorld` command does exactly what you would expect: It removes a model from the active 3D world. You call it as you would any of the other commands of a model. Likewise, `removeModifier` is a command for removing any given modifier from the model's modifier list.

rotate

You may use the `rotate` command using one of two available argument formats. The first is to rotate the model by a variable number of degrees around each of its three axes. You could, for example, write `myModel.rotate(90,0,0)`, and this would rotate the model 90 degrees in the positive direction on the x-axis. The rotation of the model would be relative to the model itself because the default relative coordinate space is `self`. You could also specify the relative coordinate space by commanding `myModel.rotate(90,0,0, #world)`. In this case, the model would rotate around the absolute x-axis of the world. Depending on the distance between the two x-axes, this could be a substantially different effect.

The other argument system for the `rotate` command would be expressed like this: `myModel.rotate(positionExpressedAsVector, AxisExpressedAsVector, angleInDegrees, relativeCoordinateSpace)`. You'll find examples of this use of the `rotate` command in the Exercise 5.2.

scale

The `scale` command is similar to the `rotate` command. It has two potential argument paradigms. You may either enter a single integer for a uniformly scaled model or individual X, Y, and Z integers to scale the object relative amounts in each of these directions. The syntax looks like either `myModel.scale(2)` or `myModel.scale(.5,3,1)`.

translate

The translate command allows you to move your model around the space. You may either move the object by a given amount in each of the X, Y, and Z directions or move the object a given distance along a vector. In either case, the vector or incremental movement happens relative to the position and coordinate space of either the model itself, the world, or another object within the world. You specify which one of these to use with the second argument in both styles of calling this command. You would either write `myModel.translate(0,10,0, #world)` or `myModel.translate(vector(0,10,0), #world)`. You could leave the coordinate space argument off, in which case the command assumes you mean to make the translation relative to the object itself.

update

Use the update command to update a model without rendering it to the screen. You may find this useful for making sure that your feet stay on the ground or your baseballs don't penetrate your bats.

These are the properties and commands that allow you to gain Lingo-based control over your 3D models, and ultimately they will become the cornerstones of your interactive 3D applications in Director. Before we move on to the other objects found in your 3D scene, I encourage you to try the following exercise. It guides you through the use of Lingo as a tool for manipulating 3D models.

Exercise 5.2:   Learning To Fly

In this exercise, I show you how to make a propeller-driven plane appear to fly through the sky using simple interactive keyboard controls. We won't add features such as failed landings leading to exploding fireballs at this point, but manipulating the model and all its children should provide ample opportunities to experiment with the model properties and commands we've explored thus far.

There are two relevant scripts for this movie. The first, the startMovie and key handlers, are in Listing 5.1, and the second, the parent script for the airplane object, is in Listing 5.2. I'll refer to these scripts in the steps as we walk through the creation of the airplane flight movie.

LISTING 5.1   The Start Movie and Key Handlers

```
1: -- Declare a global that will hold a reference to the w3d member
2: global w
3: -- Declare a global that will hold a \
```

LISTING 5.1   Continued

```
➡ reference to the airplane animation object
4: global gPlane
5:
6: -- As the movie is preparing to play
7: on prepareMovie
8:    -- Place the member reference into the global
9:    w = member(1)
10:   -- Place the airplane animation object reference into the global
11:   gPlane = new(script "plane")
12:   -- Place the object reference in the actor \
➡ list so it will receive stepFrames
13:   add(the actorlist, gPlane)
14:   --- set the keyUp and keyDown script because we want to separate
15:   --- the beginning and the end of a key press event from the keypressed
16:   -- state.
17:   the keyUpScript  = "mKeyUp"
18:   the keyDownScript = "mKeyDown"
19: end
20:
21: on stopMovie
22:   ---- Reset the world on stop so we don't go crazy testing
23:   w.resetWorld()
24:   ---- clear the globals
25:   clearGlobals()
26: end
27:
28:
29: -------------------------------Key Detection
30:
31: on mKeyUp
32:   --- set the global gPlane's pKeyLock property to 0
33:   --- this means that the key is not in a down state
34:   gPlane.pKeyLock = 0
35: end
36:
37: on mKeyDown
38:   -- if all of the relevant keys are up
39:   if  gPlane.pKeyLock <> 1 then
40:     -- save the key just pressed in tKey
41:     tKey = charToNum(the key)
42:     --- put a copy of that value in the pActiveKey property
43:     --- of the plane animation object
44:     gPlane.pActiveKey = tKey
45:     -- if the key pressed is an arrow
46:     if (tKey = 28 ) OR (tKey = 29) OR (tKey = 30)  OR (tKey = 31)  then
47:       -- set the position of the dummy model, so we can turn around it
48:       gPlane.cyclePivots(tKey)
```

LISTING 5.1   Continued

```
49:        -- lock the key state so the dummy stays in position as long as
50:        -- the user holds the key down.
51:        gPlane.pKeyLock = 1
52:    end if
53:  end if
54: end
55:
56: -----------------------------------------------End Key Detection
```

LISTING 5.2   The Plane Parent Script

```
 1: -- A reference to the w3d model
 2: global w
 3:
 4: -- -----------------------------------------------
 5: property pKeyLock  ------ Is the keyDown?
 6: property pPlane        ------ a reference to the plane model
 7: property pActiveKey ----- the last key pressed
 8:
 9: --- Create a new object
10: on new(me)
11:   ---- run the initialize handler
12:   init(me)
13:   return me
14: end
15:
16: --- The initialize handler
17: on init (me)
18:   -----Set the pPlane reference
19:   pPlane = w.model[1]
20:   -- Add each of the wheels, the propeller, and the struts as children
21:   -- of the base plane model.  This way they will all move when the plane
22:   -- moves.
23:   repeat with x = 2 to 5
24:     --- preserve world keeps the children in their current position
25:     pPlane.addChild(w.model[x], #preserveWorld)
26:   end repeat
27:   -- Slap a default texture map on the ground plane
28:   w.model[6].shader.texture = w.texture[1]
29:   -- create a dummy object called "pivot" that we can use to
30:   -- calculate the rotation of turns.
31:   nMR = w.newModelResource("pivot", #plane, #both)
32:   nM = w.newModel("pivot", nMR)
33:   --- make the new object invisible.
34:   nM.visibility = #none
35: end
```

LISTING 5.2   Continued

```
36:
37: -- every time the playback head moves between frames
38: on stepFrame(me)
39:    -- spin the propeller
40:    w.model[2].rotate(-43,0,0)
41:    --- move the plane forward
42:    pPlane.translate(-120,0,0)
43:    -- handle key response
44:    mFly(me)
45:    -- fix the rotation of the model if the plane is tilting.
46:    restoreRotation()
47: end
48:
49: -- This handler takes care of the key responses
50: on mFly(me)
51:    -- check the pActive key for a match
52:    case (pActiveKey) of
53:       28:
54:          -- If it was 28 and the lock is engaged then
55:          if pKeyLock then
56:             --- rotate the plane a bit along it's x axis - tilt the wing
57:             pPlane.rotate(2,0,0)
58:             --- rotate the plane (<around the pivot point that has
59:             ---been placed off the wing>, <on the zAxis so that
60:             ---the plane turns>, <1 degree>, <parallel to the ground plane>).
61:             pPlane.rotate(w.model("pivot").transform.position, \
➥ vector(0,0,1), 1, w.model[6])
62:          end if
63:       29:
64:          if pKeyLock then
65:             pPlane.rotate(-2,0,0)
66:             pPlane.rotate(w.model("pivot").transform.position, \
➥ vector(0,0,-1), 1,  w.model[6])
67:          end if
68:       30:
69:          ---- Dive
70:          if pKeyLock then
71:             pPlane.rotate(0,-2,0)
72:          end if
73:       31:
74:          -- Climb
75:          if pKeyLock then
76:             pPlane.rotate(0,2,0)
77:          end if
78:    end case
79: end
80:
```

LISTING 5.2 Continued

```
81: --- This is called from the keyDown handler \
 ➥ if an appropriate key is pressed
82: -- only when that key is pressed. \
 ➥ The key up handler clears the keyLock and
83: -- re-enables this handler each time the user releases a key.
84: on cyclePivots (whichWay)
85:    -- place the pivot off the appropriate wing in preparation for rotation
86:    if whichWay >28 then
87:      w.model("pivot").transform = w.model[1].transform
88:      w.model("pivot").translate(0, 1800, 0)
89:    else
90:      w.model("pivot").transform = w.model[1].transform
91:      w.model("pivot").translate(0, -1800, 0)
92:    end if
93: end
94:
95: on restoreRotation()
96:    -- create a new empty transform.object
97:    Neutral=transform()
98:    -- set the position of the transform to equal the position of the plane
99:    Neutral.position  = pPlane.transform.position
100:    -- set the rotation of the neutral\
 ➥ transform to = a neutral x,y rotation, but match the
101:    -- z rotation of the plane.
102:    Neutral.rotation = vector(0, 0, pPlane.transform.rotation.z)
103:    --- move slowly in the direction of ideal \
 ➥ transform - we'll never quite get there
104:    pPlane.transform.interpolateTo(Neutral, 6)
105: end
```

Soon we'll be able to watch our plane flying through the sky, but for now let's break the stages of building the whole movie down into steps so that it's easier to play along:

1. Open the file named 05baseFlight.dir on the CD-ROM (see Figure 5.9).

2. Import the W3D file into this movie. Place the 3D member in the first position of the main cast.

    Importing either the plane model provided on the companion CD-ROM (05MAX01.max) or one that you built yourself is fine. If you have made one of your own, be certain to include the plane, the propeller, the struts for the wheels, two wheels, and a large plane for the ground. Position the plane and all its parts substantially higher than the ground plane. Make certain to place the W3D member in cast position one (see Figure 5.10).

FIGURE 5.9

The 05baseFlight.dir movie opened in Director.

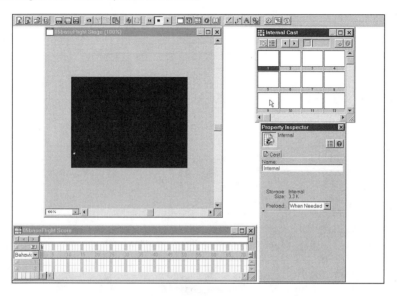

FIGURE 5.10

Importing the W3D movie.

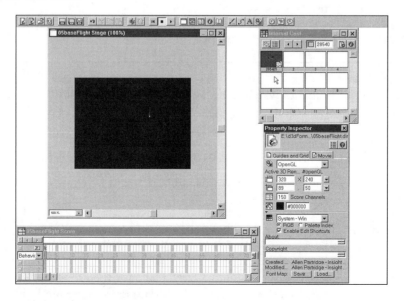

3. Drag the W3D cast member onto the score (see Figure 5.11). My file was created in 3D Studio Max, so the world and model coordinate systems are Max style—z is up and down. This means that as we work with the file in Director, we need to remember that the up/down axis is z rather than y.

4. Create a new movie script and name it **Startup**. Type the global declarations (lines 2 and 4 of Listing 5.1) at the top of the script window (see Figure 5.12).

5. Continuing in this script window, you'll need to do some prep work as the movie is first beginning. On the prepareMovie handler, assign the W3D member to the global w and create the object that will handle the animation of the plane. You'll need to add that object to the actor list so that it can receive stepframe events. Finally, set the keyUp and keyDown scripts. Your code should look similar to the code in lines 6–19 of Listing 5.1, as shown in Figure 5.13.

FIGURE 5.11

Dragging the 3D world onto the score.

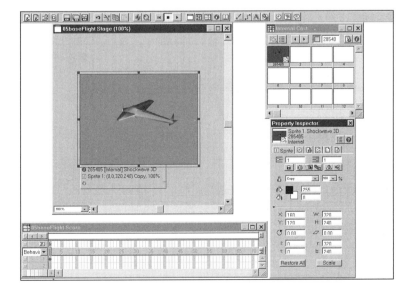

FIGURE 5.12

Global variables in the Startup script.

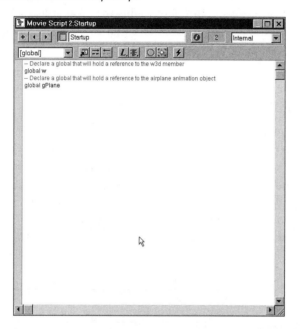

FIGURE 5.13

The prepareMovie handler.

6. When your movie stops, you'll want to reset the world and clear the globals. Add a `stopMovie` script here that can do those things for you. An example of such a script appears in lines 21–26 of Listing 5.1 (see Figure 5.14).

FIGURE 5.14

The `stopMovie` handler.

7. The final two handlers in this script are the `mKeyUp` and `mKeyDown` handlers. They respond to calls from the movie's `keyUp` and `keyDown` scripts because you told them to in the `startMovie` script. We'll need these, because we need keyboard info from the movie even when we aren't working on a field or text member. You'll find the appropriate code for these handlers, along with comments about the function of each line in lines 31–54 of Listing 5.1 (see Figure 5.15).

8. Now that you've finished the `Startup` script, make another script cast member and name it **plane**. Before you get started on the handlers, use the Property Inspector to change the script type from Movie to Parent, as shown in Figure 5.16.

FIGURE 5.15

The mKeyUp and mKeyDown handlers.

FIGURE 5.16

Making a parent script called plane.

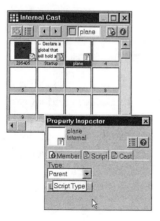

9. You are getting good at this by now, so go ahead and type in the global declarations as well as the property declarations for the parent script. Heck, go ahead and do that new handler as well. You'll find the code in lines 2–14 of Listing 5.2 (see Figure 5.17).

FIGURE 5.17

The declarations and new script for the animation object script.

10. Now if you are paying attention, you probably noticed that the new script doesn't do much. It relies on the `init` script to do the real work. The `init` script assigns values to the variables, makes the plane model the parent of all its parts, changes the gray ground plane to a pretty pink checkerboard, and makes a new invisible model in the 3D member. Go ahead and type in the `init` script as it appears in lines 17–35 of Listing 5.2 (see Figure 5.18).

11. Because we added this object to the actor list, it will receive `stepFrame` events. We'll use the `stepFrame` handler to trigger the continual rotation of the propeller, the continual forward motion of the airplane, and the variable effects of the user's key input. We'll also use it to restore the plane to smooth and level flying paths in case the user goes crazy. Type in the `stepFrame` handler as it appears in lines 38–47 of Listing 5.2 (see Figure 5.19).

FIGURE 5.18

The init *script initializes all the properties of the object.*

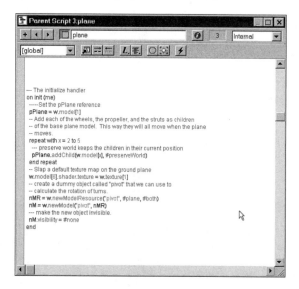

FIGURE 5.19

The stepFrame *handler.*

12. The next handler responds to key input from the player. It checks to see whether the key was in the same state (down) during the last cycle. If it was, the handler rotates the plane according to which key the user pressed. It uses a `case` statement to check which key was pressed and conditional evaluations of the object's `pLocked` property to determine whether the key was down during the last `stepFrame`. Enter the `mFly(me)` handler as it appears in lines 50–79 of Listing 5.2 (see Figure 5.20).

FIGURE 5.20

The `mFly` handler responds to keyboard input.

13. The last two handlers do a little assisting. The first of these, `cyclePivots()`, takes the invisible model we created during the beginning of this object script and plops it off to the side of the plane. Imagine that you want to turn the plane left. If you just rotate left, the plane will rapidly begin to spiral. This script manages the rotation by orbiting the plane model around an arbitrary invisible point off the side of the wing. The `cyclePivots()` handler places the center of the orbit in place. The

restoreRotation() handler returns the plane to a level flying path. It features the interpolateTo command, which is great for gently moving toward a preferred position. It also generates a Lingo transform object. Go ahead and type these handlers in now. You'll find the exact code in lines 84–105 of Listing 5.2 (see Figure 5.21).

FIGURE 5.21

The cyclePivots and restoreRotation handlers add a bit of cleanup.

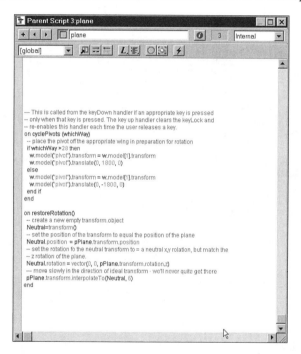

14. Now add a camera-control device that will follow the airplane around. Select the 3D sprite on stage and choose the Gear icon to open the Behavior Inspector. Click the plus sign (+) in the Behavior Inspector and select follow_camera from the drop-down menu. (I put that in there to save you some typing.) See Figure 5.22.

FIGURE 5.22

Attaching the camera.

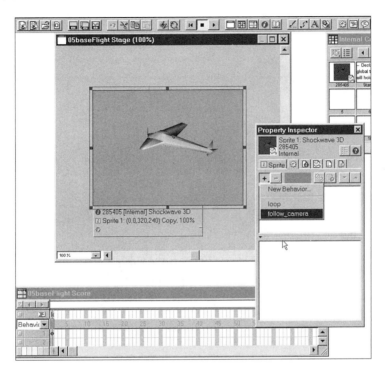

15. As soon as you release the mouse, a dialog pops up (see Figure 5.23).
    You only need to change the value of the offset vector in the top line to
    `vector (4000,-4000,3000)`.

16. Save the movie on your hard drive and then rewind and play it. Try
    moving the aircraft with your mouse keys.

17. As an extra challenge, see if you can rotate the propeller the opposite
    way or create collision detection and replace the whole animated plane
    with a burning crashed one.

FIGURE 5.23

Setting the offset distance of the camera.

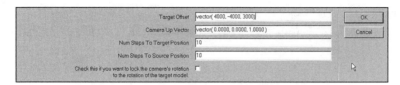

It always feels great to make things happen using only Lingo, doesn't it? Now that you've been introduced to a tiny bit of the amazing new features of Director 8.5, you are ready to explore the remaining concepts.

In the chapters that follow, I'll introduce you to each of Director's new 3D features and give you a slew of games, demos, and exercises that will help you learn to master the 3D data type.

In the next chapter, I'll begin the adventure with an introduction to cameras and lights. After all, it's impossible to see anything in these simulated spaces without them.

CHAPTER 6

Cameras and Lights

In the most practical sense, cameras and lights are absolutely necessary elements in the display of simulated 3D worlds. You need a camera to provide a view into the 3D space. You also need lights; otherwise, all the objects in the 3D world would be too dark to see.

Each element is based conceptually on physical world counterparts and, for the most part, cameras and lights behave as they would in the "real world." Learning the nuts and bolts of cameras and lights will help you understand how to control the image that players see while viewing your game.

After reading the chapter, you will

- Know the properties and methods used by cameras

- Know the properties and methods used by lights

- Understand the importance of usability as it relates to the use of cameras and lights

- Understand the fundamental concepts of lighting the game space

- Manipulate a 3D camera with Lingo

After a brief overview of transform objects and the various methods of finding and moving nodes in the 3D space, I'll present a summary of the properties and methods of cameras. You'll get an overview of the things that Shockwave 3D cameras can do, and then I'll demonstrate some camera behaviors.

In the "Working with Lights" section, I'll explain the properties and methods associated with lights in Director's 3D cast member type. Then we'll walk through several examples of using lights in your 3D members.

Time Out for a Mental Transformation

A big chunk of the work that we do with models, lights, and cameras involves moving these nodes and understanding, predicting, and assessing their relationship to one another.

I think that at this point it will prove helpful if I review the fundamental concepts that lie behind the transform of a node and the keys to understanding relationships between nodes.

It is important to know that each element expressed by the transform is expressed in terms that define that element relative to some other element in the 3D world. This is the nature of vectors. Many of the things that you find in a transform are vectors.

Now if you've been limping along so far with a limited understanding of vectors, you have probably begun to think of vectors such as the transform.position of a node as points in 3D space. Knock it off! You just can't think of it that way. It will make your life more miserable in the end.

Understanding Vectors

A vector is an expression of movement in a direction. Think of vectors as straight little paths or lines. They have a starting point, a distance traveled, a direction traveled, and an ending point. The magic trick with the written vector is that the only obvious thing expressed in the numbers you see is the ending point.

Suppose I told you that we wanted to draw a vector that could be expressed as vector(1, 1, 1), but I want the endpoint of the vector to end up at worldTransform.position vector(4, 4, 2). If you've been thinking of vectors as simple points thus far, that sentence should make your head spin. If you've been thinking of vectors as vectors, you should be fine.

Head spinning? Take a look at Figure 6.1, in which I've drawn the vector in question. You can see here that the vector originates at worldTransform.position vector(3, 3, 1). If we add vector(1, 1, 1) to this vector, we get vector(4, 4, 2). I gave you enough information to compute the proper position of the vector, but I gave it to you in a screwy format.

FIGURE 6.1

Vectors don't have to be fixed in space; they represent distance and direction.

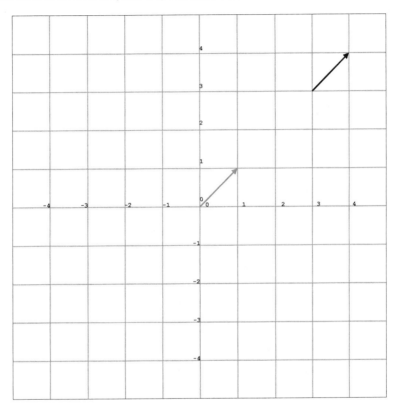

Wouldn't it have been easier if I had said, "Draw a line from vector(3, 3, 2) that moves to vector(1, 1, 1)." This is generally what you say when you do any calculation on the transform.position vector of a 3D node. The syntax for a typical translate command looks like this.

```
member(n).model[n].translate \
(vector(xUnitsMotion,yUnitsMotion,zUnitsMotion),\
  #relativeTo)
```

There are two arguments. The first is a vector representing the motion traveled, and the second is a value that helps the system determine where the vector should originate.

The #relativeTo argument is extremely important. It probably doesn't do what you think it does. The possible values of the #relativeTo argument include #self, #parent, #world, and an object reference to a node in the 3D scene.

The basic questions with any vector are where does it start, where does it end, and which direction does it travel. You cannot define a point in three-dimensional space without referring to some other point in 3D space. Don't believe me? Try it. Look around the room and try to express verbally where some object is without referring to some other object.

In the same way, all of the movements that you make with the translate() command require a declaration of relative position and declination. Because of this requirement, vectors that are offered as the argument of a translate command originate at the current location of the node that called the translate command. Remember that the syntax of a translate command looks like this:

```
w.model[n].translate(vector( x, y, z), #relativeTo)
```

The model (model[n]) has a position. This position is the position of the model relative to the model's parent object's coordinate system. It is this position that becomes the starting point for the translation vector.

The #relativeTo argument is not a reference to the fixed point in 3D space occupied by the vector (0, 0, 0) at the center of the 3D world, or to the referenced node's center. It is a reference to the directional orientations of the world or referenced node. It is like saying, "Go to the center of the #relativeTo node and make a vector line that is these vector coordinates long, in this direction. Now stick that line onto my current node's center point and tell me what position you get in the coordinate space of the parent of the node that called the transform in the first place. Finally, move this node (the one that made the translate call) to the point that you just found."

In reality, you are adding the vector in the argument to the current vector. It's just that the directional information for the vector may differ if it (the node or coordinate system that is used in the relative to argument) is relative to any node other than the parent of the one that called translate to begin with.

Now if the parent of the model/node that called translate is not world, the coordinates of the transform of the node that called translate() exist in a different coordinate space than the coordinates in which your motion is occurring.

You may observe changes in the `transform.position` of the node that made the `translate()` call that seem to suggest angular motion, when you thought you were getting straight motion. To learn the world-relative position of your model after such a change, simply call `member(n).model[n].getWorldTransform().position`—and don't forget to use "`()`" because this call to the transform is a command, not a property.

Generally the program assumes that you mean to make the adjustment relative to the node itself if you are translating a node. If you are translating a transform, the program assumes that you want to translate relative to the transform's parent node. If you want to calculate a vector that is relative to another node, or relative to the world, you'll need to let the program know. It is always a good idea to include the optional `#relativeTo` argument, just so you are certain of what you are calculating.

Any object in the space has a `transform.position` that represents its position relative to its parent. You can calculate its position relative to any other object. In the case of the world, you can simply call `member(n).model[n].getWorldTransform()`.

Rotation is handled in a similar fashion. What you want to rotate around is the most important question. This is followed immediately by questions about the alignment of the node while it rotates around the position specified.

Visualize the 3D world for a moment as a giant grid, extending in three dimensions infinitely with reference marks every one unit. The center of this world would be the place where each of three planes/grids converge simultaneously.

Now imagine that an object is added to the world—use the illustration in Figure 6.2 to help. Notice that the pivot point (center) coordinates and specifically the orientation of the object are different from the orientation of the world. As long as this object is a child of the world, its transform will be expressed relative to the coordinate system of the world.

If you add another object and make that object the parent of the original object, the transform of the child object is returned relative to the coordinate system of the parent (see Figure 6.3).

FIGURE 6.2

The xAxis, yAxis and zAxis of each node in the world are independent of the world.

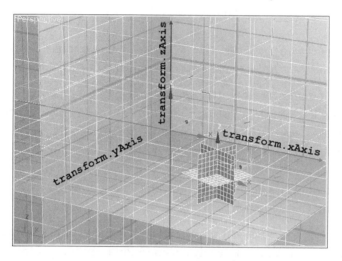

FIGURE 6.3

The position of a vector is expressed as a vector that is relative to another node in 3D space.

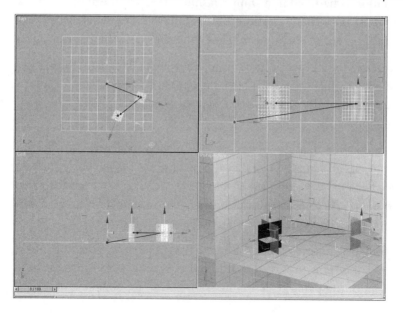

It doesn't take much imagination to see that this could quickly become confusing if you are just staring at little numerical vectors on the screen. Keep this basic concept in mind: A transform is always relative to the parent of a node. Normally the parent of the node is the world. In some cases, the parent of the node is another node. Translations may be made in the coordinate space of any node, but they always conform to the orientation of the node that issues the `translate()` command.

Now understanding the relevance of the transform is only half the battle. Let's move further with a beginning understanding of how to use some of the other data that we can get from the transform.

Up to this point, I have generally showed you the motion of a model through space by moving that model a given distance and direction (expressed as a vector) on every frame. But this is really probably not the best way to do it. Usually my models are oriented along their own positive x-axes (`xAxis`). Here's an alternative way to accomplish this motion:

NOTE

From this point on in the book you'll see me use the global variable w, rather than `member(n)` to refer to the 3D member. I do this to cut down on my typing and because I find it easy to think of world as w.

```
w.model[n].translate(w.model[n].transform.xAxis, #parent)
```

This moves the model forward along its own `xAxis`. It would move very slowly, but it would move. Now suppose that we wanted to vary the speed of forward motion. Well, we could decide to hold the relative speed of travel in a property (`pSpeed`, for example). If we change the command to multiply the normalized vector by the property `pSpeed`, we get a vector that moves in the right direction of an appropriate magnitude (length):

```
w.model[n].translate(((w.model[n].transform.xAxis) * pSpeed), #parent)
```

The only difference between this command and the first is that the direction vector is multiplied by the proposed speed in order to create a vector with the same direction, but of a greater length. In other words, your model travels farther in the specified direction the higher the value of `pSpeed`. It is equally interesting to note that this command allows pSpeed to hold negative values, in which case the model moves backward along the same direction vector.

Often this motion is enough to get things well underway, but occasionally you want to attract the nodes to one another or repel them away from one another. One obvious strategy would be to calculate the direction of a vector between the two objects and move one object along that line, either toward or away from the other object.

There are several ways to get the vector you need. The most immediately apparent method is to take advantage of the product of subtracted vectors. When you add two vectors (see Figure 6.4), you can visualize the resulting vector by attaching the tail of the new vector to the tip of the original vector in a chain. When you subtract two vectors, the result is a vector that starts at one vector's tip and travels to the tip of the other vector (see Figure 6.5). This means that subtraction not only gives you the direction vector to move, it also gives you the total distance in the form of the #magnitude or #length of the vector.

FIGURE 6.4

Adding two vectors can be illustrated as a geometric combination of the vectors by attaching the tail of the second to the tip of the previous.

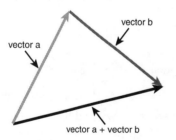

If you normalize the vector returned in the subtraction process, you can use it in tandem with a pSpeed property, just as we have in the immediately previous examples. The code would look like this:

```
directionVector  = w.model[n1].transform.position\
 - w.model[n2].transform.position
-- make the second model move toward the first
w.model[n2].translate((directionVector * pSpeed), #parent)
-- make the first model move toward the second
w.model[n1].translate((directionVector * -pSpeed), #parent)
```

```
-- make the second model move away from the first
w.model[n2].translate((directionVector * -pSpeed), #parent)
-- make the first model move away from the second
w.model[n1].translate((directionVector * pSpeed), #parent)
-- the negative speed (-pSpeed) is used to reverse the direction of the vector.
```

FIGURE 6.5

Subtracting two vectors will help you to find the direction that a given vector is pointing. It is key to attraction and repulsion.

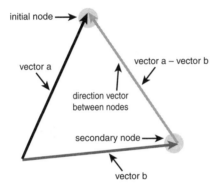

Another really handy way to find the direction vector between two nodes is to start with the pointAt() command. To use pointAt(), you need to first make certain your node's pointAtOrientation property is aligned to the model, camera, or light in a manner that is consistent with your expectations about pointing the node at another node. The obvious use of this command would be to tell the node that you want to do the pointing to point at the other node. You don't need to be that vulgar—you are after all a master in the making.

Because pointAt() is designed to work on nodes and not transform objects, we need to start with a dummy object. Create the dummy and match the dummy's transform to the transform of the actual node you intend to point. Now use interpolateTo() to move the actual node to the calculated value of the pointed transform. You need only move your character, light, or camera forward or backward along its primary direction axis in order to accomplish the chasing or avoiding maneuver from here.

If you wanted to accomplish this without turning your object toward the target node, you could simply use the `interpolate()` command to get the direction vector between the two objects and then convert the vector to a unit vector version of itself using the `getNormalized()` command. Finally, you would multiply the normalized (unit) vector by the magnitude represented by `pSpeed`. This amounts to a longhand version of subtracting two vectors, but it may lead you to a better understanding of the `interpolate` command. The syntax for a method like this would look like this:

```
directionVector = w.model[2].transform.interpolate \
(w.model[1].transform, 100).position.getNormalized()
w.model[2].transform.position = \
w.model[2].transform.position + (directionVector * speed)
```

The difference between this set of commands and simply using `interpolateTo()` is that the node would only move to the new position and not adapt the rotation changes of the target transform. The difference between this syntax and simply subtracting the two vectors is that this syntax beats around the bush and gets downright silly before getting to the point. The results of either method would be identical.

This overview should be enough to help you understand the transform methods we'll be using throughout the next several chapters. I'll return to the subject in Chapter 9, "Understanding the 3D Animation Options," as we begin to investigate Lingo-based animation.

Working with Cameras

Cameras in a 3D world are really an abstract concept used to figure out what stuff to display on that flat computer monitor and how to draw it there. It's one of the ironies of 3D representation that all the work of simulating the 3D environment is then mashed into a flat two-dimensional display.

The camera object consists of several parts. The camera has a transform that identifies its position, rotation, and orientation within the 3D world. You can adjust the various elements of the transform, just as you would for a model, to move and rotate the camera.

In Figure 6.6, I've captured the screen of a simple camera at work in 3D Studio Max. The view on the left side of the illustration is a `#left` view of the scene. The image on the right is the camera's perspective view. The pale lines forming a pyramid between the camera and the box represent the view volume of the camera. Anything that falls inside this area is drawn (projected) onto the computer screen. Those models that fall beyond the range of this area are not drawn onto the screen.

FIGURE 6.6

The view volume of the camera determines the models that are projected onto the screen.

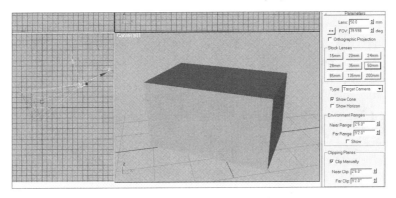

Just as the models to the left and right of the camera will be ignored during projection, models that are closer than the camera's `#hither` property or farther than the camera's `#yon` property also are clipped. Think of these as the cap and base of the pyramid representing the viewing volume.

It is also helpful to note here that there is a direct relationship between the base of the view volume and the position of a camera's backdrop. There is also a direct relationship between the top of the pyramid and the camera's overlays. Backdrops are drawn in the position of the base, and overlays are drawn in the position of the top. That is why turning the camera does not affect the position of backdrops or overlays. They are attached to the camera's projection volume.

Cameras have an up vector. This is really just common sense. If you held a real camera upside down while shooting, you would expect it to return upside-down film or video, right? The same is true here. Complex rotations often need the hinting from the camera's up vector in order to hold the camera upright while executing changes to the transform.

In Figure 6.7, I have widened the camera's `#fieldOfView` property to approximately 100 degrees. Notice that at first glance, it looks as if the camera has moved farther away from the box. It hasn't—we are simply looking at it through a wider-angle lens. This also has the effect of distorting the perspective more substantially than the first lens angle we used.

FIGURE 6.7

The same camera using a wider #fieldOfView.

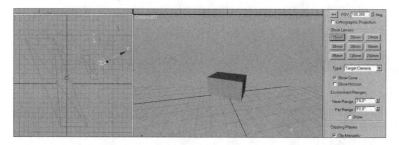

The camera is displayed on the sprite that you drop onto the stage. By default, the camera fills the entire sprite, but it does not have to be done this way. In fact, a single sprite does not have to contain only one camera. It can display as many cameras as you like. You can even add cameras from other 3D cast members. Simply add the cameras to the camera list of the sprite using the following syntax:

```
sprite(n).addCamera(member(n).camera[n])
sprite(n).camera(n).rect = rect(intleft,intright,inttop,intbottom)
```

The rect is the position, relative to the upper-left corner of the sprite (0,0), in which you want to display the camera. You can even control the movements of each camera independently as well as layer cameras over the top of other cameras. Director sorts the Z depths of the projections the same way as it does for sprites. The first camera will be the farthest back in the pile, and the highest numbered camera will be the closest to the viewer.

TIP

A sprite's 1st camera's rect can be modified, but the rect of the sprite will then show only the `clearColor` color from the camera's `colorbuffer` property settings. I use this method in *Bubble Pop Raceway*, the game featured in Chapter 9.

You may have noticed that I've used a combination of calls to `sprite.camera` and calls to `member.camera`. This can become a little frustrating. The basic rule of thumb is this: The world (member) contains the actual camera nodes, and the sprite contains only the camera projections as they actively render.

By default the sprite contains only one projection. If, however, you use the `addCamera()` command to add a camera node from the 3D member to the camera list of the 3D sprite, you may then define the rect of that camera. Used in combination, these basic elements can provide the foundations for a solid cinematic approach.

I want to briefly introduce you to each of the properties and commands supported by cameras within the W3D member and the W3D sprite. I've separated these based on those that demand calls to the member and those that require calls to the sprite.

Properties

I've listed and defined the properties of the member or the `member.camera` that may be accessed via Lingo in Table 6.1. Use the terms in this table and in Table 6.2 to work with cameras and camera properties.

TABLE 6.1   Member Camera Properties

Property	Description
colorbuffer.clearAtRender	Set this property to True to redraw everything on a blank slate every frame. Otherwise, you'll get a sort of 3D trail going on.
colorbuffer.clearValue	This property holds a Lingo color object that defines the color to be used as the blank slate for redrawing the scene each frame. This is only active if colorbuffer.clearAtRender is True.

TABLE 6.1   Continued

Property	Description
count	The count property contains the total number of camera nodes in the W3D member. This is not the same as the number of active cameras (cameras in the sprite's camera list).

Lingo provides two special member properties to help you control the rendering process of the W3D member: colorbuffer.clearAtRender and colorbuffer.clearValue. These properties are used to determine whether the projected 3D image is erased each time a new frame is drawn. If the clearAtRender property is False, animated images within the 3D member remain on the screen between frames. This leads to a sort of 3D trails effect.

Its counterpart, clearColor, determines the color that erases the whole screen if you choose to set clearAtRender to True. You may set this to any RGB color value, although it is normally black. Both clearColor and clearAtRender are properties of colorBuffer, which is in turn a property of the member. To access or set the value, use the following syntax:

```
w.camera(n).colorBuffer.clearAtRender = 0
w. camera(n).colorBuffer.clearValue = rgb(24,76,89)
```

The count property is one of the more confusing properties of the camera. This is only a property of member.camera. You cannot poll sprite.camera to give up its count property because it doesn't have one. To get to member.camera's count, use this syntax:

```
put w.camera.count
```

The properties of sprite cameras and member cameras are summarized in Table 6.2.

TABLE 6.2   Sprite and Member Camera Properties

Property	Description
The Backdrop Properties	
backdrop.blend	The opacity of the backdrop expressed as an integer between 0 and 100 representing the percentage of opacity.
backdrop.count	The total number of backdrops that are attached to the camera.

TABLE 6.2   Continued

Property	Description
backdrop.loc	The location of the backdrop in relationship to the camera's view volume base. A value of 0,0 generally centers your image on the screen.
backdrop.regPoint	The registration point of the backdrop measured from the upper-left corner.
backdrop.rotation	This property lists the degrees of rotation of the backdrop. Rotation spins the backdrop clockwise with positive numbers and counterclockwise with negative numbers.
backdrop.scale	This float allows you to get or set the scale of the camera's backdrop.
backdrop.source	Allows you to set the image source of the backdrop to the value of any texture object.
The Overlay Properties overlay.blend	The opacity of the overlay expressed as an integer between 0 and 100 representing the percentage of opacity.
overlay.count	The total number of overlays that are attached to the camera.
overlay.loc	The location of the overlay in relationship to the camera's view volume top. A value of 0,0 generally centers your image on the screen.
overlay.regPoint	The registration point of the overlay measured from the upper-left corner.
overlay.rotation	This property lists the degrees of rotation of the overlay. Rotation spins the overlay clockwise with positive numbers and counter-clockwise with negative numbers.
overlay.scale	This float allows you to get or set the scale of the camera's overlay.
overlay.source	Allows you to set the image source of the overlay to the value of any texture object.
3D Sprite Camera Position Properties cameraPosition	The position of the camera may be accessed directly via this property.
cameraRotation	This property provides direct access to the rotation of the camera.
worldPosition	The world-relative position of the camera.
Field of View Properties fieldOfView	This property stores an angle that represents the field of view of the camera in degrees.
projectionAngle	The same as fieldOfView.

TABLE 6.2   Continued

Property	Description
The Fog Properties	
fog.color	A Lingo color object that specifies the color of fog in the camera when fog.enabled is True.
fog.decayMode	The decay type of the fog. This may be [#linear, #exponential, #exponential2].
fog.enabled	This property uses a Boolean value to turn fog on or off.
fog.far	This property holds the distance in world units to the point at which the fog reaches its maximum density.
fog.near	The closest point at which fog is rendered.
Clipping Properties	
hither	This is the near clipping plane of the camera. Objects that are closer to the camera than this distance will not be drawn to the screen.
yon	The far clipping plane of a given camera. This is the point at which models will no longer be drawn (the farthest distance the camera sees).
Transform Properties	
transform	The transform object of the camera.
rotation (transform.rotation)	The rotation of the camera is also a property of the camera's transform. It contains a single vector representing the angle of rotation around each axis relative to the transform of the camera's parent.
scale (transform.scale)	The camera's scale is similar to the camera's position and rotation. Also a vector, this element represents the increase or decrease in size of the camera node.
position (transform.position)	The position of the camera is a property of the camera's transform. It contains a single vector representing the camera's position relative to the coordinate system of the camera's parent node.
Other Properties	
boundingSphere	The bounding sphere of a camera is a sphere sized to fit the extents of the camera and all its children. The property contains a list that includes the vector point at the center of the sphere and a float representing the length of the sphere's radius.
name	The name of the camera.

TABLE 6.2   Continued

Property	Description
orthoHeight	If the camera has been set to project in #orthographic mode, use orthoHeight to establish the amount of the world that will fit into a single camera view.
parent	The parent model of the camera node.
pointAtOrientation	The pointAt orientation of the camera contains two vectors. The first is the vector representing the front direction of the camera, and the second is a vector representing the camera's up direction.
projection	The style in which the image is drawn to the screen. Options are #perspective and #orthographic.
rect	By default, a camera fills the rect of the sprite with its image. You can customize the rect within the sprite where the camera is drawn. You may even draw many cameras onto a single sprite by setting their rects to different positions within the 3D sprite.
rootNode	This property let's you take advantage of the hierarchy system to display only those models you wish at any given moment. By default, the root node of a camera is the world, so the world and all its children (everything) appear in the camera's view. You may change the root node to any node in the scenegraph, so only that model and its children will appear in the view of the camera.
userData	A property that stores a property list that may be accessed and set with Lingo or with external 3D modeling software. You may store information about the node in its userData property.

As I said earlier, the backdrop and overlay may be visualized as the covers at the back and the front of a camera's viewing volume. They do not ever appear to move, because they ride along with the camera. It is as though someone stuck sheets of painted glass both very near to the camera and as far away as possible.

We saw a backdrop used in *Word Wacky 3D* in Chapter 2, "Making Plans." An overlay uses the same basic mechanisms. You can create it from any Lingo image object. You may rotate it and translate it within the parameters of the view volume. Because these layers support alpha channels, you can create visual frames for the image that allow the 3D member to be viewed through a sort of frame. You could also lay a permanent gun site across the viewer's screen or use overlays to feather the edges into your 2D interface. In our exercise at the end of this section, we'll do something like this.

Let's discuss some of the properties in Table 6.2 a little more.

The `boundingSphere` property may be accessed using the following syntax:

```
member(x).camera("cameraName").boundingSphere
member(x).camera[n].boundingSphere
```

This property may be retrieved but may not be set. It contains a two-item list. The first item in the list is a vector that represents the center of the bounding sphere. You may think, "But isn't that the same as a `transform.position`?" It isn't at all the same, because `boundingSphere` encases an object and all its children. This has two significant implications.

First, if you need to find the geographic center of a group consisting of the camera and each of its children, using `boundingSphere[1]` is an ideal solution. The second advantage is that the center of the bounding sphere will return the precise center even when an object's pivot point is not aligned to the center of the object.

The second item in the `boundingSphere` property is the length of the radius of the sphere, expressed in world-relative units. You could use this to determine the distance between an object and its most distant child, or to quickly estimate the relative size of the bounding sphere encasing the object and all its children.

The `cameraPosition` and `cameraRotation` properties are used to get and set the current `transform.position` and `transform.rotation` of the default 3D sprite's camera. These are sprite properties. Typical syntax would take the following form:

```
sprite(1).cameraPosition
```

The `worldPosition` property is a shortcut used to access but not to set the `transform.position` of this camera in world coordinates. In each case, these are shortcuts for the longer form of access via `w.camera.transform.property` and `w.camera.getWorldTransform().property`. Like all shortcuts in 3D Director, they only work with the first or default node (in this case, the default camera). If you want to get information about cameras that are not the default, you'll need to access them directly.

Imagine a line projecting outward from the camera to the top of the camera's view volume. Another line mirrors it on the bottom. The angle between these two lines is the `fieldOfView` or `projectionAngle` for perspective-projected cameras. Cameras that are projecting in `#orthographic` mode do not respond to these properties.

Fog is expensive in terms of animation performance. You will probably want to avoid its use at all costs during gameplay. That said, it is a beautiful addition to your arsenal. It is easy to use, easy to turn on and off, and runs fine on high-end machines. I highly recommend using fog to create cinematic effects, or when the environment just screams for it and you feel certain that the end machine can handle the cost. Typical `fog` syntax looks like this:

```
cameraReference.fog.color = rgb(n,n,n)
cameraReference.fog.decayMode = #linear
— possible values also include #exponential1, \
#exponential2. Linear fog stays the same density
— throughout the fog. Exponential1 is most dense \
at the far value of the fog. Exponential2 is
— most dense at the near value of the fog.
cameraReference.fog.far = 5000
cameraReference.fog.near = 1000
cameraReference.fog.enabled = TRUE
```

The best single tip I can give you about using fog is to match the color of the fog to the color of the background. This will cause things to blend together in a very cool way. If you can't match the color, at least match the value (the darkness or lightness) of the background and the fog. If the difference in value is substantial, you'll get crappy fog. A good trick for comparing color values is to convert both colors to grayscale color for a second. If the grays look close, you've got a good value match. If one of the grays is substantially darker or lighter than the other, you've got fog/background problems.

The front of a camera's view volume is the *hither* and the back of a camera's view volume is the *yon*. Only objects within the view volume of the camera are drawn, so you can use the `hither` and `yon` properties to prevent things that are too close or too far away from tying up the render engine.

This is handy in a couple of ways. Imagine that you have a game that follows a character around, watching the character from behind. The camera is positioned 500 units behind the character. It won't be long before your character walks behind a wall and the camera will be watching the wall instead of the character. You can take advantage of the camera's near clipping plane (`hither`).

If `hither` is set to 400 units, it is considerably less likely that the character will be out of our view at any time. (I actually prefer blending walls in such a case, but we'll get to that later.)

All nodes have a name. It must be a string value, and any other node cannot share it. You may use the name of a node to refer to that node.

The `orthoHeight` property controls the amount of the world that an orthographic projection camera displays. If you change the camera's projection mode to `#orthographic`, you need to set this value in total world units that you want displayed.

The normal parent of a camera is `world`, just as it would be for any other node. You may want to make some object in the world the parent of your camera. This is a very simple strategy for achieving camera motion that is tied to the motion of a model. Remember that the rotation and position of the parent will be echoed in the child, so you may find this method of camera motion far to jarring. A side effect of this method is that the model and camera are locked together so that the motion of the model is not really apparent to the camera. The camera always sees the model from the same angle. The world seems to move but the model and camera are attached.

`pointAtOrientation` is the direction in which the camera's lens is pointed by default. Changing this does not change the orientation of the lens; it simply changes the part of the camera that the `pointAt()` command uses to aim at another node. The `pointAtOrientation` property is the directional axis that is aimed at another node when `pointAt()` is called.

The `projection` property has two possible values: `#perspective` and `#orthographic`. A perspective projection will give you a 3D world that, like the one you see with your eyes every day, appears to have depth. Things get smaller with distance. An orthographic view does not do this.

Use the `rect` property to determine the size of the camera's projection. You should only set this when the camera has been added to the sprite or when the camera is the default camera. This controls the 2D display rect of the camera. You can add as many cameras as the RAM of the machine will allow. This means that you can peek into as many 3D worlds as you like from as many different camera angles as you like. To see them all at once on a single 3D sprite, simply add each camera to the camera list of the sprite and then adjust the rect of each one as discussed earlier.

The camera's rootNode is very cool indeed. Simply put, you can add and remove objects from the camera's view, simply by altering the membership of the hierarchical tree that begins with the camera's rootNode. As I mentioned earlier, every object is initially a child of the world. You can make objects children of other objects instead. You could make several objects children of the node "ground," for example. If you made "ground" the rootNode of the camera, only the children of ground would be visible in that camera. Another camera looking into the same world, with a rootNode of "world" (the default) would see all the world's objects. If you wanted to increase obstacles over time in a game but don't want to clone them, you could simply remove them from the tree that begins with the camera's rootNode.

A camera's transform property and position, rotation, and scale properties work the same as they do for any other node. The scale property has no visible effect on the camera, because the camera is not visible.

The userData property of the camera is the same as the userData property for any other node. It is a property list that may be set or accessed from either an external modeling application or from within Lingo. This property is used extensively in the *Battle Balls* game in Chapter 3, "Managing Your Story On-the-Fly."

Camera Commands

In addition to the camera properties that we are able to control with Lingo, there are also several commands that act upon the camera object and increase its usefulness. The first of these commands are supported by the 3D sprite and are outlined in Table 6.3.

TABLE 6.3   Sprite Camera Commands

Command	Description
addCamera()	3D sprites have a list of cameras. By default, there is one on the list. Use this command to add cameras from the member to the sprite's camera list. Then use the rect property to position each camera within the sprite.
cameraCount()	Use this command to get a count of the number of cameras in the sprite's camera list.

The addCamera()command adds a camera node that already exists in the 3D member to the 3D sprite. Because the sprite sorts the Z order of the cameras with the lowest-indexed camera at the back of the stack, this command appears to switch the default camera to the view of the camera you just added. Don't be fooled. Your default camera is still there; it is just behind the one you just added. Use this command in conjunction with camera.rect to place multiple camera views on the sprite.

CameraCount() returns an integer that represents the total number of cameras in the camera display list of the 3D sprite. This is notably different from the member.camera.count property. There may be 50 cameras in the member, but there is only one camera in the sprite's camera list until you add more using the addCamera() command.

The remaining commands are briefly explained in Table 6.4.

TABLE 6.4   Either Sprite or Member Camera Commands

Command	Description
Backdrop and Overlay Commands	
addBackdrop()	Adds a backdrop to the far clipping plane of the camera.
addOverlay()	Adds an overlay to the near clipping plane of the camera.
removeBackdrop()	Removes a backdrop from the far clipping plane of the camera.
removeOverlay()	Removes an overlay from the near clipping plane of the camera.
Manipulation Shortcuts	
addToWorld()	Use this command to add a camera to the world. You would only use this if you had specifically removed a camera from the world at some point.
isInWorld()	Use this command to learn whether an existing model is in the 3D world.
removeFromWorld()	Use this command to remove the camera from the world group, without actually deleting it. You could then reinstate it with the addToWorld command.
Clone Commands	
clone()	Makes a copy of a camera.
cloneDeep()	Makes a copy of a camera and all its children.

TABLE 6.4   Continued

Command	Description
3D Camera	
deleteCamera()	If used on sprite.camera, this command will remove the camera from the list of active cameras and stop the display of the camera. If used on a member, this command will delete the camera node from the 3D world.
newCamera()	Use this command to create a new camera in the 3D world.
Camera Picking	
Commandsmodels-UnderLoc().	This picking command is used to determine which, if any, models are currently under a given location on the 2D space
modelUnderLoc()	Similar to modelsUnderLoc, this picking command only returns information about the first model found beneath the 2D location.
spriteSpaceTo-WorldSpace()	This picking command may be used to calculate the 3D world space equivalent of a given two-dimensional point on the sprite's surface.
worldSpaceTo-SpriteSpace()	This command determines the sprite space equivalent of a given space within the 3D world. It is the opposite of spriteSpaceToWorldSpace().
Camera Motion	
rotate()	Use this command to rotate the camera around its x-, y-, and/or z-axes any given amount of degrees.
translate()	Use this command to move the camera object within the 3D model. It accepts a vector representing the distance and direction to be moved.
Other Commands	
autoCameraPosition()	In a 3D text member, this command (True by default) determines whether the camera is automatically positioned to see the 3D text.
pointAt()	A command used to aim or constrain the aim of a camera toward another model or node.

The backdrop and overlay commands (addBackDrop(), addOverlay(), removeBackDrop(), and removeOverlay()) are used to add and remove the backdrops and overlays that remain glued to the camera. Common uses include star-field backdrops or custom cutaway overlays that suggest all or part of the interface scheme. We'll look at an example in Exercise 6.1.

The commands addToWorld(), isInWorld(), and removeFromWorld() provide shortcuts to manipulate the scene hierarchy. You can pluck a camera (or any node) out of the world group, thus removing it from the world. A good time to do this would be when trying to slim down the number of resources that the render engine needs to fuss with during a given frame. Use isInWorld to test to ensure that you've put the node back into the world, and if you haven't, you may add it to the world with the addToWorld() command. Nodes are added to the world group by default, so you won't need these commands unless you first remove something from the world.

The autoCameraPosition() command is a toggle switch. Use it to switch on or off a preference that automatically centers text in the 3D text member camera's view. This is on by default but may be switched off using this command.

The clone() and cloneDeep() commands copy a node and each of that node's children. The difference between them is that cloneDeep() is more thorough. It also copies all the resources, shaders, and textures of the node and all the children's resources, shaders, and textures.

The deleteCamera() command is a bit tricky. As I indicated, you may use this command on either the sprite or member.camera. The effect will be very different on each. If you delete the camera of a sprite, you are removing that camera from the display list of the sprite. If you use deleteCamera() to delete a camera from a member, you are actually removing the camera and all its resources from the 3D member. Used in this manner, deleteCamera() is the opposite of newCamera(), which is used to add a camera to the 3D member.

The camera picking commands—modelUnderLoc(), modelsUnderLoc(), spriteSpaceToWorldSpace(), and worldSpaceToSpriteSpace()—are the keys to forming a nice healthy relationship between the mouse and the 3D sprite. The modelUnderLoc() and modelsUnderLoc() commands are close cousins. In a nutshell, these handy little commands let you submit a point representing a 2D horizontal and vertical position within the sprite. The function returns a list containing the model or models found directly beneath that point in 3D space. We will look at both of these commands in more detail in *Art Car Crazy Paintshop*, the game in the next chapter.

The spriteSpaceToWorldSpace() command takes a 2D coordinate within the 3D sprite's display and converts it to a 3D vector. This doesn't mean that you can use it to point at some object on the projection and get the point in space of the object—that's the purview of modelUnderLoc(). It literally returns the 3D equivalent of that place you clicked on the screen. The opposite of this command is worldSpaceToSpriteSpace(). Essentially this function calculates the 2D location of the projection of a 3D model's position vector.

Now let's walk through an exercise that is designed to give you practice manipulating cameras.

Exercise 6.1:   Over the Top and Behind the Lot

This is a good time to do some work with Director's billboard commands, play with some camera movement, and gain a more complete understanding of the camera-access procedures. Along the way you should learn a bit more about camera motion.

NOTE

I'll talk a great deal more about cameras and fine-tuning camera motion in Part III, "Putting Strategies into Action." This exercise should provide you with an overview. In Part III, we'll add some more advanced techniques, such as camera collision detection, obstruction clipping, and dynamic node management, to your bag of tricks.

During this exercise, you will be working with two files from the accompanying CD-ROM: basicFollowCamera.dir and stalkerCam.dir. Here are the steps to follow:

1. Open the basicFollowCamera.dir file now.

2. Open the Cast window. The cast should look similar to the one shown in Figure 6.8.

3. Open the first behavior, KillerCam, and have a look at the first several lines of code. I've included them here with more extensive comments:

```
--- ***NOTE **** --- This behavior requires an mCameraTimeStep()
------------------- event from a timer object.  This is a time-based
------------------- behavior, not a frame-based behavior. To convert
------------------- it to frame based - change the mCameraTimeStep
------------------- to exitFrame.
```

FIGURE 6.8

The cast contains three behaviors, two movie scripts, and two parent scripts.

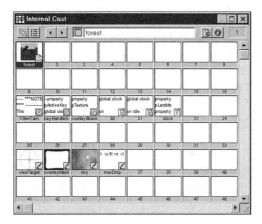

One of the more unusual things about this camera behavior is that it requires a bit of custom stimuli. This camera doesn't use the `exitframe` events sent by the movie to trigger movement. It uses a trigger sent as often as the system is able from a movie script. The movie script is set to trigger the camera motion and the ball movement on each idle cycle. If you glance at the `startMovie` script, you'll notice that I set the tempo (the movie's frame rate) to one frame per second.

This is the first time in this book that we've looked at the time-based alternative to frame-based animation. There are many solid arguments for using exclusively time-based animation, rather than frame based animation, to regulate the speed of playback of your animation. The most notable argument in favor of time-based animation is that playback on high end machines can be ridiculously fast with frame-based animation if you are not very careful. The counter to this argument is that time-based animation can seem jarring or jerky if you are not very careful about the method you use to match distances over time. In this behavior, a central clock object triggers all motion events:

```
----------ID TAGS------------
property pSprite
property pMember
property pCamera
property pTarget
```

Each of these properties store a reference to the object for which it is named. The pTarget property will hold a reference to the model that is being targeted by the camera:

```
---- VECTORS ----------------
property pOffset
property pCameraUp
property pTargetPosition
property pCameraPosition

----- INTERPOLATION ----------
property pTargetSteps
property pCameraSteps
```

These properties are used to calculate the previous position and next position of the camera each time the screen is redrawn. In order to dampen (smooth) the motion of the camera a bit, we'll divide the total distance to be covered by pTargetSteps and pCameraSteps.

The pOffset property is a vector that represents the relationship of the camera to the target object. If the camera is not in this position, relative to the object, the camera will work to get to this position. The pCameraUp property helps with the rotation of the camera by providing some hinting information during rotation. Rotating an object in 3D can cause all sorts of bizarre racking (distorting the rectangular volume of the model), tilting, tipping, and so on. The hinting is used to keep the camera's up vector pointing up during these rotations. The pTargetPosition and pCameraPosition properties are vectors that indicate the location in 3D space of the target and the camera:

```
------------------------------------
------------------------------------
on beginSprite(me)
  ---- set up the basic id info
  pSprite = sprite(me.spriteNum)
  pMember = pSprite.member
  pCamera = pMember.camera(pCamera)
  pTarget = pMember.model(pTarget)
  ----- clear the old cameras from the sprite and add a new
  ----- camera if the user asked for it.
  if pCamera <> pSprite.camera then
-- if the camera the user picked from the
-- popup dialog isn't the same camera as the
-- one the sprite is actively using, then
-- delete all of the extra cameras from the
-- sprite's camera list
    repeat with x = pSprite.cameraCount() down to 2
```

```
        pSprite.deleteCamera(x)
      end repeat
-- and add the camera that the user picked to the camera list
-- of the sprite
      pSprite.addCamera (pCamera)
-- finally, adjust the rect of the new camera
-- to fill the screen, and reduce the rect of the
-- default camera to the smallest rect possible.
      pSprite.camera(pSprite.cameracount()).rect =
rect(0,0,(pSprite.rect.width),(pSprite.rect.height))
      pSprite.camera(1).rect = rect(0,0,1,1)
    end if
```

The first portion of the beginSprite() handler assigns values to many of the properties and then switches the camera to the one that the user requested via the pop-up dialog spawned by getPropertyDescriptionList(me).

The last two lines of this handler record the current positions of the camera and the target. These positions need to be tracked every cycle in order to allow the camera to follow motions made by the model:

```
------- Record the current positions of the camera and target
  pCameraPosition = pCamera.transform.position
  pTargetPosition = pTarget.transform.position
end beginSprite


--------------------TRIGGER REDRAW
on mCameraTimeStep (me)
  mNextInterval (me)
end
```

The mCameraTimeStep() handler puts a public face on the private handler used to calculate the new position and orientation of the camera and rerecords the new position of the camera and the targeted model.

The calculation of camera movement and rotation is done by the mAutoFollow() handler. This handler starts by recording the new position of the target model. Next, it calculates the desired new position of the camera. It does so by adding the pOffset property (the desirable distance between camera and target) to the current position of the target.

The next step subtracts the vector representing the current camera position from the vector representing the proposed camera position and divides that vector by the number of steps called for in the interpolation. The user decides this during the initial assignment of the behavior to the sprite. Finally, the original position of the camera is added to the resulting vector. The camera is then moved to the calculated position (see Figure 6.9).

FIGURE 6.9

The interpolation of the camera may be visualized as a simple manipulation of vectors.

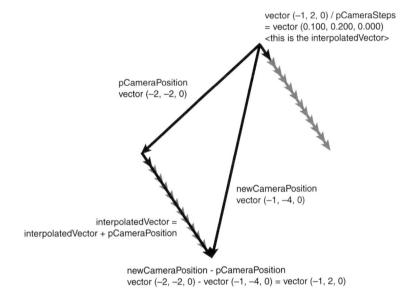

The process is similar for aiming the camera. The only difference is the position of the nodes that are being calculated. The formula is identical:

```
-------------------- FOLLOW THE MODEL
on mAutoFollow (me)
  newTargetPosition = pTarget.transform.position
  newCameraPosition = pOffset + newTargetPosition
  if( not (0 = pCameraSteps) ) then
    cameraPos = ((newCameraPosition - \
pCameraPosition) / float(pCameraSteps)) + pCameraPosition
    pCamera.transform.position = cameraPos
  end if
  if( not (0 = pTargetSteps) ) then
    cameraAim = ((newTargetPosition - \
pTargetPosition) / float(pTargetSteps)) + pTargetPosition
    pCamera.pointAt( cameraAim, pCameraUp )
  end if
end
```

4. Now let's put this movie together. Start by sliding the `KillerCam` behavior onto the W3D sprite on the stage.

5. When the behavior hits the stage, a dialog like the one shown in Figure 6.10 pops up.

FIGURE 6.10

The KillerCam behavior's property dialog.

6. Set the target model to `GeoSphere01` and the camera to `Camera02`. Set the camera-to-model distance to `vector( -1250, 1250, 150)`. Set the Camera Up Vector field to `vector( 0.0000, 0.0000, 1.0000)`—positive 1 in the Z direction and 0 on the other two axes. (The default should be fine.) Leave the Model Interpolation and Camera Interpolation values at `10`.

7. Now add the `keyHandlers` behavior. There won't be a dialog, so don't worry when nothing happens. This behavior adds user control to the ball. You will be able to control the ball using the arrow keys on your computer's keyboard.

8. Add a copy of the `overlay&backdrop` behavior. A dialog like the one in Figure 6.11 appears.

9. Using the first drop-down menu, select the image that you want to use to create the texture for your overlay or backdrop. If you use this behavior in your own movie or import additional images into this movie, you will be able to use them as backdrops and overlays as well. Set this one to "sky."

10. The second drop-down menu lets you choose whether you want this to be a backdrop or an overlay. Choose "backdrop" this time.

11. Use the third drop-down menu to define the camera to which you want to apply these overlays. Choose Camera02 so that you will be able to see your changes.

FIGURE 6.11

Use the image of the overlay&backdrop *behavior to help you set the properties of each overlay or backdrop as you work.*

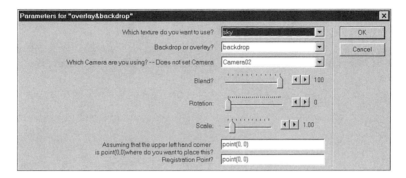

12. The Blend slider allows you to manipulate the opacity of the backdrop or overlay. Set it at 100 to make it opaque or at 0 to make it transparent. Let's leave the sky opaque, so set this value to 100.

13. The Rotation slider allows you to adjust the rotation of the overlay or backdrop. We don't really need any rotation here, so set this to 0. If it amuses you, feel free to adjust the angle on any of the overlays or backgrounds.

14. The Scale slider allows you to scale the image down to nothing or up to 10 times its size. This one defaults to 1. Values less than 1 shrink the image, and values greater than 1 increase the image by a factor equal to the value. I made all these images the same size as the display sprite, so we don't need to change this value from 1.00. If you use an outside image, you may find that playing with scale gives you a good sense of how that adjustment is being made.

15. You may set the loc and the registration point using the last two dialogs. For our purposes, the default loc (point(0, 0)) and registration point (point(0, 0)) are fine.

16. Click the OK button.

17. Grab another copy of the overlay&backdrop behavior. Set this one as follows:

```
treeDrop
backdrop
Camera02
85
```

```
0
1.00
point(0,0)
point(0,0)
```

Click OK.

18. Drop another copy of the overlay&backdrop behavior on the 3D sprite. Set it as follows:

```
viewTarget
backdrop
Camera02
40
0
1.00
point(0,0)
point(0,0)
```

Click OK.

19. Drop another copy of the overlay&backdrop behavior on the 3D sprite. Set the fourth and final one as follows:

```
overlayMask
overlay
Camera02
100
0
1.00
point(0,0)
point(0,0)
```

Click OK.

20. Rewind and click the Play button to see your handiwork.

Working with Lights

There are four types of lights in Director 3D members:

- #point—Point lights are omnidirectional light sources that originate at a given point within the 3D world. Think bare light bulb and you'll be pretty close to a point light.

- #spot—Spotlights are lights that may be aimed in a given direction and whose beams may be confined to a given angle. Think theater spotlight and you've got the right idea.

- #directional—Directional light is like a giant block of light moving through the entire plane at a given angle. The angle doesn't change. It is the same everywhere within the 3D member. Think sunlight, but the sun is stuck in one place, and you get a directional light.

- #ambient—Ambient light is meant to simulate the reflected light within the environment. In life, ambient light is the stuff that bounces off surfaces and then hits others. This is approximated in Director 3D in order to save the processor from certain meltdown.

You can use these light types together or independently to sculpt the space you will be sharing with your audience. Lighting is a combination of functional illumination, dramatic sculpture, and evocative painting. Just as the fundamental elements and principles of design dictate your aesthetic choices in the creation of other visual elements for the game, they should inspire your lighting choices.

Illumination is sometimes a narrative chore and sometimes a pragmatic one. The first role of illumination in lighting is to make certain that there is enough light on the scene for the player to interact with the space. The second challenge is to ensure that any specific information that assists the narrative is evident in the manner in which the scene is lit. If it is a bright day, the light should provide evidence of this.

Your next challenge as a lighting designer within your game space is to sculpt the objects that exist in the space. If your models look flat, the lighting is probably less effective than it could be. Try to enhance the mass of your models by accentuating highlight, midtones, and shading within the environment. As long as your efforts don't prevent the player from seeing the model, you are doing fine.

The last role of the light is to augment the overall mood of the gamespace by modifying the colors and values of the models in ways that enhance the emotional power of the game. Consider these images of a gray model, lit with just green, red, and blue spotlights (see Figure 6.12).

FIGURE 6.12

A gray model lit with colored spotlights.

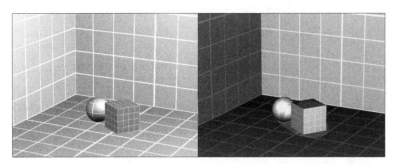

Later in this chapter, we'll take a closer look at this gray world and adjust the lights in it in order to get a better understanding of the changes that can happen when lights are altered in the 3D member.

As you begin working with lights in your 3D world, it is important to keep in mind that the expense incurred by elaborate lighting schemes might be substantial. Do yourself a favor and keep this axiom in mind: Everything must have a purpose. This works equally well for all sorts of things, but it is especially helpful in 3D modeling for games. Every polygon must have a purpose, every light must have a purpose, and every line of code must have a purpose.

The painful truth is that the prettiest solution is usually the most expensive solution in terms of optimization. This can be the case in 3D lighting, but it doesn't have to be.

Properties

Let's take a look at the properties for lighting. Table 6.5 lists light properties with brief descriptions.

TABLE 6.5   Light Properties

Property	Description
attenuation	A property of point lights and spotlights, attenuation controls the intensity through constant, linear, and quadratic attenuation factors of the light. In other words, you can make the light brighter or dimmer by adjusting the attenuation.

TABLE 6.5   Continued

Property	Description
boundingSphere	An imaginary sphere just big enough to enclose the light and all its children.
color	The RGB color value of the light that is emitted by the light source.
specular	This property determines whether the light source will cause a specular highlight on the models that it hits.
name	The name of the light.
pointAtOrientation	The direction the light is pointed and the direction that represents the top of the light.
type	The type of light may be altered by resetting this property. Director supports the following types: #spot, #directional, #point, and #ambient.
userData	A property that stores a property list that may be accessed and set with Lingo or with external 3D modeling software. You may store information about the node in its userData property.
Spot Properties	
spotAngle	Compares to the field angle property of a camera. This is the angle at which the beam spreads for spotlights.
spotDecay	This Boolean property indicates whether the beam of light diminishes in intensity as it travels farther through the 3D space.
Camera-Similar Properties	
transform	The transform object of the light.
position (transform.position)	The position of the light relative to its parent node.
rotation (transform.rotation)	The rotation of the light relative to its parent node.
scale (transform.scale)	Has no effect because the physical light has no model.
worldPosition	The world-relative position of the node.

I want to give you a little more information about these properties. The attenuation property, the intensity of a light, is only a relevant property on spotlights and point lights. The property accepts a vector as its argument. That vector lists the light's constant, linear, and quadratic attenuation. These are the factors that are used in order to calculate the dimming of light over time.

Just as in OpenGL or virtually any other 3D program, Director calculates the attenuation of a point light or spotlight using the formula `1.000 / (constant + (distance * linear) + ((distance*distance) * quadratic))`. Therefore, the total value will not exceed `1.000`. This is why extremely small values must be used to alter the attenuation of point lights and spotlights.

When the constant, linear, and quadratic attenuation factors are not given, the defaults are `vector( 1.0, 0.0, 0.0)`. This results in no attenuation and is the reason that the lights will pop down just as they reach their brightest intensity. Because the attenuation calculation mushes these numbers together anyway, I generally just set the constant to a percentage value.

The `boundingSphere`, `transform`, `worldPosition`, `position`, `rotation`, and `scale` properties are fundamentally the same for a light as they are for a camera.

A light's `color` property stores the RGB value of light that will be emitted from this source. Blending colors of light is not the same as blending colors in pigment. Even the primary colors are different. If you are not familiar with lighting color theory, you may find that your attempts to blend lights and get the results you expected are failing miserably. The subject is too extensive to cover here, but Paul Catanese has provided an outstanding overview of lighting versus pigment color theory as it applies to Director 3D in his book *Director's Third Dimension* (Sams Publishing, 0672322285). There are also several good online tutorials on the subject included in Appendix C, "Online Resources."

The arguments accepted by the `color` property is an RGB color. These take the form `rgb(red,green,blue)`. The range of each factor is 0 (none of that color) to 255 (as much of that color as possible.) Set all three to 255 and you'll get white light; set all three to 0 and you'll get black.

The `specular` property allows you to toggle on and off specular reflections. Remember that lights in a big black void would really have no effect. They have to bounce off something in order for you to see the effect of the lights. The specular reflection is that bright spot you see reflected on a typical model—it's the sheen on an apple and the twinkle in an eye. You may want to turn it off. It takes extra time to render a scene with lots of cool lighting effects. Keep in mind that it is also a big part of the illusion of 3D, and if you turn it off, you might be sacrificing a lot of quality.

The `name` and `userData` properties are the same for lights as they are for any other node. The `type` property is the key to the nature of the light node. The four types of lights are discussed more extensively at the beginning of this section.

Just as it does for any other node, the `pointAtOrientation` property stores the orientation vector for the light. This is the direction in which the light is pointing relative to itself. This doesn't tell you which direction the light is pointing relative to the world; it tells you which axis the light is pointing down relative to itself.

The `spotAngle` property can easily be compared to a camera's field of view property. Just as a camera has a view volume, a light has a projection cone. Generally the cone projecting from a spotlight's source is round at the top and bottom and forms a cone with its volume. The `spotAngle` property contains an angle that represents the degrees of spread that the cone has from its point to its base.

The counterpart to `spotAngle` is `spotDecay`. This property allows you to choose whether the spotlight will lose intensity with distance. This property is normally set to `False`. You should keep in mind that although the effect may be lovely, it is generally unlikely that you will have the CPU cycles or graphics card RAM to waste on this effect in your games.

In addition to the properties directly associated with lights, there are a few lighting properties that are accessed via the member rather than via a single light. These properties are listed in Table 6.6.

TABLE 6.6   Member Properties That Influence Lighting

Property	Description
ambientColor	This member property controls the base color value of ambient (reflected) light in the space. This isn't really reflected light; it's a general simulation of the same.
Directional Properties	
directionalColor	The color of light emitted from the default directional light in the W3D member.
directionalPreset	The angle of the default directional light in the member. Options are #topLeft, #topCenter, #topRight, #middleLeft, #middleCenter, #middleRight, #bottomLeft, #bottomCenter, #bottomRight, and #None.

These three properties are all accessed via the member using the following syntax:

```
member(n).property = value
```

Ambient light is the light in the world that has been reflected off objects and is now bouncing around indirectly. It would be far too expensive to actually calculate this in a real-time 3D engine. Director approximates these values and uses the general color, ambientColor, to establish the overall color of ambient light. In reality, the color of ambient light is determined by the combination of objects off which the light bounced. You may set the ambientColor property of the member to any RGB color value.

The directionalColor value determines the color of the default directional light that Director places into the scene via the Property Inspector. It is possible to have custom directional lights in the scene either in lieu of or in addition to this light. The possible values for directionalPreset are the same as those listed in the directionalPreset drop-down menu in the Property Inspector for the 3D member.

Now take a look at commands to use with your lights.

3D Light Commands

Like cameras, light objects support several commands. These commands are used by the light nodes to accomplish tasks related to both illumination of surfaces and orientation of the lights. There are housekeeping commands that allow you to manage your light assets and other commands that enable finer levels of control over the performance of the lights. Table 6.7 introduces the light commands.

TABLE 6.7 Light Commands

Command	Description
pointAt()	Aims the light at the node defined in the command's parameters.
World-Related Commands	
addToWorld()	Adds the light to the world group within the 3D member. You would only really need this if you specifically removed the light from the world because all nodes are initially added to the world.

TABLE 6.7   Continued

Command	Description
isInWorld()	Checks to see whether the light is in the world group.
removeFromWorld()	Removes the light from the world group but does not delete the light from the member.
Clone Commands	
clone()	Makes a copy of the light and all its children. Does not copy the resources, shaders, and textures of its children.
cloneDeep()	Makes a copy of the light and all its children. Copies all the model resources, shaders, and textures of the children.
Activation Commands	
deleteLight()	Removes the light from the 3D world and from the cast member.
newLight()	Creates a new light node and adds it to the world group.
Movement Commands	
rotate()	Use this command to rotate the light on any of its axes.
translate()	Move the light around in the space using the translate command, just as you would for a model or camera.

Now that you've seen the camera commands, the lighting commands should seem painfully obvious. The lighting commands are identical to most of the camera commands and even those that do not directly correlate—deleteLight() and newLight()—are immediately comparable. Just as you would suspect, deleteLight() is used to remove a light from the 3D member, and newLight() is used to add one to the member. Each of the remaining light commands behaves the same way for lights as it did for cameras and other nodes.

It always amazes me how completely a space may be altered by the color, value and intensity of the lights that illuminate that space. The next exercise demonstrates this effect in a 3D scene.

Exercise 6.2:   Changing the Look of a Place with Light

Find the 06ColorStudio.dir file on the companion CD-ROM and open it. Go ahead and play with the color sliders for each light. Make note of the way that colors change as you increase or decrease the RGB values of each light in the scene.

Of particular interest in this exercise is the extreme degree to which you can paint the scene with the color of the light. Explore this movie, keeping in mind our earlier discussion of sculpting and painting the space in order to establish mood, create an illusion of place and time of day, or other lighting conditions.

Flatten the scene and then maximize the visual contrast in the scene. Which do you find more appealing? Are there times when each would be appropriate? How much can you accomplish with just one light? These are spotlights; could you get the same or similar effects with only directional or point lights? Try setting each of the light's RGB values to 0 and adding a directional light using Director's Property Inspector for the 3D member. (You can type RGB values in the text field.)

Poor lighting is one of the most common mistakes in 3D games. You don't need an arsenal of lights to effectively light the space. Keep the tricks and tips you've learned here in mind as you begin to construct your own worlds.

Lights and cameras are a huge part of the 3D picture, but alone they offer us nothing to look at. In the next chapter I'll introduce you to shaders and textures and you'll have a chance to try your hand at a little 3D painting in the *Art Car Crazy Paintshop*.

CHAPTER 7

Shaders and Textures

Now that we've got eyes into our worlds and have a good idea about ways to cast light within the space, it is a great time to start investigating the ways that objects within the 3D world reflect light.

Objects are visible because they absorb and reflect light, and they appear to be different colors because they reflect different wavelengths of light. The 3D worlds we are making in Director simulate this direct relationship between lights and the objects that reflect light by simulating real-world materials.

Those materials are created from two separate components: shaders and textures. Shaders contain the information about the manner in which light should react to a material's surface, and textures contain references to detailed images that are used to generate variation in the patterns of light absorbed and reflected by a given material.

In this chapter, I'll give you an overview of Director's robust support for surface materials, and you'll have an opportunity to play with some examples from a game called *Art Car Crazy Paintshop*.

After reading the chapter you should

- Know the properties and commands associated with shaders
- Know the properties and commands associated with textures
- Understand how light and materials interact in a 3D world
- Understand the basic relationship between shaders, textures, and models

This chapter begins with an overview of the properties and commands used to manipulate shaders in a 3D world. Then we'll look at the properties and commands used by texture objects, and I'll introduce you to the *Art Car Crazy Paintshop* and explain the various handlers used to create the painting effects in the game.

Working with Shaders

Light bounces, sometimes. Most of the fun of light is in the bounce. If you look at a pattern printed into the fabric of your shirt or the tablecloth on your kitchen table, you'll see different colors. They seem tangible, and you can probably name them. Ultimately, these colors are simply visual patterns that are formed when part of the light that hits the surface material is reflected and another part of the light is absorbed.

We see the reflected part of the light, so we say, "Ooh, Beulah, look at the lovely flowers on that tablecloth." The same principal applies to the color of the walls, doors, and floors. Color is an abstract concept. It is the way we describe the phenomena of varied wavelengths of light bouncing off objects in the physical world. I suppose the fact that color is tangible to most people makes us a bit unwilling to accept the fact that it is a trick of the eye.

Shaders are virtual objects designed to re-create all the subtleties of surface materials in the physical world. A shader contains all the information necessary to calculate the manner in which a model should be rendered in order that it is perceived by the viewer as a physical object. Because the shader is the source of all this information, it only makes sense that the relationship between shaders and textures is a paternal one. Each shader may have up to eight textures. Textures are still discrete objects, but they may only be assigned to a model in the 3D world via a shader.

Properties

The best way to familiarize yourself with the items a shader represents is to dig in to the shader's properties and commands. Table 7.1 provides an inventory of these.

TABLE 7.1   Shader Properties

Property	Description
ambient	The amount and hue of light colors that are reflected by a shader. This property stores an RGB color object.
blend	This property is an integer between 0 and 100 that indicates the percentage of opacity of a given shader, assuming that you haven't switched the transparent property to False.
blendConstant	The shortcut to blendConstantList[1].
blendConstantList	A list of integers, between 0 and 100, used to determine the amount to blend a texture with the texture below it in the stack when blendSource is set to constant.
blendFunction	The shortcut to blendFunctionList[1].
blendFunctionList	The properties stored in this list come in four flavors: #multiply, #add, #replace, and #blend. Use them to determine the way a texture blends with the texture beneath it in the stack.
blendSource	This is the shortcut to blendSourceList[1].
blendSourceList	This property may be set to #alpha or #constant. The setting determines the manner in which blending will occur. If it is set to alpha, alpha channel information from the texture is used to determine how much to blend each pixel. If it is set to constant, the shader's blendConstant value is used for all pixels.
brightness	Used with the engraver and newsprint shaders. An integer between 0 and 100 that determines the amount of whitespace rendered in the engraver or newsprint shader. The default setting for this property is 0.
colorSteps	Used with the painter shader and toon modifier. You may display 2, 4, 8 or 16 colors in either the painter shader or the toon modifier. Set the number you prefer to see in the finished shader here.
density	Used with the engraver and newsprint shaders. This property takes an float between 0 and 100 that determines the density of lines or dots the shader displays.
diffuse	The diffuse color (RGB) you want to blend with the textures assigned to a given shader when you set useDiffuseWithTexture to True.
diffuseColor	The diffuse color (RGB) that you plan to blend with the first texture assigned to the first shader in a given cast member.
diffuseLightMap	Stores a reference to the texture that you want to use for diffuse light mapping. The texture reference is kept in the second position of the shader's textureList.

TABLE 7.1   Continued

Property	Description
emissive	Allows the model to glow and emit light all by itself. It does not cast light on other objects in the scene.
flat	Use this property to speed things up. You can enable flat shading rather than Gouraud by switching this one from its default, False, to True. It may not give you the same boost on all systems, but it should generally make things render faster. You will lose some realism when you switch from Gouraud to flat shading.
glossMap	Use this property to set the texture you want to use for gloss mapping. Stores a reference to a texture in the fourth position of the shader's textureList.
highlightPercentage	Used with the painter shader and toon modifier. A counterpart to shadowPercentage, this property determines the percentage of the colors specified via colorSteps that will be used in the highlight area of the shader.
highlightStrength	Used with the painter shader and toon modifier. This property takes a float between 0.0 and 100.0 indicating the brightness of the highlight. The default is 1.0.
reflectionMap	A reference to an image used to create reflections on the surface of a shader. The map will be placed in the third position of the shader's textureList.
reflectivity	Stores a float value between 0.0 and 100.0 that may be used to adjust the reflectiveness the default shader in the 3D member. The default value is 0.0.
renderStyle	Use this property to switch among the #fill, #wire, and #point style displays of the shader.
rotation	Used with the engraver shader only. This property determines the rotation offset in degrees of the engraved lines.
shaderList	A list of each of the shaders that have been applied to a given model. The number of shaders assigned to a model is equal to the number of meshes in the modelResource.
shadowPercentage	Used with the painter shader and toon modifier. This property relates to the colorSteps property of a painter shader or toon modifier and is the percentage of the assigned number of colors that will be displayed in nonhighlighted areas of the shader or modifier. The value is expressed as an integer between 0 and 100.
shadowStrength	Used with the painter shader and toon modifier. Using a float value between 0.0 and 100.0, this property indicates the relative brightness of the area of a model's surface that is not highlighted.

TABLE 7.1   Continued

Property	Description
shininess	Stores an integer between 0 and 100 that indicates the percentage of the model's surface area that is highlighted.
specular	The RGB color value of specular reflections for a given shader.
specularColor	This shortcut points to the RGB color used for specular reflections by the first shader in a 3D cast member.
specularLightMap	A reference to a texture that will be used to map specular reflections onto the shader. This will place the map in the fifth layer of the shader's textureList.
style	Available to both the painter shader and the toon modifier, this property allows you to choose the manner in which color will be applied to the model. There are three possible values: #blackAndWhite, #gradient, and #toon.
textureList	The list of each of the textures assigned to a given shader.
textureMode	This property determines the way in which a texture is wrapped around the first shader of a given model. It comes in the following flavors: #none, #wrapPlanar, #wrapCylindrical, #wrapSpherical, #reflection, #diffuseLight, and #specularLight.
textureModeList	Provides access to the textureMode property for additional textures in the shader's textureList.
textureRepeat	A Boolean property that determines whether textures wrap and repeat when the scale of the textureTransform is smaller than 1.0. This is True by default and can create decals (single non-repeating texture images that are smaller than the full surface covered by the shader) when True.
textureRepeatList	Provides access to the textureRepeat property of each texture in a given shader's textureList.
textureTransform	An independent transform that controls the position, rotation, and scale of the first texture assigned to a given shader. This transform is constrained to x and y translations and z rotation.
textureTransformList	Access to the texture transforms of each of a given shader's texture objects.
transparent	A Boolean property that toggles the shader's alpha blending on or off (True by default). Changing this property to False disables the shader's blend property.
type	Shaders come in four basic types: #standard (the default), #engraver, #newsprint, and #painter.

TABLE 7.1   Continued

Property	Description
useDiffuseWithTexture	This Boolean property allows you to combine the effects of the diffuse color with the shader's texture object(s). This is False by default.
wrapTransform	The independent transform of a shader object. Use this property to alter the wraptransform.position, wraptransform.rotation, and so forth of the shader. This form is the shortcut to the first shader in a given model's shaderList.
wrapTransformList	The transforms of a given model's shaders within the shaderList. Allows access to the wrap transforms of deeper-layered shaders on a given model.

It is fitting that the ambient property tops the list alphabetically, because it also tops the list of shader properties conceptually. The ambient color of a shader is the color that *may* be reflected when light makes contact with the shader.

May? Now that's irritating, isn't it? The key to understanding the impact of any property of a shader is in remembering that a shader is nothing without a light. Shaders, just like those walls and tablecloths, have the potential to reflect certain colors of light. If the light that hits the shader doesn't contain the colors that the shader is set up to reflect, the object/shader will not be visible. This is why changing the color of a light has an effect on the models that the light hits. The model's shader isn't changing color any more than you might expect the walls of your room to have turned red just because someone has thrown a red cloth over the lamp. Nonetheless, the walls appear red, because the filtered light that hits them contains only red light waves.

Think of the shader's ambient property this way: If the light is white, this is the color that the shader would reflect. To set the ambient color of a shader, use the following syntax:

```
w.model[n].shaderList[n].ambient = rgb(intRed,intGreen,intBlue)
```

NOTE

Here, and in most other places in this chapter, I'm giving you the syntax I prefer to use to access the property in question. There are other ways to access these properties, often called *shortcuts*. It is generally better to get into the habit of accessing these properties directly, because using the shortcuts is fairly limiting, and using a combination of shortcuts and direct access can become very confusing.

A close cousin to the `ambient` property, the `diffuse` property also contains a reference to an RGB color object. The diffuse color is blended with the texture if the `useDiffuseWithTexture` property is set to `True` and the `blendFunction` property is set to either `add` or `multiply`. You can also use it with the `blendFunction` property set to `blend` if the `blendSource` property is `constant` rather than `alpha` and the `blendConstant` property is lower than `100`. The `diffuseColor` property provides shortcut access to the `diffuse` property of the first shader of the member. Use this syntax to access these properties:

```
w.diffuseColor = rgb(50,60,70)
w.model[n].shaderList[n].diffuse = rgb(60,70,80)
w.model[n].shaderList[n].useDiffuseWithTexture = TRUE
```

A shader's `emissive` property is also filled with an RGB color object. This property determines the color of light added to the shader. It doesn't add a light to other objects in the scene; it only adds the light of the specified color to the shader of the given model. Access the `emissive` property of a given shader using the following syntax:

```
w.model[n].shaderList[n].emissive = rgb(70,80,90)
```

The `specular` property also contains a reference to an RGB color. This is the color of the highlight of a given shader if a light with its `specular` property set to `True` lights the shader. `specularColor` is a shortcut to the `specular` property of the first shader in the cast member. Set the `specular` property using the following syntax:

```
w.model[n].shaderList[n].specular = rgb(90,100,110)
w.specularColor = rgb(100,110,120)
```

The `blend` property determines the opacity of a given shader. You used the `blend` property in Chapter 6, "Cameras and Lights," to manipulate the opacity of overlays and backgrounds. The `blend` property is tied to the `transparent` property, which is a toggle switch that enables and disables all blending. To alter the `blend` and `transparent` properties of a shader, use the following syntax:

```
w.model[n].shaderList[n].transparent = TRUE
w.model[n].shaderlist[n].blend = 65
```

As you might expect from their names, a relationship exists among the `blendConstantList`, `blendFunctionList`, and `blendSourceList` properties. Each of these properties is used to determine how the blend of a texture within the shader's `textureList` will blend with the textures beneath it in the shader's `textureList and the shader's other surface properties.`

The `blendConstantList` property contains the corresponding values used to blend the texture if the `blendSourceList` property is set to `#constant`. If, for example, `blendConstantList[3]` were set to `30`, the texture in the third layer of the `textureList` would be rendered at 30-percent opacity over the texture in the second level. This would only be the case if `blendSourceList[3]` were set to `#constant`. If it were set to `#alpha`, the alpha channel information about the percentage of blending per pixel would be used to calculate the blending between the current layer and the one behind it.

Using the `blendFunctionList` property, it is also possible to blend these textures in more sophisticated ways. You can do additive blending as well as multiply, replace, or choose the regular blend option. The default value of this property is `#multiply`. Use the following syntax to work with these properties:

```
w.model[n].shaderList[n].blendFunctionList[n] = #blend
w.model[n].shaderList[n].blendSourceList[n] = #constant
w.model[n].shaderList[n].blendConstantList[n] = 60
```

The engraver and newsprint shader types treat the surface of the object differently than the standard shader. They add some custom details to the surface and the rendering process that are designed to give non-photorealistic results. These shader types have some additional properties, because they behave differently than the standard shader. You can still access all the standard shader properties, so you should think of these as additional properties that are specific to the engraver and newsprint shader types.

The two additional properties shared by the engraver and newsprint shader types are brightness and density. Open the sampleShaderStudio.dir movie found on the CD-ROM to have a quick glance at the difference between photorealistic (#standard) and other shader types.

Try typing the commands in Listing 7.1 into the message window to see quick examples of each of the following non-photorealistic shader properties: brightness, density, rotation, colorSteps, highlightPercentage, highlightStrength, shadowPercentage, shadowStrength, and style.

LISTING 7.1   Viewing Shader Examples

```
 1: put w.shader[2]
 2: -- shader("Material01") -- this is the standard shader
 3: put w.shader[3]
 4: -- shader("painter") -- this is the painter type shader
 5: put w.shader[4]
 6: -- shader("engraver") -- this is the engraver type shader
 7: put w.shader[5]
 8: -- shader("newsprint") -- this is the newsprint type shader
 9: -- with the movie running, click on the painter \
➥ hyperlink in the text field below the 3D sprite.
10: put w.shader[3].colorSteps
11: -- 2 -- most of the image is just blocks of red color
12: w.shader[3].colorSteps = 16
13: -- you will see the image change to a more detailed one
14: -- If everything is red, it is because the painter gets its \
➥ color from the first light in a scene. If the first light is red then;
15: put w.light[1].color
16: -- rgb( 255, 0, 0 ) -- you'll see this.
17: w.light[1].color = rgb(0,255,0)
18: -- you should see the image change to a green colored version.
19: w.shader[3].highlightPercentage = 70
20: w.shader[3].highlightStrength = 60
21: put w.shader[3].style
22: -- #gradient
23: w.shader[3].style = #blackAndWhite
24: w.shader[3].style = #toon
25: w.shader[3].style = #gradient
26: -- now switch to the engraver shader by clicking on the engraver hyperlink
27: -- in the text field below the 3D sprite.
28: put w.shader[4].brightness
29: -- 0.0000
30: w.shader[4].brightness = 35
31: -- notice the increase in white in the resulting 3D display
```

LISTING 7.1   Continued

```
32: w.shader[4].density = 22
33: -- brightness and density have similar effects on the newsprint shader.
34: -- You can change the index reference to shader[5] and use the hyperlinks
35: -- to navigate to newsprint if you want to try these on newsprint.
36: w.shader[4].rotation = 10
37: -- if you dont catch this one, repeat it a \
➥few times. The angle of the engraving
38: -- lines are rotating clockwise. Use 45 to \
➥get to 90 and form a vertical horizontal
39: -- crosshatch instead of the default oblique pattern.
```

Each of the `lightMap` properties is a sort of shortcut to quickly create a standard effect. The `diffuseLightMap` property places a texture in the shader's second layer, sets the mode to `#diffuse`, the `blendFunction` property to `#multiply`, and the `blendFunction` property of the texture below it in the stack (`textureModeList[1]`) to `#replace`. Each of the maps is meant to simulate the effects of patterned light reflecting off the object.

The `glossMap` property places a texture in the fourth channel. Its texture mode is set to `#none`, and its `blendFunction` property becomes `#multiply`. The `reflectionMap` property sends its texture to the third layer. It sets the `textureMode` property to `#blend`, the `blendSource` property to `#constant`, and the `blendConstant` property to 50. Finally, the `specularLightMap` property falls in layer 5. This shortcut sets the `blendFunction` property of the texture to `#add` and the `blendFunction` property of the first texture layer to `#replace`. We'll look at some examples of these in action at the end of this section.

Normally these shaders are rendered using a method called *Gouraud shading*. Essentially gradients are calculated for each face of a shader in order to give a more realistic look to the objects in the 3D space. The downside of this form of shading is that it takes a bit of time. You can set the `flat` property, a Boolean, to `True` in order to turn off Gouraud shading and use flat shading instead. Flat shading still gives variety in the appearance of the model's surface, but deviations in value are calculated on a per-polygon basis rather than gradiating the values within each polygon. The result is a sort of faceted look. Open the movie `sampleShaderStudio.dir` again and type the following command into the message window while you are viewing the standard shader version of the scene:

```
w.shader[2].flat = 1
```

The renderStyle property determines whether the image will be drawn with points or wireframe or is fully shaded. Point and wireframe display is not supported by every system, so be aware that you may not see any change as you toggle between them. To access the render style of a shader, use this syntax:

```
w.model[n].shaderList[n].renderstyle = #point
w.model[n].shaderList[n].renderstyle = #wire
w.model[n].shaderList[n].renderstyle = #fill
```

The reflectivity shortcut is used to access the shininess property of the member's default shader. The shininess property indicates the percentage of the surface of the shader that will be covered by the highlights. Note that this is not the same as saying that it represents the amount of shininess. In fact the smaller the shine, the more reflective an object will seem.

You can access these properties with the following syntax:

```
w.reflectivity = 80
w.model[n].shaderList[n].shininess = 80
```

By now, you've grown accustomed to the name of the shaderList property. This is really just a linear list that has as many items as there are shaders available to the model. The number of shaders in a model is determined by the modelResource property. Some have one; some have many. You can set all the shaders in the shader list by omitting the index and referencing the list or set any individual item by using its index number.

As mentioned earlier, even though textures are independent objects, they do not display in the 3D scene unless they are listed as the properties of a shader. Each shader may have up to eight textures (assuming that the playback machine supports that many texture layers). The layers are stacked into a list, the textureList property. You can access any of the textures in the shader's texture list by index (textureList[n]). The textureModeList, textureRepeatList, and textureTransformList properties correlate to the texture list of the shader. In other words, the third item in the texture list is referenced by the third element in the texture mode list and the third item in the texture transform list. Each refers to the same texture object and is used to set a specific property for the instance of that texture object that is attached to this shader.

In short, texture modes determine the manner in which the textures are projected onto the surface of the model. The `textureRepeat` property determines whether a texture will repeat when the image is smaller than the surface onto which it has been projected. The `textureTransform` properties store 2D x,y coordinates of the location, rotation, and scale of the texture.

The `wrapTransformList` property is the 3D cousin of `textureTransformList`. It controls the 3D transform of the texture as it wraps around the model using the shader. This one doesn't work when the corresponding texture mode in the texture list is set to `#none`, `#reflection`, `#diffuseLight`, or `#specularLight`.

Commands

Only two commands are used to work with shaders. They are fairly simple to understand, but I've detailed them in Table 7.2 for your convenience.

TABLE 7.2   Shader Commands

Command	Description
deleteShader()	Deletes a shader object from the W3D cast member
newShader()	Creates a new #standard, #engraver, #newsprint, or #painter shader object

The `deleteShader` command allows you to remove a shader object from the 3D scene. You may issue the command using the following syntax:

```
w.deleteShader("stringShaderName")
w.deleteShader(n)
```

The `newShader` command creates a new shader of the type specified in the second argument. You can create a shader using the following syntax:

```
w.newShader("stringShaderName", #type)
-- the type must be either #standard, #engraver, #newsprint, or #painter.
```

Working with Textures

A texture is your best friend and your worst enemy, all rolled into one tidy little package. You can take advantage of a detailed texture to illustrate the surface of a model with a level of visual detail that would take thousands of polygons to reproduce with the model alone. This makes the texture your very best friend. On the other hand, a texture can be substantial RAM hog, swallowing up all the available RAM on the playback machine in the blink of an eye. A texture can drag your action-packed shooter's performance down to an absurdly slow animation rate, making it a truly vile and horrible enemy.

Learning to master these little monsters is a big part of successful real-time game development. Every texture starts with an image of some sort. You could start with an image that you generate entirely in Lingo (`#fromImageObject`). You may also initialize your texture using a bitmap cast member (`#fromCastMember`). You can even bring textures in from an external 3D modeling program using the material editor found in the authoring program (`#importedFromFile`).

NOTE

Import procedures from each of the major 3D modeling packages are described in Chapter 8, "Low Polygon Modeling and Third-Party Exporters."

Properties

Most of the properties of textures are designed to assist you with optimization. Optimizing your textures works in two different directions. First, your textures will swell the size of the data file that must be downloaded or otherwise delivered to the player. If your delivery device will be the Internet, the download size of the file is critical. Large textures mean large bitmap downloads, unless these files are substantially compressed or you find clever ways to build the images during playback.

The other half of optimization is tweaking the display properties of the textures themselves. When you make a texture in Director, the original image is generally copied at three sizes in order to maximize efficiency while displaying the texture in the 3D world. If the texture draws near the camera, the larger, more accurate version of the texture is used. As the texture moves farther away from the camera, the less accurate, smaller versions of the texture are used. The process of creating multiple versions of textures and drawing the most appropriate one depending on the distance between the camera and the model is known as *mipmapping*, which is controlled by Director's `quality` property.

Finally, Director gives you direct access to the `renderFormat` property of each texture. This means you will be able to choose how many bits of each color (red, green, blue, and alpha) are used to display the image. This process can be a bit tricky, because not all video cards support the display of all render formats. However, this process does give you the opportunity to choose how your models will render on ideal systems and enables you to set a low bar for machines that just won't be able to play your games.

Take a look at the properties of textures, as shown in Table 7.3.

TABLE 7.3   Texture Properties

Property	Description
compressed	Indicates whether the image that the texture used as a source is compressed. These images aren't compressed while they are in use, but they can be before and after.
image	A reference to the Lingo image object that the texture used during its creation. You can reset the image property on-the-fly, making radically fast changes to the texture possible.
member	A reference to the member that the texture used to create itself. This property can be reset on-the-fly for rapid replacement of the texture, even animated textures.
nearFiltering	This Boolean property allows you to switch on a sort of blending feature that smoothes out the texture's source pixels as a texture is displayed at sizes larger than its original dimensions. True is on; False (the default) is off.
quality	This property gives you control over the level of mipmapping (creating multiple versions of textures). There are three potential values: #low, #medium, and #high. This determines the number and quality of copies that are made of the texture's image in order to display more size-appropriate images as the texture moves closer in the Z plane to the camera.
renderFormat	This is the value of the display resolution for the specific texture object referencing the property. It is an RGBA (or red, green, blue, alpha) color object. Add each integer, and the total will generally equal the color depth.
textureRenderFormat	The value assigned here determines the default display resolution of all the textures, assuming that the graphics card can display images at the desired resolution.

TABLE 7.3   Continued

Property	Description
textureType	This property might be more aptly named the default texture type because it stores the value of the default texture for the 3D member.
type	Textures come in three flavors: #fromCastMember, #fromImageObject, and #importedFromFile.

The compressed property determines whether the resource file of a given texture is compressed. This property is automatically updated when a texture is created from the bitmap, but you may find it useful to decompress the image earlier than the system decides to do so.

The image and member properties provide direct access to the bitmap resource of the texture. Using these properties you may alter the appearance of the texture on-the-fly. This can lead to simulated animation effects on the skinned surface of 3D objects. Use the image property for textures whose type is #fromImageObject and use the member property for those created from cast members. The syntax looks like this:

```
w.model[n].shaderList[n].textureList[n].image = lingoImageObject
w.model[n].shaderList[n].textureList[n].member = member("bitmap")
```

A texture's nearFiltering property determines whether the pixelization caused when an image is displayed at a resolution larger than the original size of the bitmap will be blended. This is a Boolean toggle switch, so you turn it on or off using the syntax:

```
w.model[n].shaderList[n].textureList[n].nearfiltering = \
TRUE -- TRUE is on, FALSE is off.
```

The quality property determines the amount and type of mipmapping that will be done to the texture. This property has three possible settings: #high, #medium, and #low. If you set the property to #low, no copies are made. If you set the property to #medium, several simple copies are made at smaller sizes. If you set the property to #high, several complex and detailed copies are made at smaller sizes.

The textureRenderFormat property of the global getRendererServices() object controls the default render format for any model that doesn't have its renderFormat property set to a specific level. More specifically, this controls the render format property for those textures which have this property set to #default, rather than set to a specific rgba value. The levels are expressed as RGBA values using the following syntax:

```
-- set the default render format for all textures \
not using a specific renderformat to #rgba4444(4 \
bits of red, 4bits of green, 4 bits of blue \
and 4 bits of alpha. (16 bits)
getRendererServices()textureRenderFormat = #rgba4444
-- set the specific texture to use the default renderformat.
w.model[n].shaderList[n].textureList[n].renderFormat = #default
-- Use 5 bits of each color, rgb, and no bits for an alpha. (16 bits)
w.model[n].shaderList[n].textureList[n].renderFormat = #rgba5550
-- Use 5 bits per color and 1 bit for an alpha channel. (16 bits)
w.model[n].shaderList[n].textureList[n].renderFormat = #rgba5551
-- Use 5 bits for red, 6 bits for green, and 5 bits for blue. (16 bits)
w.model[n].shaderList[n].textureList[n].renderFormat = #rgba5650
-- Use 8 bits for each color, but don't bother with any alpha. (24 bits)
w.model[n].shaderList[n].textureList[n].renderFormat = #rgba8880
-- Use 8 bits for each color and support an 8 bit alpha channel. (32 bits)
w.model[n].shaderList[n].textureList[n].renderFormat = #rgba8888
```

The textureType property is the shortcut to the type of the default texture, which is based on the kind of resource that used to create the texture in the first place. It either came from an imported W3D file (#importedFromFile), was created from an image object (#fromImageObject), or was based on a wbitmap cast member (#fromCastMember).

Commands

By now, the commands for working with textures should look absurdly similar to the major commands for just about every other type of object in the 3D member. Examine the pair of commands in Table 7.4.

TABLE 7.4   Texture Commands

Command	Description
deleteTexture()	Deletes an existing texture object from the W3D member
newTexture()	Creates a new texture based on a member or Lingo image object

The deleteTexture() command, as you must have suspected, deletes a texture object from the 3D cast member. The texture is removed from the world. Use this syntax to delete a texture:

```
w.deleteTexture("stringTextureName")
w.deleteTexture(n)
```

The `newTexture()` command allows you to create a new texture within the 3D cast member. It requires two arguments: the name of the new texture and the type. Use the following syntax to generate a new texture:

```
w.newTexture("stringTextureName", #type, imageOrMemberReference)
-- #type will be either #fromCastMember, or #fromImageObject.
```

Exercise 7.1: *Art Car Crazy Paintshop*

Now let's have a look at a small chunk of a game that I've been working on called *Art Car Crazy Paintshop*. This game grew out of my love for art cars and a long-time friendship with an artist who creates them.

Open the file on your companion CD-ROM named `artCarCrazy.dir`. Rewind it and click Play. Play around with the various texture tiles, rotate the car, and note that you are able to rapidly paint the surface of the car in all sorts of fun and zany ways. The primary texture swapping is handled by the `changeTexture` script, which is shown in Listing 7.2.

LISTING 7.2   The `changeTexture` Script

```
1: property pTexture
2: property pHotModel
3:
4: on mouseUp(me)
5:   if NOT the shiftDown then
6:     -- as long as they aren't holding down the shift key
7:     currModel = member(sprite(me.spriteNum).member).\
➡ camera[1].modelUnderLoc(the mouseLoc)
8:     if NOT voidP(currModel) then
9:       -- if there is a model under the mouse
10:       if NOT voidP(pTexture) then
11:         -- if the texture chip has already been set
12:         member(sprite(me.spriteNum).member).model\
➡ (currModel.name).shader.texture =\ member(sprite\
➡ (me.spriteNum).member).texture(pTexture)
13:         -- change the texture
14:       else
15:         alert "Pick a texture first"
16:       end if
17:     end if
```

LISTING 7.2   Continued

```
18:    end if
19: end
20:
21: on exitFrame(me)
22:    if rollover(2) then
23:       --- if the cursor is over the 3D sprite
24:       currModel = member(sprite(me.spriteNum).member).\
   ➥camera[1].modelUnderLoc(the mouseLoc)
25:       -- set the variable currModel to the model \
   ➥under the mouse (if there isn't one we'll get that in a sec)
26:       if NOT voidP (currModel) then
27:          -- if there is a model under the mouse
28:          if NOT voidP(pHotModel) then
29:             -- if there has ever been a model under the mouse before
30:             if currModel <> pHotModel.name then
31:                -- if the model is different than the model was last cycle
32:                member(sprite(me.spriteNum).member).model\
   ➥(pHotModel.name).shader.emissive = rgb(0, 0, 0)
33:                -- turn the old glowing model back to normal
34:                pHotModel = currModel
35:                -- set the property pHotModel so we'll \
   ➥remember which one was glowing this time, the next time
36:             end if
37:          else
38:             -- if there has not ever been a model under the mouse
39:             pHotModel = currModel
40:          end if
41:          member(sprite(me.spriteNum).member).model\
   ➥(currModel.name).shader.emissive = rgb(125, 125, 125)
42:          -- now make the model under the mouse right now, glow a bit.
43:       else
44:          --- there is not currently a model under the cursor
45:          if NOT voidP(pHotModel) then
46:             pHotModel.shader.emissive = rgb(0,0,0)
47:          end if
48:       end if
49:    else
50:       if NOT voidP(pHotModel) then
51:          if NOT (pHotModel.shader.emissive =rgb(0,0,0)) then
52:             pHotModel.shader.emissive = rgb(0, 0, 0)
53:          end if
54:       end if
55:    end if
56: end
```

The two properties associated with this behavior hold a reference to the active texture object and a reference to the model that is currently under the mouse cursor.

As the mouseUp response script begins, I strip out mouseUp events that occur while the Shift key is being held down by the user. This is done to prevent accidental painting while the car is rotating. The next few lines check to see which, if any, model is under the mouse. If there is a model under the mouse and that model is not already textured with the pattern from the highlighted pattern box, the texture is updated appropriately. There is also a little helper that asks the users to choose an initial pattern if they have yet to do so.

The next handler responds to rollovers within the 3D sprite. Basically it highlights the section of the model that the cursor rolls over in order to give the users feedback about the painting they are about to do. Users are familiar with this sort of intuitive feedback and should immediately recognize the glowing auto part as an indication that it will receive the active color.

The handler simply checks to see which model, if any, is under the cursor and makes it glow. The bulk of the work involves actually turning the glow off immediately as the mouse rolls outside the model.

This section of the game demonstrates a fairly straightforward combination of the shader's properties and the texture's properties changing dynamically in order to provide entertainment for the player. Try importing one of your own models and placing it in the position of the second sprite in place of the car model. Be sure to place the member in the first position of the cast as well.

You should find that your model works the same as the car model. This is because the scripts do not depend on the car member world to operate. They work with whatever models and shaders exist in the 3D world when it is generated.

These basic tools are truly awesome and you are beginning to get a very real sense of the power that you can hurl around with Director 8.5. In the next chapter I'll turn my attention to some ways to augment that power as I investigate and explain Low polygon modeling techniques and several of the Shockwave 3D exporters that are available to Director developers.

CHAPTER 8

Low-Polygon Modeling and Third-Party Exporters

We've talked enough about optimization now that you are likely to realize that every polygon adds to the burden the CPU must face as it attempts to bring your game to life. The process of creating 3D models from the smallest appropriate number of polygonal faces is commonly known as *low-poly (low-polygon) modeling*.

A delicate balance must be honored when creating low-polygon models for real-time games. This is because you are likely to deform the meshes during animation cycles, and you want the characters that you create to maintain some resemblance to their original form even as their knees bend and their arms pivot.

When these characters are created, they need to be converted into Shockwave 3D files to be used as W3D cast members. There are several major 3D modeling packages that support the W3D export standard, including Alias Wavefront's Maya, Discreet's 3D Studio Max, and New Tek's Lightwave. An overview of export procedures for these three software packages later in this chapter should help you address the advantages, strategies, and pitfalls of W3D exporters regardless of the 3D authoring package that you prefer.

After reading and understanding the chapter, you should

- Know the basic techniques used to determine whether a model needs to be further optimized

- Know the trinity of tools most commonly used to optimize polygons

- Know how to use exporters for Lightwave, Max, and Maya

- Understand the fundamental concepts behind optimizing animated models

- Understand the differences between the exporters created by each of the major third-party modeling software companies
- Understand how to optimize models as you build them
- Have practiced optimizing a model

In this chapter, I talk about some tricks I've learned for optimizing 3D models. I help you understand where to look for excess polygons and make decisions about how you might reduce them in your models, and then you peek over my shoulder as I build a little dragon for one of my games.

Next, we look at the process of exporting models from the major 3D packages. I walk you through the export procedures of each one and give you some handy tips about the potential pitfalls involved with using them.

Optimization

Virtually any model that you export to Director from an external authoring program will be a mesh or collection of meshes. A *mesh* is a collection of polygons (in this case, triangles) that are connected by common edges and vertices.

Allow me to paint a picture for you. Pretend that you have a magic blanket that is made of a strange and wonderful material (see Figure 8.1). This material divides the blanket into small triangular shapes that are stiff, but you can squash and stretch the edges of the triangles. In other words, the length of any edge can grow or shrink, but the face of the triangle remains flat. You can bend the blanket at any point where there is an edge between triangles, but you can't break the linking edge between two triangles (see Figure 8.2).

Meshes in the Shockwave 3D format are made out of the material from such a "magic blanket." *Optimization* is the process of reducing the number of triangles to the smallest number possible without sacrificing the illusion of form or the ability to deform that shape during animation.

The best strategy for optimizing your models involves three steps: validation, method, and exemption.

The first step, validation, is to carefully consider each polygon within the model and ask yourself whether you really need that extra face. If the edges of the polygon, or even one edge of the polygon, are not serving a specific purpose in the definition of the form, it must be optimized.

FIGURE 8.1

Polygons as they are drawn in Director 3D.

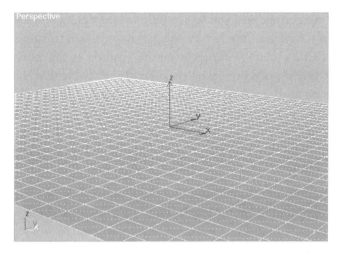

FIGURE 8.2

Manipulating triangular polygons.

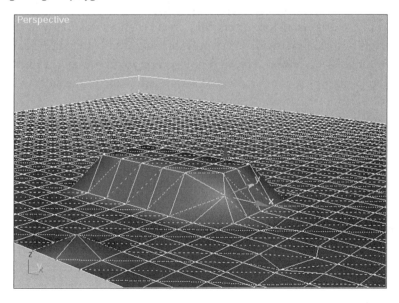

The next step, method, is to decide the best approach to reducing the polygons. This must be determined based on your eventual plans for the faces, the effect of reduction on the finished mesh, and the total number of faces that can be reduced using a given optimization strategy.

The last step, exemption, asks you to carefully consider the eventual deformation of the mesh during animation. A polygon might seem to have no purpose at the moment that you are working, given the position of the model. This doesn't mean that the polygon has no purpose. It is possible that the polygon would provide eventual accommodation for the motion of a joint. It is even possible that you will need to add some of these extra faces in anticipation of such motion.

For Every Line a Purpose

As you begin to optimize your models, you will want to validate the relevance of every edge and face within the mesh. This is a time-consuming but necessary process. Most 3D modeling packages also offer some sort of algorithmic optimization modifier that usually does not give you the effect you had in mind.

I have found such modifiers useful when working with extremely high-resolution models, or when the meshes were fairly simple with absurdly high polygons in the original. More often, they create such a mess that you find yourself reworking virtually every polygon and eventually going back to the beginning. If you have a very high polygon original, you might find that it is better to simply use it as you would a scanned image in the side and front views to aid in the construction of a model from scratch.

More often than not, algorithmic optimization leads to funky surface distortions in the finished model caused by edges that are turned in opposition to the flow of the skin. In other words, you'll get lumps on the surface of the object. These are easy enough to rectify, but they are still a bit of an annoyance.

An edge has a purpose if at least one, preferably both, of its vertices defines a point of variance in the occluding contour (the outline) of the form. If you remove the edge or one of its vertices and there is no perceivable difference in the model, you know you've done well. As you work, be realistic. Players will be more grateful for fast animation and quality gameplay than they will be that you got such amazing 3D detail in that guy's face.

We are severely limited when we consider the massive number of Internet-based computers that do not have 3D hardware acceleration, so you'll want to be certain that you keep every model as trim as you can without abandoning aesthetic qualities all together.

Steed's Trinity

Paul Steed, character modeler on Quake 3, introduced other modelers to his trinity of optimization tools in his article "The Art of Low-Polygon Modeling" in the June 1998 issue of *Game Developer* magazine. He says divide, turn, and merge (collapse and/or weld) are the most important tools in his 3D Studio Max toolkit when mesh optimization is the task at hand.

The collapse vertices command in 3D Studio Max combines one vertex with another and, in the process, reduces the polygon count as well as the vertex count. Use Edit Polygons, Merge Vertices in Maya (or the command-line `polyMergeVertices`). Using Detail, Points, Weld Average seems to simulate this effect best in Lightwave Modeler.

NOTE

Although collapse is the optimum tool for merging two vertices, its behavior becomes a bit unwieldy when you are trying to merge a cluster of vertices. To merge small clusters, you might prefer to work with the weld (threshold) tool, which allows you to merge vertices that are positioned within a given distance of one another.

To use collapse vertices in 3D Studio Max, first create a mesh. To do this, first create a primitive, then convert that to a mesh: use the Modifier Stack, Connvert To, Editable Mesh Shortcut. Then use the Selection Masking drop-down menu found under Selection Level on the Modify Properties tab to choose sub-object, vertex (see Figure 8.3). Finally select two vertices and then click the Collapse button in the Edit Geometry section (see Figure 8.4).

FIGURE 8.3

Switch Selection Masking to Vertex and select two vertices.

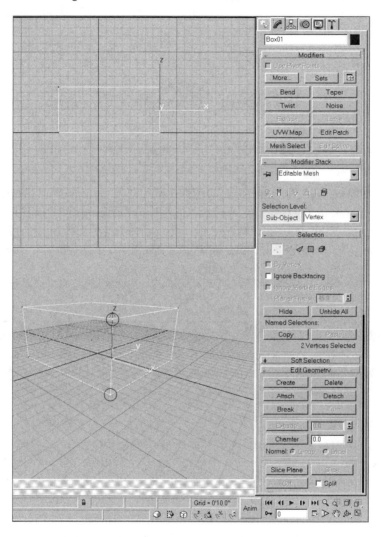

FIGURE 8.4

Use the Collapse Vertex button to combine these two vertices.

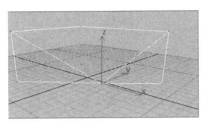

The remaining tools in the bag of tricks work with the edge of a given polygon. To work with these tools in 3D Studio Max, you need to switch the Selection Masking (Sub-Object) level to Edge (see Figure 8.5).

Sometimes you want to add vertices. Edge Divide is the perfect tool for this job. It divides the edge of a polygon in half and adds a vertex at the center point. This operation creates a new vertex and splits the original polygon into two polygons.

If the edge already joins more than one polygon, the polygon on the opposite side also is split into two polygons. To understand how adding polygons fits into optimization, remember that our ultimate goal is not simply to reduce polygons in the mesh, but to reduce polygons to the lowest number possible to effectively create a mesh that can be animated.

When the edge is selected, use the Divide button on the Modify tab in the Edit Geometry subsection. To use this tool, simply click the button and then select an edge. The edge will be split in the middle (see Figure 8.6). In Maya, this can be accomplished by using Edit Polygons, Subdivide while you are in the modeling mode and an edge is selected (see Figure 8.7).

FIGURE 8.5

Switch the Sub-Object selection masking to Edge.

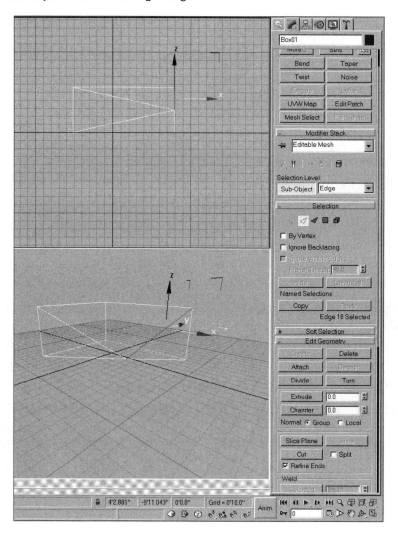

FIGURE 8.6

Use the Divide tool in Max.

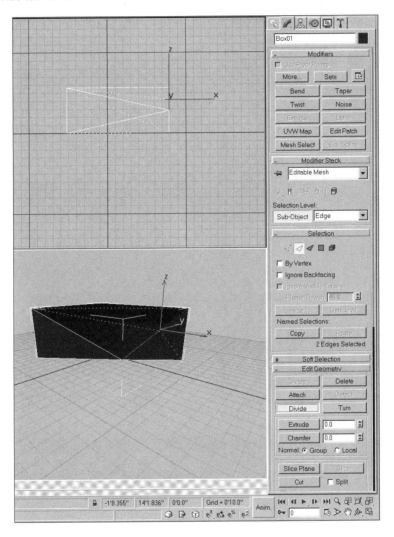

FIGURE 8.7

Use the Subdivide tool on a selected edge in Maya.

The last tool in our collection is the Edge Turn tool (the Flip Triangle Edge tool in Maya). I love this tool in a strange and haunting way. It is incredibly helpful to be able to go back into a mesh and turn the edges to ensure that the faces lay flat without bubbling and puckering.

I should mention that to actually see what you are doing in 3D Studio Max, you must make certain that the display properties are not set to Display Edges Only in the Display tab. This makes the triangles that compose the model visible for you.

In Figures 8.8 and 8.9, I've used the Edge Turn tool, by first selecting the Edge Selection-Masking tool and then choosing Turn from the properties dialog to the right. As long as that button is depressed (mint green), any edge that I click on will rotate from its current orientation within a given quad to the opposite two corners. Compare the figures to see the change in appearance before and after.

FIGURE 8.8

Compare this image of the edge prior to turning to the image in Figure 8.10.

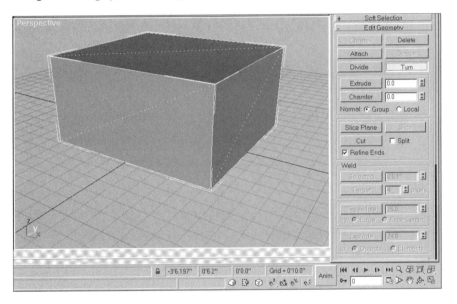

I use each of these tools to optimize the dragon model I draw later in this chapter.

FIGURE 8.9

The edge is turned from a line adjoining two opposite corners of a quadrangle to a line adjoining the opposite two corners of a given quadrangle.

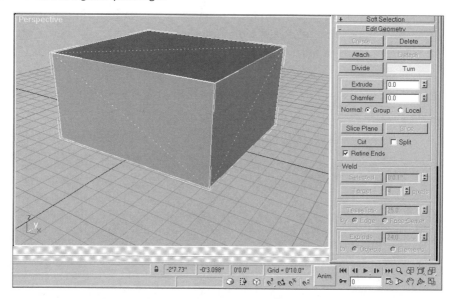

Accommodation

If you plan to bend the mesh you are creating, especially if the model's mesh will be jointed, you need to accommodate that bending to avoid strange, unwanted side effects. Consider the sample arm shown in Figure 8.10.

Your character's arms and legs will look like they are made of thin-wall metal pipes, and those pipes will collapse and crease every time you try to bend a limb.

The simple tube collapses if there are not enough appropriately aligned polygons to accommodate the bending motions. This means that your figure's knees or wrists would collapse as well without these added faces to accommodate such motion.

FIGURE 8.10

Bending a simple tube based arm at a single joint yields a bizarre collapsed-looking mesh after deformation.

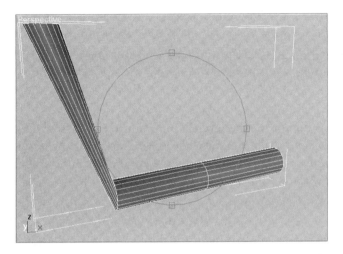

Steed suggests that low-polygon models should be created with their limbs in bent positions to ensure that adequate measures have been taken to accommodate mesh deformation and to retain the girth of the model at the joint.

I think that it is sufficient to anticipate the bend, and perhaps simulate it in your modeler, before finalizing the mesh. (This is because the use of the standard T position—arms outstretched and legs apart—makes your application of a biped considerably simpler.)

Exercise 8.1:   Building a Dragon

Now that you've seen the basic elements of low-polygon modeling, it is time to take a dip in the icy water. In this exercise, I walk you through the steps of creating a low-poly model and then creating and applying a texture map in 3D Studio Max.

NOTE

You don't have to use 3D Studio Max to follow along with this exercise, although it might be difficult to accomplish exactly the same things with another modeling package. You may have noticed that I've already suggested some parallel tools in Maya and Lightwave.

If you don't have one of these mid-priced 3D tools, and don't plan on shelling out the considerable licensing fees, you might want to consider Tabliero's ShapeShifter. This $99 wonder allows you to edit 3D from within Director (on either platform). Although it does not yet support some of the more advanced features, it certainly does seem well poised to become a fully integrated 3D authoring system for Shockwave.

It isn't difficult to see that this little 3D package could easily become the tool of choice because of the specific orientation toward Director's 3D features.

1. Draw a picture of the model that you want to create from a direct side perspective and a direct front perspective. The model needs to be the same height and proportions in each view and each drawing should use the same scale.

2. Scan your drawing into the computer, assuming that you didn't draw them there in the first place. Save them as `*.tif` files and put them in a folder where you will have no difficulty finding them quickly. If you'd rather use my sketches, you'll find them on the companion CD-ROM in the folder for this chapter. They are named `modelSketchFront.tif` and `modelSketchSide.tif`.

3. Now open 3D Studio Max and create a plane in the front view that is 120"×120".

4. Switch to the side view and create another plane that is 120"×120".

5. Open the Material Editor and work with any of the available standard shaders in the editor. Add a map to the diffuse channel of the active shader by clicking the Diffuse Map button next to the Diffuse Color selector for the material. (see Figure 8.11).

6. The map that you apply to the shader should be the model side or front view. After you've assigned the tif to the map channel, use the Assign Material To Selected button in the Material Editor to assign the material to the appropriate plane.

7. Repeat step 6 for the other image map. Make certain that you apply the front map material to the plane that you see in the front view and the side map material to the plane that you see in the side view.

8. Enable the 2-Sided check box on the Material Editor while viewing each map. This enables you to see the image from either side and from both the front and back.

FIGURE 8.12

Map the image you intend to model on the shader.

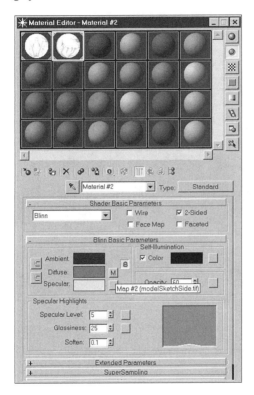

9. After you assign a map to the material, a blue-and-white-checkered cube appears in the Material Editor directly below the material preview spheres in the middle (left to right) of the window. This cube was disabled (as illustrated previously in Figure 8.11) until you completed this step. Click this cube to enable display of the map in your view panes. Now simply make certain that the view mode for your workspaces is set to Smooth and Highlights. (I like to enable edged faces in the views as well, to see the work more clearly.) Figure 8.12 shows the work at this point.

FIGURE 8.12

The planes have been assigned the materials and the maps are displayed in the window.

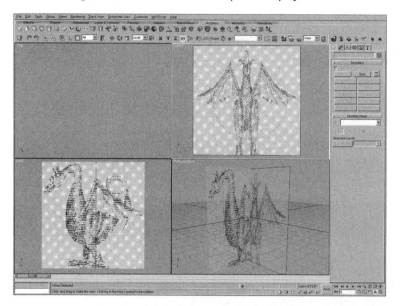

10. Now create a box like the one shown in Figure 8.13. This particular box is divided into five length sections, two width sections, and three height sections.

    As I created the box, I moved momentarily to the Hierarchy tab to move the box independently of its pivot point. I want the pivot point to remain perfectly aligned to the world. It will make my life easier when I try to work with the model later.

11. Convert the box into an editable mesh. You can do this quickly by selecting the stack of pancakes (Edit stack) button in the modifier stack section of the Modify tab. Choose Convert to, Editable Mesh from the submenu.

FIGURE 8.13

Start with a simple box.

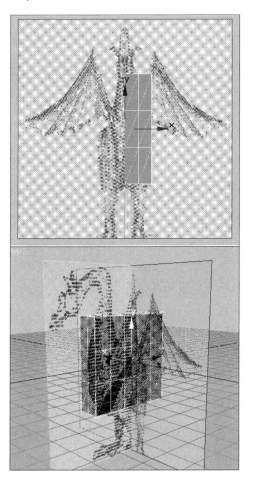

12. It's time to put those tools to work. Start moving vertices using the
    Move tool while the Selection Masking is set to Vertex. (You can use the
    little skittles button as a shortcut to vertex selection masking mode or
    choose Sub-Object Vertex from the Modify tab while your box is
    selected.)

    Make sure to watch the vertices move in all four views to ensure that
    they are going where you want them. Use the images as a guideline.
    After moving several points, you should have an image that is similar to
    the one in Figure 8.14 (similar because your image wouldn't have a neck
    yet).

FIGURE 8.14

The dragon begins to take shape as you move the vertices.

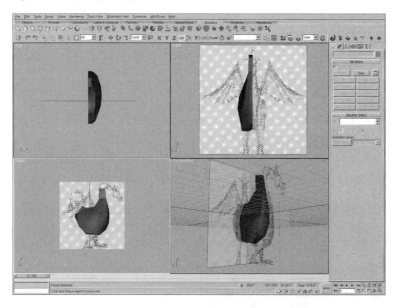

13. To create the neck and tail, use the extrude tool. Switch selection mask-ing to the face level and choose the two polygons that make the quad that will form the base of the neck.

14. Click the Extrude button and it turns that cute minty green color, indi-cating that it is the current tool. Type a value into the Extrude Depth field next to the Extrude button (I used 20 units) and then press the Enter key. (You can also pull the extrusion by hand simply by using the cursor over the face, but be careful because a new set of polygons is cre-ated every time that you release the mouse.)

15. Now, just repeat this step several times. Creating the neck was a simple matter of extruding a bit, and then rotating the plane before extruding again. Figure 8.15 shows the result.

FIGURE 8.15

The neck and head were created by repeated extrusions and making adjustments to the faces at the leading edge of the extrusion as the extrusions were executed.

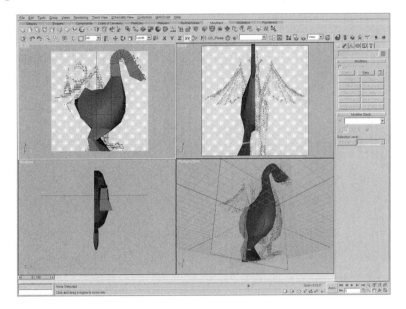

16. Switch back to vertex-level selection masking and begin to massage the points for the head. See Figure 8.16.

    We are nearly ready to make the other side of the creature. First, I want to clip away the extra faces. These are the faces that would be buried inside the creature if we simply mirrored it and attached the two boxes. The last thing that we want is to have a bunch of faces in the model that aren't even visible. The computer would still try to draw them (or at least determine that they were culled) either way wasting time on unnecessary calculations.

17. In Face selection mode, select all the polygons that will not be visible in the finished model and delete them (see Figure 8.17).

FIGURE 8.16

You need to give the head a little extra attention.

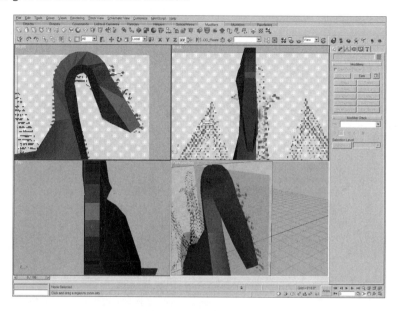

FIGURE 8.17

The extra faces are removed in anticipation of the merging of left and right sides.

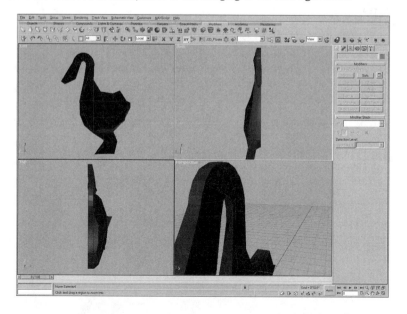

18. Finally, add a wing. I just used another simple box. I collapsed the vertices on the two ends, pushed the points around a bit, and then merged the vertices of the wing to the vertices on the side of the dragon's body.

19. Select the entire model and click the Mirror Clone button. Choose the Copy option button and offset the clone by about -94 units. (The point is to move the clone into alignment so that the two copies are ready to merge (see Figures 8.18 and 8.19).

FIGURE 8.18

The model is ready to clone.

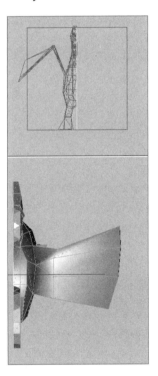

FIGURE 8.19

The model is cloned using the mirror tool and the mirrored model is moved to the correct position.

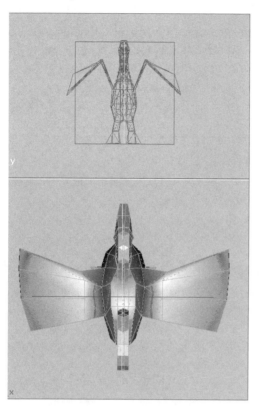

20. After the clone and the original are aligned, you need to attach them together to form a single model. Use the Attach button on the Modify tab.

21. Attaching the meshes is good enough for a still life, but if you want this mesh to deform, you need to be certain that there are no holes in the mesh. To do that, weld all the vertices of each side to their equivalent vertices on the opposite side. Use the Weld tool with the threshold set to a very low number (between .3 and .001). This should weld all the points together, but you want to keep an eye peeled as you work and collapse points where needed if there are some points that don't get welded properly.

As I work, I have already begun to optimize. I turn edges as they pucker, and often do quick renders to see the way the model will display from various angles. The process is very much like sculpting, starting from rough forms and working in greater levels of detail as I move closer to the ideal surface.

22. Remove as many extra polygons as you can while you sculpt the shape. Figures 8.20 and 8.21 feature one example of this sort of polygon reduction through vertex collapsing and/or welding.

FIGURE 8.20

Note the three triangular polygons in a place where one would suffice.

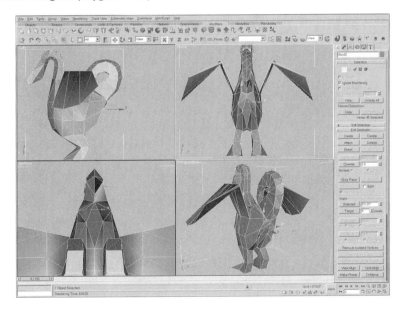

FIGURE 8.21

I collapse the extra point with one of the corners yielding one polygon instead of three.

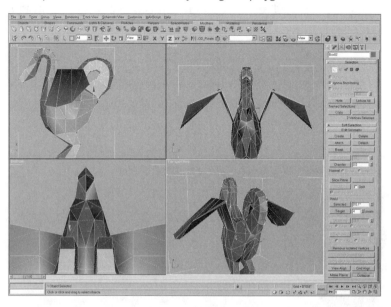

23. From here, it is all just patient polygon reduction and careful manipulation of the edges. Your results should resemble your starting image, but don't feel obliged to get an exact replica of the sketch (see Figure 8.22).

The ultimate question in low polygon modeling is always "What's the payoff to cost ratio?" Our finished dragon is 610 polygons. With a bit more careful reduction, this could probably drop down to 560 or even less. It has a close resemblance to the sketch and we should be able to paint it to get a good result.

FIGURE 8.22

The finished dragon is a close replica of the sketch, but lacks a lot of detail.

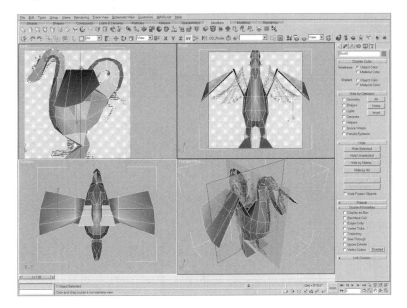

The Exporters

In this section, I walk you through the procedures involved in exporting the dragon from each of the three major modeling packages. I'm going to place a simple shader and texture on the beast, and animate him spinning in order to demonstrate the basics of each exporter. In Part III of the book, "Putting Strategies into Action," I'll explain how to create a detailed texture map for a complex model's mesh, so don't worry if you have no idea how to do it now.

Each of the major 3D modelers has an exporter either in release or beta versions. You can also use the Speed Port Xtra to convert *.obj files into *.w3d files via Director's interface. Table 8.1 contains a breakdown of the features that are currently supported by each of the big three exporters.

TABLE 8.1   The Exporters Support a Variety of Features

Feature	Lightwave	Maya	Max
Geometry	x	x	x
Cameras	x	x	x
Lights	x	x	x
Shaders			
Blinn	x	x	x
Phong		x	
Lambert		x	
Textures	x	x	x
Procedural		x	
Animation			
Keyframe	x	x	x
Bonesplayer	x		x
Toon/SDS	x	x	x
Particles			
Fog	x		
Havok integration	x	x	

Exporting from 3D Studio Max

Several limitations exist that you should be aware of before you try to export a 3D scene from 3D Studio Max into the Director Shockwave Studio format. To get a complete rundown of the limitations, consult the Max plugin Help file for Shockwave 3D exports.

The most substantial difference between the 3D Studio Max scene you create and a blank W3D in Director Shockwave Studio is in their default coordinate systems. All 3D software uses coordinate systems to express several essential qualities of the 3D space.

The qualities we are concerned with here are the orientation axes. Every coordinate system has three axes labeled X, Y, and Z, which are used to describe the horizontal, vertical, and depth dimensions and positions of the space itself and the objects found in that space.

In Director, X is width, Y is height, and Z is depth, by default. In 3D Studio Max, X is width, Y is depth, and Z is height. The 3D world isn't the only thing that is affected by this divergence in coordinate systems.

Every visible object in the 3D scene has its own coordinate system. When we begin to animate, you'll see that these individual coordinate systems are fundamental in creating interactive animations. In 3D Studio Max, the X, Y, and Z vectors (which way is up, back, and sideways) also differ from the default Lingo coordinate system.

Remember that, by default, Director labels the up-down axis as Y, whereas Max labels the up-down axis Z. This can really confuse you if you are unaware of the difference in reference systems.

There are many times when you want to modify the position of a model by applying a translation, rotation, or physics force to the model in relationship to itself. For example, you might want to apply force to a car that moves the car forward. This `applyForce (vector (0, 0, -1), #self)` command would propel a physics modified model forward along the negative Z-axis. If the negative Z-axis runs top to bottom through the car, however, the car would drop downward through the road surface as if succumbing to quicksand.

As you work in 3D Studio Max, take care to develop a strategy for aligning the axes of the model in a manner that is consistent with the methods you plan to use to animate that model in Lingo once in the Director environment. I generally align my models to their own coordinate system so that they face or point down the positive X-axis, their sides faces the Y-axis and their top and bottoms face the Z-axis. To view a model's local coordinate system in Max, simply choose Local from the Display Coordinates drop-down menu in the tool bar at the top of the Max interface.

There are many things that you could do in 3D Max (or virtually any modeling application) that will not be exported into a Shockwave 3D file. Basically, you are limited to true primitives and editable mesh models. No nurbs (nonuniform rational b-spline curves) or b-spline curves are allowed. Many of the

3D Studio Max modifiers are not allowed. These restrictions mean that you cannot use anything with nurbs, and that the exporter recognizes no primitives other than traditional primitives.

Fortunately, you can do a good deal of free-form modeling in Max and then convert the finished model into an editable mesh. I normally work fairly freely until I near the final phase of the model and then collapse all meshes to a single editable mesh. Keep in mind, however, that the more polygons you create, the longer it takes the system to draw each frame.

Keyframe animation exports information on the translation (move), scale, and rotation vectors of models. If you have Character Studio, you can export IK animation cycles using the Physique and Biped modifiers. Havok has created an Xtra that will connect the Havok 3D Max Physics Modifiers to the Shockwave 3D engine. Using the Havok Xtra is covered in Chapter 12, "Simulating Physics."

To make this description of the export process easier to follow, create a box primitive in 3D Studio Max. The Box tool is on the Objects toolbar on the far left at the top of your 3D Studio Max interface. To create a box, click the Box button and then click and drag in any of the scene views.

After you have defined the first side of the box, release your mouse and continue to drag in the other direction. You might need to switch views or move to the perspective view to see the effects of the second drag. When you have a box that you like, change your Property tab to display the object properties for the box you created.

Midway down the Property tab is a drop-down menu that lists the object and modifier stack. Choose this menu and then select the option to Convert to Editable Mesh. This enables selection masking as you work on the model.

Choose the Point Selection masking option and manipulate a few points on the mesh using the Rotate and Move tools. Now open the Material Editor and select one of the materials from the table of prefabricated materials at the top of the editor.

Make certain that the type is set to Standard, and then adjust the various qualities of the surface material as you normally would. If you want to attach a texture to the shader, assign a UVW Map modifier to the model. First decide where you want to attach the texture.

In Shockwave 3D format, textures may be assigned via the diffuse channel, but not the ambient. For a complete list of available map channels, consult the online help system in Director or the help file that came with your 3D Studio Max Shockwave Exporter.

After you have created a scene in 3D Studio Max that conforms to the recommendations for compatibility, choose File, Export from the drop-down menu at the top left of the interface. Make certain that you have made the perspective view the active view port.

An export dialog appears (see Figure 8.23). You are prompted with a Save dialog and you need to change the drop-down file format to Shockwave 3D (*.w3d) and name your file. Click the Export button. An Export Options dialog box appears.

FIGURE 8.23

The Max Export Options dialog.

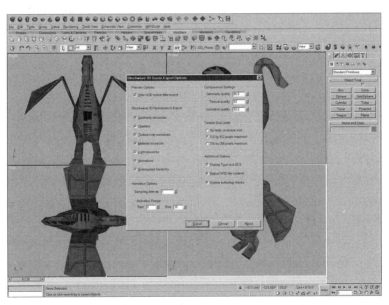

The Export Options dialog box allows you to choose the information that is to be included in the Shockwave 3D file. It also gives you the option to preview the scene after the export. The export dialog box allows you to export the 3D Studio MAX scene and to choose which elements should be included in the export. Generally speaking, you want to leave all of the default options selected.

There are instances in which data will be unnecessary. You might, for example, have no animation in a particular model, or you might have created a series of biped animations in Character Studio, but not want to export any of the models. Simply uncheck the resource you do not want to include and the exporter omits that data during the export.

The first of these resources, geometry, includes all the models and any associated bones. This includes the geometry of the bones, but not any animation cycles that have been mapped to these bones.

The next option allows you to include or exclude the shaders you have created in 3D Studio Max. You must use the Standard shader type in 3D Max. The Type option is to the right of the shader name in the Materials palette in 3D MAX.

Shaders are the root-level objects used to define the surface properties of 3D models. The shaders are parents to material and texture resources that further define the specific ways that light reacts with a model in the scene.

The material alone defines the manner in which light generally reacts to the surface of objects as well as the opacity and luminosity of the object. Textures are image resources that define color and surface irregularities for the model.

Think of the shader, texture, and the material options as linked. If you want materials or textures, you need shaders. Images used for texture maps in 3D Max are converted to streaming Shockwave JPEG's on export. The next check box allows you to choose whether to export lights.

Most of the time, you want to leave this option checked as well. Finally, you are able to choose to export animation. You might find occasions when you want to export animation without anything else; you might also find that there are times when you want to export everything but the animation routines. Simply check the box to enable the option.

Additional options on the right side of this dialog give you added control over the animation you export. Animation is sampled once per frame by default. You can decrease that interval and therefore reduce the number of samples taken.

This of course reduces file size, but also reduces the precision of the animation. You are also given control over the range of animation frames to export. You might want, for example, to export only a select few frames from a larger animation. The start and stop times listed in this dialog allow you to specify the desired range.

Finally, the animation compression option allows you to select the degree of compression that will be used on the animation data. The higher the value, the less compression will be applied to the animation data when it is converted to the W3D format.

The next element you can enable or disable is the Scenegraph Hierarchy. This data set contains all the information about the way in which the various elements in the 3D scene relate to one another. There are few reasons to turn this option off.

You may disable this option if you are exporting keyframe animation alone, or if you are working with only a single object and do not need the scene data. Usually, however, you want to leave this option enabled.

Enable Toon and SDS is the next available option. Some data must be stored with the scene to enable Toon and SDS modifiers to be employed in Director. If you are certain that you will not use either of these modifiers in your project, you may disable this option, but there is no way to use them if this data has not been included in the file on export, so you should be careful disabling this option.

Just as you can adjust the compression settings of animation, you can also adjust the compression settings of the texture bitmaps and geometry. These compression algorithms control the manner in which the data streams—that's right, *streams*—to the executable. You can also take advantage of the custom user properties to alter the order in which these items stream.

Exporting from Lightwave

The folks at New Tek have developed a robust exporter for Shockwave 3D files via their Lightwave modeler. Although the exporters are very similar, there are a few differences in the two that can be seen by undertaking a simple export.

If you have not already installed the Shockwave exporter in Lightwave 6.5b, choose Layout, Plugins, Add Plugin from the drop-down menu to the left of the Items tab. Locate and add the Shockwave exporter to the input-output plugins and the associated utility to the utilities plugins. Open the file `dragon.lws` (on this book's CD-ROM) in your Lightwave Layout tool.

NOTE

I know that it is very unlikely that you have all three of these packages. I assume that these sections will be most useful to those who have the relevant package.

Now choose File, Export, Shockwave3D Export from the File menu that correlates to the Items tab (see Figure 8.24). A dialog box like the one shown in Figure 8.25 appears.

FIGURE 8.24

Generate the Export dialog using the File menu.

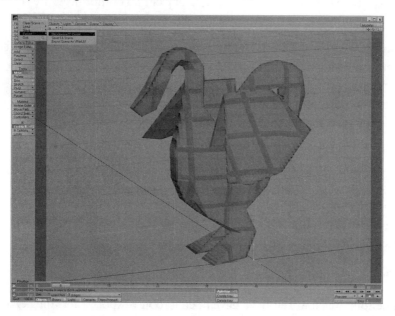

FIGURE 8.26

The Export dialog box.

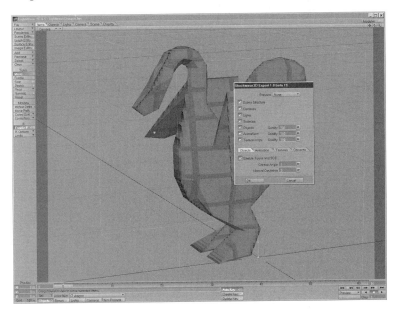

At the top of the dialog box is a drop-down menu labeled Preview. Use this box to choose the size of your preview pane, or to set the preview pane to disable preview after export, or to match the size of the preview to the size specified for the camera in its render settings.

Next, there is a series of check boxes running down the left side of the dialog. These allow you to choose which elements should be exported from the scene. This is a good thing. As we continue to work, you'll discover that there are times when you don't want the geometry from the scene—you really need only the animation or the shaders. These simple Boolean switches allow you to export (checked) or not export (unchecked) each element of your scene:

- Scene Structure: Scene Structure is the hierarchical relationships of nodes within the world. This includes parent-child relationships, information about groups, and the relationship between models and the shaders and textures that have been assigned to them.

- Cameras: This switch controls the export of cameras. If you don't have a camera into a world, you can't see into that world. Nonetheless, you might want exactly this when you begin working with heavily optimized media.

- Lights: Lights are exactly what you would expect. Lightwave supports each of the types included in Shockwave.

- Surfaces: Surfaces are the shaders.

- Objects: Objects are the models that you created. This is called *geometry* in the 3D Max exporter.

- Animations: Animations include both bone and keyframe animations.

- Texture maps: Texture maps are your textures.

The last three check boxes—Objects, Animations, and Texture maps—have variables that control the amount of compression that is performed during the export process. The integer fields to the right of each of these categories can be adjusted as you see fit. These number values are essentially percentages of quality in the finished result. The lower the value the smaller, and less precise, the finished export will be.

The next section of the dialog is divided into four specialty tabs: Objects, Animation, Textures, and Cameras. These enable you to fine-tune the settings. The first of these tabs, shown in Figure 8.26, allows you to work with the properties of objects.

The Enable Toon and SDS check box allows you to include special data about the nearby polygons that is used for these modifiers in Shockwave. Regardless of the modeler you use to export, you must check this box if you plan to use either of these modifiers in your finished program. If you don't plan to use either one, leave this disabled. The file size increases when it is on.

Use the Crease Angle setting to choose the minimum angle between neighboring normals. Polygons that are closer than this value will be merged together during the export process. Think of this as a sort of detailed compression setting that helps decide how to optimize the geometry upon export.

FIGURE 8.26

The Objects tab of the Export dialog.

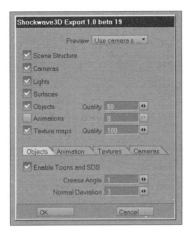

The Normal Deviation setting is a level that determines the ideal limit on the
deviation of normals from their original position. This is used to help calculate
the level of detail data during compression.

The Animation tab lets you choose whether to export both bones and
keyframes and allows you to fine-tune the sampling of the animation itself
(see Figure 8.27).

FIGURE 8.27

The Animation tab of the Export properties dialog box.

Animation is sampled based on the rate that you specify in the Interval field. This is necessary if you've used any programmatic or modifier-generated animation effects. Remember that Shockwave understands animation data only in terms of change over time to the translation, rotation, or scale of a node, so this animation can be sampled from more complex animations. Don't expect any miracles, but you can get some things out that would be hopeless without forcing the sampling. The Start and End settings control the starting and ending frames of the animation.

The translation of meshDeformations based on bone structures is not a simple parallel. New Tek recommends that you try to limit your bone-based deformations to weight-based settings in Lightwave. It also suggests that you work with weight maps rather than trying to use Lightwave's bone setup options.

The Textures tab (see Figure 8.28) features optimization tools that help you adjust the textures within your scene . Textures can be one of the biggest RAM hogs in your 3D world, so these elements can make a huge difference in your finished project.

FIGURE 8.28

The Textures tab gives you access to additional optimization tools.

The Override Size option and the corresponding Size drop-down menu enable you to choose the size limit in pixels for your finished W3D file. This allows you to optimize the bitmaps during the export process.

You can also check the Disable Alphas option to remove the alpha channels from the texture maps. This eliminates any transparency in the textures that are exported.

The Cameras tab gives you access to the remaining adjustable properties of the cameras within your 3D world (see Figure 8.29).

FIGURE 8.29

The Cameras properties tab within the Exporter dialog.

Use the Cameras drop-down menu to select which cameras you want included in the export. Then use the Fog and Backdrop settings to list those cameras whose fog and backdrops you would like to include.

When you have finished adjusting the settings, click OK and a preview of the W3D member will appear (see Figure 8.30). The preview pane is interactive. Just use your mouse to rotate around the center of the 3D world.

FIGURE 8.30

The Shockwave 3D preview window in Lightwave 6.5b.

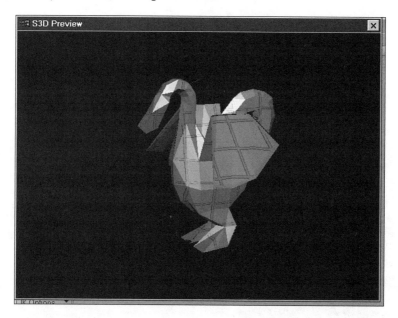

The best way to really learn about any of these bits of software is to play with them. Now that you've exported the dragon once, try doing it several times, each time changing one or two small elements on the Export dialog, and observe the difference those changes make.

Exporting from Maya

The Maya exporter has been lagging a bit behind in the race for completion, but the implementation is turning out to be worth the wait. Already the plugin supports batch exporting from the command line, making it the clear contender for the "workhorse" award.

If you haven't already done so, add the Maya plugin to the plugins directory and then use the Windows, Preferences, Plug In Manager to load the plugin. It adds its own menu, shown in Figure 8.31.

FIGURE 8.31

Use the Shockwave Export menu to choose the function that you want related to the optimization and export of W3D files.

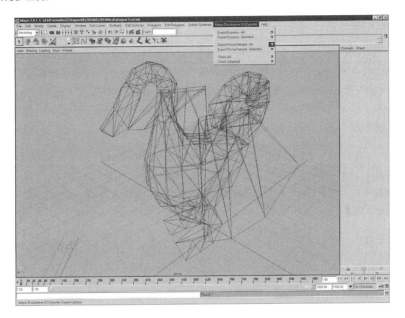

Maya's approach to the plugin for exporting W3D files is slightly different than the other two exporters, but it is an approach I wouldn't mind seeing copied elsewhere. The drop-down menu added by the plugin gives you several new tools that can be used to rapidly export and optimize scenes for export.

The foundation of this plugin is the idea that you will probably be re-exporting the files dozens, perhaps hundreds, of times as you optimize the files for the Web. Each time that you export, the file would normally need to be optimized, one node at a time, and then saved in the correct format.

Maya tracks your changes as you work and is capable of updating only those assets that have changed since your last save, thereby enabling much faster iterations. As a result, the Export Shockwave 3D drop-down menu contains the following options:

- Export Express—All

- Export Express—Selected

- Export Force Rebuild—All

- Export Force Rebuild—Selected
- Check All
- Check Selected

These options are actually very simple. Whether checking your model for conflicts or exporting, you can work with either the entire scene (All) or only the current selection (Selected). If you want to do so, you can force a complete rebuild of the file before exporting (Export Force Rebuild), or you can simply use the pre-optimized version and update only those nodes that have changed.

Maya also allows you to run a test on either the scene or the selected node(s). This is done using the Check features. For this demonstration, I'll use the Export Force Rebuild All option under the Export Shockwave 3D drop down menu, and I'll open the Options dialog box (see Figure 8.32). To open any options dialog in Maya, simply click on the shadowed square (dialog) icon to the right of the menu selection on the corresponding drop down menu. This selection was highlighted previously in Figure 8.31.

The Basic Export Options tab's first field allows you to enter the name and path of the file that you will be exporting.

The Optimization Options tab submenu includes several properties that ease your work when optimizing files for download and performance:

- Presets: The presets menu contains a few basic profiles created to help you quickly choose the most appropriate type of optimization for your target file. Use Balance Speed and Quality when you want to get average quality and reasonable playback speeds. Use Best Speed/Size when you want to reduce file size and enhance playback speeds as much as possible. Use Best Quality when you are more concerned with appearance than performance (see Figure 8.33).

  You are not limited to these preset options. You can create your own presets by modifying the mel script s3dCreateUI.mel.

FIGURE 8.32

The Export Options dialog box in Maya.

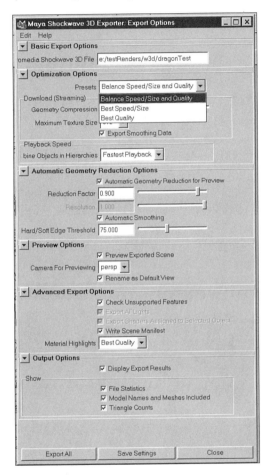

- Geometry Compression: This setting indicates the level of compression rather than the level of original detail. Lower numbers indicate higher quality and lower rates of compression. Higher numbers indicate smaller files with faster playback and reduced detail.

- Maximum Texture Size: The drop-down menu to choose the size limit for your textures. You can use this option to force texture size reduction on export just as you would in Lightwave or Max.

- Export Smoothing Data: This is equivalent to the enable Toon and SDS switches in the other two exporters.

FIGURE 8.33

The Optimization Options tab of the Maya Shockwave 3D Exporter.

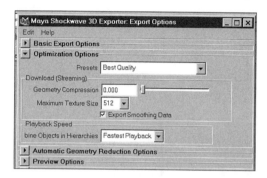

The Automatic Geometry Reduction Options tab allows you to tweak the optimization of geometry (see Figure 8.34).

FIGURE 8.35

The Automatic Geometry Reduction Options tab on the Maya Shockwave 3D exporter.

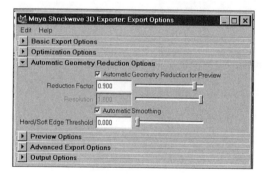

- Automatic Geometry Reduction for Preview: This check box enables level of detail in the preview window.

- Reduction Factor: This setting determines the degree of degradation based on the total distance from the camera to a given node.

- Resolution: Use this field to set the initial value of the W3D's level of detail if you have disabled Automatic Geometry Reduction for the preview. You can also toggle this value dynamically using the numerical keypad while viewing the exported scene in the preview window.

- Automatic Smoothing and Hard/Soft Edge Threshold: These options are used to soften the effects of level of detail modifications on each model. The Hard/Soft Edge Threshold correlates to the Crease Angle setting in Lightwave.

The Preview Options tab of the dialog presents options that assist you in creating the preview of the scene (see Figure 8.35).

FIGURE 8.35

The Preview Options tab of the Maya Shockwave 3D exporter.

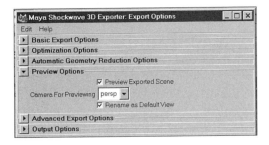

- Preview Exported Scene: The first check box allows you to disable the preview.

- Camera for Previewing: The drop-down menu allows you to choose the camera to be used for the preview.

- Rename as Default View: This check box allows you to rename the camera to the default for use in Shockwave.

The Advanced Export Options tab (see Figure 8.36) has several options.

FIGURE 8.36

The Advanced Export Options tab of the Maya Shockwave exporter.

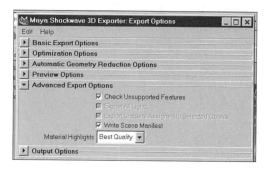

- Check Unsupported Features: Checking this box asks the exporter to look for and report any unsupported features that you have used in the scene.

- Export All Lights and Export Shaders Assigned to Selected Object: These two check boxes are enabled only if you are using the Export-Selected option (under the drop-down Export Shockwave 3D menu). This is another way in which Maya's approach to export is fundamentally different than that of the other two major exporters. In Maya, you can specifically choose individual elements to export and then adjust using these toggle switches. In the other exporters, you must limit your exports to include all items of a given type.

- Write Scene Manifest: Creates a manifest describing the composition of the scene and the hierarchy of each node. This may be useful when you are programming.

- Material Highlights: The drop-down menu allows you to optimize the shader export method depending on your target playback experience.

  The highlights are the specularity channel of the Blinn and Phong shaders in your scene. In a nutshell, you can get better looking ones with Best Quality, or faster performing ones with Best Performance. In games, we'll almost always prefer Best Performance.

The Output Options tab allows you to choose whether to display the results of the export procedure and if so, which aspects of the procedure to display (see Figure 8.37).

FIGURE 8.37

The Output Options tab of the Maya Shockwave 3D exporter.

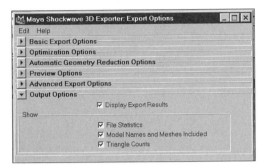

After you have finished filling in each option, simply click the Export All button at the bottom of the Export Options dialog. Note that the tools for manipulating the camera in the preview within Maya conform to the standard methods used in Maya rather than those used in the other exporter preview windows.

As with the other exporters, it is a good idea to familiarize yourself with the use of this tool if you plan to use it regularly. I recommend that you go back and repeat this procedure several times. Each time you try it, experiment with one or two elements and see whether you can observe visible differences.

If you don't have all of these exporters and would just like to see a comparison of the exported data from each modeling package, I have included a `allthree.dir` file on the companion CD-ROM that contains copies of the dragon exported from each package.

In addition to these exporters, Shells Interactive has created a wonderful editor which allows you to open and add interactivity to *.w3D files without using Director. You'll find a copy of the Shells Interactive Shockwave 3D editor on the CD-ROM in the Shells folder.

Now that you've had a chance to tinker with basic geometry and try exporting 3D content from a wide variety of authoring packages you must be itchy to try some animation. In Chapter 9, "Using 3D Keyframe Animation in Director," I'll show you how to create a basic racing game using a combination of keyframe-driven animation and Lingo.

CHAPTER 9

Using 3D Keyframe Animation in Director

There are many ways to move models around within the 3D worlds you create and manipulate in Director. It is not always the most efficient use of your time to move the models solely in Lingo. Often you will want to use a cycle or looping motion that is very complex and would be much easier to create inside a 3D modeling and animation package.

In this chapter, we'll create a couple of seriously silly soda pop–powered cars. Their twists, shakes, shudders, sputters, and back flips would take an eternity to simulate via Lingo alone. This is the perfect time for keyframe animation to step up to the plate.

After reading the chapter you should

- Know the basic properties and methods supported by the keyframe-player modifier
- Know how to attach the modifier to a model
- Know how to create keyframe-based animation in 3D Studio Max
- Understand the basic principles of keyframe animation
- Understand how to gain control over various aspects of a model's animation cycle interactively
- Understand how to animate models via Lingo

Now that we have investigated the basic units of the 3D space, I'll give you a series of examples that demonstrate and explain the powerful and timesaving animation potential that is created when Director 3D is combined with 3D

Studio Max. I'll demonstrate the methods needed for porting complex scenes from Max to Director and then show you how to manipulate the keyframe-based animations created in Max from within Director's programming and playback environment.

Along the way, I'll introduce you to the properties and methods of the keyframe animation modifier and give you quick syntax examples.

Keyframe Animation Basics

In order to help you understand the fundamental concepts of keyframe animation as it relates to Director, I'm going to define a few of the major terms and concepts that are central to keyframe animation. I want to point out that this chapter and the next may easily be viewed as close partners: Both will help you discover ways to quickly export prebuilt animation sequences and use them dynamically in Director.

The phrase *keyframe animation* is a holdover from cel (celluloid) animation, introduced by Earl Hurd in 1914. The animation process involved the creation of key cels that represented the motion of the character. The primary artist would draw these key cels and then junior artists would draw the cels in between (called, not surprisingly, the *in-between cels*).

The terms *in-betweeners*, *tweening*, and *interpolation* are all directly tied to the concept of filling in animation between key frames. The computer rather than a team of junior animators creates the in-between cels in computer animation.

In real-time 3D games, the in-between animation is basically the same. Any visible node in the space—whether it is a car or a jellybean—can change size, location, and rotational orientation. You don't need to tell the node to move 10 units per time interval. You can tell the node to move from position A to position B and expect the computer to figure out what position the node should be in when the screen is updated.

If the updates are fast enough to fool the player into thinking that the object is moving, the animation effect is achieved. This is due to a concept called *persistence of vision*—the principle that makes us believe we are watching objects in motion when we are actually seeing lots of similar still images. We only need eight images (or frames) per second to produce an animation illusion, but it is always better to have more.

You have already seen me use two major methods of animation in this book. In *Battle Ball*, I used keyframe animation to rotate each of the little balls in a continuous spinning or jumping pattern. This simple motion loop allows the balls to have fairly complex fundamental motions that don't interfere with the Lingo commands they are sent in order to translate their positions and move them around the space.

The paths that the little balls follow as they move around in the arena are determined by a behavior that the balls choose to execute in response to their emotional states. This form of behavioral animation is easily blended with keyframe animation in order to create a rich combination of motion.

In the next chapter, we'll examine another form of animation—inverse kinematic (IK) animation. Although any support for direct IK in Director is undocumented, we will look at ways to use the IK support within outside animation packages to create bonesplayer animation. Like the other types, this sort of motion may be blended with keyframe, behavioral, and simple Lingo-driven animation. I'll tell you more about bonesplayer animation then.

Generating Keyframe Animation

Each of the big three modeling and animation packages that support Shockwave 3D export (Maya, Max, and Lightwave) has export keyframe animation sequences. The changes to the translate, rotate, and scale values of each model on each frame during the duration of the exported file's timeline are saved as motions. You can access these motions using the syntax `put w.motion[n]`.

Each W3D member has an initial motion in the first index position. The type of this motion is `#none`. The result is that the first motion in the W3D member is stored in the second position. The name of each motion is equal to the name of the node with the characters `-Key` added to the end of the name. A model called `boo` would have a motion called `boo-Key` associated with it if you animated the model in your authoring package.

There will be one motion to correspond to each model you animated in the W3D scene. Examine the motions in the remaining motion index positions; they are either `#keyframe-` or `#bonesplayer`-type motions, depending on whether you used the keyframe animation tools in your authoring application or the IK animation tools.

The trick to working with keyframe animation motions can be found in Director's ability to queue and play back multiple motions on any given model. Not only can you exchange the motion of a given node for a different keyframe motion, you can create clones of motions from one W3D member in another W3D member.

This idea can easily be visualized if you imagine the sort of motion I've described for our soda pop cars. Initially I want the cars to sputter and jiggle. This motion would logically loop so that the last frame of the animation is the same as the first frame, and the viewer will not be able to detect the point when the playback jumps back to the beginning of the sequence.

At one point in the game, I want the car to jump up in the air and do a back flip. I could code this in Lingo and just add the motion of rotation and translation to the animation cycle, but it would be considerably easier to simply switch to a prebuilt animation of the car jumping up and flipping.

The problem with that solution is that you can only map one motion at a time onto a given node. There are a couple of different solutions to this problem. You could animate a series of motions for the node on a running timeline and then trigger different portions of that timeline according to your need, or you could export a series of different animations and then clone those animations as independent motions into your final 3D world.

The "running timeline" solution requires you to work carefully with the exact start and stop times of the animation segments. This option is a little simpler during authoring but a lot more difficult during playback.

The "multiple motion maps" solution takes a bit more time during authoring, but it is very simple during playback. I'm really very fond of the multiple-motion solution. This approach also allows you to rename your motions during the clone operation. You'll see an example of each of these approaches in Exercise 9.1 at the end of this chapter.

Keyframe Modifier Properties

As soon as you begin to work with a keyframe animation sequence, you need to add the keyframe modifier to the model that will be manipulated. Do this using the syntax `w.model[n].addModifier(#keyframeplayer)`.

Issuing this command enables you to access all the properties involved in keyframe animation. Some of these properties are associated with the 3D world, and some are common to both the keyframeplayer modifier and the bonesplayer modifier. The properties associated with keyframe animation are listed in Table 9.1.

TABLE 9.1   Keyframe Animation–Related Properties

Property name	Purpose
animationEnabled	A member property that allows you to toggle on and off both keyframe- and bones-based animation.
count	The total number of a given member's motions.
type	Used to set the type of a motion to #keyframe, #bonesplayer, or #none.
motion	The animation data for a given node.
playRate	The speed of the motion associated with this keyframeplayer. Negative values cause the motion to play in reverse. Numbers greater than 1 or less than -1 cause accelerated motion. Numbers less than 1 and greater than -1 yield slow-motion playback.
Transition Properties	
autoblend	A keyframeplayer and bonesplayer modifier property that determines whether the system automatically blends between motions in the queue.
blendFactor	A keyframeplayer and bonesplayer modifier property that is used only when the autoblend property is False. This determines the percentage of the motion files that should be used to blend a given motion with the next.
blendTime	A keyframeplayer and bonesplayer modifier property that is used when the autoblend property is True. This determines how much time in milliseconds should be used to blend a given motion with the next.
Reset and Lock Properties	
lockTranslation	Determines whether the member should lock the translation of the node to a given plane or set ofplanes.
positionReset	A Boolean value that determines whether the animation should be reset to the original transform at the end of a loop. This value is True (on) by default, and you usually want to turn it off (False).

TABLE 9.1   Continued

Property name	Purpose
rootLock	A Boolean property of the keyframeplayer and bonesplayer modifiers that determines whether translation commands are ignored on a given model. When this is True, the root node of a model does not translate but rotation continues.
rotationReset	A keyframeplayer and bonesplayer property that causes the model to reset to its original position on any of the axes that are offered as settings of the property. (For example, a value of #z causes all rotations around the z-axis to reset after each motion file played.)
Timing Properties	
currentLoopState	A Boolean value representing whether a given keyframeplayer modifier is set to loop the motion. This is a model.keyframeplayer property
currentTime	The time in milliseconds of the playback within the duration of the motion. This is a model.keyframeplayer property.
duration	The length of a motion in milliseconds. Duration is a property of the motion.
endTime	The last millisecond of a motion that should be played. This is a property of the playlist item.
startTime	The first millisecond of a given motion that should be played. This is a property of the item within the playlist.
offset	If the looped property of a motion within the playlist is False, the motion begins at offset and ends at endTime. If looped is True, a motion begins at offset, plays to endTime, and then loops from endTime to startTime. Use offset as a parameter of the play() function.
playing	A Boolean value that determines whether any motion associated with this keyframeplayer modifier is currently playing.
playlist	A linear list of property lists containing information about motion files that are queued up and ready to play. The first item in the list is the actively playing motion.

With a few exceptions, the properties associated with keyframe animation may easily be broken into three primary groups. These include the transition properties, the reset and lock properties, and the playlist properties.

The transition properties include autoblend, blendFactor, and blendTime. Each of these properties is used to control the nature of the transition that is created when one motion ends and the next motion begins.

One of the inherent problems in switching between one motion file and the next is that the motions do not always share translation and rotation positions when the transition occurs. If you simply jump from one motion to the next, there is a visible jump or glitch in the animation as the model suddenly pops to the beginning transform and scale of the new motion sequence.

We generally don't want popping in animation, so a method of interpolation between individual motion files is essential to the design of heavily interactive game animations. To accomplish the interpolation between motion files, we use the transition properties.

The autoblend property is a simple Boolean toggle switch that determines whether the keyframeplayer modifier should automatically attempt to resolve the interpolation. The blendTime property is the partner of the autoblend property.

A keyframeplayer modifier's blendTime property is only used when that modifier's autoblend property is set to True. In this event, the blendTime property stores a number representing the time in milliseconds that should be used for the transition.

If the time in the blendTime property is greater than the duration of the motion, the transition occurs over the entire duration of the motion file.

The blendFactor property allows you to have a more precise level of control over the manner in which motions are blended. You can set blendFactor to a high value (100) in which case 100 percent of the first motion will be entirely incorporated into the second motion. A setting of 50 will blend the first and second motions equally, whereas settings below 50 will lend more of the second motion to the first. This property of the keyframe or bonesplayer modifier is set on a per model basis, so all motions in the playlist will be treated the same way. As in baseball, this is always the active motion (the batter) and the second motion (the on-deck hitter).

The reset and lock properties are used to prevent drift during animated motion loops. One of the problems inherent in all of this math is that the models can easily begin to roll through floors or drift through walls because of tiny mathematical imperfections in the animation cycles and transitions.

Director features several keyframeplayer and bonesplayer modifier properties that may be used to prevent or reduce drift in your motions. These include the lockTranslation, positionReset, rootLock, and rotationReset properties.

The first three of these prevent various types of translation for a given node. The last one, rotationReset, restores a node to its original rotation along a given rotational axis or axes.

The lockTranslation property accepts the following arguments: #none, #x, #y, #z, #xy, #yz, #xz, and #all. Whichever axes are listed as the value of this property are ignored when the translation of the node is calculated.

The default lockTranslation value is #none, so all the axes are translated as directed by Lingo or the system by default. If you change this to any other value, one or more axes will be ignored, both by attempts to reset the position of the node along those axes via Lingo and by attempts to do so via motion animation.

This can be very handy if you want a model to move along X and Y planes but you don't ever want it to change its Z value. If Z is up and down, you might want to change the lockTranslation to #z in order to prevent the model from drifting through the floor, for example.

The positionReset property actually controls the entire transform of a given node. At the end of any given motion cycle, the default value of the positionReset property (True) causes the engine to move the node back to its original transform. This is why a walk cycle imported into Director walks a little and then jumps back to the beginning and walks again.

You normally want to switch this property's value to False in order to create animation cycles that compound their changes over time and let characters "keep on walking" without that strange little jump back to the origin.

The rootLock property is used to prevent all changes to the translation of a given node. With rootLock set to True, the model rotates and scales, but no changes occur to the position of the model. This is the equivalent of setting lockTranslation to #all.

The rotationReset property may be set to any of the following values: #none, #x, #y, #z, #xy, #yz, #xz, and #all. The default value is #all, although you normally want it to be #none. The rotationReset property is used to determine around which, if any, of the axes the rotation of the node should be reset to its original rotation.

Given a rotation that spins a model 180 degrees around its z-axis, the rotationReset default value of #all causes the model to spin back 180 degrees to 0 degrees at the end of each motion cycle. If you set this value to #none or a value that omits the z axis, the rotation around the z-axis becomes cumulative and is not reset at the end of each cycle.

Working with motions in a W3D member is very similar to working with audio playback using the sound() command. It uses a list of motions to play, just as the sound() command uses a list of audio files to play. The list of current and pending motions is called the *playlist*.

A keyframeplayer or bonesplayer's playlist property is a list of property lists. Each item in the linear list represents either the active or a pending motion animation. That item is a property list that contains all the information about the motion and the properties that should be used to determine how to play the motion.

A typical playlist might look like this:

```
[[#name: "cor002-Key", #loop: 1, #startTime: \
0, #endTime: 1000, #scale: 1.0000]]
```

Here, #name is the name of the motion. Because this is the active motion, the loop is the same as the currentLoopState. The startTime is the time that you want to begin the motion, given the duration in milliseconds of the motion file.

This is how you can play back motions that are exported in a long string of separate sequences. If you specify start and end times that call up only a portion of a total motion, you can select submotions to play and even loop from a single continuous motion sequence.

Using this model, you would animate each potential motion of the node in a single continuous motion. You would then use the startTime and endTime properties to clip the motions apart during playback. The last property in each item found in the playlist is scale, which is the same as the playRate of a given motion. The value assigned to scale affects the speed of a motion, as shown here:

Value	Speed
More than 1.000	Moves the node faster
1.000	Plays back the node at the same speed at which it was authored
Less than 1.000 and more than 0.000	Moves the node in slow motion

Value	Speed
Less than `0.000` and more than `-1.000`	Moves the node in slow motion but in reverse
`-1.000`	Moves the node at normal speed but in reverse
Less than `-1.000`	Moves the node in fast reverse

CAUTION

Be sure that you disable the `autoblend` property and set the `blend` factor to `0` if you plan to play files backward.

The `currentTime` property contains the local time of a given animation motion during playback. This time is the current time value of the motion in milliseconds. The `duration` property is the total length of a given motion, and the `playing` property tells you whether the `playlist` property of a given keyframeplayer modifier is empty. If it is empty, no motions are playing.

The `offset` property is used to determine the `startTime` of playback, when that `startTime` should be different only during the first loop of a given motion. The `offset` property may either be set to a value in milliseconds or to `#synchronized`. If it is set to an integer, the playback begins at the milliseconds specified by the integer. If it is set to `#synchronized`, the playback begins at the local milliseconds equal to the milliseconds of the motion that is being subsumed. Offset is a parameter passed to the play function.

Keyframe Modifier Commands

The commands associated with the keyframeplayer modifier are listed in Table 9.2. These commands may be split into two basic groups: motion modification and playback.

TABLE 9.2   Commands Associated with Keyframe Animation

Command Name	Description
Motion Modification Commands	
`cloneMotionFromCastMember()`	Creates a clone of a given motion in the member that called the command.
`deleteMotion()`	Removes a motion from the 3D member.

TABLE 9.2   Continued

Command Name	Description
Playback Commands	
pause()	Temporarily stops the playback of a keyframeplayer or bonesplayer modifier's current motion.
play()	Interrupts the playback of a motion if it exists and plays the given motion immediately.
playNext()	Deletes the first item from the modifier's playlist and plays the next motion in the list. If there is no other motion in the list, this command stops the playback of motions.
queue()	Adds a given motion to the last position in the playlist of a given modifier.
removeLast()	Removes the last item from the playlist of a given modifier.

The motion-modification commands are used to adjust the motion data itself, whereas the playback commands are used to alter the playlist of a given motion modifier.

The first motion modification command is cloneMotionFromCastMember(). This command is issued using the following syntax:

```
w.cloneMotionFromCastMember("newMotionName", \
"sourceMotionName", member("sourceCastMember"))
```

One of the most notable features of this command is that it is the only way to rename a motion. The other exciting feature is that you can export a given motion, such as a car idling, as you'll see in Exercise 1. This can be included in your basic 3D model.

Now if you go back to your animation package and create a new keyframe animation cycle for the same model, you can take advantage of the selective export features of your exporter and export a W3D member that contains no geometry, lights, cameras, or material information. The file may contain only animation data. You can import an array of such motion files into Director and then use the cloneMotionFromCastMember() command to load these motions into the primary 3D world.

At this point, you would have separate motions all mapped to the same nodes that could easily be assigned to the motion modifier's playlist. This is an excellent way to organize your media, and you'll see me use it often throughout this book. The one disadvantage to this procedure is that the cloning operation is a bit slower than simply launching a file with all the information pre-embedded, so you need to allocate a little load time at the start of your movie if you plan to implement this method.

The `deleteMotion()` command is used to delete a given motion from the scene.

The playback commands are used to change the playlist of a given motion modifier. They include `pause()`, `play()`, `playNext()`, `queue()`, and `removeLast()`. Each of them allows you to control some aspect of the motion playback.

The `pause()` command causes the active motion to stop playing. The `play()` command interrupts the active motion and begins playing a given motion immediately if the modifier is already playing a motion. This command simply restarts the paused motion if no motion is currently playing.

The `playNext()` command dumps the active motion and begins playing the next motion in the list. If there are no more motions in the list, it simply dumps the active motion and stops the playback of motions.

The `queue` command may be used to add motions to the playlist. You use the queue command with the following syntax:

```
w.model[n].keyframeplayer.queue\
("nameOfMotion", booleanLooped, \
startTimeMilliseconds, \endTimeMilliseconds, \
floatScale, offset)
```

Each of the arguments after the name of the motion is optional.

The `removeLast()` command simply removes the last item from a given motion modifier's playlist. In other words, if a playlist has five motions, the `removeLast()` command would remove the fifth motion from the list.

Exercise 9.1:   *Bubble Pop Raceway*

As I started to think about the best way to explain the procedures involved in keyframe animation, an idea for a game began to gel in my head. I quickly decided to experiment with this game concept, called *Bubble Pop Raceway*.

We won't bother with fleshing out the game at this point because I want to remain focused on the keyframe animation strategies. Nonetheless, I'll walk you through the process of creating and integrating several different keyframe animation sequences into a game prototype in order to demonstrate the basic principles of keyframe motion swapping.

There are some foundational principles at work in this demonstration that require careful consideration before I even begin the process of animating the models in my authoring program.

I've decided to animate the cars in 3D Studio Max and then export the motions as independent files. I could just as easily export the motions as a longer composite motion attached to the W3D, but I like the tidiness of separate motion files, and I love to be able to name the files appropriately. As long as I don't try to map a motion to a nonexistent model, I should be fine using this procedure.

If you are working with a group of models, you want to carefully evaluate any decision to group these models before you begin animating. Grouped models are converted to a single model on export. This means that a car composed of 50 models might well become a car composed of only one model when it is exported.

This is very relevant to me because my plan calls for three animation cycles per car. Each animation cycle is more rickety than the last, so I want to be able to adjust the transforms of each part of the car in order to get that jiggly, unstable feeling.

In a nutshell, I'm going to create one animation cycle of each car idling. Then I'll animate each car after a boost of energy. Finally, I'll animate each car doing a flip after another boost of energy.

It's the wiggly instability that makes all the difference in this animation sequence. If there were no independent motion for the parts of each car, I'd simply animate the car as a group and allow the exporter to merge my model into a single mesh. With the hillbilly jiggles, I need to maintain independent control over the individual parts of the car.

Now if I were to start rotating all the individual parts of the car model in Max simply by selecting all the models simultaneously and adjusting their rotation, my car would break into tons of pieces almost immediately. This is because the pivot points of the models are probably not standardized for all the parts of the car.

If these pivot points were all in the same location, I could move and rotate the car as though it were grouped in spite of the separation of the models. Therefore, whenever you want to animate a group of models that should travel together for the most part, the first step is to match all their pivot points to the same transform. This makes your Lingo life much easier and facilitates your keyframe animation process as well.

NOTE

To set these pivot points to a common location, First I selected the modify pivot point button from the hierarchy tab. Then I simply selected each model and then right-clicked the translate tool, evoking the Move Transform Type-In dialog. I then set the translation of each model to vector(0,0,0). Once the car's models all share a common pivot point, I simply move them all to the side to accommodate the other car.

Now that all the pivot points for each car are common to the car, I am able to begin work on the animation cycles. The first cycle animates the cars while idling. These are particularly rickety cars, so I want quite a bit of wobble and bounce (see Figure 9.1).

Keyframes are set every three frames, and the system is allowed to interpolate (or *tween*) the motion between these key motions. This process is repeated with different motions for each of the level-up sequences.

The export procedure for the base file is the same as the export procedures we examined in Chapter 8, "Low Polygon Modeling and Third-Party Exporters." The export procedure for those files containing only motion data is slightly different. In the Max exporter, I uncheck all the options except Animation and then export the file. In Maya, I need to select the node and then deselect Geometry in the Export Options dialog.

Once the files are all imported into Director, I need to preload all the motions into the primary 3D world. Listing 9.1 is the script I use to load the files into the world safely. The concern here is that the state of the W3D member receiving the clones must equal 4 in order to perform the cloning procedure. If the state is not 4, the cloning operation will fail.

FIGURE 9.1

The cars' rotation and translation properties are manipulated on keyframes during the animation authoring process.

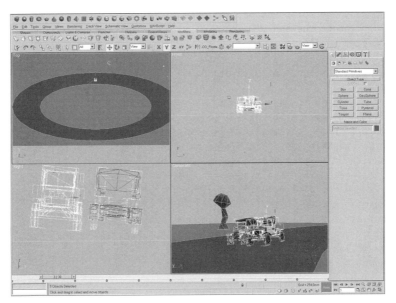

LISTING 9.1   The Motion Loader

```
1: global w
2:
3: property pIterMember -- the current member
4: property pIterMotion -- the current motion
5:
6: on beginSprite(me)
7:   pIterMember = 11 --- the number of \
     the first member with motions to clone
8:   pIterMotion = 2 --- the number of the first motion to clone
9: end
10:
11: on exitFrame me
12:   ----- The w3d will fail if you try\
          to load motions while the state is lower than 4.
13:   ---- Loop through each motion, in \
          each member one at a time, carefully checking
14:   ---- to make certain that the state \
          is 4 before you try to load the motion.
15:   --- This handler waits on this frame \
          until all of the motions have been loaded.
```

LISTING 9.1   Continued

```
16:    if w.state > 3 then
17:       --- store the name of the motion in a variable
18:       baseName = member(pIterMember).motion[pIterMotion].name
19:       --- I don't want the "-Key" part of \
               the name so I'm going to delete it.
20:       repeat with x = 1 to 4
21:         delete the last char of baseName
22:       end repeat
23:       --- Now I'm going to make a new \
               name by combining the name of the member
24:       w.cloneMotionFromCastMember((baseName&member(pIterMember).name), \
25:       member(pIterMember).motion[pIterMotion].name, member(pIterMember))
26:       ---- and the name of the original motion.
27:       --- Once I reach the last motion \
               in a member, I'll reset the cycle and move on to
28:       --- the next member. Once I reach \
               the last member I move on to the next frame
29:       --- not by commanding it, but by failing to "go to the frame"
30:       if pIterMotion < 46 then
31:         pIterMotion = pIterMotion + 1
32:       else
33:         if pIterMember < 12 then
34:           pIterMotion = 2
35:           pIterMember = pIterMember + 1
36:         else
37:           go to the frame + 1
38:           abort()
39:         end if
40:       end if
41:     end if
42:     go to the frame
43: end
```

In order to ensure that the procedure works every time, regardless of how bad the playback system is, I check the value of the member's state and delay the cloning procedure until the desired state is reached.

In lines 3 through 9, I set the values of the base member and base motion. These are the first member that I'll retrieve cloned data from and the first motion from each member that I plan to clone.

The base motion is almost always 2, because the first member is not a motion at all. The second motion in any given W3D member is the first motion you created. Think of each motion as composite tracks, each containing the translation, rotation, and scale data from a given model.

The exitFrame handler, beginning on line 11, first checks the state of the primary W3D member. This is the one with all the geometry and cameras. If the state is high enough, it clones the first motion from the first motion cast member. These motion cast members are the motion-only exported files we just imported. Notice that these W3D files are entirely black and contain no visible elements.

I hack around, kludging out names for each new motion that are based on the model name and the name of the member that is the original owner of the clone. This way, I'll be able to dynamically resolve which motion gets attached to which model and assign level-up motions dynamically based on the level number found in the name of the motion-only cast members.

The really juicy part of this code is contained in lines 24 and 25, where I clone a new motion from a given cast member and give that motion a new, unique name. This motion is now added to the available palette of motions in the primary W3D member and may be called upon (loaded into the playback queue) at any time.

Once all the motions have been loaded into the primary 3D world, I can work through a few setup commands to ensure that my animations perform as expected. Listing 9.2 contains a breakdown of the setup routines.

LISTING 9.2   The Setup Handlers

```
 1: global w
 2:
 3: property pSpeed1 -- The current speed of the first car
 4: property pSpeed2 -- The current speed of the second car
 5: property pWinna -- A flag used to trigger a go to frame event
 6: -- because you can't call go to from an event triggered with a timer
 7:
 8: on beginSprite(me)
 9:   pWinna = 0 -- setup the win flag
10:   repeat with x = 4 to 48 -- add the modifier \
      to each model, the cars are made of these 44 models
11:     w.model[x].addModifier(#keyframePlayer)
12:     w.model[x].update() -- because we are inside a repeat loop
13:     w.model[x].keyframeplayer.positionReset = \
      0 -- don't do that bounce back to position thing
14:   end repeat
15:   w.newGroup("Car01") -- group together the models that make the car.
16:   ----- Start by creating an empty group
17:   w.group("Car01").transform = w.model("FT12bdy1").transform
```

LISTING 9.2 Continued

```
18:    --- Match the group.transform to the transform of one of the members
19:    --- this is a critical step.  If we didn't \
          do this the transform would be centered
20:    --- at the center of the world and then the\
          bounding sphere and center of the
21:    --- group would be much less useful to us.
22:    repeat with z = 4 to 12
23:      ---- now add each model to the group
24:      --- clean up the playlists
25:      --- Clear the blending properties
26:      w.group("Car01").addChild(w.model[z], #preserveWorld)
27:      w.model[z].keyframeplayer.removeLast()
28:      w.model[z].keyframeplayer.autoblend = 0
29:      w.model[z].keyframeplayer.blendFactor = 100
30:    end repeat
31:    ---- rinse lather and repeat for car 2
32:    w.newGroup("Car02")
33:    w.group("Car02").transform = w.model("SEATSB").transform
34:    repeat with z = 13 to 48
35:      repeat with x = 1 to count(w.model[z].keyframeplayer.playlist)
36:        w.model[z].keyframeplayer.removeLast()
37:      end repeat
38:      w.group("Car02").addChild(w.model[z], #preserveWorld)
39:      w.model[z].keyframeplayer.autoblend = 0
40:      w.model[z].keyframeplayer.blendFactor = 100
41:    end repeat
42:    w.group("Car01").translate(2000,0,0)
43:    w.group("Car02").translate(-2000,0,0)
44:
45: end
46:
47:
48: on startCars (me, whichOne)
49:    --- Command issued by either of the acceleration keys. In fact
50:    --- there is no acceleration. There is only start, using the up keys
51:    --- assigned in the keyHandler
52:    w.animationEnabled = 1
53:    case whichOne of
54:        --- if the car starting is car 1
55:        1:
56:        --- set its speed to 1, play the silly \
              sound associated with this car
57:        --- and start its basic jiggly motion \
              using the keyframeplayer.play command.
58:        pSpeed1 = 1
59:        sound(3).play(member("car01"))
```

LISTING 9.2   Continued

```
60:        sound(3).volume = 100
61:        repeat with z = 4 to 12
62:          ---- you'll need to start each little model motion separately.
63:          ---- NOTE that you could simply group these things in Max
64:          ---- and then they would export with just one motion.  You'd
65:          ---- lose some subtlety in the playback, but the animation would
66:          ---- play back faster.  It's a pretty \
                 obvious place to optimize a piece like this.
67:          w.model[z].keyframePlayer.playNext()
68:          w.model[z].keyframeplayer.play(string(w.model[z].name)&"-Key", 1)
69:        end repeat
70:      2:
71:        ---repeat these steps for the other car.
72:        pSpeed2 = 1
73:        sound(4).play(member("car02"))
74:        sound(4).volume = 100
75:        repeat with z = 13 to 48
76:          w.model[z].keyframePlayer.playNext()
77:          w.model[z].keyframeplayer.play(string(w.model[z].name)&"-Key", 1)
78:        end repeat
79:    end case
80:    --- I'm sneaking in some new goodies here.
81:    ---- registerForEvent or RegisterScript are \
              used to create custom events triggered either
82:    ---- for individual nodes or for the world \
              member.  You specify the callback handler name
83:    ---- and the script instance. IOW, I'm \
              telling the system to tell me when each #animationEnded
84:    ---- occurs in the 3dworld.  Specifically \
              I want it to send a message to the handler named
85:    ---- resetZ inside this script (me).  The \
              resetZ script below simply adjusts the height of the model
86:    ---- keeping it glued to the road, but \
              only between animations. Why? Because I don't want to
87:    ---- lock it to the ground, that would \
              screw up the bouncy motion.  I just want to bring it back
88:    ---- down to the road after each individual \
              animation.  This would work perfectly if animationEnded
89:    ---- was triggered after each cycle in a loop.  \
              Unfortunately it doesn't work that way, so we'll have
90:    --- to invent a workaround for that with the \
              timeMs.  TimeMS allows us to set a recurring timeout
91:    --- event and associate it with a handler and a script.
92:    w.registerForEvent(#animationEnded, #resetZ, me)
93:    --- This timeMs commands an update to the \
              forward thrust every 42 milliseconds (appx 30fps).
```

LISTING 9.2   Continued

```
94:   w.registerForEvent(#timeMs, #ForwardThrust, me, 42 , 42, 0)
95:   --- This timeMs updates the height every \
         second.  Because the animation is fairly jumpy we can get
96:   --- away with it this way.
97:   w.registerForEvent(#timeMs, #resetZ, me, 1000 , 1000, 0)
98: end
99:
100:
101: on resetZ (me, whichEvent, whichMotion, whichTime)
102:   -- the world relative position in a z up world
103:   repeat with z = 4 to 48
104:     w.model[z].transform.position.z = 0
105:   end repeat
106: end
107:
108: on ForwardThrust (me, type, delta, time, duration, systemTime)
109:   ---  First check to ensure that the car has been started by the user.
110:   if sprite(1).pStarted1 then
111:     --- Store a reference to the car \
            group in a variable and check for obstacles
112:     pMyModel = w.group("Car01")
113:     --- look down to make sure they are still on the road.
114:     whichDirections = [#down]
115:     --- look to the sides and front \
            to make sure that they aren't about to hit something
116:     t = checkObstacles([#forward, #back, #side], pMyModel)
117:     if t = 1 then
118:       --- if you aren't in danger of hitting something in the road
119:       if checkObstacles(whichDirections, pMyModel) then
120:         --- if you are still on the \
              road then move ahead at maximum speed for your experience.
121:         w.group("Car01").translate(vector(0,60 + \
              (45 * pSpeed1),0), #self)
122:       else
123:         --- You are off the road.
124:         pSpeed1 = 1
125:         sprite(1).pLevel1 = 1
126:         --- Slow back down to the base experience level.
127:         --- Drive so slowly that you'd be\
              insane to try to drive beyond the grass buffer.
128:         w.group("Car01").translate(vector(0, 5 + \
              (45 * pSpeed1),0), #self)
129:       end if
130:     else
131:       ---- You are about to hit an obstacle, \
              so slow back down to base level
```

LISTING 9.2   Continued

```
132:        pSpeed1 = 1
133:        sprite(1).pLevel1 = 1
134:        --- Back up.  This is not a very eloquent \
               solution. IOW it will be fine for trees,
135:        --- but the user will easily get accidental \
               interpenetration of the cars if each
136:        --- attempts to do this at a given moment.  \
               We'll talk about more robust models
137:        --- of collision detection and simulated physics in chapter 12.
138:        w.group("Car01").translate(vector(0,-30 + \
            (45 * -pSpeed1), 0),#self)
139:      end if
140:    end if
141:    --- rinse lather and repeat for the second car.
142:    if sprite(1).pStarted2 then
143:      pMyModel = w.group("Car02")
144:      whichDirections = [#down]
145:      if checkObstacles([#forward, #back, #side], pMyModel) then
146:        if checkObstacles(whichDirections, pMyModel) then
147:          w.group("Car02").translate(vector(0,-60 + \
              (45 *  -pSpeed2),0), #self)
148:        else
149:          pSpeed2 = 1
150:          sprite(1).pLevel2 = 1
151:          w.group("Car02").translate(vector(0,-5 + \
              (45 *  -pSpeed2), 0), #self)
152:        end if
153:      else
154:        pSpeed2 = 1
155:        sprite(1).pLevel2 = 1
156:        w.group("Car02").translate(vector(0, 30 + (45 * pSpeed2),0), #self)
157:      end if
158:    end if
159: end
```

The beginSprite modifier assigns keyframe modifiers to each of the 44 models that compose the cars. Once the models have keyframeplayers, we are able to control their motions individually.

We want to be able to easily control the models that belong to each car as a group. The code in lines 15–41 is charged with this task. I create a new group for each car and then move the transform of the group to match the transform of one of the group members. This way, I avoid any strange behavior caused by off-center alignment of the group.

You can visualize the bounding sphere of a model as a giant sphere that is large enough to contain all the points of a given model, regardless of the shape. Groups are similar. They also have bounding spheres. Their bounding spheres, however, must encompass the entire groups of models. If the pivot point (transform) of a group were not centered to the group, even simple rotations would seem peculiar. This is because the objects in the group would be more like satellites out on the far edge of an enormous bounding sphere rather than objects grouped in a little cluster.

Envision this by packing a bunch of marbles into an imaginary bag. If you rotate the bag around its center, the motion of the marbles/bag group seems fundamentally logical. Now pretend that the marble bag is stuck to the side of an enormous ball.

Rotate the ball and the marble bag suddenly rushes away from you, appearing to translate huge distances. This is because the center of the rotation is now the center of the ball. Not only is the ball massive, it is also invisible.

This is exactly the sort of confusion that is created when you don't make certain that the transform of the group is in the center of the actual group of models. This sort of behavior is great if you are trying to map orbital paths in a simulated solar system, but it can be a real head-scratcher if you are just trying to turn a compound model.

In line 48, I start the cars with the startCar handler. This is really just a matter of turning on the basic motion that makes the cars jiggle, starting a sound effect, and moving the group forward at a constant rate. The translation of the car forward is bound to the level of experience of the player, so more experienced players have faster cars.

In lines 92–97 I begin several callback routines. One of the great features of Director 3D is the ability to register scripts for callback notification. In this case, I want to know when the animation cycles end so that I can move the models back down on their z-axis, thereby compensating for any drift that occurs during a given cycle.

The other events that are registered here use timeMs events to help me track and trigger events at regular intervals. This game is the first demo I've given you that is driven entirely by time events rather than by the score's exitFrame events.

NOTE

Drift is a strange and predictable side effect of animation cycles in real-time 3D. With all the calculations going on, you eventually find that some of your motions drift (float away from their intended path) over countless repetitions. You can lock elements to a given plane in order to counteract drift, but I want to have the freedom to bounce the car up and down, so locking the height of the car is not a good option for me in this case.

In Chapter 12, "Simulating Physics," I'll talk about the option to accelerate your playback and stabilize the animations on a broader range of machines using this form of event hierarchy rather than the frame-reliant method.

The `forwardThrust` handler, beginning on line 108, simply assesses collisions and moves the car according to the collisions it encounters. You may find it helpful to examine the collision handlers in the movie as well.

Now we're ready to begin swapping motions. In the game, the motion-swapping happens when you hit a token with your race car. Tokens give you extra soda pop power to run your carbonated cola car. Running into objects and veering off the road drain your energy and slow you down. I'm going to represent the bubble power with a giant bubble that bursts when you hit it.

Here are the rules I'll have to program:

- Hitting a bubble fountain causes a power-up
- Hitting another object or straying off the road causes a power-down
- Crossing the checkered banner results in victory

This should provide the foundation for a very silly race game. We won't bother with the formalities, such as automated racers, scoring, or lap counting/timing. These items are a good challenge for you to work on yourself. The handlers for the power-ups are found in Listing 9.3.

LISTING 9.3   The *levelUp* Handlers

```
1: global w
2:
3: property pLevel1 -- stores level data for car 1
4: property pLevel2 -- stores level data for car 2
5:
6: on levelUp (me, whichWay, whichCar)
```

LISTING 9.3   Continued

```
7:    --- called when a token is acquired, this \
          handler increases speed and handles
8:    -- special animation for the first couple of level increases.
9:    if (value("pLevel"&string(whichCar))) + whichWay = 0 then
10:       ---- just a safety net to check for a \
              0 value and prevent the racers from stopping.
11:       if whichCar = 1 then
12:         pLevel1 = pLevel1 + (whichWay * 2)
13:       else
14:         pLevel2 = pLevel2 + (whichWay * 2)
15:       end if
16:     else
17:       --- Add the integer to the level, \
              increasing the experience level of the player
18:       if whichCar = 1 then
19:         pLevel1 = pLevel1 + whichWay
20:       else
21:         pLevel2 = pLevel2 + whichWay
22:       end if
23:     end if
24:     case whichCar of
25:         --- if this is the second or third \
                level play some special animations by adding them to the queue
26:         --- the playNext command dumps the \
                current idling animation and the new animation plays
27:         --- once through and then the idling \
                loop is back at the head of the queue.
28:       1:
29:         if pLevel1 > 1  AND pLevel1 < 4 then
30:           repeat with x = 4 to 12
31:             w.model[x].keyframeplayer.queue\
➥ (string(w.model[x].name)&"level"&string(pLevel1 -1), 0, 0, -1, 0.5,0)
32:             w.model[x].keyframeplayer.queue(string(w.model[x].name)&"-Key", 1)
33:             w.model[x].keyframeplayer.playnext()
34:           end repeat
35:           sprite(1).pSpeed1 = sprite(1).pSpeed1 + pLevel1
36:         end if
37:         --- same story for the other car.
38:       2:
39:         if pLevel2 > 1 AND pLevel2 < 4 then
40:           repeat with x = 13 to 48
41:             w.model[x].keyframeplayer.queue\
➥ (string(w.model[x].name)&"level"&string(pLevel2 - 1), 0, 0, -1, 0.5,0)
42:             w.model[x].keyframeplayer.queue\
➥ (string(w.model[x].name)&"-Key", 1)
```

LISTING 9.3   Continued

```
43:            w.model[x].keyframeplayer.playnext()
44:          end repeat
45:          sprite(1).pSpeed2 = sprite(1).pSpeed2 + pLevel2
46:
47:      end if
48:
49:  end case
50:
51:  if whichCar = 1 then
52:    sprite(1).pSpeed1 = sprite(1).pSpeed1 + pLevel1
53:  else
54:    sprite(1).pSpeed2 = sprite(1).pSpeed2 + pLevel2
55:  end if
56: end
```

If you haven't already done so, open the file named bubbleCarRacing.dir on your CD-ROM. Rewind the file and click Play. I started the movie with a simple splash screen intended only to distract the user while I load the motion files in the background (see Figure 9.2).

Open the score window as the movie begins to play and watch the playback head. You'll notice that it stalls for a moment on frame 2. Obviously, this is where you'll find the motion-loading script. I placed the behavior in the frame channel of the score.

I know that the biggest problem users will face with a racing game of this sort is figuring out how to control the cars. I always find that the simplest communication is the best.

Icons that resemble computer keys contain the letters that should be pressed, along with symbols that indicate upward (which most people translate as *forward*), left, and right propulsion. Before the game fully loads, the player should have time to read the words "Jist use these here keys to drive," printed just above the key symbols.

Once the player reaches the play screen, the key clues remain onscreen. I never remember details like that, so I figure why not make life a little easier for the player. From the onset, I've helped the player get into the mood of the game by starting some truly goofy music and maintaining an aesthetic style that suggests simplicity, antiquity, and general zaniness.

FIGURE 9.2

The splash and score screens for Bubble Pop Raceway.

The play screen reveals two cameras simultaneously moving into position just behind the cars. There is no start light or flag waving, so the players are free to begin whenever they want (see Figure 9.3).

Drive around and see what it feels like. This is not exactly the typical race game, but I think you should be able to work from a base like this to create racing versions of just about anything.

The major concerns of such a game include counting laps, detecting and compensating for collisions, handling extreme collisions (explosions), and timing the race. You might want to present a top view of the course, limit viewing to one camera, or even try to do something similar with flying models.

FIGURE 9.3

The cameras move into position at the beginning of the race.

I've included a slightly different camera in this demo. The tracker camera follows the model in a gentle but persistent attempt to reach the model-relative vector listed in the camera offset. The camera code includes comments that explain the procedures used to create this effect.

NOTE

I have included an optimised version of this game on the CD-ROM called `bubblePopRacingWIV` that creates a very similar effect, but uses simplified models and the new "What's in View" Xtra from Shells Interactive to achieve much faster animation.

Keyframe animation, although only one tool in the arsenal that Director provides, is an incredibly powerful and versatile one. In the next chapter, we'll examine the keyframeplayer's counterpart: the bonesplayer.

CHAPTER 10

Using 3D Bone Animation in Director

One of the most exciting features included in Director's W3D member type is the ability to work with complex bone structures. This means that figures may be manipulated via underlying bonesets.

If you start with Character Studio, you can create models that have responsive mesh deformations in conjunction with these underlying bones. In other words, you can make models that walk, run, and jump, and switch their underlying motions on-the-fly.

After reading this chapter, you should

- Know the properties and methods supported by the bonesplayer modifier
- Understand the fundamental concepts of animating via bones
- Understand how to queue and control bones-based animation playback
- Know how to switch motions for a figure via Lingo
- Be able to manipulate the bonesplayer.playlist to adjust the properties of the animations

In this chapter, I talk about the process of generating and manipulating bonesplayer animation. I explain the elements that the properties and methods associated with the bonesplayer modifier share with the keyframe modifier. Then I introduce you to some additional control elements supported by the bonesplayer modifier that are not present in the keyframeplayer modifier.

I wrap things up by explaining how to use bones animation cycles within the Director environment, and how to swap motions on-the-fly.

Bone Animation Cycles

The language of bone-based animation can seem very daunting. It is full of acronyms, such as IK and FK, and abstract terms such as weight mapping and envelopes—the terms alone are enough to scare away most people.

If language of bone-based animation is new to you, don't worry. My father used to say that there was really no difference in the basic nature of any new concept. He argued that the mastery of any given field was really only a matter of learning the jargon of the field.

Although I believe that practice is also an important element for mastery of a given field, Dad had a pretty good point. All these goofy terms are really just tricks of speech. When you understand the meaning of these words, you'll be substantially closer to understanding the fundamental principles of bone-based animation.

The idea of animating a structure based on an internal skeleton is not really unique to computer animation. The prototypical animated figures that use internal bones to control the manner in which they bend and (to some degree) deform are the animals that walk the surface of this planet.

You are a perfect example of bones-based animation. Movement is not fluid for you. You don't deform the shape of your hand or fingers in order to slip them into a tight corner or under a door. The animation or movement of your limbs and digits is limited by the ability of your bones and joints to bend, twist, turn, and compress.

You support a fairly sophisticated range of motion, and one of your most interesting features is the ability to move extreme bones independently of the bones to which they are attached.

The attachment of one bone to the next, and the influence of each bone over the preceding or following bone in a chain of bones are the basis for those mysterious acronyms, FK and IK.

FK (forward kinematics) is the common term for bone-based motion involving a series of linked bones, wherein the motion of a parent influences the motion of all the children. This is remarkably similar to the principles that we have encountered in 3D animation within Director already. In Exercise 5.2, "Learning to Fly," the propeller was the child of the plane, so the propeller moved along with the plane in a constant relationship to the plane. If the parent moves, the child goes with it.

In the propeller example, there was only one limit to the attachment between propeller and plane. The propeller could spin only along a single plane relative to the plane. In FK, there can be any number of parameters assigned to lock or constrict the motion of the child bone.

In all forms of kinematics, the bones are stuck to the parent bones at the joint. Some joints allow spinning; others restrict rotation around the joint to a single plane. Some allow motion only within a given range.

FK can be separated from its close cousin, *IK (inverse kinematics)* by the manner in which the bones can be manipulated within the animation software. In FK, you move the root and the other bones will follow.

In IK, you move a virtual handle attached to the end of a string of bones and the other bones working up the chain toward the parent respond by attempting to adjust their positions to accommodate this new motion and position.

Both IK and FK are essentially animation approaches that you are not likely to attempt within the Director environment. Your exposure to these tools is likely to be confined to your animating characters in your 3D modeling and animation software.

Director supports bone-based animation forms. This means that it will recognize the bone-driven animations that you have created using these methods. You will even have remarkable levels of control over the motions of your bone-based characters within Director. Nonetheless, you will likely choose to create such animation routines in an outside software package.

Unlike keyframe animation, bone-based animation in Director supports mesh deformation. That means the mesh that creates the visible skin of your character will be able to twist and turn. An *envelope* is the weight map, or influence map, that determines the amount of mesh deformation that will occur when a given bone moves to a new position. Generating bone-driven animation cycles is basically divided into two major chores.

The first is mapping the bones to the character and assigning weight or influence to each bone. If there is not enough influence, little bits of the character will fail to travel with the mesh and you'll get bizarre effects. The figure will have huge distortions as parts of its mesh move and other points remain fixed in space.

The second chore is creating the actual animation cycles. After a character has been boned and the influence map is in place, you can create many different animation routines using the same basic figure.

I don't know of any animation package that has made this process simpler than 3D Studio Max with the addition of Character Studio. One thing to keep in mind, however, is that there is always a trade-off involved when an application simplifies a complex chore.

As an application simplifies a routine chore for the user, it must also remove many of the options that make a feature powerful. Ease of use and flexibility are generally on opposite sides of a continuum in computer software. You might find that it is far better for your purposes to choose an animation-authoring tool that allows you greater levels of flexibility.

Generating Bone Animation in Character Studio

Character Studio is a plugin component of 3D Studio Max. It is designed to simplify the creation of IK skeletons to make the work of animation easier for you.

The procedures for creating bonesplayer animations in Character Studio are not much different when exporting your bonesets to Director than they are when creating boned animations for other purposes. Basically, Character Studio is a combination of two special modifiers for 3D Studio Max. One is called biped, and the other is called Physique.

Biped creates a precalculated skeleton with some limited variation in the numbers of extreme digits and subdivisions of bone groups. Because a great deal of the work involved in IK animation is found in programming the specific limitations of each joint, using biped to quickly assign character motions to human and humanoid meshes can be a significant timesaver.

Using biped is simple. It can easily be broken down into a handful of steps:

1. Activate biped: click the Biped button on the Create palette of the Systems subsection of the property inspector. It will turn minty green.

2. In a front view (or the view that shows you the orthographic front of your model), draw a box (click and drag) starting at the bottom of your character's feet and extending to the top of your character's head (see Figure 10.1).

FIGURE 10.1

The biped has been drawn in front of a character.

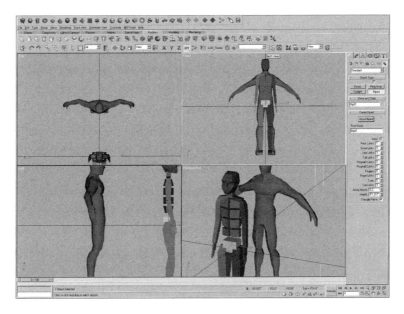

3. Select any piece of the biped and move to the Animation/Motion tab on the Property Inspector (see Figure 10.2).

4. Click the Figure Mode button to lock the biped (the purpose for this doesn't become apparent until you have mapped a motion onto your character and you need to get back to the T pose).

5. Now just adjust the scale, translation, and rotation of each element of the biped until it essentially matches the shape of your model.

6. You can use the Symmetry button in the Property Inspector to select opposing elements (both arms or legs, for instance). You can also use the Page Up and Page Down keys to move the active selections up or down the bone hierarchy.

   Note that if you want to move the entire biped, you need to use the Translation and Rotation toggles within the Property Inspector.

7. Be certain to stretch out the biped to fill the areas defining the arms, legs, feet, and hands. Be extremely careful when you get to the hands and feet. Most stray vertices get lost at the tips of the hands or feet.

FIGURE 10.2

Use the Motions section of the property inspector on the right side of the 3D Studio Max interface while any part of the biped is selected to adjust the properties of that element as well as the entire biped.

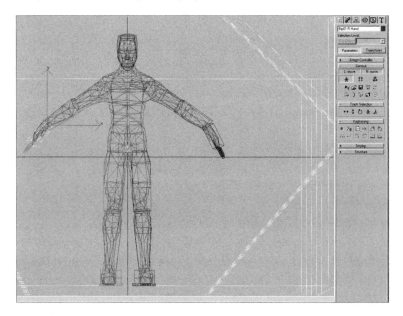

After you finish aligning your biped to your mesh, you are ready for the other half of the Character Studio suite: Physique. Physique is a skinning modifier that allows you to create rules for mesh deformation and assign those rules to the skeletons you create with biped.

Physique is also very simple to use. Just follow these basic steps:

1. Select the model mesh. Note that this does not work if you have anything but the model selected. You are assigning the physique modifier to the top of your model's modifier stack. Also note that physique must be the top modifier in the stack or the export will fail.

2. From the Modifiers subsection within the Modify tab of the Property Inspector, click the More button. This launches a dialog box that lists all the available modifiers.

CAUTION

It is no accident that I use the terms "modify" and "modifiers" in this manner. The Modify tab in the 3D Studio Max interface is denoted by the small blue macaroni noodle on the top of the property inspector on the right side of the default interface. Each of these property inspector tabs changes dynamically depending on the object that is actively selected.

The term modifiers is used to describe groups of code that may be added to a node in order to programmatically alter it's appearance, properties or behavior. Because there are loads of third party modifiers, the More button allows you to list all of the modifier objects that are known to your installation of 3D Studio Max. If you don't have Character Studio, you won't find Physique in this list. Also, note that it must be registered separately.

3. Double-click on Physique.

4. A new set of properties appears under the Physique subsection in the Modify tab of the Properties Inspector (compare Figure 10.3 to figure 10.2 to see the difference).

5. Switch to a front orthographic view of your model and zoom in on the pelvic region, where you'll see a yellow rectangle with a blue triangle in the center of it.

6. Click the baby in diapers button (the Attach To node) and it should turn a nice minty green.

7. Move your cursor over the blue diamond on the pelvis of the model and it will change to a cross hair. Click the diamond to attach the model to the biped and launch the Preferences dialog (see Figure 10.4).

FIGURE 10.3

The properties of the physique modifier appear after the modifier is applied.

FIGURE 10.4

The Physique Initialization properties dialog appears after you assign a biped to the mesh.

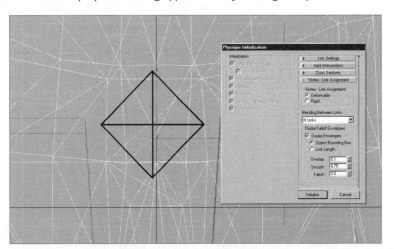

8. The default settings are fine, so just click the Initialize button. You are almost done.

9. In Max, the deformations of skin based on bone influence are visualized through envelopes. If you look at your Sub-Object Selection modes now that you've assigned the physique modifier to your model and linked it to a biped, you'll notice that you are able to select envelopes. These are like big balloons that wrap around the bones and encourage vertices that are within the balloons to move with the bone. How much influence the bone has over the vertex is determined by its position within the envelope. If a vertex is outside the envelope, it will not deform at all and you'll get bizarre spikes.

10. Still working in the Modify tab of the Property Inspector, choose Sub-Object Mode Selection and select one of the thin yellow lines on the figure. You'll see an envelope appear. The properties of the envelope appear in the Property Inspector. You'll need these in a second, but first let's see how well you did without any envelope adjustments.

11. Select the Motions tab and select any single piece of the biped. You'll need to deselect the mesh first.

12. Within the Motions palette, Click to deselect the figure mode button, and then open a motion file using the File Open button. Browse through your Max resources and you'll find some motions in the motions/mocap/bip/ folder. Choose any of these motions (see Figure 10.5).

13. After your motion has loaded, click Rewind and Play in the timeline.

14. Look for any tearing, strayed vertices, or excessive influence crossover (when the bones on one side pull too heavily on the skin of an opposing element). You'll often get crossover influence between the legs and from the underarms to the chest.

    If you have any of these problems, select the relevant envelope and adjust its inner and outer scale. You might even need to go back and redo parts of the biped. This is really just a matter of patient fiddling. Test the motions frequently to see how you are doing.

15. When you are satisfied with the influence maps, select the mesh and then delete all the motion keyframes in the timeline to get a clean slate.

FIGURE 10.5

Use the Load File button (the open folder icon) to associate a motion with the model.

Now you are ready to animate it any way that you like. Note that you could, of course, work from the animation that you have been testing with or even assign a different animation using the File Open dialog to choose alternative motion files. You can even create or motion-capture additional animations and then associate them with your model in this manner.

Bonesplayer Modifier Properties

The bulk of the properties of the bonesplayer modifier are shared with the properties of the keyframeplayer modifier. If you haven't read Chapter 9, "Using 3D Keyframe Animation in Director," you'll probably want to go back and check the sections on keyframeplayer properties and commands.

There are some properties that are unique to the bonesplayer modifier and I have listed them in Table 10.1.

TABLE 10.1   The Properties Unique to Bonesplayer

Property	Description
bone[boneID]	Used to get to each bone in a skeleton. Sometimes you will want to reference individual bones within the hierarchy to fine-tune motions.
bone[boneID].transform	The transform of an individual bone, relative to itself.
bone[boneID].worldTransform	The world relative transform of an individual bone.

Each of these properties is an element of the bone[n] property. This property is actually an object that stores the local and world transform data for any given bone. Access to the property comes through the bonesplayer of a given model, like this:

```
w.model[n].bonesplayer.bone[n].transform
w.model[n].bonesplayer.bone[n].worldTransform
```

Bonesplayer Modifier Methods

Just as the properties of the keyframeplayer and bonesplayer modifiers share many common qualities, the commands for these two modifiers share common qualities. There are two things that the bonesplayer can do that the keyframeplayer cannot. The first of these is the map() command.

The map() command is used to map motions of a given motion node onto a bone set from the bone given in the argument to the last of its child bones. You can visualize this as mapping a kick onto a soccer player's leg while continuing a running loop. Just map the kick motions onto the leg from the hips and the rest of the leg plays the kick motion set, while the unreferenced areas of the body and those that are above the bone in the hierarchy continue to play their motion unaffected. The syntax for this sort of thing would look like this:

```
w.model[n].bonesplayer.map("motion", "boneName")
```

It is interesting to note that we are not given the option to find the names of bones from within Director. You must reference a bone by its index position in the transform properties, but there is no name property for a bone. This means that you'll have to write them down and use your notes. Blech!

The other command that is unique to the bonesplayer is the `newMotion` command. We'll see how this works in the demonstration at the end of this chapter.

In the next section of this chapter, I explain the various techniques involved in manipulating, mapping, and moving bones via Lingo. These properties and commands will be used to explain and then demonstrate the basic concepts as I make a human biped stomp, romp, and wiggle his way around the 3D space.

Using Bones in Director

Now it's time to get into the world and start poking around. As we begin to make a simple biped, I can't help remembering my own excitement the first time that I made one of these little guys roam around interactively. It is an admittedly empowering experience.

Our first step involves mixing and matching motions. Next, we manipulate individual bones and groups of bones. Finally, we move on to mapping motions to root bones and other bones.

Together these basic approaches allow me to create several examples of typical real-time gameplay features. The typical over-the-shoulder 3D adventure and first-person shooter both feature many similar techniques.

As we begin to explore the methods for mapping bone animation to your models, start thinking about the sort of things that you can do with this form of interactively controlled animation.

Swapping Motions On-the-Fly

The magic of bone-based animation is not in the technology. It is in the illusion. Remember as we work that the point of all this technology is not to impress players with our cool code, it is to guide them and grab them for a few minutes or hours of entertainment. Generally, we want to encourage our audience to find immersion in our games. This means that we want to design control methods for the characters that ease players out of their awareness of the computer and the keyboard and into the fantastic world that we have worked so hard to create.

One way to minimize the interference evoked by elaborate on-screen interfaces is to use keyboard-controlled animation playback. From our point of view, as programmers, we will be changing the active animation file based on keyboard input. It is essential that you always remember that this should never be the sensation that the player has while playing.

Ideally, the players' use of the keyboard is easily learned, used, and forgotten. The best approach is to teach the users the keys in a manner that is effective and leaves a lasting impression, but also presents the information in a form that allows the users to escape into the 3D world and concentrate on the interactive adventure that they came for.

When working with a biped or humanoid character, there are a few common approaches that we take to increase the believability of the motions that these on-screen personalities perform. When we animate a walk cycle, we put together a single full stride, moving the legs from a given position through a complete left and right stride until the character's legs return to the exact position in which they originated.

The character will have moved some distance in an essentially straight line. If we want the character to be able to walk in any direction other than a straight line, we have a problem. The walk cycle animation will be looped in the playback within Director and we'll switch off the position reset. The natural result will be that the character will rapidly walk off screen in a perfectly straight line.

We could throw a camera on and follow this victim as it charges forward off to infinity, or at least as far as the number magii will allow, but we'd just see the same silly stride over and over. If we want the player to have any control over this character, we need to add the ability to rotate the model.

Now if we simply rotate the model while the biped is standing still, we'll get an absurd result. The model will turn as if it were mounted on a turntable. This is not generally how people turn. They walk or run in a given direction. The magic to the turning biped lies in the combination of rotation with an activation of the walk cycle.

This means that at the very least, we need a resting motion, a walking motion, a starting motion, and a stopping motion. We'll use the walking motion and starting motion to enable rotation from the rest position to a new rotated position. We'll just rotate in small increments if the character is already walking.

Use the following list to get a sense of the procedures involved in setting up simple walking.

1. Start the character in a resting animation loop. This should have very little motion. I like to use breathing, to give the character a little life, but I avoid any limb movement or it would be too obvious that I was looping the animation very rapidly.

2. If the user presses the forward motion key (we'll designate that later), change the motion to a single sample of the starting to walk motion and then switch to a looping walk.

3. If the user presses either turning key, the result will vary depending on the current state of the character's motion.

    • If the character is standing still, the start walking motion will be triggered and the character will be rotated slightly in the appropriate direction over several frames as long as the key remains down. At the end of the starting to walk animation, the walking loop will begin. If the key remains depressed, the character will walk in circles.

    • If the character is already walking, the system will simply rotate the model by small increments at every update for as long as the key remains down.

4. If the player presses the back key, the character will react if he is currently moving forward. This would be true if the bonesplayer animator were playing back either the "starting to walk" motion or the "walking loop" motion.

As your game grows in complexity, the patterns of motion will grow more complicated. Adding running will cause you to rethink keyboard control. You will find that checking the state of the character's motion can be a powerful procedure. If you know that a character's state is walking and the player presses the forward key, you can guess that he wants the character to go faster.

Likewise, repeatedly pressing the back key should slow a running character to a walk, a walking character to a stop, and a stopped character into a backing character.

If you add flight or underwater swimming to a character, the control system becomes even more stratified, but it can always be broken down into choices based on the current state of either the motion of the character or some combination of a character's motion and the current environment of the character.

Exercise 10.1:   Using the Bonesplayer Modifier to Swap Motions

I've prepared an example for you that swaps motions on the biped to handle the bulk of the animation. The script does rotate the character using a `rotate` command when appropriate, but all the other motion is handled by simple motion swapping.

Open the file named `motionMan.dir` on the companion CD-ROM. Rewind and click Play. You will be able to control the character using the arrow keys on your keyboard.

The motion control script that allows you to control the character using your keyboard arrows is found in Listing 10.1.

LISTING 10.1   The Keyboard Control Handler

```
 1: global w
 2:
 3: property pMyMod
 4:
 5: on beginSprite(me)
 6:   pMyMod = w.model[1]
 7: end
 8:
 9: on enterFrame me
10:   -- this is in lieu of lockTranslation because the lockTranslation
11:   -- only happens once per loop. that won't be enough for us.
12:   pMyMod.transform.position.z = 0.6252
13:   if count(w.model[1].bonesplayer.playlist) > 0 then
14:     motionState = getAProp(pMyMod.bonesplayer.playlist[1], #name)
15:   else
16:     motionState = #none
17:   end if
18:   --If the key was the left arrow
19:   case (the keypressed.charToNum) of
20:     28:
21:       -- if we are standing still or stopping
22:       if motionState = "bipedResting" OR \
➥ motionState = "bipedWalkStopping" then
23:         -- make us walk
24:         pMyMod.bonesplayer.playnext()
25:         pMyMod.bonesplayer.queue("Bip01",1)
26:       end if
27:
28:       --        rotate us to the left
29:       pMyMod.rotate(vector(0,0,5), #self)
```

LISTING 10.1   Continued

```
30:        pMyMod.update()
31:
32:        -- If the key was the right arrow
33:     29:
34:        -- if we are standing still or stopping
35:        if motionState = "bipedResting" OR motionState \
➥ = "bipedWalkStopping" then
36:          pMyMod.bonesplayer.playnext()
37:          pMyMod.bonesplayer.queue("Bip01",1)
38:        end if
39:
40:        pMyMod.rotate(vector(0,0,-5), #self)
41:        pMyMod.update()
42:
43:     30:
44:        -- IF we are stopped, walk, if we are walking, \
➥ run, if we are running, jump
45:        -- if we are standing still or stopping
46:     if (motionState = "bipedResting") OR (motionState \
➥ = "bipedWalkStopping") OR (motionState = "bipedWalkBacking") then
47:          pMyMod.bonesplayer.playnext()
48:          pMyMod.bonesplayer.queue("Bip01",1)
49:          return 0
50:        end if
51:        if motionState = "Bip01" then
52:          pMyMod.bonesplayer.playnext()
53:          pMyMod.bonesplayer.queue("bipedrunning", 1)
54:          return 0
55:        end if
56:
57:        if  motionState = "bipedrunning" then
58:          pMyMod.bonesplayer.playnext()
59:          pMyMod.bonesplayer.queue("bipedJumping", 0)
60:          pMyMod.bonesplayer.queue("bipedrunning", 1)
61:        end if
62:
63:        --If the key was the down arrow
64:     31:
65:        if motionState = "bipedrunning" OR motionState = \
➥ "bipedJumping" then
66:          pMyMod.bonesplayer.playnext()
67:          pMyMod.bonesplayer.queue("Bip01",1)
68:          return 0
69:        end if
70:        if motionState = "Bip01" then
```

LISTING 10.1   Continued

```
71:         pMyMod.bonesplayer.playnext()
72:         pMyMod.bonesplayer.queue("bipedWalkStopping",0)
73:         pMyMod.bonesplayer.queue("bipedResting",1)
74:         return 0
75:      end if
76:      if motionState = "bipedResting" OR "bipedWalkStopping" \
➥ OR "bipedWalkBcking" then
77:         pMyMod.bonesplayer.playNext()
78:         pMyMod.bonesplayer.queue("bipedWalkBacking", 1)
79:      end if
80:   end case
81: end
```

The first several lines of the handler are just declaring the global world variable and storing a quick reference to the model that we'll be working with. By line 12, I get started with the real work of the handler. The first major task is to make certain that the model stays at the same height as the plane upon which he is walking.

Now if you remember the properties of motion animation from Chapter 9, you might be thinking, "But that's what lockPosition is supposed to do." It's a good idea, usually. The only limitation that you face with lock position is that it resets the lock only at the end of the animation cycle. This means that you'll drift and then snap back to the ground plane once every cycle.

Try commenting out line 12 in your copy of the movie to see what I mean. After that line is commented out, rewind and play the movie. You won't see the effect dramatically until you try to rotate while walking or running. When you are finished, uncomment the line.

My next step is to learn the current state of animation. I want to store that state in a variable so that I can compare it to the names of various motions in order to decide the most appropriate response to any given key input.

The remaining part of the handler, lines 19–80, are a simple case statement. The statement checks whether the user is currently pressing any of the four arrow keys on the keyboard, and then reacts appropriately to any pressed keys.

The first evaluation is done for the left-arrow key. It is almost identical to the subsequent evaluation for the right-arrow key. If the model is standing still or in the process of stopping and one of the left-arrow or right-arrow keys is pressed, I dump the active motion from the bonesplayer.playlist and then add walking to the list. Then I rotate the model, whether or not it was standing still.

I can do it this way because I know that all the other motions will enable effective rotation. Only the standing still motions need to be enhanced with the walk forward routine.

The other two cases evaluate the forward and backward keys. If the player presses the forward key, the model will cycle through a series of potential motions. If it executes any one of the motion swaps, it will use return() to exit the handler. This way the various cycles can be visualized as a chain. We are simply moving the character forward or backward via a chain of motion types.

Ultimately, these motions can be controlled by the system as well. Try the following lines of code while the movie is playing to see this in action:

```
w.model[1].bonesplayer.playNext()
w.model[1].bonesplayer.queue("bipedBackflip", 0)
```

As you can see, you can easily control the active motion in the queue. If you'd like to take this even further, you might try adding a cube in the space and then using modelUnderRay() or distanceTo() commands to detect the model's proximity to the box and queue a backflip when the figure gets too close.

These commands can be easily combined with one another and with the motion mapping command to do all sorts of wonderful things. The map() command allows you to map all or part of one motion onto another motion. Try the following bit of code in the message window while your movie is playing:

```
w.model[1].bonesplayer.playnext()
headTurnWalk = member(1).newMotion("headTurnWalk")
w.motion("headTurnWalk").map("bip01")
w.motion("headTurnWalk").map("bipedWalkBacking", "Bip01 neck")
w.model[1].bonesplayer.queue("headTurnWalk", 1)
```

The playNext() command empties the active walk motion from the playlist. This should cause your motion to stop.

The next line creates a new motion called headTurnWalk. We'll use this new bone motion to combine the head turn from the walk backward animation with the walking from the basic biped motion.

The third and fourth lines map these two motions to our new motion. The last line simply adds the new motion to the playlist and asks it to repeat so that you can watch.

Director's bones animation tools are valuable and potent additions to our growing chest of toys. These commands and properties can be added to the properties and commands that the bonesplayer modifier shares with the keyframeplayer to get deep interactive and programmatic control over the characters in your real-time games.

With keyframe and bones based animation under your belt, you are clearly ready to meet the rest of the family. In Chapter 11, "Adding Abilities with Modifiers," I'll cover the remaining modifiers. I'll show you how to get vertex level control of your meshes and really start tinkering with those models and the manner in which they are rendered, dynamically.

CHAPTER 11

Adding Abilities with Modifiers

The basic building blocks of the 3D media type may be augmented further with the addition of special "modifiers." We have already seen two types of modifiers. The keyframe and motion modifiers enhance the ability of the Director 3D cast member nodes to perform specialized animation tasks.

There are also modifiers designed to extend the range of effects that are possible for materials in the 3D member, modifiers that increase the programmer's ability to optimize and tessellate meshes, and a modifier that provides substantially deeper access to each individual vertex in a mesh.

NOTE

In Chapter 12, "Simulating Physics," I'll discuss the last modifier, the collision detection modifier, as well as the Havok physics Xtra.

Although these modifiers substantially extend the range of things you are able to do with 3D in Director, they do not come without a cost. Each modifier that is added to the scene increases the load on the computer's CPU and graphics card. It is important to keep in mind that they should be used carefully.

After reading the chapter, you should

- Know the properties and methods of each modifier
- Know the limitations of excessive modifier use
- Understand the capabilities of each modifier
- Understand how models that use the modifiers may interact

In this chapter, I explain the concept of modifiers and describe the shader, optimization, and mesh-control modifiers. I give examples of most of these modifiers in use and provide a general modifier tutorial. I discuss the properties and methods supported by each modifier and then give you a chance to explore the way they work. You have the opportunity to experiment with mesh deformation and with the effects of each modifier in a 3D world.

General Modifier Usage

Modifiers are objects that include functions that are not always required for the 3D world to function. Basically a C++ object can be added to the world and may enhance the functions available to a given node.

There are plans to offer developers the ability to program custom Xtras using the Director 8.5 Xtra development kit. Some syntax is common to all modifiers, regardless of whether it ships with Director or is offered as a third-party Xtra.

You call the properties of a modifier by referring to the properties of the modifier object. Generally modifiers are assigned to individual nodes. Typical syntax then takes the form `w.model[n].modifierObject.modifierProperty`.

This one concept remains true regardless of the modifier with which you are working. Modifiers are also all added using the same syntax:
`w.node[n].addModifier(#modifierName)`.

You can get a list of all the modifiers that are available on a given system by checking the modifiers property of the W3D member:

```
put getRendererServices().modifiers
-- [#collision, #bonesPlayer, #keyframePlayer, \
   #toon, #lod, #meshDeform, #sds, #inker]
```

Each of the basic modifiers that ship with Director is designed to attach to a model object. None of them will function properly if the model does not have a valid model resource.

Two of these basic modifiers, `#keyframePlayer` and `#bonesPlayer`, are used to enhance access to the motions that are found in the 3D member. These were covered in detail in Chapter 9, "Understanding the 3D Animation Options," and Chapter 10, "Bone Animation." The `#collision` modifier is used to detect collisions between models that are using the modifier. We'll talk more about that one in the next chapter.

The remaining modifiers can be broken into three groups:

- **Inker and Toon**—These modifiers are used to enhance the rendering capacity of the model's shaders.

- **SDS and LOD**—These modifiers assist programmers with geometric optimization. The SDS modifier is used to tessellate the polygons that compose a model's surface, increasing its smoothness and often improving the quality of the display. Its counterpart is the LOD modifier, which is used to reduce the detail represented by the geometry. In essence, it optimizes the polygons dynamically.

- **Meshdeform**—This modifier grants you access to the remaining properties of each individual vertex and face within a given mesh. It provides developers with an entry point for modifying the points within a mesh without forcing a rebuild of the mesh.

Inker and Toon

These items are not simply additional shader types because they would not be possible to create without the help of special information about the neighbor relationship of polygons within a given model.

The Toon and Inker shader styles create cartoon-style and silhouette-style properties, respectively, for a given model. The properties of these two modifiers are listed in Table 11.1.

TABLE 11.1   Toon and Inker Properties

Property	Description
Toon Properties	
style	The aesthetic style of the shader. Comes in three flavors: #toon, #gradient, and #blackAndWhite.
colorSteps	Indicates how many colors should be used to create the effect.
shadowPercentage	The percentage of the color steps that will be used to represent the shadowed areas of the model's surface.
highlightPercentage	The percentage of the color steps that will be used to represent the highlighted areas.
shadowStrength	The depth of the shadows.
highlightStrength	The value of the highlights.

TABLE 11.1   Continued

Property	Description
Toon and Inker Shared Properties	
lineColor	The color of the lines.
creases	Creases are the boundaries of meshes. This is a Boolean value that determines whether lines will be drawn at given locations.
creaseAngle	The amount of deviation of face normals, expressed as an angle that must be detected in order to create a crease.
boundary	A Boolean value that determines whether lines will be drawn around the object's boundary.
lineOffset	The distance that lines are drawn away from the edge of a shape.
useLineOffset	A Boolean value that determines whether lines are offset.
silhouettes	A Boolean value that determines whether lines will be drawn around the occluding contour of the object.

Exercise 11.1:   Working with Inker and Toon Modifiers

In order for you to better understand these properties, I've set up a little movie file for you to test each of them and observe the manner in which they interact. Open the movie toonTest.dir on your CD-ROM, rewind it, and click Play. The movie automatically places the Toon and Inker modifiers on the models in the scene. We will be working with the teapot (see Figure 11.1).

FIGURE 11.1

The Toon and Inker modifiers are applied to the models in the scene.

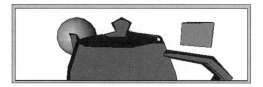

Experiment with the following commands to see the Inker and Toon modifiers in action and get a good sense of how these modifiers work. While the movie is running, type each command into the message window. Set the lineColor property first, which will help you see the other changes more clearly:

```
teapot.toon.lineColor = rgb(255,0,0)
```

This command changes the color of the lines used by both Inker and Toon to delineate the outlines of shapes and forms created by the model, including the shapes that compose the model as well as its silhouettes and boundaries (see Figure 11.2).

FIGURE 11.2

The lineColor property is changed to red.

The next two lines of code allow you to adjust the number of colors used by the shader modifier to represent mass for the model. You may set the colorSteps property to 2, 4, 8, or 16 colors. Try setting colorSteps now:

```
teapot.toon.colorSteps = 8
teapot.toon.colorSteps = 4
```

The effect of the colorSteps property should be immediately clear. The image appears to have mass, but the rendering style is limited enough to give the model that "cartoon" flavor. Figure 11.3 shows the teapot model rendered with colorSteps set to 4.

FIGURE 11.3.

The teapot rendered with toon.colorSteps set to 4.

The toon.boundary and inker.boundary properties are set to True by default. This means that the edges of any mesh are automatically outlined. The lid on top of the teapot is a great example of an edge of a mesh. Watch the lid of the teapot as you experiment with the `boundary` property of the Toon or Inker modifier attached to the teapot:

```
teapot.toon.boundary = 0
teapot.inker.boundary = 1
```

Figure 11.4 illustrates the result of turning off the boundary property of either modifier. As you can see in the figure, the outline of the object is unaffected, but the outline around the edge of a mesh (in this case, the lid of the teapot) is turned off.

FIGURE 11.4

The boundary property controls the outline surrounding the edge of a mesh.

The `toon.silhouettes` and `inker.silhouettes` properties are similar to the `boundary` property. They also control the outline, but the outline is the visual occluding contour of the object relative to the projected image. This is the outer edge of the shape as you see it at this moment. Turn off the `silhouettes` property as you watch the outer edges of the teapot:

```
teapot.toon.silhouettes = 0
teapot.inker.silhouettes = 1
```

If you need to, repeat the process a few times until you have seen the effect clearly. In Figure 11.5, I have turned `silhouettes` off but left the `boundary` property on.

Take a look at the image of the teapot in Figure 11.6. In this case, I have turned the `creases` property on and set the `creaseAngle` property to a value of `0.99`. The `creaseAngle` property must be given a value between `-1.0` and `1.0`. It represents the angle of variation in neighboring normals that is allowed before you will begin to see creases (lines representing the edges between polygons).

FIGURE 11.5

With the silhouettes property switched off, the outer edges of the image are no longer outlined.

FIGURE 11.6

Creases are rendered if you set the creases property to True.

Use the following commands to enable the creases on the teapot and experiment with different creaseAngle values:

```
teapot.toon.creases = 1
teapot.toon.creaseAngle = 0.99
sphere.inker.creaseAngle = 0.39
sphere.inker.creaseAngle = -0.39
```

The lineOffset property and useLineOffset property are used to determine the height or distance away from the surface of the model that you want to render the lines. Positive values between 0 and 100 press the lines through the skin and into the inside of the model. Negative values project the lines farther and farther in front of the model's surface. The lineOffset property of the teapot in Figure 11.7 is set to -99.

To manipulate the lineOffset property of the teapot in the demonstration movie, try entering the following commands into the message window:

```
teapot.toon.useLineOffset = 1
teapot.toon.lineOffset = -99
teapot.inker.lineOffset = 9
```

FIGURE 11.7

Negative lineOffset values can cause the apparent strength of the lines to increase.

The style property of the Toon modifier allows you to adjust the manner in which the shader is drawn. The shader is able to render in simple black and white, in black and the color attributed to the model's original shader, and in a stepped gradient of analogous colors based on values of the original shader color (see Figure 11.8).

FIGURE 11.8

The teapot is rendered in #blackAndWhite style with creases on, creaseAngle at -0.99, useLineOffset on, and lineOffset set to 19.

Try changing the #style property of the Toon modifier to each style: #toon, #gradient, and #blackAndWhite. Use the following syntax as a guide:

```
teapot.toon.style = #blackAndWhite
teapot.toon.style = #gradient
teapot.toon.style = #toon
```

The remaining properties—highlightPercentage, hilightStrength, shadowPercentage, and shadowStrength—are used to fine-tune the amount of surface area dedicated to shadow and highlight colors and to adjust the value (tint and shade) of the highlights and shadows (see Figure 11.9).

FIGURE 11.9

The teapot, with its highlightStrength *property set to 1.9.*

It is important to note that the Toon and Inker modifiers take advantage of special neighbor data that is optionally exported when you save a W3D file. This means that the data to create these effects will not be available in all W3D members. You need to make sure you enable the export of neighbor data in your 3D modeling package in order to achieve these effects.

This data is necessary in order to calculate properties such as creaseAngle and boundary. It is also necessary if you plan to use the subdivision of surfaces modifier.

SDS and LOD

Subdivision of Surfaces (SDS) and Level of Detail (LOD) modifiers are opposing arms of the same basic geometric function. The meshes are composed of polygons. They are specifically made of triangles. Every triangle that is added to a mesh has the potential to smooth its surface and possibly make the image appear more realistic. Unfortunately, each triangle that is rendered has a fixed cost in processor terms.

Because of these benefits and limitations, the SDS and LOD modifiers are available in Director to help developers optimize the performance and quality of their 3D models. The SDS modifier allows us to break the triangles up into smaller triangles, and it ideally improves the appearance of models. Because the performance of machines can vary wildly, SDS can be used to increase realism on faster machines without restricting all animation playback to such machines.

The LOD modifier is basically the opposite. It allows us to decrease the total number of polygons used to render the finished model. As a model moves farther away from a camera, it is often desirable to decrease the number of polygons used to create the illusion of the model. This way, the system does not have to work as hard, and the player may not even notice if the degradation of the model is minor enough to fool the player's eye at the given distance.

Both the SDS and LOD modifiers may be used as automatic tools that dynamically adjust their values as the model moves closer to or farther away from the camera. Each modifier may also be used to control the display properties based on events determined by the programmer via Lingo.

You generally won't want to use LOD at the same time that you use SDS because they are fundamentally opposites. You may not use the LOD or SDS modifier in conjunction with either the Toon or Inker modifier, because only one modifier is allowed access to the additional data (neighbor data) at any given time.

Tables 11.2 and 11.3 list each of the properties of the LOD and SDS modifiers and give you a brief description of their purpose.

TABLE 11.2   LOD Properties

Property	Description
auto	When this property is enabled, the LOD modifier dynamically determines the level of detail to use when displaying the model based on the model's relative distance to the came property allows you to adjust the amount of reduction that the modifier does when the lod.auto property is TRUE.
level	The level (0.00 to 100.00) of detail at which the model will be rendered. This property can only be set when auto is FALSE.

TABLE 11.3   SDS Properties

Property	Description
depth	The highest number of tessellations that will occur for this model.
enabled	A Boolean value that determines whether the SDS modifier is active.
error	The amount of error you are willing to accept in the new geometry created by the tessellation.
subdivision	There are two ways to approach tessellation, indicated by the two possible values of this property. #Uniform subdivision splits all the polygons by the same amount for each level of depth. #Adaptive subdivision splits only those polygons that are visible and only when major changes are made to the display of these models.
tension	Determines how strictly the new surfaces should stick to the existing surface.

Open the movie LODSDS.dir on the companion CD-ROM to see the Subdivision of Surfaces and Level of Detail modifiers in action. Rewind the movie and click Play. Type the following commands in the message window:

```
ball.shader.renderStyle = #wire
ball.lod.auto = 1
```

Watch the ball as it moves nearer, then farther from the camera. Although there was initially no change in the appearance of the ball, once you set the lod.auto value to 1 and click Enter, you should notice the ball changing automatically as its distance to the camera decreases (see Figures 11.10 and 11.11).

FIGURE 11.10

The ball is rendered in wireframe mode and the auto property of the LOD modifier has been disabled.

FIGURE 11.11

The auto property has been enabled.

The auto property determines whether the LOD modifier automatically establishes the appropriate level of detail that should be used to render the ball. Now try changing the bias property:

```
ball.lod.bias = 20
```

The bias property controls the level of optimization that the LOD modifier attempts to use on the object. In the startup script of this movie, I set the bias to 5. That is why the ball immediately steps into a very low quality once you set the modifier's auto property to TRUE. As you increase the bias value, it is increasingly difficult to perceive any difference in the number of polygons used to render the sphere (see Figure 11.12).

FIGURE 11.12

The lod.bias property is reduced to 5 in order to increase the rate of reduction.

Now turn the auto property off:

```
ball.lod.auto = 0
```

You may also adjust the level of detail via Lingo. To do this, simply turn the lod.auto property off and then adjust the lod.level property. The lod.level property accepts values between 0 and 100 and adjusts the number of polygons used to display the object according to its value (see Figure 11.13).

FIGURE 11.13

The lod.auto property is turned off and the lod.level property is set to 30.

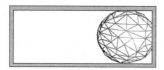

I often use lod.level to dynamically alter the resolution of a model based on the model's proximity to another model. Simply use the distanceTo() command to find the distance between the models and then set the level to a relative number between 0 and 100. Try adjusting the level via the message window now:

```
ball.lod.level = 30
```

The other major polygon optimization modifier is the Subdivision of Surfaces modifier. Fundamentally, this is the opposite of the LOD modifier. Instead of reducing the polygonal geometry of the model, the SDS modifier adds to the model's geometry.

Essentially, the modifier subdivides the triangles that make the model according to the SDS properties. Whereas the LOD modifier generally improves performance and reduces image quality, the SDS modifier generally decreases performance and increases image quality. In the message window, type the following commands to enable the SDS modifier and remove the LOD modifier:

```
ball.removeModifier(#lod)
ball.sds.enabled = 1
```

It would just be screwy to try to use both at the same time, in most cases. If you really want to, you should first disable the lod.auto property and set the LOD modifier to the level you desire.

The subdivision property determines whether the effects of subdivision should be applied to the entire model or just the bits that are visible and changing. Try setting the subdivision property to #uniform and then #adaptive:

```
ball.sds.subdivision = #uniform
```

```
ball.sds.subdivision = #adaptive
```

To explore the effects of the SDS error property, type the following into the message window (see Figures 11.14, 11.15, and 11.16):

```
ball.sds.error = 50
```

```
ball.sds.error = 2
```

```
ball.sds.error = 100
```

FIGURE 11.14

The sds.error property is set to 50.

FIGURE 11.15

The sds.error property is set to 2.

FIGURE 11.16

The sds.error property is set to 100.

The `tension` property may be seen in effect by using a similar set of commands. A ball does not give us the best test bed. I set the tension of a teapot using these commands in the message window:

```
ball.sds.tension = 50

ball.sds.tension = 2

ball.sds.tension = 100
```

Figures 11.17, 11.18, and 11.19 show the results. You'll notice that with low `tension` values, the teapot seems to have loose skin, whereas high settings make the surface overly taut. Each of these was done on a teapot with an `sds.depth` setting of 2. If you try to do this in the Toon movie, as you'll note that I did, be certain to remove the Toon and Inker modifiers from the teapot first.

FIGURE 11.17

The sds.tension property is set to 2.

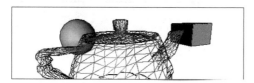

FIGURE 11.18

The sds.tension property is set to 50.

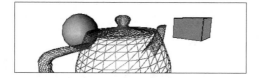

FIGURE 11.19

The sds.tension property is set to 100.

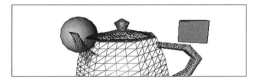

Together these two geometry-adjusting modifiers add a great deal of flexibility to the media that developers are able to deliver to the players. It is possible to load extremely low polygon placeholders and steadily increase the complexity of the models, even as the player has already begun to interact in the 3D world.

As you work, keep in mind the fine balance that has to be maintained between the quality of the image and the speed of the animation. These two modifiers are often critical tools when you are trying to ensure rapid animation on less-than-optimum machines.

Meshdeform

The most complete, dynamic access to the elements of a given mesh can be obtained by adding the meshdeform modifier to a model. This amazing little widget enhances your access to the components of a mesh. Lingo control of a model without the meshdeform modifier is basically limited to control of the translation, scale, and rotation of the entire mesh.

With the meshdeform modifier, it is possible to get and set the values of each vertex within the mesh, allowing you to dynamically alter the form of the mesh itself. A complete list of the properties and commands supported by the meshdeform modifier is given in Table 11.4.

TABLE 11.4   Properties and Commands of the Meshdeform Modifier

Property/Command	Description
mesh.count	The total number of meshes in the model.
face.count	The total number of faces within either a given mesh or a given model.
mesh[n].colorlist	A list of the colors of each face in the given mesh.

TABLE 11.4   Continued

`mesh[n].face[n].neighbor`	A list of data about a given neighbor. This is generally a list of four items: `meshIndex`, `faceIndex`, `vertexIndex`, and `flipped`.
`mesh[n].vertexList`	The list of vertices that compose the model's mesh.
`mesh[n].normalList`	A list of the normals (vectors running perpendicular to given front faces).
`mesh[n].textureLayer.add()`	Use the `add()` command to add a blank texture layer to a given mesh.

I'll use most of these properties in the next section, "Exercise 11.2: Twist and Shout." For the most part, these elements are exactly what they appear to be. In most cases, the property stores a list.

The `colorList` property is a list of RGB color values that represent the default color of each face in a given mesh. The `neighbor` property stores a list of the mesh and the neighbor's face index number.

Every mesh is composed of triangles. The position of these triangles in the simulated space is defined by the position of each of the three vertices that pin the corners of the triangle. The area inside the triangle is the face of the polygon, and the direction of the normal determines which side of that face is the front and which is the back.

This data can easily be expressed as a list of vertices for any given mesh. This list of vectors, representing the positions of each vertex, is called the `vertexList`. The list of directions that determine which side of each face is the front and which is the back is called the `normalList`.

The last element in this cluster is the `textureLayer.add()` command. The meshdeform modifier supports modification of the `textureLayer` coordinates. You can use the `textureLayer.add()` command to add new texture layers and then create custom texture maps to determine the manner in which a texture is drawn onto the surface of your model.

In Exercise 11.2, I'll walk you through some Lingo that will modify a mesh using the meshdeform modifier. The Lingo has been built in to a behavior, so you'll be able to play with some parameters and experiment with their impact on the movie's model, or you can move the behavior to your own movies and see how your own models respond to the twisting behavior.

Exercise 11.2:   Twist and Shout

The following example will give you a chance to experiment with several of the properties of the meshdeform modifier. I've created a simple behavior that may be attached to any model in order to rotate the vertices of the model, thus creating a twisting appearance. The code for the behavior in this example is shown in Listing 11.1.

LISTING 11.1   The Twist Behavior Handler

```
 1: global w --- the world
 2:
 3: property pModel -- the model you want to twist
 4: property pSteps -- stores the current iters
 5: property pDirection -- The current direction
 6: property pX -- the amount of twist on the x
 7: property pY -- the amount of twist on the y
 8: property pZ -- the amount of twist on the z
 9:
10: on beginSprite(me)
11:    -- set up the basic parameters
12:    w = member(1)
13:    pModel = w.model(pModel)
14:    -- add the meshdeform modifier
15:    pModel.addModifier(#meshdeform)
16:    pDirection = 1
17:    pModel.visibility = #both
18:    pModel.shader.blend = 40
19:    pSteps = 1
20:    -- avoids a 0 value error
21:    if pX > 0 then
22:      pX = pX * 0.0001
23:    end if
24:    if pY > 0 then
25:      pY = pY * 0.0001
26:    end if
27:    if pZ > 0 then
28:      pZ = pZ * 0.0001
29:    end if
30: end
31:
32: on twistBox
33:    --- store a couple of copies of the vertexList
34:    pVList = duplicate(pModel.meshdeform.mesh.vertexList)
35:    tVList = duplicate(pModel.meshdeform.mesh.vertexList)
36:    -- Adjust the rotation value to a reasonable size.
```

LISTING 11.1   Continued

```
37:    if pX > 0 then
38:      pXd =  0.05 * (pSteps)
39:    else
40:      pXd = 0
41:    end if
42:    if pY > 0 then
43:      pYd = 0.05 * (pSteps)
44:    else
45:      pYd = 0
46:    end if
47:    if pZ > 0 then
48:      pZd = 0.05 * (pSteps)
49:    else
50:      pZd = 0
51:    end if
52:    --- for each vertex
53:    repeat with iter = 1 to pVList.count
54:      t = transform()
55:      --- rotate the vertex by the amounts calculated.\
             It twists because the vertices on opposite
56:      -- sides of the box are oriented in opposite directions.
57:      t.rotate(pVList[iter].x *pXd, pVList[iter].y *pYd, pVList[iter].z *pZd)
58:      tVList[iter] = t * pVlist[iter]
59:      tVList[iter].z = tVList[iter].z + (tVList[iter].z * (pZ *  pSteps))
60:      tVList[iter].y = tVList[iter].y + (tVList[iter].y * (pY  * pSteps))
61:      tVlist[iter].x = tVList[iter].x + (tVList[iter].x * (pX  * pSteps))
62:    end repeat
63:    -- now just set the vertex list to the new list we've created.
64:    pModel.meshdeform.mesh.vertexlist = tVList
65:    if pSteps = 7  OR pSteps = -7 then
66:      pDirection = pDirection * -1
67:    end if
68:    pSteps = pSteps + pDirection
69:    pModel.rotate(-2,0.5,0,#self)
70: end
71:
72: on exitFrame
73:    twistBox()
74: end
```

Open the file named meshDeform.dir on your CD-ROM. Rewind the movie and click Play. The gelatin is jiggling because I've attached a behavior that instructs it to rotate each vertex in short animation cycles. The twisting is created because the opposing faces of the box are oriented in opposite directions.

Stop the movie and open the Behavior dialog for the twist behavior. You can adjust the amount of rotation around each of the axes. Once you've made adjustments to the parameters, rewind the movie and play it again to see the changes you've made.

There is very little limit to the level of control you can achieve given the added muscle of the meshdeform modifier. For example, you could create a game that enables mouse-based manipulation of individual points within a mesh or an animation that transforms primitive shapes into a myriad of mathematically driven images.

Now that you've seen the bulk of Director's new 3D features, I can't wait to walk you through the really gnarly world of simulated physics and collision detection. In the next chapter, I'll show you a couple of great new ways to handle collisions in your 3D scene, lending your games a key component.

CHAPTER 12

Simulating Physics

When people talk about simulating physics in a 3D game environment, they are normally talking about simulating rigid body dynamics. Rigid body dynamics is a means of describing the way gravity, friction, force, and velocity affect solid matter.) For example, a ball falls to the ground and then bounces, or pool balls are struck by a cue and then bounce off each other and the table bumpers because force and or gravity cause them to move, friction slows their motion, elasticity causes them to bounce when they impact with another solid object (rigid body).

There are a couple of ways to enhance Director's ability to handle the simulation of rigid body dynamics.

Director 8.5 includes a collision modifier that has the ability to detect limited collision events and begin the process of responding to the intersection of two models. Alone, this is a huge feature for game development, but Director also ships with the Havok Physics Xtra.

This Havok Xtra provides ways to detect collisions between models and enables the system to respond to those collisions in plausible ways. In this chapter, I'll introduce you to these marvelous toys.

After reading the chapter you should

- Know the properties and methods of the collision modifier
- Know how to set up a collision-monitoring handler
- Know the basic properties and methods supported by the Havok Xtra
- Understand the capacity and limitations of collision detection and resolution
- Understand the capacity and limitations of rigid body dynamics simulations using the Havok Physics Xtra

One of the most amazing features supported by the W3D format is collision detection, which provides a foundation for creating rigid body physics resolution in Director. The Havok Physics Xtra adds rigid body dynamics to the arsenal of tools at your disposal.

In this chapter, I talk about using the collision modifier in Director Shockwave Studio. I walk you through the basic concepts behind collision detection and point out some of the hazards you might encounter as you use collision detection in your games.

In the "Using Havok for Physics" section, I introduce you to the Havok Physics Xtra for Director. I walk you through the basics of the Havok plug-in from within 3D Studio Max to create an HKE file that may be imported into Director and used to establish rules for a rigid body simulation in Director. Then I introduce you to Havok's robust Lingo support and show you how to control the Havok Xtra with Lingo alone. Finally, I show you a real-life example of the Havok Physics Xtra.

The Collision Modifier

Collisions are the heart and soul of most real-time games. In the real world, solid masses do not pass through one another. In 3D simulations, there is usually nothing to prevent such bizarre events. Because we normally don't want the balls to pass through the bumpers on the virtual pool table, knowing when the two models have collided is an essential element of developing the game.

This is also the case with bullets and projectiles in a first-person shooter. It is needed with bodies in a combat game and with the terrain in a radical skateboarding simulation. If your world is interactive, players will try to pass through solid objects, and a major part of your development process will involve collision detection and resolution.

In this section, I introduce you to the basic methods of learning about the collisions that occur between models in your 3D world. I focus on collision detection rather than collision resolution at this point. I'll go into more depth about resolving collisions in Part III, "Putting Strategies into Action."

The last of the modifiers that may be attached to nodes in Director is the collision modifier. This modifier allows us to receive notification when a collision occurs either between any two objects using the modifier or between a specific model and any other model that is using the modifier.

The modifier can be set to resolve collisions automatically, or you can take advantage of the notification system to make your own decisions about collision resolution.

The most common problem with collision detection and resolution is the interpenetration of models. When the bounding spheres of two models interpenetrate or the two models themselves interpenetrate, collision events occur. (In the next section, I show you how to disable the collision modifier temporarily to avoid this problem.)

Normally resolution refers to the process of responding to the collision event in a manner consistent with physics and consistent with the behavior and locomotion of the objects that collided.

Director's collision-resolution system simply prevents interpenetration of any two models that have the modifier attached and have their respective `resolve` properties set to `TRUE`.

Simply put, if the `collision modifier's resolution property` for either object is `TRUE`, the model that is animating cannot move into the bounding sphere, bounding box, or mesh of the other model. It simply stops.

Tell Me If I Hit Something

The first step in using the collision modifier is to assign it to each model for which you want to receive collision events. Adding the modifier is simple and parallels the addition of any other modifier. Here's the syntax:

```
w.model[n].addModifier(#collision)
```

The modifier features several properties that may be adjusted in order to alter the manner in which a model responds to and reports collisions. These properties are listed in Table 12.1.

TABLE 12.1   Basic Properties of the Collision Modifier

Property	Description
`enabled`	Determines whether collisions are actually detected. You can toggle this property off if you want to disable collisions on a given node.
`immovable`	Determines whether a given model may be moved during a collision resolution.

TABLE 12.1   Continued

Property	Description
mode	The type of geometry that will be used by the collision modifier to determine whether a collision occurred. Comes in three flavors: #sphere, #box, and #mesh.
resolve	Determines whether the system will attempt to resolve the collision for the object automatically.

You may switch the modifier's detection of collisions on and off using the enabled property. The syntax is fairly straightforward:

```
w.model[n].collision.enabled = 0
```

The immovable property can assist you with optimization. Any model that is not moveable will not be calculated when the determination of interpenetration is occurring. This is roughly the same thing as registering only mobile objects to receive collision events.

The mode property of the collision modifier is the geometric form that will be used to determine whether the model has collided with anything. The #sphere mode represents collisions of the bounding sphere of the model. A sphere drawn to a size that is large enough to enclose its most extreme points determines a model's bounding sphere. This mode is the least expensive to calculate.

The #box option uses a bounding box. Similar to the bounding sphere, a box is formed that encases the entire model. This is often a better choice when the model is not fundamentally rounded.

The #mesh option is the most accurate but far more expensive than the other options in terms of performance. If you need precise collisions on concave objects, you may need to choose this option.

TIP

Changing the scale of a model that will use any form of collision detection leads to an unreliable physics simulation. You will probably find that the system reacts to the collisions as if the models were the size of the model resource rather than the size of the actual model.

The resolve property determines whether the collisions will resolve automatically. Essentially this stops all animation on the models that experience a collision at the point of impact. This seldom works for our purposes in games, because at the very least we want a player's character to be able to slide along the surface of a given model.

The collision modifier supports the creation of callbacks to generate custom event notification whenever a collision occurs between two or more objects that are actively using the modifier. You can set up the collision callback handlers using any of the commands in Table 12.2.

TABLE 12.2   Callback Handlers

Command	Description
registerForEvent()	Member command that is used to register a given script and handler to receive events of the specified type.
registerScript()	3D node command that is used to register a given script and handler to receive events of the specified type.
setCollisionCallback()	A shortcut to the registerScript(#collideWith) command. Used on a specific node's collision modifier, this command registers the node that calls the command to receive #collideWith messages for collisions with any other node bearing the collision modifier.

We've used the registerForEvent() and registerScript() commands already when we created timeout objects in *Bubble Pop Raceway* in Chapter 9, "Using 3D Keyframe Animation in Director." Using either of these commands, you supply the #collideWith or #collideAny argument in order to determine whether you want to receive notices only when the model collides with specific other models or whenever the model collides with any other model. In general, collideAny is dark and evil magic that will cripple most systems just by thinking about it.

We always want to limit collision reporting to collisions with those mobile objects that are relevant at the moment. This is because there are considerably fewer calculations involved in figuring out which models are colliding with a few specific other models than in determining which models are colliding with any other models. Often, though, we don't really care.

Visualize a game of pool. Do you care that the surface of the table is colliding with the bumpers or the pockets? No, of course you don't. It would be a silly waste of processor and graphics card resources to calculate and report these collisions, but it would be quite useful to know when any of the balls are colliding with any of these elements.

I would want to put collision modifiers on all these models, but I would only want to deal with resolving the collisions between the balls and the objects they encounter.

To set up a typical collision callback using the `setCollisionCallback()` shortcut, use the following syntax:

```
w.model[n].collision.setCollisionCallback(#handler, scriptInstance)
```

The handler should match the name of the handler you are using to receive the callback and respond. You cannot use `updateStage()` commands within your collision callback handler.

Also, `scriptInstance` should contain a reference to the script object that is handling the callback. If the script that set up the callback is a behavior and the resolution handler is within the same script, you can just use `me` in the conventional sense. If the script is within a movie script, use `0`, and the system will search for the first global handler or the correct name. If the script is within an instance of an object, use a reference to the object. Here are examples of the syntax for each of these approaches:

```
-- Using me, (assuming that you normally \
use me in your behavior scripts) tells
-- the system to use the same script that just called setCollisionCallback()
w.model[n].collision.setCollisionCallback(#catchCollisions, me)


-- Using 0 tells the system to go to the movie scripts and look for one.
w.model[n].collision.setCollisionCallback(#catchCollisions, 0)


-- Using a reference to an object is another option. You could birth a
-- collision monitoring object that just floats \
about in ram waiting to respond
-- to collision callback events.
w.model[n].collision.setCollisionCallback(#catchCollisions, objectRef)
```

Once the collision event occurs, the collision notification is sent to your custom collision-resolution handler, which receives a bunch of information about that collision event. This batch of information is called *collision data*, and the collisionData object has several properties. Each of these properties stores a specific type of information that proves useful as you try to respond to the collision event. Table 12.3 provides information about each of the properties of the collisionData object.

TABLE 12.3   Properties and Methods of the *collisionData* Object

Property or Method	Description
collisionNormal	A direction vector representing the direction that the object was traveling when the collision occurred.
modelA	The first model in the collision.
modelB	The other model in the collision.
pointOfContact	The world position where the collision occurred.
resolveA()	Overrides the resolve property. This command allows you to override modelA's resolve property by passing a Boolean value (1 for resolve anyway, 0 for don't resolve.)
resolveB()	Overrides the resolve property. This command allows you to override modelB's resolve property by passing a Boolean value (1 for resolve anyway, 0 for don't resolve).

You may access any of the properties or methods of the collisionData object using the following syntax:

```
put collisionData.propertyOrFunction -- use (arg) if a command.
```

The collisionNormal object contains a direction vector that represents the trajectory of motion at the moment of impact. This will come in very handy when we are ready to calculate the angle of deflection or bounce off solid objects.

The collisionData object also includes references to the models involved in the collision. You can find these references by polling the modelA and modelB properties of the object.

The final property in collisionData is pointOfContact. This is the place in 3D space—expressed in world units—where the collision occurred.

The functions `resolveA` and `resolveB` may be used to complement the `resolve` property. Essentially you can use these to override a model's `resolve` property and get the model to adopt the `resolve` setting of the model it bumped into.

Resolving Collisions

Now I want talk about resolving collisions within the limited parameters of a ball or similar object bouncing off a fixed or immobile object. (In Part III, I'll discuss the more detailed options related to collision resolution and steering behaviors as well as collisions between two objects that are not immobile.)

We know now that the collision callback gives us some basic information about a collision between objects and about the details of that collision. To resolve that collision in its simplest possible form, we need only set the `collision.resolve` properties of the models to TRUE.

This causes the models to stop the moment they make contact. Even if you attempt to move them via Lingo, using the `translate` or `rotate` commands, the objects will not move into one another as long as their collision modifiers' `resolve` properties are TRUE.

This is not generally enough for enticing gameplay. It is considerably more common that you will want the collision between two objects to trigger some more complex reaction. The order of such events may usually be broken down into the following sequence:

1. Begin animating normally.
2. Detect a collision between two relevant models.
3. Temporarily disable collision detection.
4. Interpret the collision data and respond appropriately.
5. Reenable collision detection.
6. Continue normal animation.

In Exercise 12.1, I'll demonstrate this procedure as we go back to the ball in the forest and bounce it off the trees. You may recall that we've already done this. I bounced the ball off trees using `modelsUnderRay()` in the first chapter. The critical difference here is that we will be using the collision modifier to detect the collisions, and we will be using a more sophisticated response system to determine how we should respond to a collision event.

The core of this response lies in determining the deflection vector that is most appropriate for the ball as it bounces off the surface of the tree.

We could factor in the velocity of the ball and the elasticity of the ball and the tree. However, we aren't going to bother with this. Realistic physics do not always make enticing gameplay.

The right solution to any problem in a game is always the one that does the job with the least possible cost to the processor and the highest possible realism or appropriateness. Finding the balance is important, and this is a case where excessive calculations wouldn't add substantially to the realism of the bounce.

We need two bits of information to calculate the deflection vector. We need to know the direction in which the ball was moving before the collision and the direction of reverse force (which is essentially the normal—the vector representing the direction that is perpendicular to the face plane of the geometry—of the specific face on the tree that was hit). Figure 12.1 provides a visual guide to these elements.

FIGURE 12.1

The basic elements used to calculate the deflection vector.

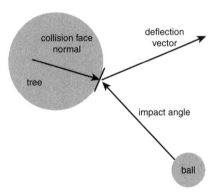

To find the deflection vector, simply subtract the `impactAngle` value from the impacted surface's normal. There are, of course, some additional considerations that must be made when you start working with actual models. Therefore, the example in Exercise 12.1 is designed to demonstrate some of the real-world problems you will face as you work to bounce models off one another in your simulations.

Exercise 12.1: Back to the Forest

Open the `collision.dir` movie on your companion CD-ROM to see a demonstration of a ball bouncing off trees with the collision modifier. Rewind and click Play. You may use the keyboard arrows to accelerate the ball's motion and to steer it.

The first thing you will notice is that this ball is rolling and bouncing off the trees. If you are observant, you may even notice that the direction of the roll remains logical (it rolls the way a real ball would) regardless of the direction in which the ball is moving or has been bounced.

The ball isn't actually rotating. I mean that the ball is not rotating along its x- or y-axis. It only rotates along its z-axis in order to steer around the space. "But I can see it rolling," you might think. That's because I'm rotating the `wrapTransform` of the texture in order to simulate rolling without disturbing the orientation of the model on the x- and y-axes.

Most of the handlers in this movie are identical or similar to handlers we've already discussed. The new material is found in the collision response handler in Listing 12.1. I used the `setCollisionCallback()` command to instruct the system to call this handler, called `bang()`, any time that the ball hits another object with the collision modifier attached.

LISTING 12.1   The Collision Response Handler

```
 1: on bang(me, collisionData)
 2:    -- Store the collision normal in easy to read variable format
 3:    impactAngle = collisionData.collisionNormal
 4:    -- find the face for the tree's surface.
 5:    face = (w.modelsUnderRay(w.model[1].transform.position, \
➥ impactAngle, 1, #detailed))
 6:    -- make certain that the ray found a face.
 7:    if count(face) > 0 then
 8:       -- find the faceNormal
 9:       facePerp = face[1].isectNormal
10:    else
11:       -- if we didn't see tree, use a default normal
12:       facePerp = impactAngle * -1
13:    end if
14:    -- make that bouncing sound.
15:    sound(8).play(member(string(random(2))))
16:    -- calculate the deflection vector by subtracting \
➥ the face normal from the impact angle
```

LISTING 12.1   Continued

```
17:   deflectionVector = (impactAngle - facePerp)
18:   -- now because we need to rotate the ball to \
➡ orient it to the deflection vector we have
19:   -- to calculate the angle equivalency of the \
➡ deflection vector on the up and down axis.
20:   tangent = float(deflectionVector.x)  * float(-deflectionVector.y)
21:   -- basic trigonometry - the tangent of theta \
➡ is equal to the opposite side / the adjacent
22:   -- then just calculate theta (the angle) using atan()
23:   theta = atan(tangent)
24:   -- convert from radians to angle in degrees
25:   angle = radToAngle (theta)
26:   -- now rotate the ball (the +180 inverts the angle for the bounce)
27:   ball.rotate(0,0, (angle + 180))
28:   -- disable collisions for a second
29:   ball.collision.enabled = 0
30:   timeOut("resetCollision").new(1000, #resetCollision)
31:   -- increase the speed of the ball at this \
➡ new direction to create rough bounce.
32:   sprite(1).pVelocity = sprite(1).pVelocity + 10
33: end
```

When the collision is detected, this handler is triggered. I first store the impactAngle value into a more manageable variable. Then I use modelsUnderRay() to find the face that was hit. Because I'm doing fairly rough collisions, I may not always find a face on the tree. This means that I need to have a safety net. In line 12, I tell the system to simply reverse the direction of the ball if it doesn't see what it hit. This is not the cleanest solution to this problem, but it is fast.

It would be cleaner to cast multiple rays to the front left and right and then use that data to determine the appropriate deflection vector. We'd see much better glancing bounces.

Line 15 calls the sound event, which randomly selects a sound file to play. Next, deflectionVector is calculated and then converted into an angle expressed in degrees. This represents the angle of rotation around the z- (up and down) axis. I use this to rotate the model to the appropriate orientation.

The ball's collision modifier is then disabled to prevent multiple events within milliseconds and to avoid the ball getting stuck to trees. I set a clock to wake the collision modifier back up after 1 second. In most cases, this leaves everything functioning perfectly well.

The command in line 32 resets the velocity of the ball in order to give it a bit of a boost as it deflects. This is meant to exaggerate the bounce off the tree and has the added bonus of moving the ball away from the collision area regardless of the speed at which the ball was moving when it hit the tree.

As you can see, the collision modifier can be a powerful tool in game development within Director. We'll talk about more sophisticated methods of resolving collisions in Part III.

Unfortunately, the collision modifier does not really simulate the effects of rigid bodies and their physical properties. For this reason, Director ships with the Havok Physics Xtra.

Using Havok Physics Xtra

Havok Physics Xtra is a phenomenal tool that augments the 3D world by adding a wide array of features, commands, and properties to the world and its models. This Xtra essentially adds the ability to work with rigid body dynamics within Director and Shockwave.

The Xtra may be accessed via Lingo, or physics properties may be set using the Reactor plug-in for 3D Studio Max. You may also use combinations of these access methods.

In this section, I introduce you to the basic methods and properties supported by the Havok Physics Xtra, explain the process of authoring rigid body groups in Max, and introduce you to the basic concepts of manipulating these physics-enhanced models via Lingo.

The Havok Xtra enables the simulation of rigid body dynamics, which means you can use this Xtra to create simulated worlds that include rigid objects that respond to the simulated effects of gravity, friction, force, and torque.

You can also use the Xtra to create springs (objects, attached to two other objects, that have a preferred rest state that when squashed or stretched will attempt to return to that rest state) and dashpots (really tight, zero-length springs, both linear and angular.) The Xtra introduces several new commands and properties that allow specialized control over simulated physics and makes these commands and properties extremely simple to use.

The downside of this Xtra is that you need to have users download it from the Web if they haven't already done so. For serious game players, this won't be an issue. It could, however, be a major concern for a potential client, so it is important to keep this limitation in mind as you plan your delivery.

Table 12.4 lists the properties of the Havok Xtra. Because this is an Xtra and not a modifier, there are some fundamental differences in the ways we work with it. Therefore, I've divided this table into member properties, rigid body properties, spring properties, and dashpot properties.

TABLE 12.4   Havok Physics Xtra Properties

Property	Description
Member Properties	
angularDashpot	A list of the angular dashpots.
collisionList	A list of objects currently colliding. Includes modelA, modelB, the world-relative collision point, and the contact normal.
deactivationParameters	The level at which an object's motion is small enough for the system to disable it until the object is stimulated by another collision.
dragParameters	A two-item list of the linear and angular drag for the simulation.
gravity	A vector representing the currently assigned force of gravity within the simulation.
initialized	A Boolean value that reveals whether the Havok object has been initialized.
linearDashpot	A list of the linear dashpots.
rigidBody	A list of each rigid body contained in the Havok physics simulation.
scale	The scale of the 3D world.
simTime	The total time in milliseconds since the beginning of the simulation.
spring	A list of the springs.
subSteps	Additional calculations may be made by breaking up the time steps into these sub-units.
timeStep	The duration of time in milliseconds between animation updates within the simulation.
tolerance	Indicates how much pad there is around objects in order to prevent interpenetration due to ambitious animation distances. It's like an invisible bumper around a given mesh.

TABLE 12.4 Continued

Property	Description
Rigid Body Properties	
active	Any rigid body may be either active (TRUE) or inactive (FALSE). If the object is inactive, it does not move or respond to environmental physics until acted upon by another object.
angularMomentum	Mass multiplied by the magnitude of the rigid body's angular velocity.
angularVelocity	The speed and direction in which a given rigid body is rotating, expressed as a vector.
centerOfMass	A vector representing any offset from the rigid body's pivot point to the center of mass.
corrector	This property actually holds a reference to the corrector object, which in turn has the following properties: #enabled, #level, #maxDistance, #maxTries, #multiplier, and #threshold. This property modifies the behavior of the correctorMoveTo() command.
force	The amount of pressure or pushing that is acting upon a given rigid body.
friction	Access to the amount of friction that the rigid body must overcome in order to slide across another object.
linearMomentum	Mass multiplied by the magnitude of the object's linear velocity.
linearVelocity	The speed and direction in which the object is translating, expressed as a vector.
mass	The mass of the object in kilograms.
name	The name of a rigid body.
pinned	Sticks the rigid body to its location. The object does not move unless it is specifically released.
position	Provides direct access to the world-relative position of the rigid body, expressed as a vector.
restitution	Indicates the bounce or elasticity of a given rigid body.
rotation	Provides direct access to the world-relative rotation of the rigid body, expressed as a vector.
torque	Indicates the amount of angular force or pressure that is acting upon the rigid body.

TABLE 12.4   Continued

Property	Description
Spring Properties	
damping	Indicates the speed at which restoration to restLength should occur.
elasticity	Indicates the springiness of the spring and the strength of the spring to return to its rest length.
name	The name of the spring.
onExtension	A Boolean that determines whether the spring will attempt to return to its rest length when the spring is extended.
onCompression	A Boolean that determines whether the spring will attempt to return to its rest length when the spring is compressed.
pointA	A vector representing a position relative to the first rigid body in a given spring to which the spring should be attached.
pointB	A vector representing a position relative to the second rigid body in a given spring to which the spring should be attached.
restLength	Indicates the ideal length of the spring (the length that the spring tries to return to when force is removed).
Dashpot Properties	
damping	Controls the speed with which the dashpot returns to a rest state.
name	The name of the given dashpot.
pointA	The attachment point relative to rigid body A of the dashpot.
pointB	The attachment point relative to rigid body B of the dashpot.
rotation	The angle in which the angular dashpot tries to remain between world space and a given rigid body.
strength	Controls the pull to return to the rest state.

As you can see, the Havok Xtra provides you with extremely deep access to the properties of rigid bodies within a given simulation.

NOTE

If you are considering working with the Havok Xtra, I strongly urge you to read the documentation that comes with the Xtra and that is available for download on the Havok Web site at
`http://www.havok.com/xtra/`.

It is the methods of the Xtra that really get things moving. Using Havok's built-in methods enables you to move objects within the world in a new manner. Up to this point, we have used keyframe or scripted incremental translations to move our models around. In a physics-based simulation, we can apply forces to objects and then allow those objects to move in response to the effects of physics on them.

To see the list of functions of any Xtra in authoring mode, simply type the following command into the message window, substituting the name of the Xtra for `"havok"`:

```
put interface(xtra "havok")
```

Director returns a list of the functions, but they aren't very well documented in this case. Table 12.5 provides a quick overview of their purposes.

TABLE 12.5   The Functions of the Havok Physics Xtra

Function	Description
Member Functions	
deleteAngularDashpot()	Removes the object of the given name from the physics simulation.
deleteLinearDashpot()	Removes the object of the given name from the physics simulation.
deleteRigidBody()	Removes the object of the given name from the physics simulation.
deleteSpring()	Removes the object of the given name from the physics simulation.
disableAllCollisions()	Disables collisions between a given rigid body and all the other rigid bodies in the scene.
disableCollision()	Disables collisions between the two given rigid bodies.
enableAllCollisions()	Enables collisions between a given rigid body and all the other rigid bodies in the scene.

TABLE 12.5   Continued

Function	Description
enableCollision()	Enables collisions between the two given rigid bodies.
initialize()	Used to set the initial values of a blank Havok cast member.
makeAngularDashpot()	Creates a new angular dashpot.
makeFixedRigidBody()	Creates a new rigid body, with a mass of 0, from a given model.
makeLinearDashpot()	Creates a new linear dashpot.
makeMovableRigidBody()	Creates a new movable rigid body of a given mass from a given model.
makeSpring()	Creates a new spring.
registerInterest()	Allows for the setup of collision callback handlers for collisions between given models.
registerStepCallback()	Creates a callback handler to notify of advancements in the simulation time step.
removeInterest()	Stops the recording and notification of collision events for the given rigid body.
removeStepCallback()	Removes the referenced callback for time intervals.
reset()	Resets the Havok "*.HKE" cast member to its initial state.
shutdown()	Stops the physics simulation and flushes it out of memory.
step()	Moves the simulation ahead by the given time increment.
Rigid Body Functions	
applyAngularImpulse()	Applies rotational force around the given axis of the given magnitude. The effect is immediate.
applyForce()	Like the name implies, this function applies a force to the rigid body. A force takes time to affect the rigid body.
applyForceAtPoint()	Applies a force to the object at a point (specified by an offset vector) other than the center of the object's mass.
applyImpulse()	Similar to a force, but the effect of an impulse is immediate.
applyImpulseAtPoint()	Similar to applyForceAtPoint() but the effect is immediate.
applyTorque()	Applies rotational force around a given axis of the given magnitude. The effect is not immediate.

TABLE 12.5　Continued

Function	Description
attemptMoveTo()	Returns TRUE if the attempted move to a position and a given axis angle does not interpenetrate another model. Returns FALSE if interpenetration would be the result.
correctorMoveTo()	Attempts to move the object to a noninterpenetrating position and axis angle using impulses.
interpolatingMoveTo()	Similar to Lingo's interpolateTo() function, but this function auto-corrects if interpenetration occurs.

Now that you've seen the basic things the Havok Physics Xtra is designed to do, I'm going to show you some examples. I'll walk you through the creation of a little dice demo inside 3D Studio Max, and then we'll use some default Havok and Director behaviors to breathe life into the simulation. Next, we'll use Lingo to tweak the dice demo, and finally we'll create a Havok-enhanced version of the bouncing ball from the beginning of this chapter.

Havok: From Max to Shockwave

The first thing you need to do to use the Havok Xtra is to install the Havok behaviors by moving them into your Director Libs folder. These behaviors are very helpful when you start working with the Havok cast members.

There are two ways to bring Havok physics into play in Director: by importing an HKE file from your favorite modeling and animation package or by inserting a new blank HKE file within Director.

In this section, I'll describe the former method using 3D Studio Max and the Havok plug-in to create the HKE file. I'll walk you through the steps that were required to create the havokViaMax.dir demonstration file that's on your CD-ROM.

Open the movie now. Rewind it and click Play to see how the dice work. Use your mouse to left-click and drag each of the dice independently. Note that the dice obey the laws of gravity and respond to collisions with one another.

I created this W3D file in 3D Studio Max, using the Havok plug-in to generate a rigid body group and then adding each of the dice to the group. I put a Havok plane where the ground plane is drawn and then added it to the rigid body group.

I set the weight of each of the dice, exported them, and then imported them into Director. Once in Director, I added a Havok initialize behavior and a move model action with a left-mouse trigger.

The only custom work in the whole movie is the artwork for the dice. All together it took about 30 minutes. Most of the time invested was in Photoshop making die faces. My point is that the Havok Xtra costs you a little extra download time, but the functions that are added to the game can be really magnificent.

The specific procedures involved in exporting the Havok file from your 3D modeling environment vary depending on the plug-in you use and the modeling software you are working with. You may not even have a software package that is capable of exporting HKE files. Fear not, there is still a very viable way to bring Havok into your game. In the following exercise, I'll explain how to create a rigid body dynamics simulation from scratch using only Director.

Exercise 12.2:   Using Havok with Lingo

Follow each of the steps in this exercise in order to generate your own custom physics simulation using Lingo (I've supplied you with a general-purpose 3D member to get you started):

1. Open the file labeled havokViaLingo.dir on your CD-ROM.

2. Using the Insert drop-down menu, choose Insert, Media Element, Havok Physics Scene. You should see a new cast member appear in the first available slot in the cast. It sports that cool Havok icon.

3. Give your physics scene member a name. For this exercise, call it havok.

4. Now you have to initialize the member. (This part is tough.) Choose Window, Library Palette from the Window menu at the top of the interface. Click the Cast Selection button on the upper-left hand side of the Library Palette and select the Havok Setup Cast.

   Note that if you didn't add these to Director's Libs folder earlier, you'll need to close Director and add them now. Put them in Director 8.5\Libs\Havok in order to find them easily and then restart Director and reopen the movie.

5. In the Setup cast, you will find two behaviors called Havok Physics. One is followed by the characters (HKE), and the other is followed by the phrase (No HKE). Drag the one named Havok Physics (No HKE) onto the 3D sprite on the stage. A dialog like the one shown in Figure 12.2 will appear.

FIGURE 12.2

Setting the parameters for the Havok Physics (No HKE) behavior.

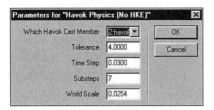

6. Set the dialog properties as they appear in the figure:

The Which Havoc Cast Member drop-down menu should point to the Havok cast member you created.

The Tolerance setting is used to determine how much space or invisible buffer should be created around objects in order to discourage inter-penetration during collisions.

The Time Step setting is used to determine the time in milliseconds that should be calculated between time steps. In this case, the simulation will be called upon to update the display once each frame.

The Substeps setting is the number of subdivided calculations you want the system to make between time steps. The more time steps, the more correct the simulation, but the tradeoff is a big slowdown in performance.

The World Scale value is the scale of the world relative to Havok's default scale, which is 1 unit equals 1 meter. The setting 0.0254 converts the scale to 1 inch per unit. (Table 12.6. contains a quick reference for Havok scale conversions.) Click OK.

TABLE 12.6   Havok Scale Conversions

Original Scale	Havok World Scale Setting
1 parsec	30856770000000000.0000
1 light year	9460500000000000.0000

1 astronomical unit	149598550000.0000
1 nautical mile	1852.0000
1 mile	1609.3440
1 kilometer	1000.0000
1 furlong	201.1680
1 cable	182.8800
1 Hectometer	100.0000
1 chain	20.1168
1 fathom	1.8288
1 meter	1.0000
1 yard	0.9144
1 ell	0.8750
1 foot	0.3048
1 hand	0.1060
1 decimeter	0.1000
1 centimeter	0.0100
1 inch	0.0254

7. Grab the `Make Fixed Rigid Body` behavior and drop it on the 3D sprite. A dialog like the one shown in Figure 12.3 appears.

FIGURE 12.3

Setting the parameters for the `Make Fixed Rigid Body` behavior.

8. Set the dialog properties as they appear in the figure:

   Set Which Model to `Plane01`. We are using the fixed rigid body on the plane because we don't want the ground to move.

   Leave the Restitution (bounciness) value set at `0.3000`, the default.

Leave the Friction value set at 0.3000, the default.

It is important to note that because the plane is made of vertices that all are aligned on the same plane (it's coplanar), we need to set the Type parameter to Concave rather than any of the convex options. Click OK.

9. Grab the Make Moveable Rigid Body behavior and throw it on the 3D sprite. Select GeoSphere01 from the Which Model drop-down list (see Figure 12.4) and accept all the other parameters' default settings. Click OK.

FIGURE 12.4

The parameters for the GeoSphere behavior.

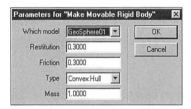

10. Grab one more Make Moveable Rigid Body behavior and throw it on the 3D sprite. Select Cylinder01 from the Which Model drop-down list and accept all the other parameters' default settings. Click OK.

11. Switch your Library palette to the Havok Control cast. There you'll find a behavior called Move Model. Add the behavior to the 3D sprite and accept the default values in the Parameters dialog (see Figure 12.5) by clicking OK.

FIGURE 12.5

Default values for the Move Model behavior.

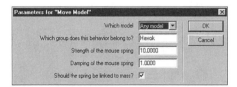

12. Switch your Library palette to the 3D Triggers tab and grab the mouseLeft trigger. Drop this trigger on the 3D sprite. The default parameters (shown in Figure 12.6) are perfect, so click OK.

FIGURE 12.6

Parameters for the mouseLeft trigger.

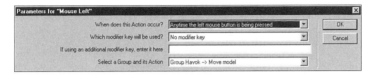

13. Rewind the movie and click Play. Grab and drag either the tree or the ball to watch the physics in action.

Although we did take advantage of a bunch of prebuilt behaviors in this exercise, these are fundamentally no different from behaviors that you might build yourself to access the methods and properties of the Havok Xtra.

The potential for collision and physics bring Director's 3D game potential right to the bleeding edge of Web-centric 3D. Now that you've had a chance to poke around with most of these new 3D features, you are probably anxious to start making some more substantial games.

In Part III, I'll let you watch over my shoulder and guide you through parallel exercises as I create a detailed real-time 3D game. We'll go into much greater detail regarding the creation of specific 3D features and creation of real-time game elements than we have in any of the previous examples as we span four chapters with a single real-time 3D game.

PART III

Putting Strategies into Action

Spend a month hovering over the back of my chair
and eavesdropping on my phone calls as I include you
in every sordid detail surrounding the design and
creation of a real-time 3D game for Shockwave.

CHAPTER 13

17 Keys: Week One

I'm taking a different approach to the chapters in this part of the book. I think learning new skill sets is sometimes made easier by following along with people who are using those very skills—people who can also talk their way through a project so that you not only see what's being done but also get a sense of the thought process involved.

So, welcome to inside my head. I'm giving you an all-access backstage pass to my brain while I go through the creation process of a real-time 3D game called *17 Keys*. Each chapter in Part III, "Putting Strategies into Action," is a series of journal entries documenting the evolution of this game's development.

Day One

I hate that "blank page" feeling I get when I am about to start a new project. It is absurd, really. When I'm in the middle of a project, I invariably have thousands of ideas each day that would make fabulous games, but the moment I'm actually sitting down to begin creating the game I've decided to pursue, I get that "What's next?" feeling. Know what I mean?

I know what's next. I've decided to pursue the idea of a real-time 3D game. I have tons of ideas for the game and a good solid sense of where it should go over the next month. As usual, however, I haven't done a terribly good job of organizing or assembling these ideas. I really need a good treatment and a solid spec.

I could easily spend six months on these elements alone, but that won't pay any bills, so I'm going to give myself an independent developer's schedule. I've got one week. It makes sense to do it this way because I have about a month to complete the project, and this puts just about one quarter of the total project effort into planning. That is a good planning-to-action ratio. I don't have to work entirely in a vacuum. I work with several people who can help, and you may hear me talk about them from time to time as we move forward.

Meet My Team

My game company, Insight Interactive Games, is a collection of artists, developers, and programmers. Sophia Varcados is a talented illustrator and graphic artist. Sophia works with me on most of my projects. She has a genuine knack for kid-centric images and is a genius with animal illustration. Sophia has done the graphics for my most successful efforts, and I'll probably ask her to do the texture maps for at least some of the characters in *17 Keys*.

Vincent Argentina is a brilliant young Director 3D developer. Vinnie is the sort of guy who breathes in broken code and exhales miracles. He's the only person I've met who shares my peculiar ability to dream code solutions that actually work when I wake up.

Matt Kew is a wonderful Flash designer and musician. He will be helping with the audio for the game and may even help me overcome my Flash phobias enough to integrate a little Flash.

These people are my greatest strength. It is always important to surround yourself with people who are more clever, creative, and gifted than you are. They will bring out the best in you and your project. More important than their talent is the fact that they are all good people and good friends. Never enter into a business agreement with someone you don't trust—or don't like. The benefit is never worth the cost.

So now that you've met everyone, I had better get to work. I need to start by knocking together a treatment for the game and then move on to some sketches and the spec.

Writing the Treatment

I know that I want this game to include an engaging story that enhances the gameplay. That means that I don't want the story to get in the way of gameplay. I also don't want the gameplay to be devoid of purpose (story.)

I want this thing to be driven by the narrative, but I don't want the exposition to be passive. What's more, I want to do it all without ever bringing the polygon count above 3,000 visible polygons. I'm such an easy guy to please. I'm going to follow the same path to create the treatment and spec that I suggest in Chapter 2, "Making Plans," although the resources are included with the spec.

17 Keys

17 Keys is a single-player online action-adventure game. It is intended for teens through adults. Similar in gameplay to many action-adventure style games, this one will feature a series of episodic elements that combine an expanding narrative with puzzles, challenges, and arcade elements.

17 Keys is unique because of its visual style and its roots in ancient Celtic mythology and Roman tradition. It will be a fantastic journey. It is a surprising and whimsical world that has little respect for the laws of nature, physics, or logic.

Platforms

The game will be designed to run on Mac OS 9.1 and higher as well as Windows 95 and higher. Users will require a graphics card that supports OpenGL or DirectX 7 or higher. The game will run in software mode, but we won't make any promises about performance in this mode. Users running in software mode will be encouraged to change their mode to a faster one.

The game will run in Macromedia Shockwave 8.5. It will be delivered online via initial and subsequent streaming downloads. The initial download will not exceed 650KB. Subsequent streams will be limited to 300KB packets, which should stream while the user is noninteractive or distracted. Cumulative limits should remain under 10MB, and users should be given the option to download the entire game in a PC or Mac executable version.

Players

17 Keys is designed for single-player gameplay. The game will generally be played online in order to allow network download of the initial game and subsequent levels.

Scoring will be handled through a central game-scoring server. Players who remain online during gameplay will be able to compare their score to the scores of other players.

OVERVIEWS

Ask yourself these questions while writing an overview of the game. What style of game is this? To what audience will it appeal? What other games could be compared to this one? What are the differences between the proposed game and the others?

PLATFORMS

Ask yourself this question while choosing the target platforms for the game: On which computer platforms will the game run? Give specific operating systems and versions. Realize that the broader your support, the more time this will cost you.

PLAYERS

Ask yourself these questions while choosing the number of players for the game: How many people will be able to play the game at one time? If more than one, is this an online game? Will it be networked?

Interface

Because the player will most likely interact with this game using a keyboard and mouse, I'd like to take advantage of this peculiar combination of tools. Most of the gamespace will be comprised of the 3D window, capable of displaying third-person, map, and first-person views of the world.

The outer edge of the display will contain 2D sprites that create (or appear to create) sliding control racks. Usually the triggering of such a rack will disable the screen so that the player may examine the contents of his pack or adjust game settings. During arcade-style episodes, the 3D screen will remain active and the rack will display updated stats that help the player understand his interaction with the game elements (usually point-and-shoot combined with scoring data in the rack).

Overlays will be used to indicate scoring and life force, and onscreen effects will be combined with sound effects to demonstrate painful encounters with enemies or obstacles. Occasionally, characters will encounter and speak with others. The dialogue will appear in a slide-in rack with an icon representing the character speaking off to the side of each line of dialogue.

In the tradition of the early action-adventure games for personal computers, the player will be allowed to type in questions, and a simple text-parsing engine will attempt to match these queries to reasonable replies.

Walkthrough

FADE IN

EXT. VILLAGE – NIGHT

A bizarre dragon-man (Liam) exhales a blast of flame and reels back as the cheering of a bloodthirsty mob swells. Hints of human and not-so-human faces form a ring around the panicked creature as he squares off against an aged man in traditional wizard's clothing.

LIAM

What more could you want of me, Wyrick?

INTERFACE

How will the player give and get information from the application? What mechanisms will you use to help the player know what is happening? What mechanisms will you use to make play more fun and less work?

WALKTHROUGH

Describe the manner in which the game will be introduced to the player. Will there be backstory or cinematics? Will there be credits or instructions? Will the player be given the opportunity to adjust any preferences? What will a typical game be like? Use screenwriting style to unify the elements and create scripts for typical cinematics or narrative exchanges.

▼

The old man grins a wry, rotten-toothed grin and rears back his wand. The blast from the thin metal rod is improbably green and swells in size as it approaches young Liam. He reaches for a shield but is slowed by his wounds and meets the bulk of the blast head on. A green orb surrounds his paralyzed frame. Electric charges lock the orb to the ground.

WYRICK

Didimus unus, geminus unus. Unus scindo. Unus scindo geminus. Auctoritas…gravitas…severitas. Didimus unus, geminus unus. Didimus unus, geminus unus. Unus scindo. Unus scindo geminus. Didimus unus, geminus unus.

As the old man's crackling mantra continues, the ball emits an ever-escalating, pulsing glow. The stiff figure inside shudders and suddenly screams. His body separates and tears as the orb splits into two. However, he is not severed in the conventional sense. Half of him becomes man, and half becomes dragon. Music swells as both man and dragon fall to the ground in separate heaps.

The ancient sorcerer laughs as the dragon, LIDO, disoriented and furious spits a ball of flame at AMED, the other half of his former self. Amed raises his shield and draws his blade. The injured dragon inflates and rises to the air, lunging toward the camera as the screen fades to black.

SLATE: *17 Keys*

The title screen offers the player the opportunity to check his configuration and keyboard/mouse control settings. It will also introduce him to the sliding-racks system by using the same racks to display these parameters. An optional help screen will be available via this introductory slate as well. The start buttons will allow the player to choose whether he wants to play the game as Amed or Lido.

If he chooses Lido, he will be taken to the forest with Lido already in flight. If he chooses Amed, he will find him running through the forest. The player will be able to control either character using the keyboard arrows or the W, A, S, and D keys. These control methods should feel fairly intuitive to most players.

WALKTHROUGH
CONTINUED

▼

The player now has a serious problem. An early encounter with his former other half will demonstrate that the relationship between them is not good. The opponent will try to attack the player's chosen character and take whatever tokens he has gathered from the world. The heart of the problem is that his opponent has no memory of them or their former life as one creature.

As if this weren't enough to deal with, Wyrick's minions are scattered throughout the forest looking for the player's character and will attack whenever they encounter him. Finally, there are various obstacles and puzzles presented by the forest itself.

As the player begins to travel throughout the space, he may learn from any number of villagers that the only way to restore his former self and defeat the evil Wyrick is to find the sacred keys and unlock the obelisk. He must also do so with the cooperation of his other self.

The story engine will find a way to introduce the narrative concepts to the player by planting the exposition in the dialogue of virtually any character the player encounters early in gameplay. Ideally, these expositional elements will be triggered by conflicts between the player and the character he meets.

A Typical Encounter with a Minion

An alarm sounds and a strange sort of portal slides onto the main viewport into the 3D world. This will replace the top view map if a map is currently in place. Within the portal a first-person camera will display the forest with a strange red glow. Camera motions will mimic the motions of the minion as it approaches.

Minions vary greatly in size and strength, but they are all based loosely on forest or village groundcover objects. If either hero destroys a minion, it reverts to its proper form and is then sometimes usable as a game token. For example, PATECK, a third-level minion of Wyrick, is born of an owl. A battle with Pateck might transpire as follows.

EXT. FOREST – NIGHT

Lido hovers above the ground for a moment and then lands gently on two legs. He walks slowly through the dense trees searching for precious food.

WALKTHROUGH
CONTINUED

▼

He hears a strange and alarming noise and senses that he is not alone. The player controlling Lido is aware of this sense, because a discolored second view of the forest has slid into the viewing area. As player and dragon work to reorient themselves, Pateck strikes with a magic bolt from amid the darkened forest.

The dragon returns the favor with several balls of fire, and the struggling minion squeals and then vanishes, only to be replaced by a beautiful owl.

OWL

Thank you.

PLAYER (LIDO)

Who are you?

OWL

That's a bit personal don't you think?

PLAYER

What happened?

OWL

Full of questions aren't you?

This continues until either the player triggers some important information or becomes frustrated and moves on. Characters will frequently be designed to return questions with questions in order to encourage feelings of conflict within the player. Eventually the player will realize that exchanging information will help secure new information.

A Typical Encounter with a Villager

Villagers are naturally predisposed to various emotional states that will strongly temper their choices. Although some villagers do have food or other tokens to trade, most simply have information.

WALKTHROUGH
CONTINUED

▼

A discussion with a villager is similar to a discussion with a forest creature, although a villager will always have something, either physical or emotional, that he or she will want from the character.

If the player provides the villager with what he or she is after, the villager will no longer be motivated to give the player any information. The player must negotiate with the villager and only offer portions of the desired goods; otherwise, the villager will win the negotiation and the player will walk away empty handed.

A Typical Death of Either Heroic Figure

When either Lido or Amed is defeated, the physical body will simply collapse and then fizzle to transparent. There will be no graphic displays of deaths, and no vivid sense that the character has been killed. This is just an end to the life force meter and the beginning of either a new round or a new game.

The Big Boss Battle with Wyrick

This will be typical of big boss battles in adventure games. Any attempt to tackle the wizard Wyrick before the player has converged back into Liam will be met with immediate death.

Once the pair are reunited, and Liam has sufficient magical powers, he will be able to square off against Wyrick. Even then, however, the battle will be a tough twitch-finger fight. It will be the sort of shoot-and-evade classic that leaves your fingers numb.

Objectives

The player wants to find the keys, visit the sacred obelisk, reunite himself with his broken half, and put an end to the reign of the evil wizard. His immediate wants will also include collecting food, gathering money, buying weapons, learning how to reunite himself, and finding shelter.

If the player wants to survive, he'll avoid battles with enemies who are more powerful than he is and work to increase his battle skills.

WALKTHROUGH
CONTINUED

OBJECTIVES

List and explain the objectives that a typical player would have while playing the game. What sort of things will the player try to do? What will/should the player want?

Entities/Sprites

Here's a list of the characters and entities in the game:

- *Liam.* The combined dragon-man hero of the game. The combining of Liam's two halves is the goal of the game.
- *Amed.* The man part of Liam, more boy than man.
- *Lido.* The dragon part of Liam.
- *Wyrick.* The ancient sorcerer who plagues this forest.
- *Minions of Wyrick.* A myriad of dark creatures, including trolls, ogres, and spiders.
- *Villagers.* The rough hewn and earthy residents of the village.
- *Forest creatures.* A fantastic assortment of animals, birds, and reptiles. Some are dangerous; some not.

Chrome

The overall look of this game will be starkly separated into two distinct visual styles. The animatics/slate elements will have a charcoal drawing freeze-frame aesthetic. They will be a sort of cross between comic books and classical drawings. The animatics will not be full-motion video. They will be comprised of a series of still drawings, sound effects, and music. Some of the drawings will be in black and white and some in color.

The actual game will be much less detailed. Although there will be some logical crossover from the drawings, it is not that important for the characters to match perfectly from still to 3D. The 3D models will be very simple and very low polygon. We'll rely on texture maps to reveal the characters convincingly and try not to get too hung up in the geometry of characters within the 3D space. The focus here will be on animation—both speed and effectiveness of motion/collision. The color palette of the 3D space will be fairly bold and fairly simple.

The architecture of the village should suggest medieval age dwellings and businesses. Clothing on characters should be roughly the same period, although there is plenty of room for whimsy in the approach to either.

Overlays and racks should be semitransparent, and the overall aesthetic of the interface should reflect the architecture and costume. It should have a hint of magic, and plenty of silliness. It shouldn't take itself too seriously.

ENTITIES

Who or what are the characters in this game? Is there anything unusual about them?

CHROME

Describe the overall aesthetic style of the game. Does it have a look? Does its appearance refer to a location, historical period, or artistic style? What is the color palette? Are there any patterns, shapes, forms, or textures that are prevalent or repeat in the chrome?

Day Two

I finished up the treatment yesterday and began contacting the members of the team I plan to work with on this project. I can't help thinking about some of the specific problems I've given myself with the various elements in this treatment, and I have to admit that I'm a bit concerned that some of the features may be overzealous, given the time frame.

I'm particularly concerned about the text-parsing engine. Both Vinnie and I have been dreading putting one of these things together, but I really do think that even a mediocre one would at least give us a chance to explore the algorithms and perhaps begin to build a library. I'm not concerned about most of the rest of it, although I do think there may be more art to create than is reasonable for Sophia alone, so I'm bracing myself for some long nights of drawing ahead.

One of my major goals for this project is to do a good job of integrating narrative and historical (exposition) elements into the game without resorting to voiceovers and other passive forms of exposition. I think that the opening animatic gets us off to a great start on that account, and if we simply maintain that philosophy throughout the game, we should be fine.

Permit me to explain this point in a bit more detail. If it isn't fresh in your mind, go back to the walkthrough section of the treatment for *17 Keys* and examine the description of the opening animatic. This section is written in typical screen-writing format because games and films have a good deal in common.

One of the first things I teach my screenwriters is that you never write novels in a screenplay's action sections. Those are the paragraphs that describe the events that are occurring onscreen. Often young writers want to express the inner feelings of the characters and explain the rationale that a given character has for making a given choice. They will write phrases such as "He thinks that she is right." This is silly, given the end medium.

A screenplay script is intended for film. Any description of action should be limited to descriptions of things that the audience can see. The same principle is true for games.

The audience must learn narrative concepts, inner thoughts, and expositional elements as the result of some outward expression. This is best served up as the result of conflict.

Imagine this opening battle with the wizard presented in a different manner. Suppose that I simply recorded a voiceover with a person telling us the story of a man-dragon who was split into two parts by an evil wizard during a fierce battle.

This would not be nearly as effective. Why? Because the audience doesn't have any stake in the conflict. In the voiceover version, the audience is told everything in an uninvolved, passionless blurb. If the audience knows everything about a given moment onscreen, it doesn't have any need to remain engaged. You have to leave some part of the algorithm unsolved or variable. It's the guessing about the unexplained moments that keeps an audience interested.

The reason that these expositional elements are best revealed through moments of conflict is similar. Conflicts inherently leave an element unrevealed. The victor in any given conflict is always unknown. The other advantage that conflict brings to the table when the goal is the revelation of some vital element of exposition is justification.

"Why now?" is a beautiful, haunting, and imperative question. Why does your character choose to reveal this important exposition now? Most of the time, obvious or passive exposition can be exposed (pardon the pun) with this one simple question.

If there is conflict, the exposition can almost always emerge as a result of one character's attempt to win the negotiation, but when no conflict exists, the audience will not see a justification for the exposition and will immediately lose interest in the game, story, or film.

The reason I wrote the opening battle scene was to teach the player that he needs to avenge this action and rejoin with his other half. If I do my job correctly, the player will only see a cool battle.

Exercise 13.1:   Writing Active Exposition

Try the following to get you thinking of ways to write active exposition. Write a walkthrough of a space that is likely to create conflict and reveals exposition actively. Use the walkthrough of *17 Keys* to guide you. The following is a summary of the basic elements of screenwriting/game scripting to help you lay out your description:

- Slug lines are lines that denote the location and time of day of a given scene. There should be one slug line every time you change location or time of day.

Slug lines are always written with every character in capital letters. They always begin with either EXT. or INT. to denote whether the scene is exterior or interior.

Slug lines have three parts: the exterior-interior label, the location, and the time of day.

- Action paragraphs are normally formatted paragraphs that describe exactly what the audience or player will see onscreen. In games, these paragraphs can include descriptions of the interface and options. These paragraphs are limited to descriptions of events and actions and should never include discussions of themes or interior motivations.

  The first time a character is included in an action paragraph, that character's name appears entirely in capital letters.

- Dialogue is divided into two parts: the character's name designation and the line itself. The name always appears a single space above the line and tabbed to a point that places the left edge of the name against an invisible centerline. This is not the same as centered. The dialogue lines are tabbed in by one or two tabs from the left margin and are inset from the right margin by the same amount. They look a bit like block quotes.

- Each of the three previous elements is separated by a blank line.

Day Three

I've begun work on the technical specification (spec) for the game. There are a couple of things that rise to the top of my list of concerns.

I realized some time ago that the key to my vision for narrative management involves using a device I call *story flocking*. Flocking is the behavior of birds and or animals that causes them to travel/move in groups that are fundamentally ordered.

I introduced this concept early in the book (you may remember the brief discussion of narrative management models in Chapter 1, "The Story: How Much Is Too Much"?), and now want to explain it in more detail. So what the heck does the flight patterns of birds have to do with managing the delivery of story elements during gameplay?

The narrative-management object is free to encourage and discourage meetings between the hero and other characters in the game. One approach to encouraging encounters between agents and the player is through creating physical and conceptual steering behaviors that will guide adversarial agents toward one another.

In flocking, each agent is assigned behaviors that control his navigational decisions. The flight of birds is essentially autonomous, once it begins. In a similar sense, conflicts that are designed to increase the player's awareness of the history, traditions, conventions, and goals of the game may be encouraged by providing autonomous agents with dynamically controlled behaviors that increase the chances of a confrontation.

In a spatial sense, no matter where the character travels in the world space, the important conflicts (represented by various agents within the gamespace) flock toward him. The narrative-management object controls the properties of the autonomous agents that determine their avoidance or attraction and guide them toward confrontations and eventual negotiations with the player.

In general, coordinating the narrative elements of the game with the steering behaviors of autonomous agents has several advantages and several pitfalls.

The advantages include limited CPU cycles compared to more sophisticated models that attempt to form neural nets and root through massive databases to make narrative decisions and coordinate narrative elements with a player's level of experience.

The pitfalls are that the narrative does in fact remain fairly fixed. Although the order in which a player encounters episodes remains flexible, the episode remains fairly static and the player needs to encounter a given number of similar conflicts before the system allows him to be exposed to more taxing confrontations.

As you become accustomed to working with computers, this pattern of loss of freedom and dynamics as a tradeoff for control seems more and more familiar. Virtually any program or aspect of a program becomes less flexible the easier it is to work with.

In *17 Keys*, we'll work to accomplish a feeling of control and randomness by making the common elements difficult to discern while putting as much freedom as possible into the choices of the agents without completely abandoning our need to communicate some ideas to the player.

If we were working on a much longer development cycle or with a much larger team, I'd push these boundaries. As it is, I think that these restrictions must be in place if we are to finish the game within a reasonable timeframe.

In a practical sense, this means that as I create the spec for the game I'll be working to balance my desire to integrate the story seamlessly with the available resources and time. I've included the complete spec for *17 Keys* in Appendix D, "*17 Keys* Technical Specification."

Day Four

I should probably keep planning, but I'm so excited about this game that it's getting harder and harder not to just dive in. I'm going to do some sketching today, so I probably won't have much to write. I'll show you the sketches as I finish them.

First, I want to get a rough idea of the lowest possible number of polygons on a human-like model. Figure 13.1 shows this sketch.

FIGURE 13.1

A basic map of polygons on a humanoid figure.

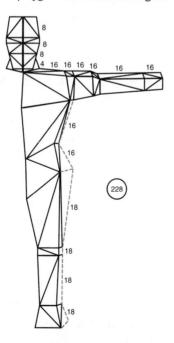

I think I can do it with fewer than 250 polygons, but I'll have to see how it animates. I don't have much faith in the underarm or waist joints, and I hope that there is no need to do much with the neck. The ankles will never work well as illustrated here. There are lots of problems, but I want to keep the count insanely low. Figure 13.2 shows a sketch of another version of my model.

FIGURE 13.2

Polycount study of a humanoid with dragon wings.

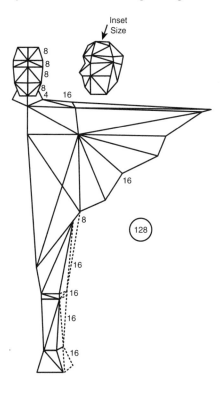

Polygon counts in typical game characters generally range from 600 to 1,200 polygons when the character is displayed in full detail. In Shockwave, I'll want to go as light as possible.

I'm going to need to really look at this carefully to see whether I can get the shape right with this few polygons. It would be great if I can, because the battle between Wyrick and Liam is technically the most complex in terms of animated models onscreen at one time.

I have a fairly clear image in my head of Liam standing solemnly after a victory, in semi-silhouette, looking a bit smug. This sketch (see Figure 13.3) is my earliest stab at that image. I want him to look satisfied but still a bit unresolved. The image should suggest finality, but leave open the question of exactly what happened to Wyrick.

FIGURE 13.3

Rough idea for the glory shot of Liam.

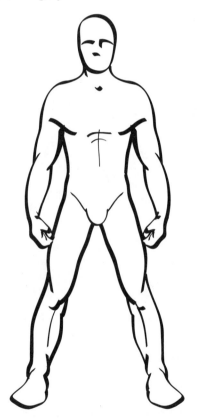

Amed's face is not completely human. Even after the split, he retains some dragon/reptilian characteristics. The real puzzle then is how to make him look heroic without losing some reference to his total personae. I did a couple of sketches of him (see Figures 13.4 and 13.5) to get my mind moving in that direction and to give a little guidance to Sophia.

FIGURE 13.4

Thinking about Amed's face.

Villains are traditionally asymmetrical. The key to making a character look evil involves making the eyes different sizes and asymmetrical as well as making the nose crooked. We all pretend that we don't judge people by their appearance, but we do. At least we do in animation and games. Figures 13.6 and 13.7 show my first sketches of the sorcerer Wyrick.

FIGURE 13.5

More thoughts about Amed's face.

FIGURE 13.6

Wyrick casting a spell.

FIGURE 13.7

Wyrick's face.

All the minions of Wyrick will share a model resource. My sketch for this is shown in Figure 13.8. I'll probably have to flush out the head and joints a bit but I think it could come in under 200 polygons.

FIGURE 13.8

Polycount study for the typical minion of Wyrick.

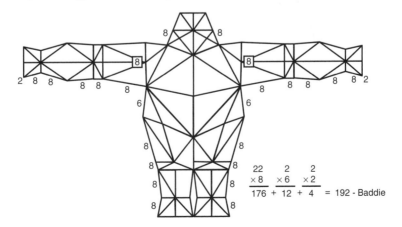

The quadruped will be scaled to make a large variant and a small variant. The bird will have an evil skin and a good skin. Changing texture maps on the same models to convey completely different images can be a very powerful tool. It allows you to conserve development-time and runtime resources. There are several other incidental models in the game, but I'm not terribly worried about how to conserve polygons on these items. Figure 13.9 shows my sketch of these creatures.

FIGURE 13.9

Study for the polygons in the bird and quadruped.

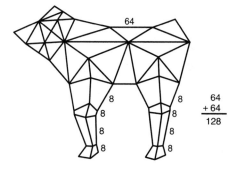

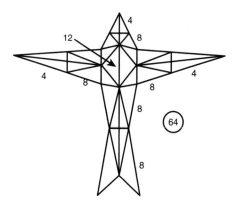

The next step for these models is to start building them and creating textures. I want to do a little more preliminary testing during this planning phase before I commit to a collision detection and resolution method. I'll work on that tomorrow.

Day Five

Collision, collision, collision! I've been begging for months now for a way to detect which models are within a given camera's view frustum. Eden Sochat, from Shells Interactive, listened to my pleas and built an Xtra called "Whatsinview" that does just this.

The Xtra is cross-platform and Shockwave safe, so it is a viable option for this project. This is a simple Xtra. It has one function: It returns a detailed list of all the models currently in view of the given camera within a given member. In practical game-creation terms, the implications are terrific. One of the biggest problems involved in collision and proximity detection is limiting the range of models that should be analyzed. Let me paint a picture.

Pretend that we have a complex world with dozens of cabins and hundreds of trees, a village, a host of bad guys, creatures, and a "big boss" bad guy. This world will drop Shockwave to its knees if we try to display everything at one time. If we divide the world up into a grid of areas, however, we could theoretically display only those objects within the viewing range of the camera.

The easiest way to determine what the user is able to see is to examine a list of the items within the camera's view. If we spot the ground plane for a given grid section, then we could just switch on all the models for that area. Likewise, we could switch off the models for another grid that's no longer in view.

An even more exciting use of the Xtra involves the use of steering behaviors. The view volume of a camera is a cubic region defined by the field of view angle, the hither (near clipping plane), and the yon (far clipping plane.) It's like a big pyramid, and the objects that appear in this pyramid are what the Xtra reports. Because of this, we can create a custom camera designed to only see the items we want to detect collisions on and then clip the view frustum to meet our ideal collision parameters.

Cameras have a root node that allows the models that will display in a given camera to be specifically set. That means that we can choose to ignore certain models—ones that we don't care about colliding with. I ran a few tests and found that using ray casting to find models in my path dropped my performance from 30 frames per second to less than 10 frames per second in a world with about 2,500 polygons, whereas using the Whatsinview Xtra had a barely perceivable performance effect.

I'll want to do some more testing, but I think that this may be the foundation of collision detection within *17 Keys*. It is fast and accurate, and at 64KB, the download is not really a concern. It is roughly one tenth the size of Havok's physics Xtra, and using it may allow me to fool the player while I stream in more sophisticated solutions, such as Havok, in the background.

The only downside of the Xtra is that it isn't packaged at this point. That means it could cost me quite a bit of money to put together a certified online delivery version. The plans for this game call for free distribution, so I'm not thrilled about the prospect of spending $400 for a VeriSign class C certificate.

To create an Xtra that will download automatically to the user's machine, you need to use the Macromedia Xtra Developer's kit. You also need to hold a Class C VeriSign license in order to convince VeriSign that it is safe to download the Xtra. The packaged version of the Xtra may then be added to a download site and referenced by Director's Xtra list. It creates the magic dialog that pops up as the Xtra downloads, telling users that the Xtra is being distributed by a certified group or company.

If you'd like to learn more about programming or packaging Xtras, visit the Xtra developers section of the Macromedia Web site at `http://www.macromedia.com/support/xtras/`.

The other option is to provide an alternative installation method for the Xtra. I did some tests this morning, and putting it in with InstallShield is a breeze. Because we will probably be asking users to download and install at least one other package, I think we could easily just combine these elements. It will make the Mac version a little harder to create, but I think we'll find a way to manage.

I still want to perform some tests using the Whatsinview Xtra to do advanced steering and collision detection in a real-world environment. I think at this point that the best approach is to go ahead with Whatsinview as plan A and to use Havok as plan B.

Collision Resolution

The real questions are, how will the characters react to collision events and how will enemy characters be encouraged to track down other characters in the scene? My plan for collision resolution for characters in the game is to treat keyboard and mouse direction input as requests. In other words, I plan to accept the player's input and then calculate whether such a move is legal. If it is legal, the translation/animation will run as requested; if it isn't legal, the collision engine will calculate the nearest legal vector to the request and move in that direction instead. This should enable sliding along walls and other sorts of things that are typically problems.

I have been inspired to create steering behaviors that are largely influenced by Craig Reynolds' "Steering Behaviors for Autonomous Characters" (`http://www.red3d.com/cwr/steer/`). This is a brilliant summary of 2D steering behaviors, and I'm sure you'll see how easily most of these concepts can be applied to 3D space when we are using a view volume to define collisions.

On Schedule?

Before I finish my notes for the week, I think I should say a bit about the schedule for development. You never really know how long it will take to make a game. Sure, you can run some typical formulas and calculate about how much time it should take, but you just cannot predict how smooth a given development cycle will be. A month is not enough time to develop the game I propose here. Even working with a small team, we will not be able to finish all the features. This sort of problem is not atypical, but it is important that you recognize upfront that you are not ever likely to accomplish everything you work toward within a narrow window of time.

Because we aren't accountable to a producer for this game, the problem is minor. If we were working under a contract, this overestimation of our prowess would be a serious issue. We'd spend a fortune in uncompensated hours trying desperately to satisfy unattainable goals. When you estimate your project's timetable, write down your ideas and then triple the time for each aspect of the project. Do the same with expenses. Keep in mind, the less you spend on a project, the more time it will cost you. The relationship is almost invariable.

Producers will be happy to learn that you're ahead of schedule. They will be seriously irked if you are late. They will also have hundreds of "notes" for you once you give them a project to test. Plan for these mishaps, setbacks, and delays, and you'll do well. We're planning to reach a stable 1.0 version of *17 Keys* by the end of our one-month development marathon. Subsequent versions of the game may include features that were left out of the initial cycle, and over time the game will grow in complexity and, hopefully, become more and more exciting to play.

Sophia is starting on the animatics this weekend, and Matt has already begun the sound effects and music. Vinnie and I are meeting today to make plans for the 3D models and the animation cycles, which is next week's adventure.

CHAPTER 14

17 Keys: Week Two

The plans for this week are fairly straightforward. I'm scheduled to build the models and begin animation, Sophia is working on storyboards, Matt is working on sounds, and Vinnie and I plan to work out an approach to world optimization, which Vinnie will then optimize. By the end of the week, we hope to have a functional version of the world and be well on our way to detecting and responding to collisions.

Day One

Collaboration is a truly powerful, adventurous, and life-affirming way to get a big project done in record time. However, it is also a bit like herding cats. I love the people I work with. They are all wonderful, generous people. I think that I would go mad if they weren't. That said, it is a constant battle to stay ahead of everyone's schedule and keep abreast of the latest work. I always make the same mistake. I assume that I can manage the project and contribute to it. This is a terribly naive assumption. If it is at all possible, get someone else to manage and direct your project, or make certain that you aren't responsible for any of the actual work.

A good deal of my time today has been spent updating everyone on the state of affairs. I imagine that this will be the case every week. Organizing roles and figuring out who has time to perform each job is a huge task. It would be insane if we weren't working from some sort of plan.

Talking with everyone at least this often gives each person a chance to ask questions and share a bit in the flushing out of the overall dream.

The hardest and most beneficial thing to realize going into any project with a group is that every member of a collaborative team is (or should be) better at his or her skill set than you are. You have to trust them all to do what they say they will do, when they say they will do it, and with a quality that surpasses anything you could do on your own.

Today is one of those days when I have to swallow my pride, ignore my doubts, and do my part to the best of my ability. To make matters worse, both Vinnie and Matt are better 3D modelers than I am, and I drew the short straw on creating all the low-polygon models. This would be fine if I hadn't been completely insane when estimating the polygon counts. Vinnie tried not to laugh when he saw my estimates and said, "Uh, these are supposed to animate right?"

He was, of course, absolutely correct. I have to say, though, that as the day moves on, I'm feeling more and more confident. I started with the smaller models, hoping to at least meet my low-poly goals on these. First up was the shield (see Figures 14.1 and 14.2). You will find the shield on the accompanying CD-ROM listed as shield.max.

FIGURE 14.1	**FIGURE 14.2**
A wireframe view of the shield.	*A Gouraud Shaded view of the shield.*

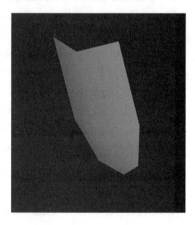

As I make each file, I'll be capturing an image of the faces using the Texporter utility plug-in. If you don't already have it, you can find it online at http://www.cuneytozdas.com/software/max/texporter/. It is a free plug-in that allows you to snap shots of unwrapped textures. Sophia will paint the snapshots and then return them to me so that they can go into the finished models. This isn't much of a big deal when the geometry is simple, but as I go I'll show you some tricks that allow you to unfold and recombine your models using a combination of this plug-in, the UVW map modifier, and the morph tool.

The finished shield model uses eight triangular polygons to form the shape of the shield. Both sides will need to be rendered, so the damage is roughly equal to 16 polygons when the shield is added to the character's visible elements. The shield is essentially a plane that is divided into two mesh sections vertically and two mesh sections horizontally. I pulled the points to form the shape.

The sword was a bit more difficult to make because I wanted it to have some thickness in the environment (see Figures 14.3 and 14.4). The sword model, which may be found on the CD-ROM under the name sword06.max, is composed of 16 faces. It started life as a rectangular box, with two divisions vertically and two horizontally. I collapsed the points along the blade side and kept many of the points for the handle.

FIGURE 14.3	**FIGURE 14.4**
A wireframe view of the sword.	*A Gouraud shaded view of the sword.*

NOTE

The sword file is named `sword06` because it is the sixth version of the sword. Absolutely every file that we do is named using this sort of convention. In the case of game files, we anticipate more than 100 versions, so we name the original file `gameName001.dir` and escalate the file number for each revision.

With the sword and the shield under my belt, I felt considerably more confident and I decided to move on to more sophisticated fare. I created the bird creature shown in Figures 14.5 and 14.6. You may notice in Figure 14.5 that I've started embedding notes to Sophia within the texture map file. Anything in the voids is not going to render onto the model, and it's a perfectly good way to let Sophia know what I'm thinking about for the model and to provide any technical details that may help her along the way. In the case of this bird, I want to make certain she realizes the bird has no distinction between top and bottom as it is currently rendered.

FIGURE 14.5

The wireframe template used to plan the texture map for the birds.

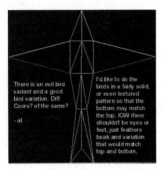

If you check the summary info, found under the file menu in 3D Studio Max, on the `bird10.max` file on your CD-ROM, you'll find that the finished bird model uses 42 faces. I'm very pleased with this. The bird was box-modeled as well, using the poly-map diagram as a backdrop. I collapsed most of the points along the side of the initial box and extruded a wing to the left. I've included the versions on the CD-ROM so that you may follow this process in 3D. Look for the files named `bird01.max` through `bird09.max` to see the entire process in stages.

FIGURE 14.6

A Gouraud Shaded view of the bird.

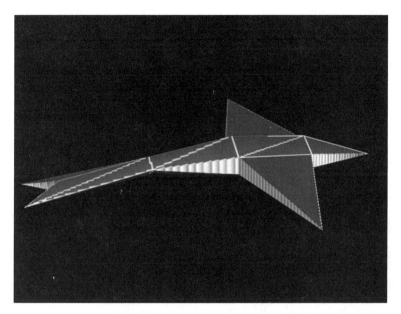

Day Two

I usually start my day between 3:00 and 4:00 a.m. I just thought I'd mention it to help set the scene and give you a sense of my schedule. I don't get up at 3:00 a.m. because I'm a compulsive workaholic. I get up then because it is quiet, and I can think better when it is quiet.

I work in a comfortable chair. After a while, you'll find you have a lot of problems with your back and legs if you don't invest a little money in comfortable chairs and appropriately sized, ergonomic desks.

I'll work until about 1:00 p.m., then I go for a swim and chill out for a while. I take care of just about anything else I need to do before coming back to the computer in the evening. My average day includes about 16 hours of work. I try to incorporate lots of breaks and interruptions. After a while, you begin to stagnate if you don't break away from your project a bit.

Today I'm finishing up the models for the game. Next on the block is the cabin model. Vinnie is probably going to do some additional architectural types, but we want to see how game performance goes before we make any firm decisions. The cabin model is the first of the models to require a different face on each side of the object (see Figures 14.7 and 14.8).

FIGURE 14.7

The texture template for the cabin model enables Sophia to work on each side of the building.

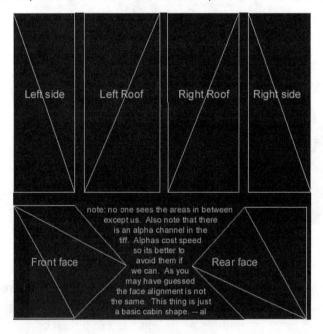

This is a great opportunity to show you exactly how I use the Texporter plug-in to make a precise map of the surfaces of the model. To create the sort of map you see in Figure 14.7, I cut the cabin model up into small chunks and then made a clone of these bits. I've listed the steps here for your convenience.

1. Select any given mesh model.

2. Choose the sub-object selection mode: Polygon.

3. Select one or more polygons from the object, being careful to take only faces that share the same general projection plane. (In the case of the cabin, that splits the object up into six parts.)

FIGURE 14.8

The image is mapped to the exact texture coordinates of the cabin.

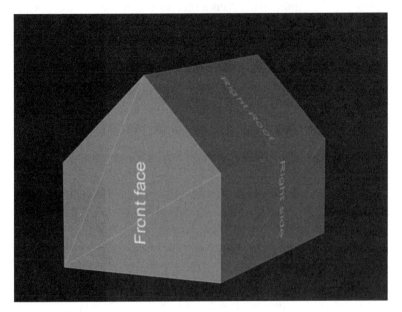

4. Choose Detach from the Edit Geometry submenu on the Modify tab of the properties options. A dialog will appear. Give the new face object a name that is sequential. (I use a, b, c, and so on.) This is important because you will need to remember the order of detachment later.

5. Repeat the detachment step for every face in the model until there are no faces remaining. Do not delete any faces or vertices.

6. Once you have detached and renamed all the polygons, deselect the sub-object selection button and press the Delete key to delete the original object. (Yes, there is still an object even though it no longer has any faces.)

7. Group the new models together and give them an appropriate name.

8. Clone the group and slide the clone off to the side. Move to the Display Properties tab and freeze and/or hide the cloned group. We'll use it again later.

9. Now ungroup the original polygons and translate/rotate them in the front face view. Move them so that they all form a nice, neat layout like the one in Figure 14.7. Make certain that all the faces (normals) are pointing toward you in the front view.

10. Once the polygons are arranged appropriately, select the first object you broke off. In my case, this would be "a."

11. Now click the attachList button and choose the second object. In my case, this would be "b." Repeat this step for each of the original face objects until all the originals are attached to one another.

12. Add a UVW map modifier with planar projection to the stack of this combined model. Adjust the modifier until the planar projection is covering the entire set of faces.

13. Using the Utilities tab of the Property Inspector, select the More button and then scroll to the bottom of the list of additional Utilities that pops up in the center of your screen. You'll find the Texporter plug-in listed there if you've downloaded and installed it. Choose the Texporter tool.

14. When the tool is added, a parameters section will appear on your Utilities tab. With the combined object selected and the UVW modifier in place, set the appropriate size for your texture in the Parameters dialog and then click the Pick button. The next object you select in the scene will be used to plot a texture map, and the map will appear in a render window.

15. Save the texture map in an appropriate location so that you can use it as a template to paint your texture using your favorite 2D paint tool.

16. Now for the magic. Unhide and unfreeze the cloned group. Ungroup the members of the group and attach them as you did the group of originals. Be certain to start with the first one ("a01" in my case) and work sequentially.

17. Turn off the attachList function and then select the laid out version of the model. (Don't forget to turn off the attach function.)

18. Move to the Create tab of the Property Inspector and choose Compound Objects from the drop-down menu under the Geometry subsection. Click the Morph button. Additional parameters will appear, and you will see a Pick Target button. Click the button and choose the cloned model. Your model will snap back to it's original shape but retain its texture map.

19. Now you need to delete the clone.

20. Next you should collapse the stack of the remaining model back into a single editable mesh. When you select the model, you'll see the morph targets in the Modify tab. Select the top morph target and then use the drop-down Stack menu to choose Edit Stack. Once you have the dialog that allows you to control the stack, simply choose Collapse All.

21. Finally, if this model will do any mesh deformation (a bone-based figure, for example), you will need to weld the vertices back together in order to prevent tearing. Select the entire mesh using the sub-object selection mask for vertices. Set the weld threshold to an appropriate value, and press the weld selected vertices button. You should see the vertices drop to a significantly smaller number.

I've included all the cabin models on the CD-ROM so that you can follow along with the process. If you'd like to try this procedure, begin with `cabin02.max`.

The next series of models included the quadrupedal animal, the minion, the typical human figure, and Liam. Most of these were based on box models as well, although the turning, sculpting, and alterations got pretty extreme in some cases.

The quadruped is created from 156 faces. I'm fairly concerned about animating the beast. I fear that the legs will collapse horribly, but I've been working fairly successfully with weight-mapping specific regions of bone structures in order to avoid collapsing joints, so I'll give it a whirl. I can always come back to it and flush it out a bit. The quadruped model, named `quad36.max`, can be found on the companion CD-ROM. Figures 14.9 and 14.10 show different aspects of this creature.

The minion is comprised of 150 faces. I'm certain that it won't move correctly, but I feel a bit cocky about the polygon count. I suppose I really shouldn't given its ludicrous shape, but I'm pretty sure it will give the desired effect, and it amuses me quite a bit. The minion model, named `minion12.max`, can be found on the companion CD-ROM. Figures 14.11 and 14.12 show how the minion is coming along.

FIGURE 14.9

A perspective view of the quadruped.

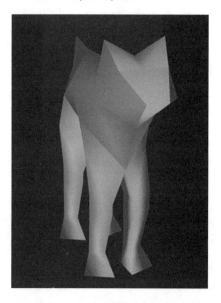

FIGURE 14.10

The quadruped's captured texture map.

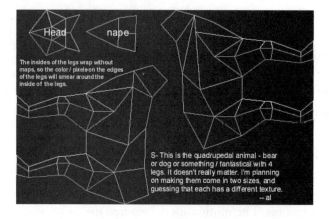

FIGURE 14.11

The minion's captured texture map.

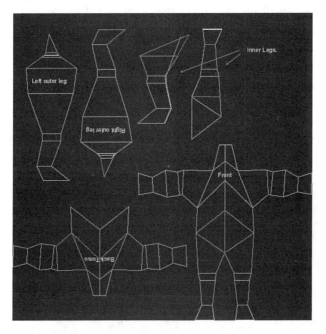

FIGURE 14.12

A perspective view of the minion.

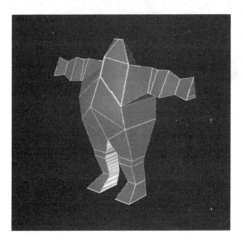

The basic human model went very well (see Figure 14.13). I've never been able to get one below 490 faces prior to this effort. This one is 352 faces (see Figure 14.14), and I feel confident that I can get it to animate well. It has good joints for accommodation under the arms, at the elbows, and along the hip sockets and knees. It's neck is a bit tight, but I think it will work well. At 352 faces, it should be staggeringly fast onscreen. The humanoid model, named `humanoidBody29.max`, can be found on the companion CD-ROM.

FIGURE 14.13

A perspective view of the basic human model that will be used for all the humanoids in the game.

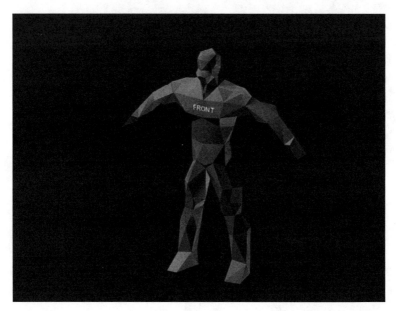

Liam's model is based entirely on this one and is just a few polygons larger to accommodate the wings (see Figure 14.15). I'm very concerned about the wings and the way they will respond to the animation. I'll do some early tests tomorrow to see how they look. Liam's model, named `liamBody41.max`, can be found on the companion CD-ROM.

FIGURE 14.14

The humanoid's captured texture map

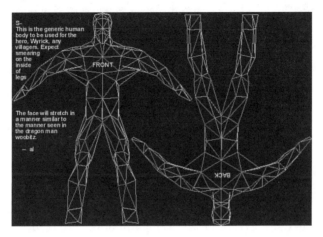

FIGURE 14.15

A perspective view of Liam.

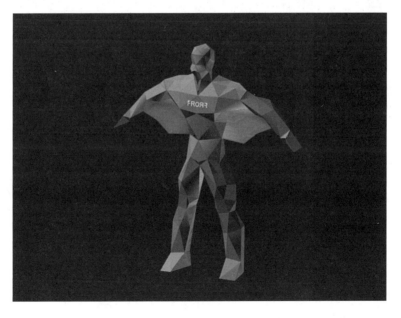

Modeling has gone well. There are quite a few more incidental pieces to bring together if time permits, but the bulk of the creatures are ready to go, and with varied textures and scales, we should be in pretty good shape.

Day Three

I love the way that projects begin to fall together just as you are about to collapse in a babbling heap of angst and confusion. Vinnie and I had a chance to discuss the game—specifically gameplay—for hours today. It was a fantastically helpful experience. I don't think I realized until now how helpful it is to talk about the game and explain my ideas to someone who can reply with immediate and thorough questions.

As I was forced to restate concepts in varied ways to clarify my thoughts; it helped me find flaws in the plans, discover opportunities for enhanced gameplay, and solidify my own understanding of the project.

Developing Environment

The most substantial revelation of the day came because of a very simple series of questions. What goes where? How much world is there? What is the scale? Vinnie's innocent questions sparked off a whirlwind in my head as I realized that I had a very solid conceptual understanding of the gamespace but a very limited physical and spatial understanding of the space. It sounds stupid, I know, but I had pretty much conceived of it as an island with a big monument in the middle and other stuff around. That isn't very helpful information for someone who is planning to help me lay out the environment.

I had known for quite a while that I would try to lay out the environment, whatever its specifics, in some sort of logical grid. The reason for this was entirely pragmatic. I don't want to overtax the system, so I planned to move the trees of the forest from one cell to the next as the player travels from one area to another. To visualize this, imagine a checkerboard from the top. Mentally place a game piece in the middle of the board. There are eight squares that touch the cell your game piece is sitting on. Four of these are diagonal and four are directly adjacent. Now move the piece in your mind. Note that the adjacent and diagonal squares are now different.

This is exactly how the game will dynamically configure the forest. Only those cells that are diagonal or adjacent to the cell where the player is currently standing will actually contain architectural and forest models. This makes it possible to move 27 trees around rather than generate 300 trees.

The logistics of this maneuver are a bit complicated. Essentially we will use fog and the clipping plane to prevent the user from seeing anything farther away than one cell. This means that the radius of the player's vision is one cell and that the maximum distance the player is able to see never allows him to see that the forest is not drawn beyond the neighboring cells. You could easily use a similar strategy to create a maze or race game.

Animating

After the meeting with Vinnie, I began work on animations. I did animation cycles for the minion, the humanoid, and Liam. These are all pretty simple and follow the basic procedures I outlined in Chapter 10, "Using 3D Bone Animation in Director." I did enough tests to determine that there were some problems with the joints deforming and then went back in to the models to work on that problem. I found that if I adjusted the specific deformation properties of parts of the body, I could force enough rigidness into the torso to get acceptable animation out of the models even when altering the envelopes wasn't sufficient.

To adjust the deformation properties of bones in Max, simply set the Envelope parameter to Rigid instead of Deformable. You can access this property by choosing the Envelope sub-object from the physique properties of a biped. If you want to see this in action, open the file on your CD-ROM named `LiamBody31.max`. Select the figure and then choose sub-object, envelope from the drop-down menu. Click an arm or leg and notice that the envelopes for these elements are red. You may also note that the Envelope parameter is set to Deformable. Now click the torso. Its envelope is green. This is because it has been set to employ a rigid Envelope parameter.

Using these settings will allow you to prevent the crushing of objects you don't want to deform, even when they are adjacent to objects that you do want to deform.

Day Four

Are you ready to play? Vinnie came through with the first hunk of game today. It has some fog issues because the combination of a large two-face plane and flat shading are a bit too much for many 3D graphics card to handle, but I think we'll be able to work that out.

Exercise 14.1:   The First Play

Try this one, but I caution you that your graphics card may not respond well to the fog issues. The file is called `031TokensOutOrig.dir`.

Use the W, A, S, and D keys to navigate and use the O key to switch to an overhead camera (P key switches back to the perspective view.)

If the performance of fog using your graphics card is perfect it will be hard for you to understand the concern at this point. If however your card is among those that exhibit the flashing you'll immediately see that the trees are being rendered with different fog effects than the ground plane.

In addition there will be flashes as you move the figure (rectangular box) around the screen using a combination of the mouse and the W, A, S, and D keys.

Details, Details, Details

Moving on, I clean up the fog and start working on a beach side solution. I've added the collision for the lower-end graphics card. You can see the results so far in the file named `035TokensOut.dir` on the CD-ROM.

I still have failing collisions on the trees, and I've dropped the grass down too low beneath the beach, so we'll have to work on valid and reliable methods of drawing these two elements. We should be able to do a layered texture, but we have had some difficulty getting matching performance on all test machines, so we are fighting with multiple planes, and the Z depths aren't reliably drawing themselves.

One of the reasons I wanted to create the last several chapters of the book in this format was to let you see all these issues as they arise. Game development is as much reliant on your ingenuity and stubborn ability to work around unforeseen obstacles as it is about creativity and discipline. I often hear people complain about the lack of a feature or a bug in Director. This is the price you pay for dependence on a development platform that is as varied as Director. You have to be willing to roll with the punches and do your best to work around things that aren't going as you imagined that they should.

Debugging Along the Way

My original tree model responds well to collisions with the test box. The test box model is created on-the-fly. The additional trees are all created on-the-fly, yet the dynamically generated tree models do not respond to collisions with the test box. This is the sort of thing that calls for slow procedural debugging.

I find that the best way to debug a problem like this is to comment all the code in any of the relevant handlers as I work my way through the commands, just as the computer does. It's important to remember that the computer is really, really stupid, and ultimately bugs are normally the result of you making an assumption that was incorrect or expecting the computer to do something that it simply doesn't know it is supposed to do.

When I comment the code, I work through it one line at a time. I try to explain it as though I had not written it. Believe me, after a few years of this, you'll be glad you left notes for yourself. You won't remember how a certain handler works, and you'll end up forced to relearn the program's deep, dark secrets.

Aha! Open the movie named `037TokensOut.dir` and drive your little box over to the right until you see a row of trees. Perfect collision. The brute force handler in Vinnie's setup script was fine for plain-old models, but collision-sensitive models need to be handled more delicately; otherwise, they'll disable themselves in order to avoid a meltdown.

I found the culprit by commenting the handlers one at a time until I finally discovered that the offending handler was clearly the one that moved the trees into position using a "`transform.position =`" command. Collision-enabled models have several methods built in to support movement so that they might find the best result that doesn't lead to interpenetration.

In this case, we should probably use Havok's `rigidBody.attemptMoveTo` handler to move the trees as close as possible to the correct position. Another apparent problem is the use of pinning. I pinned the tree down. You can move a pinned rigid body, but only if you unpin it first and then move it. I'll have to do quite a bit more fidgeting before we are going to see this work as expected.

Array Work

Among the more annoying facts we must face in this project is that we really also need to build an array to store the positions of objects in the space. I'm starting one now, but it will be quite an undertaking. It would be simple to store all the points where objects are positioned in a field and then retrieve the lists at runtime. The problem with the trees is that they need to know two properties. First, they need to know where they are positioned. Second, they need to know which original model they should use. This is because ultimately there will likely be more than one type of tree, and it would be very odd if the player came back to the same spot to find that some sort of massive landscaping had been done in only a matter of seconds.

I'm moving back to animation tomorrow and hope to catch up on the collision work next week.

Day Five

I received the storyboard images from Sophia via e-mail today. They were exactly what I was hoping for. I was elated. I couldn't help myself; I set to work immediately, writing out the captions and speech bubbles, and I began corresponding with her about the various details.

I had worked out the images originally using about 20 frames to tell the story and fill in details. As I began to get practical, I realized that only five images were needed to tell the story. I asked Sophia to draw these five images:

- Wyrick casting a spell.
- Man and dragon splitting apart.
- Reconvergence of man and dragon.
- A victorious and recombined Liam.
- A defeated player on the ground in a heap.

The game will use brief animatics (varied shots of storyboards with limited motion and transitions) to fill in the narrative at various key moments. Because some of the images used will be repeated in more than one animatic sequence I will be able to use fewer images than you might think.

The first sequence will be done with only two images and the title and associated slates. The first image is the wizard casting a spell on the dragon-man (see Figure 14.16). The second image is the man and dragon pulled apart (see Figure 14.17). This makes it tougher to be certain that people will get what's happening, but we'll make do with a voiceover if absolutely necessary.

FIGURE 14.16

Sophia's original drawing of Wyrick casting a spell.

FIGURE 14.17

Sophia's sketch of Liam splitting into Amed and Lido.

The second animatic will be done with three shots of two images. The first image is shown first from a long view and then from extremely close up. The image features the two, man and dragon, blending back together (see Figure 14.18). The next image is a glory shot of the recombined dragon-man—comic book style (note that this will also be used for the fifth animatic). Figure 14.19 shows the victory image.

FIGURE 14.18

Sophia's drawing of Liam's reconvergence.

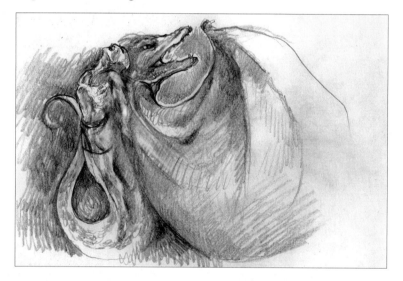

The third, fourth, and sixth animatics have been combined into a single image. A tragic/melodramatic image of a crumpled heap (see Figure 14.20) that is dragon-man/dragon/man—shouldn't matter—against a threatening forest skyline. The fifth animatic is a repeat of the last image in the second animatic.

I immediately began experimenting with text in the images to augment the comic book style and press the narrative further into the scenes. I chose a fairly rough hewn font, and using Photoshop threw in some text areas that didn't overrun the image but provided some separation. Figures 14.21–14.25 show the modifications I made.

FIGURE 14.19

Sophia's sketch of Liam as the victor.

FIGURE 14.20

Sophia's drawing of the defeated lump of player.

FIGURE 14.21

The modified version of Wyrick casting a spell.

FIGURE 14.22

The text-enhanced version of Lido and Amed splitting apart.

FIGURE 14.23

The modified version of Lido and Amed rejoining.

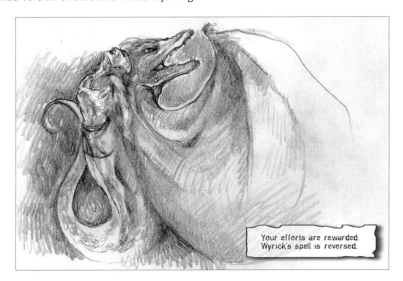

FIGURE 14.24

The text-enhanced version of a victorious Liam.

FIGURE 14.25

The modified version of a failed player.

I really like the effect. I've sent Sophia copies of the modified versions and hopefully she'll approve of the added copy. She'll probably want to change the text bubbles or the positions. They are all done as layers in Photoshop, so moving and changing things is not really any big chore.

What an amazing week. There is still a lot of work to do, and we haven't quite reached our goals, but I feel fairly confident that we will. Vinnie's contribution to dynamic world asset management has added tremendous speed to the game, and Sophia's artwork is proving to be a major asset.

Next week I'll be working more on collision but focusing on the gameplay features. Sophia has already begun work on the texture maps, Matt is hard at work gathering sounds, and Vinnie will be optimizing the game for performance.

CHAPTER 15

17 Keys: Week Three

I've been thinking quite a bit about various aspects of gameplay going into this week and several major revelations have come to me. First, I don't have the least bit of desire to implement the game in a dual-role manner as discussed in the treatment. It's seemed a bit wrong-headed from the onset of the project, but I've had a lot of trouble figuring out how to work the narrative via the action in a manner that seems logical together.

I realized today that the solution had been kicking me in the head for more than a week, but that I hadn't really been listening. I have been struggling with the problems that are created by having one creature that flies through the space and another that walks. I know that I want a dragon and I want to simulate the flight of the dragon. I also know that Amed (the humanoid) and Lido (the dragon) need to cooperate in order to rejoin into Liam (power-up) and defeat the evil Wizard.

The solution is fairly obvious if I step back from assumptions and just listen to the needs. If the player starts the game as Amed, and then plays until he has gathered enough magic and knowledge to trigger an arcade-style challenge (in which he plays the role of Lido), victory over the challenge can logically lead Lido to share his wealth with Amed. This will facilitate the re-convergence of the two characters.

Technically speaking, this removes the interaction with Lido from the normal world of the game and gives the player a chance to play a targeting shooter within a flight simulator during the game.

I often find that jumping immediately to solutions, rather than focusing on the specific needs and expectations, causes a problem in game development. It's easy to become bogged down in the details of implementation. It's important to step as far away from the project as you can and think about it in broad, general terms in order to catch this sort of thing before you've run too far down a dead-end road.

Day One

Collision was still plaguing my existence last week and this week initially looked as if it would offer me little assistance. I know a couple of important things about the Havok collision and physics simulation Xtra. I know that the objects to which I'm attaching physics modifiers should be registering and resolving collisions with this silly box, and I know that they are failing.

In Havok, collisions shut down for a given rigid body if that rigid body is inter-penetrating another rigid body when the physics engine begins the simulation. This is logical only if you think about it. If a tree is embedded in a car when you begin the simulation, Havok will simply ignore the physics of the tree and the car because neither could possibly be correct given their current state.

I can guess that the major problem that I was having with collision on my trees is that they were being switched off, because of to some interpenetration that occurred during their initial and subsequent placements. After some experimenting, I realized one important thing: Vinnie had set all the trees to land in their relative positions using the brute force method
`w.model[n].transform.position = vector( x, y, z).`

You cannot move Havok models via standard Lingo commands after they have been created as rigid bodies. You must use one of the Havok rigid-body methods to move the models to their space. The problem was that we were moving these trees often, and we couldn't afford to move them "near" the right location. We needed the trees to land in the correct positions.

My solution was to add and remove the Havok modifier from the trees dynamically. This solution comes with a future caveat: We'd like to stack and stagger these functions over a series of screen updates because we know that it takes some time (at least a couple of seconds) to accomplish the task, and the action of adding and removing the modifier from 18 to 27 models at one time can bog down the system.

I've listed the code that accomplishes this in Listings 15.1 and 15.2. The `InitForestLut()` handler creates a quick lookup table that allows me to search for the tree models that are used in each of the environment's 81 cells. There are three trees in each cell. As you look at the table, you might note that it is a list of 81 lists. The list position determines the cell, and the integers within each list reveal the numbers used in the tree model's name. The first item, for example, is a list containing the numbers 1, 2, and 3. This means that in the first cell, the tree models "tree1", "tree2", and "tree3" are used in this cell to display the trees in the environment. Using this system allows us to change the tree models as we continue to flesh out the design.

LISTING 15.1   The `InitForestLut` Handler

```
 1: global w, gHavok, gForestLut
 2:
 3: on initForestLut (me)
 4:   gForestLut = \
 5: [[1, 2,3], [4,5,6], [7,8,9], [1, 2,3], [4,5,6], [7,8,9],\
 6: [1, 2,3], [4,5,6], [7,8,9], [10,11,12], [13,14,15], [16,17,18],\
 7: [10,11,12], [13,14,15], [16,17,18], [10,11,12], [13,14,15], [16,17,18],\
 8: [19,20,21], [22,23,24], [25,26,27], [19,20,21], [22,23,24], [25,26,27],\
 9: [19,20,21],[22,23,24], [25,26,27], [1, 2,3], [4,5,6], [7,8,9], \
10: [1, 2,3], [4,5,6], [7,8,9], [1, 2,3], [4,5,6], [7,8,9],\
11: [10,11,12], [13,14,15], [16,17,18], [10,11,12], [13,14,15], [16,17,18], \
12: [10,11,12], [13,14,15], [16,17,18], [19,20,21], [22,23,24], [25,26,27],\
13: [19,20,21], [22,23,24], [25,26,27], [19,20,21], [22,23,24], [25,26,27],\
14: [19,20,21], [22,23,24], [25,26,27], [1, 2,3], [4,5,6], [7,8,9], \
15: [1, 2,3], [4,5,6], [7,8,9], [1, 2,3], [4,5,6], [7,8,9],\
16: [10,11,12], [13,14,15], [16,17,18], [10,11,12], [13,14,15], [16,17,18], \
17: [10,11,12], [13,14,15], [16,17,18], [19,20,21], [22,23,24], [25,26,27], \
18: [19,20,21], [22,23,24], [25,26,27]]
19: end
```

LISTING 15.2   The `enviroUpdate` Handler

```
1: on enviroUpdate me
2:   --initialize local variables
3:   s = sprite(1)
4:   x = w.model(s.pPlayModel).transform.position.x
5:   y = w.model(s.pPlayModel).transform.position.y
6:   if voidP(gForestLut) then
7:     initForestLut(me)
8:   end if
9:
```

LISTING 15.2   Continued

```
10:    ------------------------------------------define borders
11:    -- negative X
12:    if x <= 0 then
13:      gHavok.deleteRigidbody("testBox")
14:      w.model(s.pPlayModel).transform.position.x = 0
15:      gHavok.makeMovableRigidBody("testBox", 1.00, TRUE)
16:        -- lock the model into an imaginary box \
➡ that defines the edges of the island
17:    end if
18:    -- positive X
19:    if x >= s.pPlayAreaWidth then
20:      gHavok.deleteRigidbody("testBox")
21:      w.model(s.pPlayModel).transform.position.x = s.pPlayAreaWidth
22:      gHavok.makeMovableRigidBody("testBox", 1.00, TRUE)
23:    end if
24:    -- negative Y
25:    if y <= 0 then
26:      gHavok.deleteRigidbody("testBox")
27:      w.model(s.pPlayModel).transform.position.y = 0
28:      gHavok.makeMovableRigidBody("testBox", 1.00, TRUE)
29:    end if
30:    -- positive Y
31:    if y >= s.pPlayAreaLength then
32:      gHavok.deleteRigidbody("testBox")
33:      w.model(s.pPlayModel).transform.position.y = s.pPlayAreaLength
34:      gHavok.makeMovableRigidBody("testBox", 1.00, TRUE)
35:    end if
36:
37:    -------get current square for update
38:    --column
39:    repeat with xSquare = 1 to s.pWidthSubDivisions
40:      if x > s.pWidthSubSection  * (xSquare - 1) and x \
➡ <= s.pWidthSubSection * xSquare then
41:        column = xSquare
42:        exit repeat
43:      end if
44:    end repeat
45:    if x <= 0 then column = 1
46:    if x >= s.pPlayAreaWidth then column = s.pWidthSubDivisions
47:    --row
48:    repeat with ySquare = 1 to s.pLengthSubDivisions
49:      if y > s.pLengthSubDivisions  * (ySquare - 1) and y \
➡ <= s.pLengthSubSection * ySquare then
50:        row = ySquare
51:        exit repeat
```

LISTING 15.2   Continued

```
52:     end if
53:    end repeat
54:    if y <= 0 then row = 1
55:    if y >= s.pPlayAreaLength then row = s.pLengthSubDivisions
56:    w.camera("overhead").transform.position = vector(((s.pWidthSubSection * \
➥ column) - s.pWidthSubSection*.5), ((s.pLengthSubSection * row) - \
➥ s.pLengthSubSection*.5), 900)
57:    --get actual square
58:    currentSquare = (row * s.pLengthSubDivisions) - \
➥ (s.pWidthSubDivisions - column)
59:    --  put currentSquare
60:    --fog cuts off all but 3x3 squares
61:    activeSquareList = []
62:    activeSquareList.add(currentSquare)
63:    activeSquareList.add(currentSquare + 1)
64:    activeSquareList.add(currentSquare - 1)
65:    activeSquareList.add(currentSquare + s.pWidthSubDivisions)
66:    activeSquareList.add(currentSquare + s.pWidthSubDivisions + 1)
67:    activeSquareList.add(currentSquare + s.pWidthSubDivisions - 1)
68:    activeSquareList.add(currentSquare - s.pWidthSubDivisions)
69:    activeSquareList.add(currentSquare - s.pWidthSubDivisions + 1)
70:    activeSquareList.add(currentSquare - s.pWidthSubDivisions - 1)
71:    --get rid of non existing squares
72:    repeat with deleteTrees = activeSquareList.count down to 1
73:      if activeSquareList[deleteTrees] < 1 or activeSquareList[deleteTrees]\
        ➥ > (s.pWidthSubDivisions * s.pLengthSubDivisions) then
74:        activeSquareList.deleteAt(deleteTrees)
75:      end if
76:    end repeat
77:    if s.pActiveArea <> activeSquareList then
78:      s.pActiveArea = activeSquareList
79:      bodies = gHavok.rigidBody
80:      --put trees where they should be in the active space
81:      if count(activeSquareList) > 0 then
82:        tList = []
83:        repeat with x = 1 to count (activeSquareList)
84:          add(tList, gForestLut[getAt(activeSquareList, x)])
85:        end repeat
86:        --      put tList
87:        repeat with x = 1 to count(tList)
88:          visibleTrees = tList[x]
89:          repeat with y = 1 to count (visibleTrees)
90:            if (voidP(gHavok.rigidBody(("tree")&visibleTrees[y]))) then
91:              nothing
92:            else
```

LISTING 15.2　Continued

```
93:            gHavok.deleteRigidBody(("tree")&visibleTrees[y])
94:         end if
95:      end repeat
96:   end repeat
```

Vinnie created the bulk of the enviroUpdate handler. Later in the handler, he uses a case statement to check the lists of the cell locations against the positions in which trees should be placed. I imagine that we'll switch the case statement to use the lookup table if we have time. If you want to see the whole enviroUpdate handler, consult the file named 17Keys110.dir on the CD-ROM.

In lines 3–5, Vinnie initializes his local variables pointing to the base 3D sprite and the horizontal and depth positions of the default model. On lines 6–8, I create the lookup table if it hasn't already been created.

On lines 10–36, Vinnie does a great job of defining the boundaries of our 3D world and stopping the default model if the player tries to head out to sea. I'm so fond of this method that I'm retrofitting a couple of other games with this feature, which is absolutely elegant in its original form. The form you see here is modified by my first use of the remove-and-replace method of integrating Havok collision resolution with Lingo-based movement control. As you can see, on line 20, I simply remove the rigid body from the Havok simulation. Remember that the Lingo control simply fails if the model has been created as a Havok rigid body. After I've removed the model from the Havok simulation, I move the model with Lingo and finally reassign the model to the simulation.

This way the box continues to detect and resolve the collisions with trees, but I can also control aspects of box motion via the Lingo engine.

Beginning in line 39, Vinnie creates a quick mathematical survey to determine the spatial cell that the base model is within, and then redesigns the world as needed. If you want to see what I mean, open the file 17Keys110.dir and click Play. Now press the O key on your keyboard. Use the W, A, D, and S keys to move your model and watch as the world rebuilds around the current location of the model.

The big change here from last week is that I've added functional collision with the trees. The trick to that can be seen in lines 82–96. I've added these few lines to the handler to build a list of trees that are active using the lookup table I created in the previous listing.

I start by creating an empty list (`tList`) and then I fill it with the lists of numbers that correspond to the tree models used in each visible cell. It's important to note that `tList` is just a list of the cell tree lists, and that it holds only the lists of cells that are visible at this moment.

After these lists are stored into the variable `tList`, I go through `tList` and take out each individual number. I place each number into a variable called `visibleTrees` and delete the model from the Havok list of rigid bodies (if the model was a rigid body to begin with). In the last part of this very large handler (not shown in Listing 15.2), the trees are thrown out into appropriate positions and, finally, the Havok rigid bodies are re-created to allow the collisions to function normally.

Our in-house tests are showing OpenGL frame rates well above 50 frames per second, so, although we continue to kvetch about the problems with fog and strange side-effects of spotlights, we are a pretty pleased bunch of developers tonight.

Day Two

Matt called early enough to wake the dead this morning, and gave me a quick overview of the sounds he has created thus far. He's uploading them at this moment, and I plan to spend some time today working through them and nailing down our approach to the audio elements of the game.

Sound always scares me. It is big. In many cases, it is much, much bigger than anything else in your project and its effect on Shockwave-delivered games and multimedia widgets can be devastating. It's easy to get greedy with sound, and Matt makes me feel greedy because he gives me good things to work with.

As I've said before, the other edge of the scary sound sword is that your project will seem hollow and unprofessional without a decent audio component. You need the sound, you love the sound—you just wish it would go on a serious data diet.

I've included the sounds that Matt created on the CD-ROM in the Sounds folder that corresponds to this chapter. I've sorted through this first batch and found several that might work well for the game. I'm particularly fond of the spooky ones.

In their raw form, the files are much too large to use in the game. I'll need to convert them to Shockwave audio files in order to compress them, and I might want to stream in only those sounds that are absolutely necessary to play the game in the beginning. I can always stream in more images and sound in the background while the game is being played, but the cost can be substantial on low-end systems.

Converting the roughly 20MB of files that I liked from their original form to Shockwave audio brought them down to about 130KB. They are still a bit hefty, but that's a substantial enough improvement for now.

There is something about sound that begins to set the tone for me, even more substantially than the visual elements of the game. I have always turned to music and sounds for inspiration while I draw and paint. I suppose the two are related.

The eerie sounds and forest creature grunts and twitters seem right for the space, especially given the work that Vinnie has been doing to combat the evil OpenGL fog issue. I'll tell you more about that tomorrow.

Day Three

Bugs. Bugs bite. Except that no one calls them bugs. They call them outstanding issues, unexpected performance, or facts of life. There is a lot of craziness surrounding bugs, both from the perspective of the developer and from the perspective of the company that makes the software that is "exhibiting anomalous behavior." The truth is that it would be impossible to predict every single use that a developer will tax Director with. The software is extraordinarily accessible and unusually powerful. This is a very volatile combination.

The more power a developer is given to dig around in the software and make it do unexpected and wonderful things, the more likely it is that the software will fail in strange and astonishing ways.

I'm a bug magnet. It's one of the reasons that I like to test beta versions of software. I was trained as an artist; therefore, I'm the perfect test case for Director. I don't think like a programmer in the conventional sense, so I'm very likely to break the software. Naturally, I'm telling you this because my plans have been foiled, not by a bug, but by "unanticipated performance."

I had planned to mask the far reaches of the forest with a thick layer of fog. It soon became apparent that this simply would not be a serious option, but not because of any of the logical reasons. Fog is not too slow, at least not for our expected low-end systems, and it doesn't turn funny colors or fail altogether.

Unfortunately, fog does seem to rely heavily on the OpenGL acceleration in OpenGL-based systems that when the video card is old, ill designed, or low on RAM, it renders with extremely varied density.

The only reliable method we have found to repair the issue is to raise the mesh density on the offending model (the ground plane) to a level so absurdly high that it would severely hamper our performance.

After quite a bit of fighting with the fog, I suggested that we consider moving to an entirely nighttime game. I imagined that we could get the same eerie feeling with a couple of spotlights attached to the primary game model. Unfortunately, this method ultimately suffered from the same bizarre mesh density reliance.

Finally, through persistence, Vinnie came up with a viable solution. We are adding layers to the ground texture that mimic a spotlight, and discolor the ground with the hue of the torch (an added bonus of the nighttime setting).

Now it's important to realize that I'm one of those freaks who read Douglas Adams religiously as a kid. I actually own Starship Titanic (the interactive game that Adams scripted for Simon and Schuster and the Digital Village). After thrilling me with the *Hitchhiker's Guide* trilogy, Adams wrote the genuinely lame *Dirk Gently's Holistic Detective Agency* and the truly inspired *Long Dark Teatime of the Soul*. In both of these novels, the central character leads his life under the bizarre assumption that everything happens for a reason. Given this notion, he simply allows events to lead him, no matter how little volition he is left with.

I bring up this poor goofball because I often find myself religiously following the same basic philosophy when I'm developing a new project. I know that it doesn't make much sense. I suppose that I think that the subconscious will ultimately find a better solution than the conscious mind. This torch-bearing figure is a much better solution for us. In addition to the obvious visual benefits, it brings dramatic *chiaroscuro* (contrasting values of dark and light) to the scene and gives me a perfect torture device/motivator. The torch is a device that allows us to suggest that the light within the scene is motivated by some real object. There is a particle burst in the heart of the torch that suggests the flame. On the surface, the function of this torch is to limit the amount of the world that the player can see. This means that we don't have to draw and calculate as much of the world.

In the player's fictional experience, the purpose of the torch is to light his path. It immediately opens the door for us to a world of possibility when it comes to player motivation. Real torches, after all, are not permanent. They eventually lose their flame. You could drop it, it could be extinguished by rain, or someone could take it from you. All these things make for good solid gameplay. They all involve challenges for the player. The challenges are rooted in the narrative of the world, and they all seem immediately plausible.

Willing or not, just like Douglas Adams' hero, I find myself accidentally steered toward great solutions.

Day Four

I've got one thing on my mind today: the rack. Most games feature some sort of token acquisition—stuff you pick up, pick off, or pick apart. This game is no exception. I plan to have a trading rack form the central communication device for the game. I want to keep any text during gameplay to a minimum, so I want to handle trade encounters and specialty object manipulation by using a simple rack that slides in below the main gameplay screen whenever the player wants to attempt to negotiate with another character in the game space.

I know that the player can collect 17 keys. He may also collect and store 17 money units, so it is immediately apparent to me that it would be beneficial if the remaining tokens could fit in a single row of 17 units.

I created the image in Figure 15.1 in Adobe Photoshop simply by drawing lines, filling the border with a bit of one of the storyboard sketches, and then applying an Eyecandy inner-bevel filter to round out and soften the edges.

FIGURE 15.1

The base image for the rack.

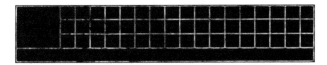

The position of the lines within the image is not at all accidental or arbitrary. I want the interface to have a rough-hewn flavor, but ultimately I'll need to build very simple repeat loop-based handlers to build the display dynamically with imaging Lingo. This means that the exact position of every cell in the rack must be in a very predictable location. The total height of the rack will be 120 pixels, and the total width will be 640 pixels.

I divided that space up into a grid that was 30 units high and 32 units wide. Using the grid, I placed the lines on the image. This means that I can find the horizontal position of any cell simply by multiplying the cell number minus 1 (the first cell starts at 0) by 32. The same method can be used to find the row heights, but by using 30 pixels rather than 32.

Listing 15.3 contains the basic handlers that are used to create the rack on-the-fly. If you'd like to follow along in Director, open the movie called 17keys112.dir.

LISTING 15.3   The Global Rack Object Scripts

```
 1: global gRack
 2:
 3: property pMagic
 4: property pFood
 5: property pWater
 6: property pWine
 7: property pMoney
 8: property pKey
 9:
10: on new (me)
11:   if voidP(gRack) then
12:     init(me)
13:   else
14:     alert ("Rack Problem Movie script 6")
15:   end if
16:   return(me)
17: end
18:
```

LISTING 15.3   Continued

```
19: on init(me)
20:    pKey = []
21:    pMoney = []
22:    pWine = []
23:    pWater = []
24:    pFood = []
25:    pMagic = []
26: end
27:
28: on addToken(me, whichType, whichToken)
29:    case whichType of
30:      #magic:
31:        whichType = pMagic
32:      #food:
33:        whichType = pFood
34:      #water:
35:        whichType = pWater
36:      #wine:
37:        whichType  = pWine
38:      #money:
39:        whichType = pMoney
40:      #key:
41:        whichType = pKey
42:    end case
43:
44:    if ilk(whichType) = #list then
45:      add(whichType, whichToken)
46:    else
47:      alert "Yikes, addToken movie script 6" && string(ilk(whichType))
48:    end if
49: end
50:
51: on drawTokens(me)
52:    rackImage = member("rack").image.duplicate()
53:    ---row 1
54:    ----------------magic
55:    if (count(pMagic) > 0) then
56:      tokens = count(pMagic)
57:      if tokens > 5 then
58:        tokens = 5
59:      end if
60:      repeat with column = 1 to tokens
61:        rackImage.copyPixels(member("m").image, rect(96 + ((column -1)\
➡ * 32), 2, (96 + ((column - 1)* 32 )+ \
➡ member("m").rect.width),  28), member("m").rect)
```

LISTING 15.3   Continued

```
 62:     end repeat
 63:   end if
 64:   ----------------food
 65:
 66:   if (count(pFood) > 0) then
 67:     tokens = count(pFood)
 68:     if tokens > 4 then
 69:       tokens = 9
 70:     else
 71:       tokens = tokens + 5
 72:     end if
 73:     repeat with column = 6 to tokens
 74:       rackImage.copyPixels(member("f").image, rect(96 + \
➥((column -1) * 32), 2, (96 + ((column - 1)* 32 ) + \
➥member("f").rect.width),  28), member("f").rect)
 75:     end repeat
 76:   end if
 77:   ---------------- water
 78:   if (count (pWater) > 0) then
 79:     tokens = count(pWater)
 80:     if tokens > 4 then
 81:       tokens = 13
 82:     else
 83:       tokens = tokens + 9
 84:     end if
 85:     repeat with column = 10 to tokens
 86:       rackImage.copyPixels(member("h").image, \
➥rect(96 + ((column -1) * 32), 2, (96 + ((column - 1)* 32 ) + \
➥member("h").rect.width),  28), member("h").rect)
 87:     end repeat
 88:   end if
 89:   ----------------- wine
 90:   if (count(pWine) > 0) then
 91:     tokens = count(pWine)
 92:     if tokens > 4 then
 93:       tokens = 17
 94:     else
 95:       tokens = tokens + 13
 96:     end if
 97:     repeat with column = 14 to tokens
 98:       rackImage.copyPixels(member("w").image, rect\
➥(96 + ((column -1) * 32), 2, (96 + ((column - 1)* 32 ) + \
➥member("w").rect.width),  28), member("w").rect)
 99:     end repeat
100:   end if
```

LISTING 15.3   Continued

```
101:    --- row 2
102:    ------------------ money
103:    if (count(pMoney) > 0) then
104:       tokens = count(pMoney)
105:       if tokens > 17 then
106:          tokens = 17
107:       end if
108:       repeat with column = 1 to tokens
109:          rackImage.copyPixels(member("$").image, rect(96 + \
➥((column -1) * 32), 32, (96 + ((column - 1)* 32 ) + \
➥member("$").rect.width),  58), member("$").rect)
110:       end repeat
111:    end if
112:
113:    -- row 3
114:    ------------------ key
115:    if (count(pKey) > 0) then
116:       tokens = count(pKey)
117:       if tokens > 17 then
118:          tokens = 17
119:       end if
120:       repeat with column = 1 to tokens
121:          rackImage.copyPixels(member("k").image, rect\
➥(96 + ((column -1) * 32), 62, (96 + ((column - 1)* 32 ) + \
➥member("k").rect.width),  88), member("k").rect)
122:
123:       end repeat
124:    end if
125:    member("rack copy").image = rackImage
126:    sprite(2).member = member("rack copy")
127: end
```

The properties declared in lines 3–8 hold lists of the tokens that have been retrieved by the player during game play. We use this list to calculate how many tokens of each type to place on the display rack, to test for player experience, and to determine whether a player may move beyond a given challenge.

The lists are also used to determine what items a player may trade with other characters to obtain weapons, torches, food, and magic.

Lines 10–17 are used to birth this new rack control object. It either calls the init script (returning a reference to the object) or exits with an alert to the developers warning us that something is broken.

TIP

> If you use alerts, errors, or puts of any form, don't get into the habit of treating them too lightly. I've heard plenty of horror stories from developers who were a little sick of making a given genre of games and therefore would name the handlers, errors, and other elements within the closed portion of the game with various inappropriate and profane terms. This is fine until you get an unexpected error proclaiming the absence of a profane handler or cast member. I frequently use alerts to warn of problems in a given script. In this instance, it is equally important to avoid inappropriate names.

The `init` handler sets the value of each of the object's properties to a blank list. The `addToken` handler (beginning on line 28) adds the model number of a token to the appropriate type list. The `drawToken()` handler (starting on line 51) is the workhorse of this script. Each time it is called, it draws all the appropriate icons onto a copy of the rack using imaging Lingo.

The handler begins by making a copy of the rack member. If I drew all over the original, I wouldn't be able to take away tokens. Now, it might look complicated from here, but it is just repeating the same basic work for each different type of handler. When you see code like this, your instinct should say, "This code needs to be optimized." It certainly does. There is no reason that we couldn't write a subroutine that takes a few arguments to handle the loops for each type of token. We'll probably get to that for the 1.x upgrade of the game.

Each of these subroutines counts the number of items in the property's list, and then places the proper icon on the rack in an appropriate position for that particular icon.

The last two lines of this handler update the image of the member and then the member of the sprite. This causes the updated version of the member to display on screen.

I've also started manipulating the tokens and prepping them to handle collisions. They'll disappear when the character contacts them and add themselves to the rack. That should be perfect for tomorrow.

Day Five

I'm continuing my struggle with animating the figure of Amed. I have moved quite a way down a path that gives the character more interest, especially in his face. He even had a tail for a brief time before I laughed myself silly and cut the darn thing. There's a shot of his new head in Figure 15.2.

FIGURE 15.2

Amed's new head.

A big part of the problem has been that I just hate the look of the shot staring at his backside the entire time. It is the single worst possible angle to view both the model and the animation. Eventually, I came to my senses and changed the angle of the camera.

My next task is the torch. Vinnie and I have talked about the torch a good bit, and I have the sense that I want to attach the particles either to the hand bone or to the torch prop. It seems to me that this will be easiest if I just attach it to the hand bone.

I simply add a couple of lines to the rotations and movements script. The new code first stores the transform of the hand bone in a variable called `tran`, and then moves the particle to a new position one world unit above the position of the bone.

```
tran =m.model("amed").bonesplayer.bone[16].worldtransform
m.model("particles").transform.position = \
vector(tran.position.x , tran.position.y , tran.position.z +1)
```

You can see the effect in motion in the movie 17Keys112.dir on the CD-ROM.

The most difficult part of implementing bones and keyframe-based motion in a game is not stacking and managing the playback of motions. It is handling the rotation and translation resets of the models.

In this case, we are pursuing a strange new path. Normally, I would allow the bones-based motion to move itself around the space, and there would be little to no slipping of the feet across the ground plane. In this case, I need to ensure that the bone cycles don't go anywhere that the test dummy can't go. To do that, we are locking the translation of the animated figure to the translation of the now-invisible box that we tested with in earlier versions of the game. This means that slipping across the ground plane is about to become a significant concern.

We have a massive week ahead of us. I have to get serious about interface graphics (the rack icons look like someone spit up a fruit salad). I also have to design and create the flight-simulating arcade shooter, handle the interaction of characters and trading process, and start integrating all the animation.

Vinnie will be hard at work optimizing the world and beginning the weapons and magic algorithms. He has some very cool plans for torches that become magic wands and other special effects.

Sophia should be delivering the textures for the bulk of the characters and architecture, and Matt will be moving ahead with the remaining sounds.

CHAPTER 16

17 Keys: Week Four

Hold on to your hats, I've got a crazy week in store. It's already clear that we won't finish the game this week as scheduled. Don't worry, though, I'm adding an epilogue to this chapter that will bring you up to speed on the changes to the game beyond this week, and the commented code for the finished game is on the CD-Rom. I have heard projects like this one referred to as ambitious. That is an ironic name for them. Just as my appetite is always bigger than my stomach, my imagination is always bigger than the outcome.

Even so, I'd rather stretch too far and miss, than shoot for something easily attainable and succeed at creating yet another clone of *Pong*. Don't get me wrong; there isn't anything wrong with *Pong*. It's a classic. I just don't have any interest in reinventing simple games when there is so much room for more investigation of more complex games.

Day One

I began the week still working on Amed and several other animations. But the real task is not fussing with animations; it is stepping up to the plate on gameplay issues. The first major undertaking at hand is to design and implement the negotiation engine that will make it possible for players to trade the goods in their rack for the objects they find in the world.

Let's dive right in and have a look at this code in action. The source for the rack object is in Listing 16.1. This object is used to manage the various tokens that the player acquires during the course of normal game play.

It is divided into six handlers. The first two handlers are used to invoke the object and initialize its properties. The next three are used to add, encumber (hold as potentially spent), and subtract tokens from the rack. The last handler is used to draw the tokens on the rack. The tokens are drawn to the rack using imaging Lingo, in a method that is slightly more complex than the one introduced in previous versions of the game.

LISTING 16.1   The gRack Handler Controls the Current State of the Rack

```
 1: global gRack, gGameEventManager
 2:
 3: property pMagic
 4: property pFood
 5: property pWater
 6: property pWine
 7: property pMoney
 8: property pKey
 9: property pEncumbered
10: property pExPts
11:
12: on new (me)

13:     init(me)


14:     return(me)
15: end
16:
17: on init(me)
18:     pKey = []
19:     pMoney = []
20:     pWine = []
21:     pWater = []
22:     pFood = []
23:     pMagic = []
24:     pEncumbered = []
25:     pExPts = 0
26: end
27:
28: on addToken(me, whichType, whichToken)
29:     case whichType of
30:       #magic:
31:         whichType = pMagic
32:       #food:
33:         whichType = pFood
34:       #water:
```

LISTING 16.1   Continued

```
35:        whichType = pWater
36:      #wine:
37:        whichType   = pWine
38:      #money:
39:        whichType = pMoney
40:      #key:
41:        whichType = pKey
42:    end case
43:    if ilk(whichType) = #list then
44:      add(whichType, whichToken)
45:    end if
46:    pExPts = pExPts + 1
47: end
48:
49: on subtractToken(me, whichType)
50:    case whichType of
51:      #magic:
52:        whichToken = pMagic
53:      #food:
54:        whichToken = pFood
55:      #water:
56:        whichToken = pWater
57:      #wine:
58:        whichToken   = pWine
59:      #money:
60:        whichToken = pMoney
61:      #key:
62:        whichToken = pKey
63:    end case
64:    if count (whichToken) > 0 then
65:      deleteOne(pEncumbered, (whichToken[(count(whichToken))]))
66:      deleteAt(whichToken, count(whichToken))
67:      drawTokens(me)
68:    end if
69: end
70:
71: on encumberToken (me, whichType)
72:    case whichType of
73:      #magic:
74:        whichToken = pMagic
75:      #food:
76:        whichToken = pFood
77:      #water:
78:        whichToken = pWater
79:      #wine:
```

LISTING 16.1   Continued

```
80:        whichToken  = pWine
81:     #money:
82:        whichToken = pMoney
83:     #key:
84:        whichToken = pKey
85:    end case
86:    if count (whichToken) > 0 then
87:      if NOT (getOne(pEncumbered, (whichToken[count(whichToken)]))) then
88:        add(pEncumbered, whichToken[(count(whichToken))])
89:        gGameEventManager.credit(#add, whichType)
90:      else
91:        deleteOne(pEncumbered, whichToken[count(whichToken)])
92:        gGameEventManager.deductCredit(whichType)
93:      end if
94:      drawTokens(me)
95:    end if
96: end

97:
98: on drawTokens(me)
99:    rackImage = member("rack").image.duplicate()
100:    ---row 1
101:    -----------------magic
102:    if (count(pMagic) > 0) then
103:      tokens = count(pMagic)
104:      if tokens > 5 then
105:        tokens = 5
106:      end if
107:      repeat with column = 1 to tokens
108:        if getOne(pEncumbered, pMagic[column]) then
109:          rackImage.copyPixels(member("m").image, rect(96 + \
➡ ((column -1) * 32), 2, (96 + ((column - 1)* 32 )+ member("m").rect.width)\
➡ , 28), member("m").rect, [#blendLevel: 95])
110:        else
111:          rackImage.copyPixels(member("m").image, rect(96 + \
➡ ((column -1) * 32), 2, (96 + ((column - 1)* 32 )+ member("m").rect.width),\
➡   28), member("m").rect)
112:        end if
113:      end repeat
114:    end if
115:
116:    -----------------food
117:
118:    if (count(pFood) > 0) then
119:      tokens = count(pFood)
```

LISTING 16.1 Continued

```
120:    if tokens > 4 then
121:       tokens = 9
122:    else
123:       tokens = tokens + 5
124:    end if
125:    repeat with column = 6 to tokens
126:       if getOne(pEncumbered, pFood[column - 5]) then
127:          rackImage.copyPixels(member("f").image, rect(96 + \
➡ ((column -1) * 32), 2, (96 + ((column - 1)* 32 ) + member("f").rect.width), \
➡ 28), member("f").rect, [#blendLevel: 95])
128:       else
129:          rackImage.copyPixels(member("f").image, rect(96 + \
➡ ((column -1) * 32), 2, (96 + ((column - 1)* 32 ) + member("f").rect.width), \
➡ 28), member("f").rect)
130:       end if
131:    end repeat
132:    end if
133:    ----------------- water
134:    if (count (pWater) > 0) then
135:       tokens = count(pWater)
136:       if tokens > 4 then
137:          tokens = 13
138:       else
139:          tokens = tokens + 9
140:       end if
141:       repeat with column = 10 to tokens
142:          if getOne(pEncumbered, pWater[column - 9]) then
143:             rackImage.copyPixels(member("h").image, rect(96 + \
➡ ((column -1) * 32), 2, (96 + ((column - 1)* 32 ) + member("h").rect.width), \
➡ 28), member("h").rect, [#blendLevel: 95])
144:          else
145:             rackImage.copyPixels(member("h").image, rect(96 + \
➡ ((column -1) * 32), 2, (96 + ((column - 1)* 32 ) + member("h").rect.width), \
➡ 28), member("h").rect)
146:          end if
147:       end repeat
148:    end if
149:    ----------------- wine
150:    if (count(pWine) > 0) then
151:       tokens = count(pWine)
152:       if tokens > 4 then
153:          tokens = 17
154:       else
155:          tokens = tokens + 13
156:       end if
```

LISTING 16.1   Continued

```
157:     repeat with column = 14 to tokens
158:         if getOne(pEncumbered, pWine[column - 13]) then
159:             rackImage.copyPixels(member("w").image, rect(96 + \
➥ ((column -1) * 32), 2, (96 + ((column - 1)* 32 ) + member("w").rect.width), \
➥ 28), member("w").rect, [#blendLevel: 95])
160:         else
161:             rackImage.copyPixels(member("w").image, rect(96 + \
➥ ((column -1) * 32), 2, (96 + ((column - 1)* 32 ) + member("w").rect.width), \
➥ 28), member("w").rect)
162:         end if
163:     end repeat
164:   end if
165:   --- row 2
166:   ------------------ money
167:   if (count(pMoney) > 0) then
168:     tokens = count(pMoney)
169:     if tokens > 17 then
170:       tokens = 17
171:     end if
172:     repeat with column = 1 to tokens
173:         if getOne(pEncumbered, pMoney[column]) then
174:             rackImage.copyPixels(member("$").image, rect(96 + \
➥ ((column -1) * 32), 32, (96 + ((column - 1)* 32 ) + member("$").rect.width), \
➥ 58), member("$").rect, [#blendLevel: 95])
175:         else
176:             rackImage.copyPixels(member("$").image, rect(96 + \
➥ ((column -1) * 32), 32, (96 + ((column - 1)* 32 ) + member("$").rect.width), \
➥ 58), member("$").rect)
177:         end if
178:     end repeat
179:   end if
180:
181:   -- row 3
182:   ------------------ key
183:   if (count(pKey) > 0) then
184:     tokens = count(pKey)
185:     if tokens > 17 then
186:       tokens = 17
187:     end if
188:     repeat with column = 1 to tokens
199:         if getOne(pEncumbered, pKey[column]) then
200:             rackImage.copyPixels(member("k").image, rect(96 + \
➥ ((column -1) * 32), 62, (96 + ((column - 1)* 32 ) + member("k").rect.width), \
➥ 88), member("k").rect, [#blendLevel: 95])
201:         else
```

LISTING 16.1 Continued

```
202:        rackImage.copyPixels(member("k").image, rect(96 + \
➥ ((column -1) * 32), 62, (96 + ((column - 1)* 32 ) + member("k").rect.width), \
➥ 88), member("k").rect)
203:        end if
204:      end repeat
205:    end if
506:    member("rack copy").image = rackImage
207:    sprite(2).member = member("rack copy")
208: end
```

The handlers in this healthy-size script begin with a declaration of a series of property declarations. These properties, found in lines 3–8 of Listing 16.1, are references to lists of the tokens that have been acquired by the player as he searches the forest and village.

An appropriate collision event triggers the addToken handler; the token that was hit is removed from the game world and its 2D representation is added to the rack.

Adding tokens to the rack is the easy part. Later in the game, the player will want to negotiate with villagers to barter for goods and information. Handling this sort of bartering in a seamless and simple manner is essential to maintaining an easy-to-use, low-interference interface.

I decided that it made sense for a player to click on an object that he wants to trade (or a series of objects) and that those objects should be considered encumbered (or on the table). If the offer is not high enough, the villager says so, via the text interface, and if the offer is sufficient, the system informs the player that he has purchased the item.

I wanted to maximize the flexibility within this negotiation process, so rather than simply accommodate tit-for-tat trades, I created a universal credit system that underlies these negotiations.

If the player goes to the shop and tries to buy a red torch, he is prompted to pay three pieces of gold. In a simple version, this would mean that the player needed to collect three pieces of money and then use them to acquire the torch. This system is inherently smarter because it knows the relative value of all the items in the player's pack.

If the player has enough water and food, and offers these instead, he might just as easily purchase the torch with these items. The system is also as typically unkind as the real world. There is no change for overpayment and the shop-keepers gladly take your most valuable items in exchange for even the cheapest product.

Encumbered tokens are drawn to the rack at a diminished opacity. This should suggest to the reasonably experienced user that these items are offered, but not yet accepted. Clicking on an item a second time, if the offer is refused, restores the item to the user's rack. If the offer is accepted, the offered tokens are removed from the player's rack.

Take a look at the first several lines of code in the addToken(), subtractToken(), and encumberToken() handlers. This is the sort of code that normally is cleaned up during the last several days of a project. I'm referring specifically to lines 29–41, 50–63, and 72–83. These case statements are redundant. Remember that whenever you see the same several lines of code in more than one place, it's a sure-fire clue that you should have a subroutine dedicated to that function. In this case, the code simply converts symbols to the lists to which they refer.

The drawTokens() handler, beginning on line 116, is a bit more sophisticated than it was the last time you had the chance to look at it. This has been done primarily to facilitate the drawing of the tokens with multiple potential states. The tokens may be blended or drawn at full opacity. Lines 126–138 illustrate a typical treatment of these elements.

Each element in the list of relevant tokens is checked. If the element is discovered in the encumbered items list, it is illustrated with an added blend argument augmenting the copyPixels() command. This added argument appears at the end of the copyPixels() command as a list of optional parameters. In this case, the #blend parameter is set to 95. This is enough to do the job and communicate the interim state of the token to the player.

Tomorrow, I push ahead on the token acquisition and bartering commands. I begin to integrate the village and the shops into the game space and work out the details of object negotiation.

Day Two

It occurs to me that a shopkeeper doesn't really need legs if you put him behind a counter. (Hey, there are a lot of polygons in a good pair of legs.) I've abducted the low-polygon man from the bonesplayer demos in Chapter 9, "Using 3D Keyframe Animation in Director," and cut off his legs just above the knee. Don't worry. He didn't suffer much.

Today, I'm working on the major game event management script. It's the script for an object that hovers around in RAM providing useful code and information for the many widgets that are hard at work trying to amuse and befuddle the player.

I'll just get it well underway today. I won't finish the handler. There will no doubt be quite a bit more to do in future versions of the game. The script, shown in Listing 16.2, is used in conjunction with the token lookup table script, the game clock script, and the rack script we looked at yesterday.

LISTING 16.2 The Game Event Manager Script

```
 1: global w, gHavok, gRack, gGameClock
 2:
 3: property pSaleTorches
 4: property pTorchCosts
 5: property pTokenCosts
 6: property pCredits
 7: property pPrice
 8: property pSaleItem
 9:
10:
11: on new(me)
12:   init(me)
13:   return me
14: end
15:
16: on init(me)
17:   -- the Text that is used to describe the \
➥ requested price of the product is the first item \
➥ in the relatively named list.
18:   -- the second item in the list is the \
➥ relative cost in common world units. This way \
➥ players can counter offer
19:   -- other items with a similar value \
```

LISTING 16.2   Continued

```
➥ in order to work around the system.
20:    -- water == 5 common units
21:    -- food == 8 common units
22:    -- wine == 9 common units
23:    -- money == 10 common units
24:    -- magic == 35 common units
25:    -- keys == 50 common units.  It's nearly \
➥ impossible to get a key back
26:    -- once sold, and you need all 17 to win. \
➥ As in life, all things are more
27:    -- expensive to buy than they are worth \
➥ to sell. Why is that?
28:    pTorchCosts = [#red:["3 Pieces",30], #wood: \
➥ ["5 Pieces",50], #silver: ["4 Pieces & 1 Magic Amulet",75], \
➥ #gold: ["5 Pieces & 3 Magic Amulets",155]]
29:    pTokenCosts = [#water:["1 piece": 8], \
➥ #food:["1 piece": 15], #wine:["2 pieces": 14], \
➥ #money: ["2 pieces": 20], #magic: ["5 pieces": 50], \
➥ #key: ["10 pieces": 100]]
30: end
31:
32: on broadCastSell(me, howMuch, whichItem)
33:    pPrice = howMuch
34:    pSaleItem = whichItem
35: end
36:
37: on broadCastBuy(me, goodsList)
38:    if pCredits > pPrice then
39:      ---- transfer the item
40:      transfer(me, goodsList)
41:    else



42:      member ("displayText").text  = \
➥ "That is not enough!"
43:    end if
44: end
45:
46: on shopEntry (me, whichCollisions)
47:    whichShop = whichCollisions[1]
48:    if sprite(1).pEnabled = 1 then
49:      sprite(1).pEnabled = 0
50:    end if
51:    outFitShop(whichShop)
52:    go to frame "shop"
53:    gHavok.deleteRigidBody("testBox")
```

LISTING 16.2 Continued

```
54:    w.model("testBox").transform.position \
➡ = vector( 50.3502, 88.7788, 1.2000 )
55:    gHavok.makeMovableRigidBody("testBox", 1.000, TRUE)
56: end
57:
58: on outFitShop (whichOne)
59:    put whichOne
60:    case whichOne of
61:      "structure1":
62:        put 1
63:        setTorches(#red, #wood, #silver)
64:      "structure2":
65:        put 2
66:        setTorches(#red, #gold, #wood)
67:      "structure3":
68:        put 3
69:        setTorches(#gold, #wood, #silver)
70:      "structure4":
71:        put 4
72:        setTorches(#gold, #wood, #red)
73:      "structure5":
74:        put 5
75:        setTorches( #red, #gold, #silver)
76:      "structure6":
77:        put 6
78:        setTorches(#red, #wood, #red)
79:      otherwise:
80:        alert "Problem in parent script \
➡ 11 with model name argument "& string(whichOne)
81:        halt
82:    end case
83: end
84:
85: on deductCredit (me, whichToken)
86:    case whichToken of
87:      #magic:
88:        tCredit = 35
89:      #food:
90:        tCredit = 8
91:      #water:
92:        tCredit = 5
93:      #wine:
94:        tCredit = 9
95:      #money:
96:        tCredit = 10
97:      #key:
98:        tCredit = 50
```

LISTING 16.2   Continued

```
 99:      otherwise:
100:         put whichToken
101:    end case
102:    pCredits = pCredits - tCredit
103:    member("displayText").text = ""
104: end
105:
106: on credit (me, addSubtract, whichType, whichGoods)
107:    --  this first bit stores a list \
of the total number of items of each type
108:    offerString = ""
109:    offerList = [#water: 0,#food:0, \
➡ #wine: 0, #money: 0, #magic: 0, #key: 0]
110:    repeat with iter = 1 to count (gRack.pEncumbered)
111:      case TRUE of
112:        (gRack.pEncumbered[iter] contains("tokenH")):
113:          offerList[#water] = offerList[#water] + 1
114:        (gRack.pEncumbered[iter] contains("tokenF")):
115:          offerList[#food] = offerList[#food] + 1
116:        (gRack.pEncumbered[iter] contains("tokenW")):
117:          offerList[#wine] = offerList[#wine] + 1
118:        (gRack.pEncumbered[iter] contains("token$")):
119:          offerList[#money] = offerList[#money] + 1
120:        (gRack.pEncumbered[iter] contains("tokenM")):
121:          offerList[#magic] = offerList[#magic] + 1
122:        (gRack.pEncumbered[iter] contains("tokenK")):
123:          offerList[#key] = offerList[#key] + 1
124:        otherwise:
125:          nothing
126:      end case
127:      --- so we can help the user by telling \
➡ them about offers that they have put on the table
128:    end repeat
129:    repeat with iter = 1 to count(offerList)
130:      if offerList[iter] > 0 then

➡ string(getPropAt(offerList, iter))
131:      else

132:      end if
133:      if tVar <> "" then
134:        offerString = offerString & tVar &" "
135:      end if
136:    end repeat
137:
138:    displayText = "You offer"&& offerString
```

LISTING 16.2   Continued

```
139:    member("displayText").text = displayText
140:    --------------------------------END DISPLAY OFFER
141:    if addSubtract  = #add then
142:      ------ the player is putting some tokens out to negotiate
143:      case whichType of
144:        #magic:
145:          tCredit = 35
146:        #food:
147:          tCredit = 8
148:        #water:
149:          tCredit = 5
150:        #wine:
151:          tCredit = 9
152:        #money:
153:          tCredit = 10
154:        #key:
155:          tCredit = 50
156:        otherwise:
157:          put whichType
158:      end case
159:      pCredits = pCredits + tCredit
160:      --    alert string (pCredits) && "credits"
161:    else
162:      ------ a game ai is taking some \
  or all of the offered items.
163:      --- in this event the second \
  argument (whichType) actually is an integer
164:      -- representing the required amount \
  in common units - that way you can buy stuff
165:      -- with things other than money
166:      howMuch = whichType
167:      if pCredits > howMuch then
168:        pCredits = pCredits - howMuch
169:        transfer(me, whichGoods)
170:      end if
171:    end if
172:
173: end
174:
175: on setTorches (a, b, c)
176:    pSaleTorches = []
177:    add (pSaleTorches, a)
178:    add (pSaleTorches, b)
179:    add (pSaleTorches, c)
180:    repeat with x = 1 to 3
181:      member("shop").model("torch0" & x).shader = \
```

LISTING 16.2   Continued

```
➥ member("shop").shader(string(pSaleTorches[x]))
182:   end repeat
183: end
184:
185: on torchRequest (me, whichType)
186:   whichBarterIndex = pTorchCosts[whichType][2]
187:   whichValue = pTorchCosts[whichType][1]
188:   if sprite(2).locH > 640 then
189:     sprite(2).toggleRack()
199:   end if
200:   displayText = "That's a " & string (whichType) \
➥ && "torch.  I need " & whichValue
201:   member("displayText").text = displayText
202:   broadCastSell(me, whichBarterIndex, whichType)
203: end
204:
205: on offerToken(me, whichToken)
206:   gRack.encumberToken(whichToken)
207:   offergoodsList = []
208:   repeat with x = 1 to count(gRack.pEncumbered)
209:     case TRUE of
210:       (gRack.pEncumbered[x] contains ("tokenH")):
211:         add(offergoodsList, #water)
212:       (gRack.pEncumbered[x] contains ("tokenF")):
213:         add(offergoodsList, #food)
214:       (gRack.pEncumbered[x] contains ("tokenW")):
215:         add(offergoodsList, #wine)
216:       (gRack.pEncumbered[x] contains ("token$")):
217:         add(offergoodsList, #money)
218:       (gRack.pEncumbered[x] contains ("tokenM")):
219:         add(offergoodsList, #magic)
220:       (gRack.pEncumbered[x] contains ("tokenK")):
221:         add(offergoodsList, #key)
222:     end case
223:   end repeat
224:   broadCastBuy(me, offergoodsList, pSaleItem)
225: end
226:
227: on addBaddie(me, whichCount)
228:   w.model("minionBip").addToWorld()
229:     sprite(1).pMinionModelToFollow = w.model("minionBox")
230:   w.model("minionBip").addModifier(#bonesplayer)
231:   w.newModel("minionBox", w.modelresource("testBoxResource"))
232:   w.model("minionBox").transform.position = \
➥ w.model("minionBip").transform.position
233:   w.model("minionBox").addModifier(#meshdeform)
```

LISTING 16.2 Continued

```
234:    gHavok.makeMovableRigidBody("minionBox", 1.000, TRUE)

235: end
236:
237: on transfer  (me, goodsList, pSaleItem)
238:    repeat with whichGoods = 1 to count (goodsList)
239:      gRack.subtractToken(goodsList[whichGoods])
240:      deductCredit(me, goodsList[whichGoods])
241:    end repeat
242:    displayText = "You purchased "
243:
244:    case pSaleItem of
245:      #red:
246:        --- a really cruddy torch
247:        w.model ("torch").shader = w.shader("red")
248:        -- change the torch skin to red \
➡ and then add 5 minutes to the torch clock
249:        remainMs = gGameClock.pTorchLife.time - \
➡ the milliseconds
250:        gGameClock.pTorchLife.period = \
➡ remainMs + (60 * 5 * 1000)
251:        displayText = displayText & "a red torch "
252:      #wood:
253:        -- change the skin to wood and add \
➡ 15 minutes to the clock
254:        w.model ("torch").shader = \
➡ w.shader("wood")
255:        remainMs = gGameClock.pTorchLife.time - \
➡ the milliseconds
256:        gGameClock.pTorchLife.period = remainMs + \
➡ (60 * 15 * 1000)
257:        displayText = displayText & "a wood torch "
258:      #silver:
259:        -- silver and 30 more minutes, note that \
➡ the time is added to the clock
260:        w.model ("torch").shader = w.shader("silver")
261:        remainMs = gGameClock.pTorchLife.time - the milliseconds
262:        gGameClock.pTorchLife.period = remainMs + (60 * 30 * 1000)
263:        displayText = displayText & "a silver torch "
264:      #gold:
265:        -- gold skin, 60 minutes
266:        w.model ("torch").shader = w.shader("gold")
267:        remainMs = gGameClock.pTorchLife.time - the milliseconds
278:        gGameClock.pTorchLife.period = remainMs + (60 * 60 * 1000)
269:        displayText = displayText & "a gold torch "
270:      #water:
271:        displayText = displayText & "water "
```

LISTING 16.2   Continued

```
272:      #food:
273:        displayText = displayText & "food "
274:      #wine:
275:        displayText = displayText & "wine "
276:      #money:
277:        displayText = displayText & "money "
278:      #magic:
279:        displayText = displayText & "magic "
280:      #key:
281:        displayText = displayText & "a key "
282:      otherwise:

283:   end case
284: member("displayText").text = displayText
285: end
```

This massive script is divided into the following handlers:

- **new()**   This handler simply calls the initialization subroutine and then returns a reference to the object script.

- **init()**   A subroutine that initializes the property values and other variables for the object.

- **broadCastSell()**   Game entities issue this command when they have something to sell. It sets the *on the table* properties to equal the item that the game entity is selling for the cost that the entity requests.

- **broadCastBuy()**   The player issues this command every time he clicks on a 2D token in the rack. The token is added to the encumbered list, the value is calculated, and the offer is eventually either accepted or rejected. If the bid is accepted, the transfer() subroutine is called; otherwise, the player sees a message denying his bid.

- **shopEntry()**   Collisions with a village shop trigger this handler. It then refers the actual setup of the shop interior to the outFitShop() subroutine before doing some general housekeeping.

- **outFitShop()**   This subroutine fixes the shop interior to display the correct types of torches on the wall. Different shops sell different objects. Right now, they all sell torches. In future versions of the game, they will probably sell other items as well.

- **deductCredit()**   The active credits (pCredits) are the integer counterparts to encumbered tokens. The deductCredit() function removes the credit amount represented by a token that has been either withdrawn or spent.

- **credit()**   The credit handler adds the integer value of a token to the total active credit. This (the active credit) is the integer counterpart of the encumbered tokens.

- **setTorches()**   The setTorches() subroutine sets the torch skins to the colors provided in the argument. This handler simply converts the symbols to strings and assigns the shader of the string name to the appropriate torch on the wall of the shop.

- **torchRequest()**   When called, this handler informs the player of the cost of a torch that has been offered for sale. The torch offered becomes the active sale item and its cost becomes the active cost.

- **offerToken()**   This handler is called when the player offers a token in exchange for an item on the table. It sends the final request to the broadCastBuy() subroutine.

- **addBaddie()**   This is the first of the handlers designed to trigger escalating adversaries in the game. This one calls up minions of the evil Wizard as the player gains experience.

- **transfer()**   The transfer handler seals the deal. It accepts the final barter and changes the player's configuration to invoke the new items that have been acquired.

As I continue to work out the details of interaction in the game space, I'll be putting additional code into this object. It is the logical place to centralize any data or command that relates to the gameplay experience.

Listing 16.3 contains the script for the game's time-management object. I've centralized the timeout objects within this object for convenience. Before we are through, there will be a fairly wide array of timer objects controlling all sorts of events in the game. Keeping them all here makes the programming a bit easier to follow.

LISTING 16.3   The Clock Object Centralizes Control of Timers

```
1: global w, gGameClock, gRack, gGameEventManager
2:
3: property pTorchLife, pHunger, pGameState, pTensionClock, pWanderClock
4:
```

LISTING 16.3   Continued

```
 5: on new (me)
 6:   if voidP(gGameClock) then
 7:     init(me)
 8:     return (me)
 9:   else
10:     alert "Object gGameClock Exists"
11:   end if
12: end
13:
14: on init(me)
15:   pTorchLife = timeout ("torchLifeClock").new\
➥ (60 * 15 * 1000, #torchOut, me)
16:   pGameState = 1
17:   pHunger = timeout("hunger").new(60 * 12 * 1000, #hungry, me)
18:   pTensionClock = timeout("tension").new(60 * 3 * 1000, #testLevelUp, me)
19:   pWanderClock = timeout("wander").new\
➥ (3 * 1000, #updateWanderVector, sprite(1))
20: end
21:
22: on torchOut (me)
23:   --kill the torch light
24:
25: end
26:
27: on hungry (me)
28:   -- do hunger & thirst calculations here
29:
30: end
31:
32:
33: on testLevelUp (me)
34:   case TRUE of
35:     (gRack.pExPts > 10):
36:       if pGameState = 1 then
37:         pGameState = 2
38:         gGameEventManager.addBaddie(1)
39:       end if
40:     (gRack.pExPts > 20):
41:       if pGameState = 2 then
42:         pGameState = 3
43:         gGameEventManager.addBaddie(2)
44:       end if
45:     (gRack.pExPts > 30):
46:       if pGameState = 3 then
47:         pGameState = 4
```

```
48:          gGameEventManager.addBaddie(3)
49:       end if
50:    end case
51: end
```

Although this script does contain a few simple handlers, it is likely that even these will eventually be moved to the game event-management script. The conceptual purpose of this object is to handle the timers. At most, it might also be viewed as a good home for time-based escalations.

I've left two handlers, hungry() and torchOut(), here to catch the events in anticipation of more substantial handlers later this week or early next week. (Since this is the last week of our planned game development period, an epilogue at the end of this chapter tells you how the game comes out and gives you a chance to explore the finished game and its code.)

The testLevelUp() handler is used to initiate adversaries (minions) within the game space. It checks to make certain that the player has gathered some tokens and looked around a bit, and then launches minions against the unsuspecting player. Of course, the minions just wander around bumping into things at this point, but we are getting there.

Tomorrow, I'll add some of Vinnie's particle effects to the mix so that we can start blowing flames and spitting fireballs.

Day Three

Last week, I gave Vinnie a brief run-down of my hopes for the weapons fire effects in the game and he smiled and headed off to his lair. I expected to hear from him today with some samples and I was not disappointed. This is probably a good time for you to have a peek at some of the things that we've added this week. Open the movie 17Keys232.dir on your CD-ROM. Rewind and play. Move the mouse left or right to rotate the figure. Use the W key to walk.

Now type the following into the message window:

```
sprite(1).torch2()
sprite(1).torch3()
sprite(1).wyrickAttack1()
sprite(1).wyrickAttack2()
sprite(1).torch1()
```

If you want to get a closer look at Vinnie's particle effects handlers for these effects, check them out in the particles cast member. I'll walk you through some of the highlights in Listing 16.4.

LISTING 16.4   The `torch1` Particle Effects Handlers

```
 1: property m                              --member reference
 2: property pTorch1OutCount               --put out torch1
 3: property pTorch1, pTorch2, pTorch3   \
➥ --flag that this type of torch is in use
 4: property torch1OutDelayCount           \
➥ --*******DO NOT NEED WITH TIMEOUT OBJECTS****
 5: property pFlameOffNow                  \
➥ -- flag to kill the flame on command


 1:  on torch1 me
 2:    m=sprite(me.spritenum).member
 3:    m.deleteModelResource("torch1")
 4:    m.deleteModel("torch1")
 5:    torch1 =m.newModelResource("torch1", #particle)
 6:    m.newModel("torch1", torch1)
 7:    sp=.75
 8:    torch1.emitter.minspeed=sp
 9:    torch1.emitter.maxspeed=sp*1.5
10:    torch1.emitter.angle = 40
11:    torch1.emitter.numParticles = 200
12:    torch1.lifetime=500
13:    torch1.texture = m.texture("particle")
14:    torch1.tweenmode=#age
15:    torch1.drag=2
16:    --makes cool effect
19:    torch1.blendrange.start = 100
20:    torch1.blendrange.end = 20
21:    torch1.sizerange.start= 0.15
22:    torch1.sizerange.end= 0.125
23:    m.model("torch1").parent = m.model(sprite(1).pPlayModel)
24:    m.model("torch1").translate(.6,.5,0, #self)
25:    m.model("torch1").rotate(0,0,90, #self)
26:    m.shader("shadow").blend =  60
27:    m.shader("particleAlphaLightColor").blend =  30
28:    pTorch1 = TRUE
29:    pTorch1OutCount = 0
30:    pFlameOffNow = FALSE
31:    sendSprite(1, #lightColorChange,rgb(255,255,0),rgb(255,25,0))
32: end torch1
33:
34: on updateTorch1 me, panAngle, backWindMotion, sideWindMotion
```

LISTING 16.4 Continued

```
35:    upWind = 5
36:    backWind = (backWindMotion * upWind) + panAngle
37:    sideWind = (sideWindMotion * upWind) - panAngle
38:    if sideWind <> 0 then upWind = 3
39:    upWind = upWind - abs(backWind)
40:    if upWind < 2 then upWind = 2
41:    if upWind = 5 then upWind = 5 + (random(9) - 5)
42:    m.modelResource("torch1").wind = vector(upwind, sideWind, backWind)
43: end updateParticles
```

Even though I am particularly fond of the spitting flame balls, I think that the flame from the torch is particularly impressive and interesting. The bulk of the effect is no different than most of the work that you've seen earlier in this book. The interesting bit comes in the updateTorch1 handler, which adds wind to the particles to simulate the effects of motion and wind-generated motion on the flames emitting from the torch.

The wind argument is passed as a vector that guides the flame. To really appreciate this effect, open your movie again and click Play. Wait for the flame to die out on the torch. Now light it up again using the command **sprite(1).torch1()** in the message window. Spin to the side quickly to see how nicely the flame grows out of the stem.

Day Four

We are handling the load of files, resources, and media in this movie in a slightly different manner than normal, which might be of interest for you. The code is certainly not complex at this point, although I expect it to grow substantially before we are ready for prime time. The loadFile command allows you to load all of the media from an external W3D member into a Director movie. You can accomplish this in Shockwave by placing the W3D member in the target system's dswmedia (downloaded Shockwave media) folder.

In Listing 16.5, you can see the manner in which I use the loadfile command to load the models into the Shockwave member. There are a couple of substantial advantages to developing the movie in this manner. The most immediate and substantial of these is that the media is not embedded in the executable. This means that I don't have to hard code the internal references to the media. I can simply point to the correct file and keep working, rather than manipulating every instance of a sprite on stage and carefully checking for broken filenames and so forth in the code. The second major advantage is that the file downlads can be handeled separately.

LISTING 16.5   The `loadFile` Command in Action

```
1: on exitFrame me
2:    if member("17Keys").state < 4 then
3:       go to the frame
4:    else
5:       member("17Keys").loadFile("17KeysBase316.W3D", TRUE, TRUE)
6:    end if
7: end
```

One of the most important things to remember when using the `loadfile` command is that the state of the member that is receiving the data must be greater than **3** before you begin loading media.

The Boolean arguments (TRUE and TRUE) at the end of the command tell the member that I want any identically named files to be overwritten with the newer data, and that I want the system to dynamically rename resources if needed.

I have a ton of tweaking, fixing, integrating, and finishing work to do today. It is the sort of ditzing that makes anybody crazy. I always find that at this (heck, at virtually any) stage of a project that it is helpful to remember the law of big uglies.

Move as far away from the project as you can get—physically, psychologically, emotionally. Now ask yourself, "What is the biggest single abomination that I see?" because it is a given that every aspect of your project is a complete failure and will never meet your standards. Make a list of the big uglies. Then make a list of the slightly less-critical uglies. Then create a list of the marginally uglies, and so on.

Now you simply start working on the big uglies and throw the remaining lists out the window because you are hugely unlikely ever to get to them. (Only partially kidding.)

I know that this sounds like an insane process, but I promise that it does work. It is a good, solid way to prioritize the remaining challenges, and to keep the pile of chores from becoming overwhelming.

Day Five

Well, it's here. Today is the last day of my crazy experiment. Don't get me wrong, we aren't going to stop work on the game here, but the month is up and the chronicle ends here. I have to admit that I'm a bit disappointed. I could easily use another month (perhaps two) to finish implementing the proposed feature set, and yet I have to also say that some of the work at hand is really, really good. The project is enormous, and it will benefit from several serious revisions.

I doubt that we'll set any performance records on software-based machines, but on midrange to low-end OpenGL-compatible graphics cards, the animation in the game still averages more than 50 frames per second. This is well above the early estimates, and really does suggest that over the next few years, we will see some eye-popping things done with Shockwave 3D.

I am also not disappointed. One of my foremost hopes for this portion of the book is that it provides a sort of honest window into the life of an independent developer in the midst of creating a game. Programming, designing, and managing these projects are crazy, unpredictable ventures. The fact that we're behind on our goals is typical for such work, even at the most substantially funded and equipped levels.

I have a lot left to do from here. I'll be continuing to integrate new models, animate and integrate fight algorithms, work on the story engine and perfect the download and delivery systems. I'll be integrating life meters for each character so that the players can monitor their status as well as their enemies' status during battles. I'll be working on collision detection for the weapons array and integrating weapon firing into the gameplay interface. I'll be designing and implementing the battle models and forum for the ultimate battle between Liam and Wyrick and probably developing new weapons for this exciting contest.

I'll work on the animals of the forest and the arcade interlude featuring Lido the dragon. I'll incorporate some intelligence and pathfinding skills into the control objects for the bad guys and the forest creatures, and perhaps even add one of those cool eye-of-the-villain cameras I've imagined for the game.

Vinnie wants to work on the animation routines. The run and back cycles are in serious need of help. (Their weight maps are distorting the heck out of the figure.) He'll also probably help with more particle weapons and perhaps even some particle-based obstacles. Sophia is continuing work on the skins for all the models, and will no doubt want to give the interface a once over when she's finished with the skins. Matt has plans for recording live actors to capture voice-like mumbling that can help set the scene.

Many of these features will continue to develop even after we've brought the first version of the game out for public consumption. We'll trim features that we think are too expensive to implement at this time, only to add them a few weeks down the road. You will find the latest version of the game in the studio at `http://insight.director-3d.com/studio/`.

Epilogue

Three weeks later...

I played the game and enjoyed it for the first time this week. Amusing yourself is certainly not the best test for success in a game, but it always gives me a hint that things are starting to come together. Specifically I was surprised to be attacked, and enjoyed the encounter—shooting flames at the giant minion and retrieving the tokens he had so viciously stolen from me in a prior encounter brought me right into the story.

This is exactly the interaction that should exist between the player and the game. I was angry with that character, because he had stolen from me. I wanted to get him back and retrieve my possessions. I was afraid that he might hurt me, and that my torch might go out. I was thinking about my health and hunger—whether I was too weak to fight. My understanding of the game space was informed only by the scene and by the stoplight meters that flicker away my status as the events of the game unfold.

Several aspects of the game have changed over the past three weeks, so go ahead and open the file `17keys260.dir` on your CD-ROM. Rewind and click the Play button.

The first thing that you'll notice is that the storyboards are now giving the player a quick overview of the game's back story. There is very little text here, just a couple of quick images along with brief descriptions to establish the pretext and then launch the player into the game. I've added some of Matt's sounds to enhance the immediate experience. Once the opening animatic is complete, the system moves to the title slate.

The title of the game is just as important as either of the opening storyboard images. In order to accomplish the game's objective—to reuinite Lido (the dragon) and Amed (the humanoid) and to destroy Wyrick—the player must collect all 17 keys.

The entire title sequence including the animatic lasts about 12 seconds. There are four words after the first storyboard and nine words after the second. Every choice in the opening sequence centers on concise, active communication of the story. The captions are written in present tense in order to accent the sense of action. Finally the music that I selected for the title sequence is intended to lend a sense of urgency and mystery to the events unfolding on screen.

Adding Icons and Meters

Once the titles are complete the game begins. I have added meters to display the player's vital statistics. The heart icon and the red meter represent the player's active life force. Players lose life force points when attacked or if they become too hungry. When the life force meter reaches zero, the game ends.

The flame icon and the yellow meter represent the relative charge of the weapon (the torch). The meter is always relative to the total original time allocated to that torch. This means that even torches that last for an hour use the same display space as those that last only a few minutes. Torch life is tied to weapon use. If the player has accessed a silver or gold torch and uses the flame thrower or fire ball weapons, the torch loses life span.

The food icon and the green meter represent the hunger/thirst of the player. The player's hunger/thirst is tied directly to his ability to take hits from adversaries. Well-fed players are much less subject to abuse than weak, underfed players. If the food meter falls to a low enough level, the character begins to starve and lose life force points.

Player Controls

The player controls the character in the game world using the six basic input mechanisms. The w-a-s-d key cluster is a traditional convention in games to facilitate control of the 3D environment. Using these keys along with the mouse, the player can easily navigate the character through the space. The final input is the spacebar. The spacebar is used for fighting and weapons fire.

Hold down the w or s key to make your character walk and try to walk into one of the tetrahedron (pyramid-like) shaped tokens on the ground. Whenever the system needs to communicate information to the player, the rack either displays that information or flys in and then display that information. As you acquire the token, you'll see the rack slide onto the stage over the top of the meters. Arrows on the rack indicate usability by changing the cursor to a finger. When the user clicks on either the out arrow or the in arrow, the rack toggles its position.

The player may also obtain information about his position in the game space by watching the map. A small orange dot indicates the current position of the character in the world.

Run around for a while and gather some tokens. Try not to get more than 10 at this point. Eleven tokens triggers an enemy launch and you may not be ready for that yet. Soon you'll realize that your torch has gone out and you are struggling to find your way through the dark forest. The character needs another torch if he is to survive any sort of battle.

Go to the village on the island's southwest corner. Go into one of the shops and buy a torch. A silver one is fun if you can afford it, but giving up a key would mean guaranteed loss of the game. Once you leave the shop with a silver torch you'll find that you now possess a flame-throwing weapon. (The gold one lets you spit fire balls.) Grab a few more tokens and you'll find that someone has taken an interest in you.

The Bonus Round

If you defeat three of Wyrick's nine evil minions, you may purchase the dragon amulet in one of the shops and play the bonus round from the viewpoint of Lido, our hero's dragon half. This arcade-style shooter lets you fly over the island where you will find that there are several tokens floating out of reach of the ground in bubbles. Flame the bubbles to drop them into your rack.

Once you have collected all of the keys, the dragon and man will be reunited and your new character will be ready for the ultimate battle with the evil wizard.

Planning: Necessary and Irrelevant

When I first began work on this book I polled members of the dirGames-L mailing list to try to find a logical pattern in the approach that different developers used to design and create games. There was absolutely no consensus, but one of the most accurate and consistent replies was that the act of planning was necessary and irrelevant. You need to plan, in order to try to hold down costs and to try to visualize your game effectively. You also need to flex and bend in order to remain adaptive and responsive to the needs of your development team and the realities of your schedule.

Games evolve as much as they are designed, but having that guideline in place can give you a solid model to grip when things start to get chaotic. It is important not to confuse adaptability with a rejection of design. You need both of these elements in order to bring your game together in a timely manner. There is no sense in gripping madly to a design concept that turned out to lack any playability whatsoever, and there is no logic in rejecting planning just because some of those plans may not come to fruition in the manner that you anticipated.

By examining the game in light of its fundamental dramatic and game-play qualities we were able to create a game that immerses players into an environment. That environment allows the players to discover and invent narratives and to experience heightened emotions as they work to accomplish the character's goals.

In Chapter 1, "The Story: How Much Is Too Much?" I discussed this need for narrative and game-play to coexist and complement each other's strengths. I believe that we are moving in that direction with efforts like this one.

In the future we will probably try to take those aspects further. We'll try to build greater levels of intelligence into the game, bring in additional heroic characters, and possibly even introduce a multi-player version.

In the next chapter, I'll introduce you to some of the fundamentals of marketing your game to your audience.

CHAPTER 17

Selling and Marketing Your Game

I have a news flash for you: You aren't likely to get rich developing games. Even if you do come up with the greatest marketing icon in history, the odds are firmly against your being the individual carrying home the profit.

After reading this chapter, you should

- Understand the the basic concepts that developers use to form business agreements with producers.
- Experiment with the impact of out-of-place elements in your game.
- Understand the real-life business and marketing limitations of independent game development.
- Anticipate the marketing strategies that you may use to sell and promote your games.

Business has some pretty universal rules. The first, and most relevant to you as an independent developer of small but fantastically cool games, is that "he who bears the risk, reaps the rewards."

That means one good reason that you would want to work on these things independently is that you can take home a larger portion of the payoff. You work for several months without substantial compensation, foregoing the convenience and reliability of a regular paycheck because you want to receive the bulk of the money that is paid for your game.

The other reason to work independently is simple. You are free to do as you please. You can decide what sort of work you do on any given day and how much work you'll do. It's not paradise, but it's very liberating.

The down side to working for yourself is that you've got to come up with people who will buy your stuff. That isn't always easy. There are a couple of things that you should keep in mind.

First, remember that Director preceded the World Wide Web and it is still the number one choice for cross-platform CD-ROM development. Developing in Director means that you can do it faster than the next guy and on a much tighter budget. Shockwave is still the only viable, universal plug-in to provide sophisticated interactivity via the Web.

If you think that your game might make a marketable CD-ROM, you should move in the direction of publishing that CD. If you think that your game might do better as a Shockwave game, you should begin investigating online opportunities. These can be tough to find, but they are out there.

They'll Buy It If You Sell It

However, the real strategy to success in this, and any business venture, has nothing to do with the delivery media or the game positioning strategy. It is really dependent on your ability to work effectively with the people that you encounter each day. The strategies that guide you to successful projects are summarized in the following sections.

Solicit

It is not uncommon to design games for a company to try to seduce the company into working with you. If you know of a company online that features games and that uses games that are similar to (ideally worse than) your games, contact that company's Web administrators and offer to show them a sample game.

They'll probably give it a look. They might even like it. At worst, you have a game that you developed to show to client X. Now you can show that game to others.

Befriend

Make friends with other developers. Often, a developer's first gigs come from other people's overflow. Use the mailing lists and patiently and faithfully answer any questions that you can. Be respectful and polite, and soon you'll find that you've made some good friends.

Inquire

Ask, ask, ask. You cannot inquire too much about the potential for contracts with various groups, Web companies, or publishers. Don't harass a single company, but you shouldn't stop after one rejection either. Make certain that you are reasonably well prepared and then go for it.

Admire

Work with people who are smarter than you, better than you, and kinder than you. Team up with cool people who are willing to tolerate your mediocrity because you'll handle the contracts. Just be sure that you let them know that you admire their work and respect their gifts. Tell them how grateful you are as often as you are able.

You have to sell yourself, your company, and your games every chance that you get. You might think of this in the inverse sense: "They couldn't possibly buy it if you don't make any attempt to sell it." How could anyone buy what he hasn't seen? If you decide to do independent development, you are your only representative.

Match the Client to the Target Audience

You can figure out what sort of games clients might be willing to license, buy, or publish by the sort of audience their other products generally are geared toward. Don't try to sell a gruesome first-person shooter to a company that sells safety equipment for toddlers. It doesn't want it.

In this spirit, you can make a product more appealing to a potential client by placing its products, or images and media that reflect positively its products, within your game. Put images of stuffed plush toys in your game, and hyperlink them to similar or identical products on the client's Web site.

Leave opportunities within the game for corporate sponsorship through advertising or product placement. If your client is a soft drink company, offer to include a virtual soft drink dispenser within the game space (for an additional fee, of course).

Also, remember to be sensitive to the potential client's target audience. If you are trying to sell a "road kill" game to a veterinary medical supply chain, you have really lost track of reality. Respect your clients and treat them as you imagine they would treat their customers.

Commit and Exaggerate

One solid way to ensure that your game stands out among the thousands of other games in the marketplace is to develop game elements that stand out in a crowd. It is always a good idea to make a solid aesthetic choice and then completely commit to that choice. The most common design mistake is to approach a design element with a tentative, reserved hand.

If all your aesthetic choices are timid, your game will be timid. You need to be certain that the choices that you make are bold enough to be noticed, recognized, and appreciated. There should be visual elements within your game that are immediately recognized and associated with your game.

One way to ensure that you achieve this level of commitment is to exaggerate the choices that you make. You obviously want to be careful with exaggeration of the aesthetic elements. It can be very difficult to find a good balance between an appropriately exaggerated image and a distorted and distracting one. As a general rule, you should make certain that the purpose of the exaggeration is consistent with a commitment to the objective that you started with. If you don't commit to the idea, neither will the audience.

Make your idea bigger than you think you should. You will probably think that your choice is going too far. Relax. Push that choice as far as you can and then give it some time. There are really very few factors that will limit the freedom you have to exaggerate your choices.

Possible, No—Consistent, Yes

It doesn't matter whether your idea would work in reality, it only matters that it works given the context of your game. This might seem like a laughably obvious statement. Nonetheless, I often hear game developers fretting over some minute point of physics or world representation that has nothing to do with the effectiveness of gameplay in their game.

The concern expressed is, inevitably, that the element is just not realistic.

"Yes, but is it consistent" is my standard reply.

It has to work for the world you make, not for the real world. It needs to work only within the context of the world that you have created. It doesn't matter one bit if the idea that you are working with—physics simulation or interface mechanics—has anything at all to do with reality. It simply must conform to the consistent rules of the space in which the game is played.

I say *must*, but I really mean something entirely different. The rule of plausibility, like all rules, was made to be broken. If you break this precept, the player (your audience) will make special note of the exception.

Try adding an out-of-place element to your game to deliberately lend emphasis to that specific element. This could also help to distinguish your game and help it carve a unique niche in the market.

Managing the Details

If you plan to take money for your games, get a lawyer to help you draw up contracts that you can use to define the relationship between yourself and your clients. Your clients might have contracts as well.

NOTE

I am not an attorney. The ideas expressed here are intended only to give you a general overview of the concepts, and do not replace the advice of a lawyer.

In general, you want your contract to include the following basic information:

- The Parties

  Who are the parties involved in the agreement? This generally includes the names and addresses of the businesses that will enter into the agreement.

- The Established Facts

  A statement of facts and motives for the contract. What do you do, in general? What does the client do? What do you want from the client? What does the client want from you?

- The Terms

  The agreements (generally includes definition of terms). What things do you agree to do for the client, and what things does the client agree to do for you?

- Grant of License

  To what extent does this contract give the client license to use/display your software? If applicable, this section might also grant you license to use materials provided by the client.

- Reservation of Rights

  What rights to said materials and software do you and the client retain? Do you forfeit all future access to all your software in any form, or do you merely forfeit immediate access?

- Territory

  Where is this contract valid? Is it valid worldwide or only in certain regions or countries?

- Client Responsibilities

  What things is the client required to do and what are the repercussions if the client fails to complete these tasks?

- Developer Responsibilities

  What things are you required to do and what are the repercussions if you fail to complete these tasks?

- Copyright

  United States Copyright Law 201(b) has a clause often requested by clients that gives the client the copyright because the work is done "for hire." As a general rule, you want to avoid signing off on that one because you lose your rights to the materials generated, including your source code.

- Content Restrictions

  Are there any restrictions that you place on the type or style of content that you are willing to produce?

- Billing Procedures

  What are the exact procedures and terms that you use for billing? How much is required at what point in the project? This should include dates, rates for late fees, and any other relevant information about the financial arrangement.

- Data Ownership

  Who owns the data after this project? This is related to copyright and might be combined.

- Creation Procedures

  This area describes the exact procedures, details the proposal, and is likely to contain a reference to your treatment and spec. It should include a calendar with deadlines and an overview of the terms for making changes and reporting bugs.

- Right of Approval

  This allows you and the client the right to halt the project if either party contributes material that either party feels would damage the reputation of the company.

- Selling Price and Terms

  If the client will sell your product, this section includes that information; otherwise, your price and terms would appear here. If appropriate, this area also includes references to royalties and advances.

- Term of Agreement

  During what timeframe is this agreement valid?

- Warranties

  Will either you or the client provide warranty for the software or for any component part of the software?

- Service and End-User Support

  Will you or the client provide end-user support for the product?

- Governing Law

  Every contract in the U.S. is governed by the laws of the state in which its proponent resides. This is the state that your company is primarily located in.

- Termination

  What happens when either party terminates the agreement? Does the developer get to keep the money spent on the project so far?

Even in this simplified form, the contractual obligations can seem daunting. Do yourself a favor and get a lawyer to take care of the contract. This has the added bonus of giving you a chance to discuss options for your company and to assess your personal liability in the event that you launch some unwanted chaos upon the face of the Internet.

As you consider your rights under any contract whether generated by you or generated by someone else try to keep your rights and your concerns foremost in your mind. It is easy to get so excited by the prospect of a contract that you take absolutely anything that is offered. The problem shortly thereafter becomes apparent. It can cost you money to create a game if you haven't carefully considered all of the implications of the contract.

Especially easy-to-neglect areas within these contractual elements are your rights regarding characters, game concepts, and other intellectual property that you generate during the course of creating the game. Be very careful to make certain that you are not at risk of losing your exclusive rights to intellectual property. Your ideas, your programming skills and your creativity are your chief assets and it would be unwise to surrender them for a quick buck.

What Next?

After all of these cautions and legal hurdles you may find yourself wondering "Why would anyone bother doing this?" If this book has been your first exposure to Director or to 3D computer animation, you may be feeling a bit numb. Don't panic.

Take your time with these new tools. Start with simple projects and work from the code and behaviors you've already learned. There is really no end to the number and type of games that you can create. As I discussed in Part I, the best place to find those ideas is in every day life. So put down this book and go spend some time with family and friends. Find something that makes you laugh, or fascinates you and your big idea for that cool new game won't be far behind.

PART IV

Appendixes

APPENDIX A

Treatments and Technical Specifications

This appendix contains the full text of the treatment/spec documents discussed in Chapter 2, "Making Plans." They may give you some ideas for approaching your own planning process.

n-Virae Interactive Entertainment Device Treatment and Spec

n-Virae is a multiplayer real-time/role-playing and strategy game set in a fantastic world of bizarre and colorful images. It bears some faint resemblance to the things we experience every day. *n-Virae* has a painted, surreal look. Buildings, trees, landscapes, and skies all seem almost possessed with personalities and faces to express them; in the right situation, these things will come to life.

Overview

Aimed at the upper elementary and junior high–aged teen, *n-Virae* is a nonviolent community experience. Players assume identities within the environment, which are partially of their own design and partially predetermined. The identity the player takes on becomes a sort of virtual costume and character. A player's entire experience may be dramatically altered depending on the character he or she becomes. Certainly the player's perception of this world will be altered depending on the character he or she becomes.

There is no real limit to the number of characters that will be assigned to players in the *n-Virae*, although it should be noted that, at this point, it's more practical to plan for groups of fewer than 50. Characters are generated when the players start the game. There is so much room for genetic variety and mutation that the resulting characters cannot really be predicted. Advanced players will be able to influence and design the genetic makeup of new characters, and most players will be able to conceive children.

This game has some similarities to *Creatures*, although the multiplayer aspect as well as some fundamental differences in the look and feel, interface design, and goals of the game set it apart from *Creatures*. *n-Virae*'s closest cousin in the contemporary game landscape is *Everquest*. Like *Everquest*, *n-Virae* is a multiplayer online role-playing game (RPG). Think of either one as a sort of 3D Multiuser Dungeon (MUD). The similarities between the games end there. Most notably, *Everquest* is often violent and has artwork of a markedly different style.

It is possible to do the following in the *n-Virae* game space: compete, explore, chronicle, procreate, band together in teams, communicate, eat, get sick, get well, spread diseases, transcend your immediate level of existence, discover archeological artifacts, create enhanced or false lore, and commit crimes.

This is a never-ending game, because the *n-Virae* environment will evolve with use. Users who transcend several levels will eventually earn the right to design new characters and press them on the newborns (users just entering the game.) Along the way, users will have the opportunity to chronicle their experiences in story stones (rocks in the scene that have the ability to store and share text messages), thus adding their own adventures to the mythical backbone of this place.

Platforms

Target platforms for *n-Virae* are Windows 9*x*, NT, and 2000 as well as Mac OS 8.1+. The basic engine for the game will be developed in Macromedia Director 8.5. The Macromedia Director Multiuser server version 3.0 creates the connections between players across the Internet. We will modify various aspects of the display, depending on the playback capacities of the systems that attempt to play the game. Players will be given the option to customize their interface for speed or allow the computer to do the customization for them. They will be warned if their custom settings will likely result in performance issues. Multiuser communications will be transmitted through a central host over IP and UDP, depending on the potential for error checking for the specific action. It is possible that we may try to port the game to Shockwave.

Players

n-Virae is a multiplayer experience. As such, players inside the game environment may interact with one another and the environment in a variety of ways. The short-term goals of the game are survival and growth, although players may choose varied goals depending on their own interests. Fifty players may exist in each *n-Virae* space at any given time. People may join sessions that are public as well as generate private password-protected sessions. Users play the game over the Internet.

Interface and Chrome

The primary screen will be a 3D view of the *n-Virae*. The animations are well developed and the multiuser interactions will provide the added benefit of interpersonal communication among players. The art style is based primarily on Friedensreich Hundertwasser and Leon Bakst, the architecture of Gaudi, and the style of the Art Nouveau period. Characters will be 3D sprites, presenting their communications as text in the interface bar beneath the 3D portal. A major goal of the project is to allow this bar to become as minimal an influence as is humanly possible.

A small translucent control pad will give players access to their journal, their map, and an overview of their character's health, hunger, and disposition. This pad will float over the 2D portion of the interface. The 3D area must be protected from any crossover to 2D rendering at all costs. The onscreen character will respond to the player's requests to move via mouse and keyboard commands.

We will take advantage of the often severe lighting of the 3D environment and the universally fauvist color palette to create a 2D background that provides an elegant transition to the 3D world.

Startup

The game plops users in random locations on the first level. By default, it tries to place them in empty areas so that a first-time player is not faced with a crazy person within the first few seconds of play. Players are given no information and are left to fend for themselves, although a first-time player who is rapidly starving or dying of sickness may encounter a sentient game element that points out these problems and suggests remedies. They are almost equally as likely to encounter a twisted game entity that suggests flawed solutions or demands things in exchange for the information.

Objectives

The object of the game varies according to the desires of the player. Generally speaking, the objectives within the game are to survive, procreate, form friendships, transcend levels of existence, uncover the past, and act bravely in order to be added to the mythology of the environment and to create the player's own lore.

Entities

Entities in the game are world objects, characters, *n-Virae* sentient beings, and environmental influences.

World Objects

World objects include the following types:

- Archaeological artifacts
- Written history
- Art objects
- Magic charms
- Talismans
- Amulets
- Cultural artifacts
- Newspapers
- Guide books (maps of sections of the *n-Virae*)
- Food
- Vegetable
- Dairy
- Meat
- Water and wine

Characters

The game engine generates characters automatically when the user first begins the game. Visually, there are only a handful of character appearances.

Hunger

Hunger has the following qualities in the game:

- Increases over time
- Decreases when fed
- Increase is amplified when effort increases
- Health polls this property whenever a negative health impact is generated
- Strong characters get hungrier faster and must eat more
- Intellectuals suffer from an unbalanced diet

Health

The player cannot have perfect health, strength, and intellect. Genetic make-up limits the amount of these to a formula consisting of not more than 60 percent of each, unless a percentage of one element is forfeited. The hero could therefore be 100-percent healthy, but the player would have to settle for a combination of strength and intellect that's 40/40, for example. Magic items that can heal are available. There are also herbs and potions in the world that may heal certain problems.

Physical Strength

Tied to other genetic properties, physical strength cannot be perfect without a sacrifice. Great strength causes great hunger.

Intellect

Tied to other genetic properties, intellect cannot be perfect without sacrifice. Intellectuals daydream. On the other hand, a low intellect can lead to difficulty understanding things; the player may not even be able to read.

n-Virae **Sentient beings**

There are some simulated life forms in this environment that are sentient, but they may be classified as non-characters. They fall under this category for various reasons, but mostly because they are not quite like the sort of sprites you would expect to find in a world like this.

Story Stones

All the legends and myths of this place are stored here permanently. There are empty stones and full stones. The player can add to an empty one. The player can mark any full stone as a liar. Unfortunately, they are very sensitive—if the player calls an honest story stone a liar, it will attack them. If they survive the attack, it will forever speak ill of them.

The only way to make amends with an angry story stone is to find it a mate and carry the mate back to it. Be certain to discuss this with the stone ahead of time, in order to find out what it is looking for in a mate.

Memory Trees

Memory trees hold secret clues to the location of lost archaeological artifacts. They never lie. They don't often speak either. A memory tree knows about artifacts from the time of its birth forward, although it may not wish to speak about every secret.

Firewater

Firewater causes visions when consumed. These visions are bizarre and disconnected, and they leave the player disoriented and weak. The only known benefit of drinking firewater is that sometimes, players will see visions of secret hiding places while under the influence. These hiding places are invisible to players who are not under the effects of firewater.

Fortune Spider

Good-luck fortune spiders bring the player good luck, and bad-luck fortune spiders bring the player bad luck. The problem is that it is very difficult to be certain which kind the player has encountered.

Features

The following features are supported during the game:

Feature	Purpose
Speak and listen	Text-based, computer-enhanced/altered chat.
Move character	Mouse and keyboard control of onscreen character movements.
Read journal	Read the things that the system has written about the journey thus far and read self-generated comments.

Feature	Purpose
Write in journal	Write in a journal.
Read guidebook	If the player finds a guidebook, they may use it as a map to portions of the landscape.
Read myth from the story stones	The player can learn the mythology of any level from its story stones.
Add myth to the story stones	The player can add to the mythology of any level by writing new legends in the stones, but they must be careful—the stones don't like liars.
Eat	The player can eat the food they find or buy. It could serve them well or it may make them sick.
Drink	Wine or water. The effects differ. Both are important. Both can be dangerous.
Deceive	People write about the things that happen here, so the player had better get away with it if they try to deceive.
Collaborate	The player will be rewarded for working with others. Besides having more power to drive off an attack, the player will win friends and influence other characters. Heroes have many friends.
Heal	Find the right herbs or magical objects and the player may gain the power to heal the sick and crippled.
Infect	If the player is carrying a disease, they may infect the weak players that they come into contact with. The worst of these situations is becoming biotoxic. The player's name and location will be published in the newspapers, and it will become an act of heroism to destroy them.
Obtain objects	There are tons of objects that can hinder or help the player's progress.

3D Resources

The game will require a large assortment of low-polygon three-dimensional models. In order to ease translation, all models should be created in 3D Studio Max and exported as W3D files or merged into a central Max file.

Character Models

All characters are humanoid, but not human. They are a cute variant of human, all clearly the same sort of creature. They must be low-poly models (not to exceed 400 polygons per model). They should be texture mapped on the diffuse channel with UVW mapping modifiers assigning the maps to channel 1. The following six characters must be created:

- Small intellectual male
- Small intellectual female
- Medium agile male
- Medium agile female
- Large muscular male
- Large muscular female

Each character will be attached to a 3D Max biped using the physique modifier to attach the mesh to the biped. The biped-enhanced character should be resting in the default T pose.

The following default motions should be generated for each character (note that it may be possible to use the same motions for more than one character):

- Walk
- Run
- Duck
- Crawl
- Jump
- Lie down
- Idle standing
- Idle sitting
- Over-the-shoulder turn to query the player

Motions should be exported separately from the characters. It is imperative that strict attention to naming conventions be adhered to, in compliance with the requirements of the 3D engine, in order to ensure that the animations will be read correctly by the system.

World Sentient Beings

The world sentient beings are much less mobile animations than the characters and will therefore be triggered keyframe animations rather than boned IK (mesh deformations based on the motion of an internal skeleton). All sentient beings should begin and end each animation cycle in exactly the same pose. All animation cycles for each sentient being must use the same model in the same scale. This is because we will need to swap the model objects on-the-fly in order to switch between keyframed animations of a single sentient being. The default pose, combined with matching transforms, will allow us to seamlessly shift between animations for these creatures.

Stones

The story stones are just simple rocks with room for a face, or at least a mouth. Only the mouth moves. They do have limited mobility, but it is mostly through transform of scale and rotation. Their mouths are either open or closed by default, depending on their status, so there will need to be two versions of each of the story stone cycles—one with the mouth open as a default, and one with the mouth closed as a default.

It is important to note that these stones may need to attack a player. I'm imagining that they expand and attempt to bite the player. This means that collision detection on the inside of the enlarged biting mouth may become an issue. Like all the sentient beings, the story stones should mumble gibberish. When their mouths move, the translated text appears below. Their animation cycles should include the following:

- Default pose (mouth closed)
- Default pose (mouth open)
- Mumbling animation
- Eat attack
- Angry mouth pursed
- Happy and in love

Trees

The memory trees are very simple tree models. They are each alike and are simply glorified cylinders with some symbolic tree properties. They have a face worked into their bark and mumble just like the stones do. They have only one default state: eyes closed, mouth shut. They require the following keyframe animation cycles:

- Default pose

- Alert pose

- Mumbling pose

Water

Firewater is just an alpha channel of moving water. It doesn't do anything special. It has user-defined properties that determine its effect on the characters who come into contact with it.

Spiders

It is hard to tell by looking at the spiders whether they are good-luck spiders or bad-luck spiders. They are very small when compared to most other objects in the game space. They run or stand still. They will need the following animation cycles:

- Running

- Standing

Tokens

A host of tokens may be acquired in *n-Virae*. Each of these must be modeled as a very primitive 3D object. It is important that the style of the tokens match the overall style of the *n-Virae*, and it is essential that these tokens remain low poly (10 to 20 polygons maximum). The following tokens are used in the game space.

Written History

This is a book. It should have a symbol on the cover that is iconic and relates to the game promotional imagery. This should be a simple cube with a texture map. It obviously needs to be scaled to the proportions of a book. Opening one of these books takes the player to a 2D art screen. The book is never seen opening or lying open.

Art Objects

Although there will be more than one art object, they all should look the same. Each object appears as a statue about one-fifth the size of a character and in the shape of a character. These should come in different materials—wood, metal, precious metal, ceramic, and glass.

Talismans

These are primitive pyramids in different materials. They come in the following varieties: rock, water, fire, lightening, wind, and rain.

Amulets

These are necklaces with symbols carved into them that seem to bear iconic relevance to the following: visibility, charm, wisdom, speed, flight, and vision.

Newspapers

A newspaper is a folded plane with a texture map; it is written in an illegible language. The system will translate for the player. A newspaper is a powerful tool that includes articles about the heroic actions of players, information about plagues and other obstacles in the environment, and (perhaps most disturbing) an up-to-the-minute account of births and obituaries.

Guidebooks

These are like the history book, only with a map on the cover in place of the icon.

Vegetables

As yet unnamed, these are distorted, textured green spheres. They simply disappear when eaten.

Eggs

These are white or powder-colored egg-shaped objects of various reasonable sizes.

Meat

A texture-mapped meat shape. Same deal as other foods.

Water and Wine

This is really just a cup. The system knows which is which.

The Environment

The environment is a mostly level forested setting. This may be as developed as time will allow. Ideally, the development team will create at least one small village (say, six shops) and a cottage in the woods. It would be nice to have other architectural forms, but this is not necessary. It is necessary that there be some opportunities to find water, such as a lake or two and perhaps a fountain.

Data Structure

The network services object handles all access to the server and all communication between clients. Its functions include connecting, reading and writing data, listening for incoming network operations, and parsing incoming connections for commands.

The 3D world services object takes care of the functions needed in order to make the 3D objects move and interact with each other. These include camera manipulation, lighting, model animation, model transformation, and loading/unloading of 3D models and worlds.

The intelligence services object handles the gameplay elements of the experience. Included is the analysis of user actions in order to determine the degree of success or failure of various actions, the analysis of user health, intelligence, strength, and hunger properties, storage and retrieval of narratives, and creature/user interaction.

Rules

The rules governing actions in the game are based on behaviors assigned to objects that will poll the properties of all the objects involved in the proposed action. The environment will then enable, enhance, or disable actions based on the rule sets of the environment. In this sense, the environment is the gatekeeper of all actions.

Object Interaction

Object interaction will happen as follows:

- The game alerts environment sentient beings of the location of the player's character.

- The game searches for world objects/characters in the player's field of view and displays them to the player.

- The game records and broadcasts the player's location.

- Environmental sentient beings check their history with the player and run modified routines when appropriate.

- Environmental sentient beings check their proximity rules for handlers and run them if they are triggered by the location of the player.

- Environmental sentient beings perform routine memory and related functions in response to player interaction.

- The player interacts with the object.

- The game engine stores a memory of player actions and performs a heuristic test to determine the degree of success of the player.

- When the player has reached the predetermined level of success, a passage to the next level becomes available.

- When a character interacts with other players, all commands are processed through the central game engine—this is both to allow transmission of the result to the Internet-linked opponent and to allow continued AI interference.

- Overall game history is stored on a third-party server to allow for continuation of the game over great spans of time.

Methods and Properties

Name	Description

`mCameraTrackModel(<"modelName">,`
`<VectorDistToModel>,`
`<booleanLockModelToModelRotation>,`
`<percentDegreeOfMotionTolerance>,`
`<integerTimeSteps>)`
This behavior must be attached to the active 3D world sprite. Calls to the functions of the behavior should reference the
	Spawns a behavior dialog when attached that allows us to choose which model we want the camera to follow and what the vector to the camera from the model should be. It also provides a check box to enable rotation, matching a slider to set the degree of wiggle room given to the model before the camera starts to match the movement, and another

Name	Description
sprite—for example, `sprite(1)`. `mCameraTrackModel("arg", arg2)`. If there are fewer than five arguments, the handler will assume that the omissions are from the end of the list.	slider to allow us to choose the number of frames used by the behavior to get to the new camera position when the model moves quickly. The behavior accepts the following arguments: `<"modelName">`—Accepts a string or an integer representing the model within the active 3D member that should be tracked. The value is stored in a property called `pCameraTarget`. `<VectorDistToModel>`—Accepts an integer in default world units representing the distance/vector of the camera to the model. The value is stored in a property called `pCameraDistanceToTarget`. `<booleanLockModelToRotation>`—Either `True` or `False`, this argument determines whether the camera will be locked to the rotation of the model being tracked. If this property is `True`, the camera will always return to the same rotational relationship with the model. If this property is `False`, the camera will maintain the distance vector from the object, but it will not orbit the model when the model turns. The value is stored in a property called `pCameraLockRotation`. `<percentDegreeOfMotionTolerance>`—A rating from 1 to 100, this property determines the amount of wiggle room the model is given before the camera takes action. The value is stored in a property called `pCameraTolerance`. `<integerTimeSteps>`—Determines the number of frames over which the camera-realignment procedure will occur. The smaller the number, the more radical the camera movement. The value is stored in a property called `pCameraReactionTime`.

`pCameraTarget`	`access = get/set`
	`sprite(a).pCameraTarget = modelRef`
	`default = member(x).model[1]`

Name	Description
pCameraDistanceToTarget	access = get/set sprite(a).pCameraDistanceToTarget= vector(x,y,z) DefaultVector = vector(250,250,100)
pCameraLockRotation	access = get/set sprite(a).pCameraLockRotation = 1 default = 0
pCameraTolerance	access = get/set sprite(a).pCameraTolerance = 50 default = 0
pCameraReactionTime	access = get/set sprite(a).pCameraReactionTime = 20 default = 10
mMoveCharacter(<whichCharacter>, <whichMotionName>, <vectorDirection>) This behavior must be attached to the active 3D world sprite. Calls to the functions of the behavior should reference the sprite—for example, sprite(a). mMoveCharacter ("arg", arg2). If there are fewer than three arguments, the handler will assume that the omissions are from the end of the list.	This behavior does not use a dialog when added to the object. When called during playback, the behavior accepts the following arguments: <whichCharacter>—A reference to the model within the active 3D world that will be moved. This value is stored in the property pActiveCharacter. <whichMotionName>—A reference to the animation cycle that will be used for the movement. This value is stored in the property pActiveMotionCharacter. <vectorDirection>—The direction that the model should be pointing for the movement. This value is stored in the property pActiveMotionDirection. It is important to note that this behavior needs to be able to stack these motions into the bonesplayer modifier playlist. We'll use another behavior to abort such movements if the stack is too deep and therein keep control over the immediate motion. This could, however, get tricky, especially with the need to rotate the models in order to get the bipeds moving in the intended directions.

Name	Description
pActiveMotionCharacter	Access: get/set sprite(a).pActiveMotionCharacter = modelRef default: member(a).model[1]
pActiveMotion	Access: get/set sprite(a).pActiveMotion = motionRef default: member(a).model[1].bonesplayer[1]
pActiveMotionDirection	Access: get/set sprite(x)pActiveMotionDirection = (vector(1,0,0)) default: (vector(-1,0,0))
mStopCharacter(<whichCharacter>)	This behavior does not use a dialog when added to the object. When called during playback, the behavior accepts the following argument: <whichCharacter>—The model within the active 3D world that will be stopped. This value is stored in the property pActiveCharacter.
mKeyAnimateCharacter (<whichKeyCharacter>, <whichKeyAnimation>, <vectorDirection>)	This behavior does not use a dialog when added to the object. When called during play back, the behavior accepts the following arguments: <whichKeyCharacter>—The model within the active 3D world that will be moved. This value is stored in the property pActiveKeyCharacter. <whichKeyAnimation>—The animation cycle that will be triggered. This value is stored in the property pActiveKeyAnimation. <vectorDirection>—The direction that the model should be pointing for the movement. This value is stored in the property pActiveKeyDirection.
pActiveKeyCharacter	Access: get/set sprite(x).pActiveKeyCharacter = modelRef default: member(x).model[1]

Name	Description
pActiveKeyAnimation	Access: get/set sprite(x).pActiveKeyAnimation = keyMotionRef default: member(x).model[1].bones- player[1]
pActiveKeyDirection	Access: get/set sprite(x).pActiveKeyDirection = vec- tor(x,y,z) default = vector(-1,0,0)
mCollisionManager (<whichCharacter>,<collisionData>)	This behavior does not use a dialog when added to the object. When called during playback, the behavior accepts the following arguments: <whichCharacter>—The active character model. The one for which we want to resolve collisions and figure out whether the character is in the area of some game object. This value is stored in the property pCollisionCharacter. <collisionData>—The list of data that the collision modifier delivered to the handler. The collisionData is returned as a list consisting of modelA (the first model involved in the collision), modelB (the other one), pointOfContact (the world-relative point of the contact), collisionNormal (the direction of the collision between models). This value is stored in the property pLastCollisionData. Note that this one requires us to set up the collision callback handler to be this script and then to parse the collision data, tossing out the irrelevant collisions and keeping the good ones. Every model that needs to be detectable under this scheme needs the collision modifier attached. Then there will need to be a large case statement drawn up that will allow us to state the results of a collision between given objects.

Name	Description
	A part of the thinking here is that we can use large invisible spheres attached to various objects or perhaps just a single one attached to our character—yes, that's better—and detect collisions off the larger sphere in many cases. If the character is close to a rock or tree, that may trigger it, but the character would have to touch a piece of meat to trigger eating it.
	This is an on `exitFrame` kind of a beast, so it is important that we optimize it. Make certain that only the relevant items are being checked.
	We'll probably check it for the sphere of influence on one frame and for the actual character on the next so that we don't slow things down too much but still get good responsiveness to collisions.
pCollisionCharacter	Access: get/set sprite(x).pCollisionCharacter = "mod" default = member(y).model[1]
pLastCollisionData	Access: get sprite(x).pLastCollisionData default : NA
mBroadcastModelChange(<#cast>, <"modelName">,<model.transform>, <"motionName">) or mBroadcastModelChange(<#world>, <[worldDataList]>)	This behavior does not use a dialog when added to the object. When called during play back, the behavior accepts the following arguments: <#cast>—This argument needs to toggle the remaining args and alters the madness to the method. The #cast value signals that this is a change to a character or world-based object. This value is stored in the property pBroadcastType. <"modelName">—This is the name of the model that will be transformed in all the other instances of the game all across the Net. The value is stored in the property pBroadcastModel. <model.transform>—A Lingo transform object that gives the position, rotation, direction, and scale information for the object. The value

Name	Description
	is stored in a property called pBroadcastModelTransform.
	<"motionName">—The name of the bonesplayer or keyframe-based motion that the character used to make its most recent change. This value is kept in a property called pBroadcastModelMotion.
	or
	<#world>—If the world argument is offered, the behavior will expect the next argument to be a list containing all the information necessary for the server to update its information tables on the state of the world.
	<worldDataList>—The value is stored as a property list in the property pBroadcastLastWorldList.
pBroadcastModel	Access: get/set sprite(x).pBroadcastModel default : member(y).model[1]
pBroadcastModelTransform	Access: get/set sprite(x). pBroadcastModelTransform default : an empty transform object
pBroadcastModelMotion	Access: get/set sprite(x). pBroadcastModelMotion default: member(x).model[1].bones-player[1]
pBroadcastType	Access: get/set sprite(x). pBroadcastType default : #cast
pBroadcastLastWorldList	Access: get/set sprite(x). pBroadcastLastWorldList default : [:]

Word Wacky 3D Treatment and Spec

Word Wacky 3D is a wild-paced, scream-at-the-monitor-with-your-friends, roll-the-dice-and-make-a-word game. The dice in this game are not covered with dots. Each face of the die displays a single letter of the alphabet. Simple to use, this game gets faster and wilder the longer you play it. In an effort to shift the demographic of the game to pop-culture teens and twenty-somethings, it will have a retro-70s aesthetic.

Overview

The game punishes your mistakes heartlessly and rewards your success generously. The better you perform, the more time and rounds you are awarded. If you perform badly, you will lose both time and opportunities. The challenge is to beat the clock at least and pummel the clock if you want to go far. The faster you play, the more points you'll earn. Earn enough, and you'll be granted longer clocks and additional rounds. *Word Wacky 3D* is a digital house of cards. Players need intellect, skill, concentration, speed, and luck to defeat the ever-racing timer and master the wheel of words.

One player at a time may play the game. It has that gather-around flavor, encouraging others to watch, taunt, and shout out genuine as well as misleading answers.

Platforms

Target platforms for *Word Wacky 3D* are Windows 9*x*, NT, and 2000 as well as Mac OS 8.1+. The basic engine for the game will be sprite-based and developed in Macromedia Director 8.5. The display will be 3D.

Interface

I want the game to have an edgy, techno-organic feel. It should be strange and slightly retro-70s. It should feature a color palette of deep purples and analogous colors with complementary lights and glowing alarms.

There are several aspects of gameplay that must be reflected in the interface. I've listed them here, separating them into informational and input elements.

Information Elements

Several elements within the interface provide information for the user about the current state of the game. These include the following:

- A visibly running timer. Players lose LED lights every 2 seconds in the normal mode but lose lights faster if things are going badly.

- A visibly reducing round counter (limits total rounds).
- The current state of the dice.
- The current score (replaces the Roll button after a round begins).
- Bonus notification (flashes in the Roll/Score position for 2 seconds when a bonus is achieved).
- Illegal submission alarm(s) or score reduction that flash in the Roll/Score position when an illegal action is detected.
- Possible correct answers taunting the player. (Note: Move this feature to the round summary.)
- Round summary screen, showing successful and failed answers with complete points breakdown, round by round. (This is an optional feature.)

Interface Elements

The widgets within the game that the player is able to interact with are as follows:

- Roll button.
- Information button. This button explains how to play as well as displays copyright and creation information.
- Quit button.
- Keyboard and mouse input alphabetical characters.
- Sum button, which appears in the Word button position at the end of any given round and stays until the Roll button is clicked. This button leads to a text-only screen summarizing the actions and results for each round. (This is an optional feature.)

Startup

After the splash screen, the game launches directly to the playing screen. The clocks are stopped, but the dice are dancing. The Information button and Quit button are always enabled. The keyboard input is disabled. There are 3D dice spinning on their own axes; each is spread in a circle around the central display. It looks like a Ferris wheel with chaser lights.

Objectives

The player clicks the Play button to stop the dice and begin a round. Once the dice have landed, the player must create words, three to six characters long, using only the characters on the face of the dice. After each visible die is clicked, the dice move into the display position on the bottom of the interface in the next available slot. If the player hits the Word button and the word is valid, the score is increased and the dice are reset. Normal rounds last 60 seconds. All players are given five rounds at the beginning of the game. Players may earn additional rounds if they earn high-enough scores during any given round. Rounds are lost when a player earns too few points during a given round.

Resources/Entities

I'll need one die (cube), with each of its six sides mapped as a single mesh. There will be no mesh deformation, so this will be a 12-polygon model. The interface will be drawn onto a backdrop. The lights will be 3D objects floating in front of the backdrop. The buttons will be 2D sprites above the 3D world.

This should not be a substantial performance problem because there is very little work for the 3D renderer to do. I'll change the appearance of the buttons and other items by swapping the textures on-the-fly. The remaining entities are graphics created in Photoshop and audio files:

- Base backdrop
- Light bulbs
- Roll button (up, down, hover)
- Score sphere (base, integers—one per index)
- Word button (up, down, hover, disabled)
- Info button (up, down, hover)
- Quit button (up, down, hover)
- Background audio track (ticking/time urgent)
- Lights-out audio reinforcement
- Roll button–clicked audio

- Dice-rolling audio (optional)
- Score-change audio (positive, negative)
- Bonus audio
- Cheat audio
- Button-clicked audio

Rules

The rules for the game are fairly simple. Players submit words using only available letters. The words must be found in the onboard dictionary. The words must be between three and six characters long. Players need to click the Word button in order to validate a given word. Players may not use a single die more than once per word, use characters not on the dice, use a word more than once per round, or spend longer than 60 seconds per round (except where bonus time is awarded.)

Functions, Handlers, and Properties

It is reasonable to divide the proposed program into five basic subsections, as defined by their functions:

1. Data Management
   a. Lookup tables
      - Dictionaries
      - 3D position data
      - Game history log
      - Interface states
2. Game Logic
   a. General
      - Initialize Game
      - Reset Game
      - Reset Round
   b. Validation

- Check duplicates
- Check invalid characters
- Check invalid words
- Check illegal duplicate character use
- Record valid words

c. Score

- Add points
- Subtract points
- Add bonus points
- Reset points

d. Round counter

- Add rounds
- Subtract rounds
- Reset rounds

e. Timer

- Start clock
- Change max time/round
- Pause clock
- Reset clock

f. Navigate

- Jump to frame
- Record frame state
- Get frame state

3. 3D Interface

a. Dice

- Spin dice
- Wheel rotate dice
- Land dice

- Fly out dice
- Rack dice

b. Lights

- On
- Off
- Chase
- Reverse
- Echo clock

4. 2D Interface

a. Button swap

- Up
- Down
- Roll

b. Text swap

- Up
- Down
- New text

c. Round display

- New text

d. Score display

- New text

5. Audio

a. Controls

- Play
- Queue
- Stop
- Volume
- Fade

The first group, Data Management, will contain information that we need to check in order to keep the game on track. As the game is played, we'll store and retrieve information from the Data Management object.

The second group, Game Logic, is the largest. It contains six subsections of its own. This object will handle all the game's rules of play and respond to user inputs. It is organized into subsections that further specialize the jobs it must do during game play.

The third and fourth groups will handle the display elements of the game. They will work in conjunction with the Data Management object and the Game Logic object to change the appearance of the screen.

The final section is devoted to audio. Because Director's built-in audio systems are able to do everything we need, we'll just use those.

This tells me that I'll need to build four objects for this game. I will be able to get started using the public methods specified here:

Method/Property	Description
mInitGame()	Clears global variables and sets all media to the default values. Builds the array of dice and places faces on each one.
mRollDice()	Rotates the dice models on two axes. Stops the rotation in a position that leaves the dice aligned appropriately to the camera. Records the active faces into a list that is accessible to validation handlers.
mResetGame()	Resets the game to its default state. Erases score information, action-tracking information, and dice roll data.
mValidateWord()	Tests a submitted word against the following: (a) the dictionary, (b) the valid characters, and (c) duplicate words this round.
mSwapButton()	Sets the appropriate button/state to the backdrop cast member with imaging lingo.
mLight()	Sets the appropriate light/state to the backdrop cast member with imaging Lingo.
mAlarm()	Creates an alarm.
mMoveDice()	Moves the appropriate dice to the requested position. Either down to the next available display slot in the word rack or back up to its default position.

Method/Property	Description
mResetRound()	Resets the game without erasing the scribe data or round information.
mAlterClock()	Keeps time and sends time data to the round clock. Triggers all timing-related subroutines.
mAlterRound()	Changes the current round and/or the total number of rounds available.
mAlterScore()	Changes the current score.
mScribeActivity()	Write info to the log about a word submitted and the results of its validation effort.
mScribeAlternatives()	Writes info to the log about the words that the user could have used in a given round, but did not use.
mJump()	Moves the playback head to a specified location in order to access info or summary screens. Also tracks navigational information, such as pauses, timers, and so on.
mPressButton()	A button state and action script. I'll probably just use the default.

APPENDIX B

Composition Basics

When designing the interface for your game, you want to keep in mind the fundamental elements and principles of design. You should use the elements according to the rules laid out in the principles to achieve a cohesive composition that helps the users figure out what the heck to do, what the game is about, and where they are headed. Figure B.1 shows several of the basic elements of design.

Here are the basic elements of design:

- Point
- Line
- Shape
- Form
- Color
- Texture
- Mass

In performance events and interactive media, we add one more element: kinesis. This element is only relevant when a change over time occurs within the design.

Here are the principles of design:

- Balance
- Focus (dominance)
- Unity
- Contrast
- Rhythm (repetition)

FIGURE B.1

Balance, focus, unity, contrast, and rhythm combine to create interesting and engaging compositions.

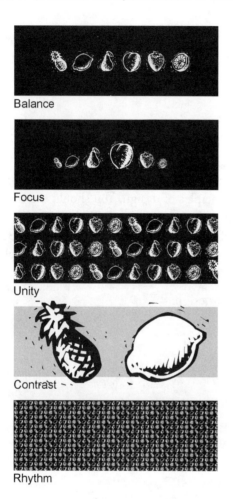

Balance

Focus

Unity

Contrast

Rhythm

The Elements of Design

An easy way to visualize the elements of design is to think of them as the tools artists use to make compositions. These are the units you use to make an image or to sculpt a form. They are used according to the concepts presented in the principles of design. If you had a design tool bag, it would contain the tools discussed in the following sections.

Points and Lines

A *point* is a position in space, defined by its relationship to some other point. A *line*, in design, is the edge of a shape. That may seem a bit odd, but if you pause for a second and look up, you'll probably be able to see an example. Look for a corner wall and make a mental note that there is a line where the two walls meet. Now look closer. There is no line there. There are only two walls (shapes), and where they come together our minds add a line. These imagined outlines, the things that many people draw when they move to depict an object, are called *occluding contours*.

Shapes

A *shape* is a self-contained geometric or organic unit in two-dimensional space. You could think of a shape as anything defined by lines. Positive shapes are things that appear to advance in a composition; negative shapes are things that appear to recede.

Forms

Forms are the result of multiple shapes combining to suggest complex images. Most of us have seen PBS cartoonists teaching children to draw forms by referring to the geometric primitives that compose the form.

Color, Texture, and Mass

A *color* is a hue. *Texture* is the visual or physical surface quality of an object. *Mass* is a whole three-dimensional object or a visual representation of an object that suggests weight.

Kinesis

The last element is unique to the design of dynamic events. *Kinesis* is motion or the potential for motion. Each of our design elements is dynamic. Never let yourself forget that we have to imagine the form in motion.

Principles of Design

The elements are the things we may use to make a composition. The principles by which we apply these tools are the real tricks to making effective compositions. The following sections define these principles.

Balance

Balance comes in several flavors. A thing is balanced when each of its elements appears to have the same mass. Most compositions are balanced asymmetrically, meaning there are different shapes and forms on either side of imagined midpoints. We generally think of such imagined midpoints as left and right halves. For our purposes, you will learn to consider these proportions in all three dimensions.

Focus

Focus and dominance are two sides of the same coin. We will use some of the tricks of dominance to get players to focus on the elements we need them to notice.

Without any sort of dominance, variety, or contrast, players would see a very plain, monotonous image. If we change the size, the color, the texture, the shape, the alignment, or even the line of just one of these elements, players will have no trouble knowing where to focus their attention.

Unity

Unity brings the elements of the composition together. If you make the lines, shapes, and colors appropriate to the content and style of the image, your work will have unity. Unity's antithesis is *contrast*, but you can have both at once. Contrast places opposite elements next to one another.

Rhythm and Contrast

Using rhythm, or repetition of visual elements, is one way to achieve both unity and contrast simultaneously. Simply repeat the contrasting elements a few times, and a unified pattern of contrast emerges.

APPENDIX C

Online Resources

General Director-Related Web Resources

The following are online resources that specialize in providing information to the community of Director developers.

Macromedia

http://www.macromedia.com

The mothership is your first stop when you want to get the latest information about updates or examine any of the extensive technotes in the online support center. The site includes a wide array of support and training documents that can augment your library. There are also links to Xtras that may help with that pesky missing feature.

Director 3D

http://www.director-3D.com

Director 3D is the meeting place for all things related to Director and 3D. The site is community owned and operated and features tutorials, news, and developer profiles.

Director Online

http://www.director-online.com

This is a longstanding and active site dedicated to the development of intelligent and engaging news, features, and tutorials for working with

Director and, more recently, Flash. Although the focus is not entirely on Director, the site is a regularly updated serious investigation of development issues in Director.

Director University

`http://www.directoru.com/community`

This site is a new model for the Director development community. Parts of the site are available to the entire community, and others are restricted to subscribers (for a $99 annual fee.) The resources are solid whether you are a subscriber or not.

Director Web

`www.mcli.dist.maricopa.edu/director`

The oldest of the Director support sites, Director Web has a longstanding tradition of providing powerful information for the community and lending a voice to individuals working on various projects. The site is home to Direct-L, the largest and most volatile of the Director mailing lists. The Direct-L archives are among the first places I search when I need information about a feature or problem.

Mediamacros

`http://www.mediamacros.com`

A solid news source, along with several links to behaviors and code of all sorts. You need to log in to the site as a member to get the full effect, but you'll probably find it worth the two minutes of effort to join the group.

Havok Xtra Support

`http://www.havok.com/xtra/`

Everything you need to get started working with the Havok Physics Xtra.

Listserves

There are literally dozens of mailing lists that focus exclusively on Director development. The two I have found the most directly related to 3D game development in Director follow.

dirGames-L

`http://nuttybar.drama.uga.edu/mailman/listinfo/dirgames-l/`

This is by far the best possible resource for anyone developing games in Director. Did I mention that I host this list along with Nathan Hruby and Andrew Cherry? Even so, people other than myself will confirm that dirGames-L is the bomb. As long as your comments and questions are about games, these folks will be your favorite humans in no time.

3Ddirector-L

`http://www.trevimedia.com/mailinglists/`

Terry Schussler, renowned Director and Flash trainer, has put together a very successful list dedicated to anything 3D and Director. The list is sometimes a bit Lingo heavy for beginners, but it is a very good place to get a question addressed regardless of the complexity of the inquiry.

Meet the Gang

Several developers who are active in the Director development community have created Web sites that include demonstrations of their work. A few of these follow.

Barry Swan

`http://www.theburrow.co.uk/d85/`

Barry's site is also home to the T3D engine, which Barry created. It is a testimony to the rapid following that a serious individual developer may generate when he is willing to take on major challenges and still provide tons of quality feedback to the community.

Charles Forman

`http://www.setpixel.com`

A solid collection of advanced demos and tutorials on a range of topics, including imaging Lingo and isometric game development.

CleverMedia

`http://clevermedia.com/`

Brian Robbins and Gary Rosenzweig (author of *Advanced Lingo for Games* and four other books on Flash and Shockwave) are the main points of visibility in the community behind this active site. Check out the 3D game gallery.

Den Ivanov

`http://cleoag.shockteam.com/`

Terry Schussler calls Den Ivanov "a world-class Flash developer." Take one look at the "Shockwave stuff" on his site and I think you'll agree that he's about to become known as a world-class Shockwave developer as well.

Al Partridge

`http://insight.director-3d.com/`

You may already have guessed that this is a link to my site. You'll find the latest info on this book as well as many additional examples, games, and demos, complete with code.

Jim Collins

`http://venuemedia.com/mediaband/collins/smhome.html`

Bow your head before you enter. This is home to one of the most amazing pixel pushers I have ever seen. His artistry and technical expertise blend together into a single stunning package that will make the hair stand up on the back of your neck.

Paul Catanese

`http://www.skeletonmoon.com/private/tron/interface.html`

Paul has written the most amazing book on Director 3D I have read. On his site, you'll find some great examples and information about his various projects.

NoiseCrime

`http://www.simtek.dircon.co.uk/mm/deightfive/`

`http://www.simtek.dircon.co.uk/`

NoiseCrime's lair is a must-see for any serious 3D game developer. He has done several demos in Director 8.5 and was a major groundbreaker in the world of 3D within Director long before 3D was natively supported by Director. He has been making 3D applications in Director for as long as just about anyone out there. The early examples are truly inspirational. Be sure to check out *Sonic Rush Racers* and then marvel that it was made long before Director supported 3D.

Nonoche

`http://www.nonoche.com`

You'll find the infamous Frenzyrith on this site. It is an amazing, fast-paced game that really takes advantage of Director's 3D features. Nonoche has also done extensive work with imaging Lingo.

Robert Walch

`http://www.entermation.com/games/minido.html`

Robert has done some amazing work combining Director's real-time 3D with the networking capacity of the multiuser server. *Mini-Do Man* is required gameplay for any Director developer.

Squid Soup

`http://games.squidsoup.com/gameset.html`

Squid Soup makes commercial Shockwave games both in 2D and 3D. Visit the site to see a wide range of online examples.

Thomas Higgins

http://www.shockwavemovies.com/

Tom's site is full of solid tutorials and engaging info, including a list of many undocumented features in Director 8.5.

Ullala

http://www.ullala.at/

This is the strange and wonderful home base of Ullala. You will find all sorts of information and animation here. You'll probably want to go there right away to download Ullala's famous 3D Property Inspector. It is a fantastic addition to your 3D toolkit.

3D Tutorials and Communities

Tons of great magazines, online communities, and tutorials are available on the Web that will help you develop your 3D modeling and animation skills. Here are a few that stand out.

3D Café

http://www.3dcafe.com

An enormous collection of online models, tutorials, and feature articles about everything 3D.

3D Ark

www.3dark.com

A magazine and collection of resources and tutorials related to 3D modeling and animation.

3Dluvr

http://www.3dluvr.com/content/

3Dluvr is a wild site full of engaging discussion forums, great tutorials, interesting high-quality 3D images and animation, and news and information about the world of 3D development.

Ultimate 3D Links

http://www.3dlinks.com/

Contains news and information about 3D and a collection of references to online tutorials and demos.

Turbosquid

http://www.turbosquid.com

Turbosquid is a fantastic tool created to enable simple media sales and purchasing. You can upload and sell or download and buy all kinds of graphics, sounds, animation sequences, and 3D models via the Turbosquid custom interface. This site hosts a wide variety of 3D-related content created by a huge and growing number of 3D artists. Media may be purchased or sold via the service.

Game Sites

Several online resources are dedicated to the technology, art, and business of creating games. My favorite game sites online include the following.

Amit's

http://www-cs-students.stanford.edu/~amitp/gameprog.html

It doesn't take much time in game development before you'll find yourself at Amit's. Here you'll find a huge collection of intelligent and important articles that explain the basic technological concepts behind much of the motion algorithms and intelligent agency heuristics you'll need to create good games.

Digital Game Developer

http://www.digitalgamedeveloper.com/Htm/HomeSet1.htm

An online magazine specifically geared to the game development community. It includes a discussion forum and feature articles.

Loony Games

http://www.loonygames.com/

Sure this site has gone dormant, but it doesn't matter. The archives alone are worth the visit. This was once a thriving Web community magazine, and the articles in cold storage are still a huge source of information.

Flipcode

http://www.flipcode.com/

News and resources related to game development. The site includes features, columns, and forums.

Game A.I.

http://www.gameai.com/ai.html

An online community that focuses on the development of A.I. for games. The site includes a magazine-style interface, discussion forums, and links to A.I.-related demos online.

Gamedev

http://www.gamedev.net

Game development industry news and information is updated daily on this news magazine-based site. You'll find plenty of links to demos and tutorials as well as job listings and other goodies.

Gamasutra

http://www.gamasutra.com

The latest news, information, resources, and contacts for game developers, generally tied to the C and C++ markets. There is substantial crossover between concepts and media, and this site is home base to information about the Game Developers Conference as well as *Game Developer* magazine.

APPENDIX D

A Large Scale Spec

This appendix contains the full text of the technical specification discussed in Chapter 13, "*17 Keys*: Week One."

17 Keys Technical Specification

The game will support the interactive features listed in Table D.1.

TABLE D.1 *17 Keys* Game Features

Feature	Actions
Hero features	Run, walk, stand, jump, defend, attack, get, put, use, equip, speak, listen, sense, eat/drink, die and when playing as the dragon fly or as the man, swim.
Autonomous agent features	Run, walk, stand, jump, attack, defend, get, put, use, speak, listen, and die.
Interface features	Track life force, view map of environment, view acquired objects, view speaking individuals, view equipped objects, invoke special aim mode, switch camera to first person, solve puzzles, and shoot tokens in arcade simulations.
Environment features	Dynamic scene loading based on grid and dynamic collision management based on proximity. Dynamic lighting and audio based on narrative management goals.
Token features	Visibility and animation.
Effects	Particle bursts for flame effects, magic spells. Particle rings for magic spells.

Resources

The proposed game will require a host of resources including 3D models, sound effects, 2D artwork, and other interface elements, which are listed in Table D.2. Names used here should be used to identify working documents related to any given resource.

TABLE D.2   Cinematics: Still Images with Transitions and Music

Image	Description
Opening	See treatment. Nine shots needed: Dragon-man, crowd, wizard, dragon-man failed defense, dragon-man encased in field, wizard pulls dragon-man apart, dragon attacks man, man rebuffs, dragon flees.
Reconvergence	The dragon and the man form an alliance and magically reconverge. Five shots needed: man, dragon, blend long shot, blend close up, combined glory shot.
Early death dragon	The dragon dies prematurely. One shot with active zoom needed: Dead dragon face shot zooms to long shot.
Early death man	The man dies prematurely. One shot with active zoom needed: Dead man face shot zooms to long shot.
Victory	The dragon-man defeats the wizard. One shot still needed: Dragon-man stands over defeated wizard.
Failure	The dragon-man loses his battle against the wizard. One shot still needed: The wizard stands over the defeated dragon-man.
Audio	
Forest noise	Background noise of forest sounds, crickets, or clicks and whirs—that sort of thing.
Village noise	Background noise. People working, clanging, rumbling, hawking their wares—that sort of thing.
Wizard cave or castle noise	Background noise of eerie winds and spooky creaks.
Underscore loop casual	A reasonable loop, around 20 seconds with possible variations to prevent monotony that suggests a casual forest walk. All of the loops should follow a theme.
Underscore loop cautious	Same basic sound as the casual loop but with a hint of caution. Something is not quite right about this place.
Underscore loop battle	Same theme as previous but with a strong sense of urgency and threat. There is fighting going on.

TABLE D.2   Continued

Image	Description
Underscore loop tense	Repeats the theme but adds considerable tension. Should cause the player to feel paranoid.
Underscore loop intense	Shifts the pitch and sounds desperate. Not the same as fighting in the sense that this sounds like panic.
Music for cinematics	Should share elements with the loops stylistically but could be considerably more customized. No cinematic should be longer than 30 seconds; ideally, they will not exceed 20 seconds.
Dragon call	Sound of a dragon?
Footsteps (three types)	Three variations on footsteps needed. Will be attached to different types of characters. Could be rate-shifted. Should be just one step, so it can be matched to the animation regardless of the loop. Likely to get cut.
Scary critters (three types)	Three different sounds, like guttural mumbling for the creatures that are encountered in the forest. These sounds should be threatening.
Good critters (three types)	Three sounds of forest and village creatures that demonstrate goodness. Should feel safe and welcoming.
Scary minions (three types)	The sound of three minions of Wyrick. These are frightening and angry-sounding guys.
Good villagers (three types)	Three sounds of good and helpful villagers. Should be voice like but not specific vocal utterances. Indistinguishable voices.
Slates	
Insight	Insight Interactive logo over art.
Title	*17 Keys* title and art.
Credits	Credits over art.
Options	Options screen, including the ability to set render mode, change the audio levels for background noises and music, and the ability to change key assignment.
Help	A brief rundown of the basic control conventions in the game, over art.
Models	
Lido	The dragon model. See features for supported animations. Needs custom skin. Polycount not to exceed 300.

TABLE D.2   Continued

Image	Description
Amed	The human hero model. See features for supported animations. Needs custom skin. Polycount not to exceed 300.
Wyrick	The wizard model. See features for supported animations. Needs custom skin. Polycount not to exceed 300.
Villager 1	A generic male villager. All three villagers will use the same model but with separate skins. See features for supported animations. Needs custom skin. Polycount not to exceed 300.
Villager 2	See previous.
Villager 3	See previous.
Minion 1	A generic minion/deformed villain. All three minions will share the same model but will have different textures to create the illusion of difference. See features for supported animations. Needs custom skin. Polycount not to exceed 300.
Minion 2	See previous.
Minion 3	See previous.
Animal 1	A bird-like creature. Polycount should not exceed 100.
Animal 2	A badger-like creature. Polycount should not exceed 100.
Animal 3	A bear-like creature. Polycount should not exceed 100.
Bad critter 1	An evil bird-like creature. Shares its model with the good bird but has a distinctly different skin.
Bad critter 2	An evil twin to the badger. Very different texture map but based on the exact same model.
Bad critter 3	An evil twin to the good bear. Same model, different texture.
Trees	A tree. Not to exceed 60 polygons.
Bushes	Bush textures applied to rects. Not to exceed 12 polygons.
Land	Simple planes. Not to exceed 32 polygons.
Hill	Simple hills; may be cut for polycount reduction. Not to exceed 24 polygons. All hills are based on one hill model resource.

TABLE D.2 Continued

Image	Description
Shop 1	A building that represents a business in the village. Shares the model resource with the other shop and the cottage. Not to exceed 12 polygons; each of these is entirely reliant on texture to differentiate them. Doors do not open, but a triggered door will transit a player inside the structure. (I know it's cheesy, but we are on a heck of a tight geometry budget here.)
Shop 2	See previous.
Cottage	See previous.
Evil wizard's cottage	See previous.
Pond	A translucent moving texture map. Note this is a very likely candidate for the chopping block.
Evil cabin interior	Interior of a box with specialty texture maps to paint an image of the space. Avoid internal geometry wherever possible.
Shop 1 interior	See previous.
Shop 2 interior	See previous.
Cottage interior	See previous.
Food	Small cube, textured to suggest some food item, boxed or other. Not to exceed 12 polygons.
Drink	Small cylinder, not to exceed 12 polygons.
Sword	Twelve-poly limit.
Shield	Twelve-poly limit.
Key	Four-poly limit.
Magic Talisman	Four-poly limit.
Money	Yet another tetrahedron. Four-poly limit.

Handlers

Table D.3 names and defines the proposed handlers for the project. This gives us some sense of the scale of the programming and provides a method for programmers to maintain as much consistency as possible throughout the duration of the development cycle.

TABLE D.3   Methods for *17 Keys*

Name/Syntax	Definition
mTracker()	Over-the-shoulder camera.
mStalker()	First-person camera.
mSunlight()	Changes the level of daylight.
mMagic()	Particle effects for at least three levels of magic spells.
mFlame()	Particle flame bursts in at least three levels.
mProjectiles()	Three levels of flung or fired objects.
mVisible()	Gets or sets the visibility of a given model.
mLoadWorld()	Loads all the appropriate models for a given section of the world grid.
mUnloadWorld()	Unloads all the appropriate models for a given section of the world grid.
mCheckGrid()	Checks the current location of the cameras in grid units should be loaded.
mPan3DAudio()	Adjusts the audio pan according to the position of a referenced object relative to a second object.
mAttach3DSound()	Adjusts the volume of a given sound relative to its distance from the camera.
mUpdateLifeForce()	Updates the life force property of a given character and, if appropriate, alters the display information for that model's life force indicator.
mUpdateMap()	Updates the map to reflect the current data about the 3D world and the player's position.
mUpdateRack()	Updates the acquired objects' and weapons' information in the player's rack.
mUpdateText()	Updates the display text.
mAnalyzeText()	Analyzes the text entered by the player and attempts to form a response based on the tables that match conceptual words and phrases to potential responses.
mDisplayRack()	Slides out the rack, complete with up-to-date information.
mDisplayPip()	Displays the picture-in-picture window. Can display the map view or alternative camera views.
mDisplayText()	Displays a text message for the user. Includes an image update to the rack to cue the user about the identity of the speaker.

TABLE D.3   Continued

Name/Syntax	Definition
mEraseText()	Erases the text in the display field.
mDisplayTarget()	Displays the targeting overlay for arcade-style interludes.
mHighlightModel()	Highlights a given model.
mKeyAnimate()	Plays a given keyframe animation for a given model.
mBoneAnimate()	Plays a given bonesplayer animation for a given model.
mAttachCollision()	Attaches the collision modifier to a given model.
mDetachCollision()	Detaches the collision modifier from a given model.
mSeek()	Steering behavior that causes the given model to move toward a given other model. Uses a combination of path-finding and world cognizance to avoid obstacles and seek out the given target model.
mAvoid()	Steering behavior that causes a given model to move away from another given model.
mWander()	Steering behavior that causes a given model to wander around aimlessly. Retains some knowledge of direction to avoid totally random and erratic motion.
mFeel()	A given character's agency uses this function to accept and analyze data regarding impacts from falls, attacks, and any other event that causes a touch-based sensation or injury.
mHear()	A given character's agency scripts use this function to accept and analyze data regarding the audible objects in the environment.
mSpeak()	A given character's agency uses this function to output speech to the player or to other characters.
mSense()	Used to trigger awareness of a general or supernatural sensation.
mEat()	Registers and responds to things that a given character eats.
mHunger()	Reports hunger events to the character's agency scripts.
mDie()	Cleans up work to display and resolve the death of an agent and the removal of its model. Includes updates to scoring and game-level data.
mAttack()	Used to attack a given character with a given weapon.
mDefend()	Used to defend a given character against a given attack.
mAcquire()	Used to acquire a given object.
mEquip()	Used to move a given weapon or tool into the player's active tool set.

TABLE D.3   Continued

Name/Syntax	Definition
mStore()	Used to return an equipped tool to a player's storage rack.
mUse()	Causes the player's character to use the currently equipped tool or weapon on a given object or an object within a given proximity.

GLOSSARY

A

action   The psychologically driven actions of characters that are intended to yield a reward.

P **active3dRenderer**   One of the available 3D renderers that is currently in use.

C **add()**   A command used by the meshdeform modifier to add a texture layer.

C **addBackdrop()**   A command used by a camera to add a backdrop.

C **addCamera()**   A 3D member command used to add a camera.

C **addChild()**   A 3D member command used to add a child to any given node.

additive color   Also known as *lighting color theory*. Red, green, and blue primary colors are blended to make white light. The more color, the closer you get to white.

C **addModifier()**   A 3D member command used to add a modifier to any given node in the 3D world.

C **addOverlay()**   A 3D camera command used to add an overlay to a given camera.

C **addToWorld()**   A 3D member command used to add a node to the world group within a given 3D member.

AI   Artificial intelligence. A colloquial term for *intelligent agency*. The illusion of intelligence generated by sophisticated, object-oriented programs designed to respond to input dynamically.

aliasing   Jagged edges that appear in digital images because the pixels are unable to display diagonal lines effectively.

alpha channel   A color channel used to store information about the opacity/transparency of an image.

P **ambient**   A variety of light; reflected light. Light that has bounced or reflected off one or more surfaces, or light that simulates such reflected light. A #standard shader property

P **ambientColor**   The default color of simulated ambient light of the 3D member.

anti-aliasing   The process of reducing the visible impact of aliasing on digital displays.

P **angle**   A property of the emitter object that determines the degree of deviation from the emitter's direction that particles may travel.

C **angleBetween()**   A vector math command that returns the angle between the first vector and the second.

P **animationEnabled**   A property of the 3D member that determines whether keyframe and bonesplayer animations will play back in the member.

ASCII   American Standard Code for Information Interchange. A common format for handling text on computers; a common file format used for the storage of 3D data by a variety of 3D modeling packages.

aspect ratio   A ratio that describes the comparative height and width of a rectangular area.

P **attenuation**   The intensity of a point light or spotlight expressed as a property. A vector that indicates the constant, linear, and quadratic attenuation factors of a point light or spotlight.

P **auto**   A property of the LOD (Level of Detail) modifier that determines whether the level of detail used to display the model will be determined dynamically based on the relative distance between the model and the camera.

P **autoblend**   A keyframe and bonesplayer modifier property that determines whether the modifier blends between the previous motion and the one moving into the lead in the queue.

P **autoCameraPosition**   A property of the 3D text member that determines whether the camera used to display the text should automatically center the text in its view frustum.

P **axisAngle**   A bipartite property that lists the rotation of a transform in terms of rotation around an axis rather than as a vector. It takes the form [axis vector, angle of rotation].

azimuth   Ancient mariners used this term to describe rotational maneuvers such as panning and side-to-side motion.

B

B-spline   The letter *B* is for Bézier. A B-spline is used to calculate a curve by averaging a series of points that generally exist beyond the curve itself. It's a very efficient way to model a curve.

P **back**   A property of the 3D box resource. It determines whether a back should be placed on the box resource.

P **backdrop**   An object that follows the camera and sticks to the farthest point of the camera's view volume, like a billboard. A camera property.

backface culling   Removing or neglecting to render faces that are not within the view of the camera because they are hidden on the back sides of various objects in the scene.

background noise   Ambient sounds that seem native to the environment.

backstory   The setup for a given game. The expositional elements culled into a presentation of information for the player.

balance   An item is balanced when each of its elements appears to have the same mass.

base map   The primary texture map used by an object to display its surface detail.

P **bevelDepth**   A 3D text member property. Determines the size of any beveled edge that is added to the extruded text.

P **bevelType**   A property of a 3D text member. Used to determine whether the text will have a bevel and, if so, whether that bevel will be rounded or flat.

Bézier spline   See *B-spline*.

P **bias**   A property of the LOD modifier. This property determines the relative effect of the LOD modifier when the modifier's auto property is set to TRUE.

bilinear filtering   A method of mipmapping that's simpler and faster than trilinear filtering.

billboard   An overlay or backdrop that is attached to the front or back end of the camera's view frustum. It provides a way to attach images to the camera so that they do not appear to move when the camera changes position.

bit depth   The number of bits used by a given color palette to display its colors.

bitmap   A method of storing image data wherein individual pixels and chunks of color data are approximated in order to give a good representation of the desired image.

P `blend`   A shader, backdrop, or overlay property used to determine the opacity of the image.

P `blendConstant`   A shader property used to determine the percentage of blend of a given texture when certain criteria are met.

P `blendConstantList`   A list of `blendConstant` values for each texture assigned to a given shader.

P `blendFactor`   A bonesplayer and keyframeplayer animation property that sets the level of blending that will occur between different motions when `autoblend` is false.

P `blendFunction`   A shader property that determines the type of blending to be used on a given texture.

P `blendFunctionList`   A list of `blendFunction` values for each texture assigned to a given shader.

P `blendRange`   A property of particle model resources that determines the start and end `blend` properties of the particles.

P `blendSource`   A shader property that decides whether the blending information from a texture's alpha channel or a constant value is used to determine opacity for the texture.

P `blendSourceList`   The `blendSource` values for each texture assigned to a given shader.

P `blendTime`   A property of the animation modifiers that assigns the time interval of the transition between animation motions in milliseconds.

bone   A base 3D element that can only be authored in an external package.

K `bonesPlayer`   The animation modifier that controls IK bone motions.

P `bottom`   A property of the `#box` model resource that determines whether the box should have a bottom.

P **bottomCap**   A cylinder model resource property that's used to choose whether the bottom of the cylinder has a cap.

P **bottomRadius**   A cylinder model resource that determines the radius of the base of a given cylinder.

P **boundary**   A property of the inker and toon modifiers that determines whether a line will be drawn around the edges of the object.

bounding box   The cubic area that encompasses the entire volume of a given model; the smallest cubic region that includes all aspects of a model's mesh.

P **boundingSphere**   Similar to a bounding box. The smallest sphere that encompasses every element of a mesh.

P **brightness**   A property of the newsprint and engraver shaders that picks the amount of white to blend in with the surface pattern.

C **build()**   A 3D command used to construct a mesh.

P **bytesStreamed**   A 3D member property that lists the amount of a given 3D member that has been loaded into the playback device.

C

K **camera**   A 3D element. The object that creates a viewing projection in order to translate the 3D data into a readable form for the viewer.

C **cameraCount()**   A 3D sprite property that determines the total number of cameras assigned to a given 3D sprite.

P **cameraPosition**   A shortcut access to the position vector of the first camera in a sprite or member's camera list.

P **cameraRotation**   A shortcut access to the rotation vector of the first camera in a sprite or member's camera list.

Cartesian coordinates   A method of describing position and rotation in a three-dimensional space.

cast   The media that will be used in a Director movie or Shockwave file.

P **child**   A hierarchical subjugate of another node; the offspring or dependent of a given node. A node or transform that inherits position and rotation information from another node, commonly called a *parent*.

P **clearAtRender**   A property used to determine whether the color buffer is cleared at the end of each frame.

P **clearValue**   If the clearAtRender property is TRUE, this property determines the color used to clear the screen between frames.

clipping plane   The near and far planes, perpendicular to the camera, that form the nearest visible space and farthest visible space for a given camera view. The front and back ends of the camera's view frustum.

C **clone()**   A command that creates a copy of a given node and all its children.

C **cloneDeep()**   A command that creates a copy of a given node, all its children, and all its resources and its children's resources. Shaders and textures assigned to the node are copied as well.

C **cloneModelFromCastmember()**   A 3D member command that clones a given model from a second cast member and brings it into the first member.

C **cloneMotionFromCastmember()**   A 3D member command that copies motion files from a second cast member into an initial cast member.

K **collision**   A modifier used to determine whether a given node has come into contact with (intersected the same space) another model or node.

K **collisionData**   Data returned by the collision modifier when a collision event occurs.

collision detection   Any of the many processes used in real-time 3D games to determine whether there has been an intersection of virtual models or agents.

P **collisionNormal**   A property that is expressed as a vector that demonstrates the vector of a given collision.

P **color**   1. The color of a camera's fog. 2. The RGB color value of a given light.

P **colorBufferDepth**   A property that determines the precision setting of the user's hardware output buffer.

P **colorList**   A property of the mesh model resource that determines the color of each face's corner.

P **colorRange**   The beginning and ending RGB color values of a particle's color.

P **colors** This property is used to set mesh face colors one at a time.

P **colorSteps** A toon and painter property used to state the maximum number of colors used to display the shader.

P **compressed** Tells whether the member resource for the texture is compressed.

concave A shape that if covered by a piece of cloth would leave a large empty void, like the inside of a bowl.

conflict The common ground that marries stories and games. The fundamental need for interference and negotiation that drives engaging stories.

contrast A distinct difference between local elements.

convex A shape that if covered by a piece of cloth would not leave an empty void, like an orange. The bulk of the surface points of the object would be at or near the cloth covering.

P **count** A 3D node property used to determine the number of elements of the given type.

P **creaseAngle** A property of the inker and toon modifiers that determines the amount of impact creases in the geometry have on the modifiers. This determines the angle at which creases are highlighted or drawn by a given modifier.

P **creases** Enables or disables the drawing of lines at the creases in the geometry when the inker or toon modifier is assigned to a model.

C **cross()** A vector math command that returns a vector that is perpendicular to both vectors.

C **crossProduct()** See cross().

P **currentLoopState** A property of either animation modifier that indicates whether the motion is looping.

P **currentTime** The playback position of the motion in milliseconds.

D

P **debug** A 3D model property that allows you to switch to a debug display mode.

P **decayMode** A fog property that determines the method used to draw the fog.

declination The other side of azimuth. An ancient mariner's term for pitch or tilt rotation.

C `deleteCamera()` A 3D member command used to remove a camera from the camera list or to remove a camera from the 3D member.

C `deleteGroup()` A 3D member command used to remove a group from the hierarchy.

C `deleteLight()` A 3D member command used to remove a light from the world.

C `deleteModel()` A 3D member command used to remove a model from the world.

C `deleteModelResource()` A 3D member command used to remove a model resource from the 3D member.

C `deleteMotion()` A 3D member command used to remove a motion from the 3D world.

C `deleteShader()` A 3D member command used to remove a shader from the world.

C `deleteTexture()` A 3D member command used to remove a texture from the world.

P `density` An engraver and newsprint shader property that adjusts the number of lines and dots used to draw the surface area pattern.

P `depth` A property of the SDS modifier that determines the number of levels of subdivision that may occur.

P `depthBufferDepth` See `colorBufferDepth`.

P `diffuse` A color that may be blended with the diffuse texture.

P `diffuseColor` The shortcut to the `diffuseColor` property for the first texture assigned to the first shader in the member.

P `diffuseLightMap` An image used to modify the effects of diffuse light on a shader's surface.

P `direction` A property of the emitter that states the vector of motion traveled by the particles as they exit the emitter.

P `directionalColor` The RGB color value of the color assigned to the default directional light created in the member via the Property Inspector.

P `directionalPreset` The general angle of the default directional light of a given member.

P **directToStage**   A property that determines whether to allow the 3D Xtra to draw directly onto the stage, bypassing Director's draw buffer.

P **displayFace**   A 3D text member property used to choose which of the faces of the extruded text will be rendered.

P **displayMode**   A property of a text member that determines whether the text will be rendered as a 3D member or as text.

C **distanceTo()**   A 3D command used to calculate the distance between two vectors.

P **distribution**   A property that decides how the individual particles within an emitter are spread out at their birth.

C **dot()**   A 3D vector math command that is used to multiply each of the items in a pair of vectors.

C **dotProduct()**   See dot().

P **drag**   A property of the emitter object that is used to calculate the impact of gravity, wind and other forces on the particles.

C **duplicate()**   Makes a copy of a vector or transform object.

P **duration**   The length, in milliseconds, of a given 3D motion.

dynamic sound   Spatialized or interactive sound. Sound that changes based on either user input or environmental factors within the 3D space. Sound that seems to come from a motivated direction.

dynamic cameras   Cameras that are able to project images of the world from dynamic positions. In some cases, these cameras follow a model; in other cases, they respond to user input. They usually integrate some form of self-control in addition to user input.

dynamic lighting   Lighting that self-adjusts or adjusts based on user input; lighting effects that assist the narrative or gameplay through dramatic or subtle changes.

dynamic narrative management   Changing the story as the player moves through the game. The dynamic narrative manager is able to adjust plot points, characters, and story decisions based on the player's choices in the game.

E–F

[P] **emissive**   The color of self-generated light or glowing on a 3D model.

[K] **emitter**   A particle generator. The object that determines the properties of particles emitted from a given point or region and based on a particle model resource.

[P] **enabled**   1. A collision modifier switch to allow or disallow the collision modifier on a given node. 2. Turns fog effects on or off for a given camera. 3. A Boolean switch that will turn the subdivision of surfaces either on or off for a given model.

[P] **endAngle**   A property of 3D sphere and cylinder primitives that allows you to generate partial hemispheres.

engine   The playback device used to draw the real-time 3D data to the screen and calculate the relative properties of the nodes in simulated 3D space.

environment mapping   Modifying the appearance of the 3D scene by simulating backgrounds with camera effects and backdrops.

[P] **error**   A property of the SDS modifier that determines the fault tolerance of the system when models are drawn that use the modifier to increase the complexity of geometry.

exposition   The part of a narrative that is used to communicate historic facts to the player or audience.

[C] **extrude3D()**   A command used to create an extruded type model resource in a 3D member that is based on extruded 3D text from a text member.

[P] **face**   The surface of a polygon; the shaded portion of a polygon.

[P] **far**   The farthest point at which fog should be rendered.

feedback   Audio or video encouragement that the interface gives the users in order to reinforce their education as they investigate an interface.

[P] **fieldOfView**   The angle of spread of the camera's view volume. Measured from the camera to the top of the projection plane and then from the camera to the bottom of the projection plane.

[P] **flat**   A property of a shader used to determine the shading method—either flat or Gouraud.

flocking   A computer simulation of animal behavior that is often used to demonstrate the power of simple behaviors to dictate complex actions.

[P] `fog`   A camera effect that adds procedural blending of a given color into a volumetric area equal to camera's view volume.

[P] `front`   The front of a box model resource.

forward kinematics   A form of bone-based animation.

fov   Field of view. See `fieldOfView`.

frame buffer   The place that the video card stores information about the display image while it is being generated.

frame rate   The playback speed of the animation measured in frames per second.

frustum   The pyramid shape created by the view volume; the visible display region in 3D space.

G-H

[C] `generateNormals()`   A mesh model resource command used to build a list of the normals for every vertex in the mesh.

geometry   The vertices, faces, and transforms of the models in the scene.

[C] `getBoneID()`   A command used to get the index value of a given bone.

[C] `getHardwareInfo()`   A command used to generate a list of information about the user's hardware configuration.

[C] `getNormalized()`   A vector command that divides each item in the vector by the magnitude of the vector.

[C] `getRendererServices()`   Provides access to the renderer services object. You can then poll individual properties of the object.

[C] `getWorldTransform()`   A command that returns the world-relative transform of a given node.

gimbal lock   Looking straight up or straight down causes the rotation systems to freeze and the objects to take on a two-dimensional form. Gimbal lock happens because some of the math needed to calculate the position of objects requires division, and division by 0 is illegal. You'll know it when you see it: The images start to skew and distort and then appear to be 2D quads rather than 3D images projected on a 2D plane. Sometimes it even crashes your computer.

K **glossMap**   A texture map used to simulate gloss lighting.

Gouraud shading   A method of face shading that calculates varied values for the shader across the face.

P **gravity**   A property of the emitter. In particle emitters, it is the direction in which a simulated force pulls particles.

P **group**   A property used to combine multiple models into a unit that may be collectively manipulated.

P **height**   A property of box or cylinder model resources used to determine the height of a resource in world units as well as the vertical dimension of a texture map in pixels.

height map   A texture map used to determine displacement or vertical deviation in terrain mapping.

P **heightVertices**   A property of a box model resource. It determines the number of vertices along the height of the box primitive.

hierarchy   The organizational structure of nodes in the 3D world.

P **highlightPercentage**   A property of the toon and painter shaders that determines the percentage of available colors that will be used for the highlight areas.

P **highlightStrength**   A property that determines the brightness of the highlight on a toon or painter shader.

P **hither**   The nearest visible position of a camera's view volume. A camera property that contains the value of the near clipping plane of a given camera's view volume.

I–K

C **identity()**   A transform command used to set a transform back to its original values.

C **ilk()**   A command that returns the type of a given object.

P **immovable**   A collision modifier property used to set the mobility of a given model in response to a collision event.

K **inker**   A modifier that allows you to work with a specialty shader called *inker*.

C **insertBackdrop()**   A camera command used to move a backdrop into a given position in the backdrop stack of the camera.

C **insertOverlay()**   A camera command used to move an overlay into a given position in the overlay stack of the camera.

C **interpolate()**   A 3D transform command used to calculate a percentage of the transform between two objects.

interpolation   An animation term that describes the process of calculating the in-between motions necessary to move an object from a given position to a second position.

C **interpolateTo()**   A 3D transform command used to move a transform a percentage of the transform between the two objects. Position and rotation are interpolated.

C **inverse()**   A transform command that returns a copy of the node's transform with the rotation and position vectors inverted.

inverse kinematics   A bone animation system that allows for quick animation and animation modifications.

C **invert()**   A command that flips the rotation and position of the given transform.

C **isInWorld()**   A 3D command that is used to determine whether a given node is still a child of the world group.

K **keyframePlayer**   The animation modifier that grants you control over the properties of a given keyframe motion.

L

P **left**   The left side of a box model.

P **length**   The length of a box or plane model resource in world units as well as the magnitude of a given vector.

P **lengthVertices**   The total number of vertices along the length of a box or plane model primitive.

P **level**   An LOD modifier property used to determine the percentage of detail to reduce.

P **lifetime**   An emitter property that controls the total time that particles are displayed.

K **light**   A 3D element used to illuminate the models within the space.

line   The path between two or more points; the edge of a shape.

P **lineColor**   A toon and inker property that chooses the color for lines.

P **lineOffset**   The distance from the edge of the model before the lines are drawn.

C **loadFile()**   A command used to load the nodes found in a given 3D file into the current 3D member.

P **loc**   The location of the registration point of a backdrop or overlay relative to the upper-left corner or the camera's display rect.

P **lockTranslation**   A property of the animation modifiers used to lock translation along a given plane.

light map   A texture map used to simulate light effects on the surface of a given model.

Lingo   Director's proprietary scripting language.

LOD   Level of Detail. The process of dynamically decreasing the detail of a model by optimizing (reducing) polygons based on the relative distance between the camera and the model.

K **lod**   The Level of Detail modifier. Used to decrease geometric complexity of the meshes dynamically.

P **loop**   1. A Boolean property that states whether the first motion found in a given cast member will repeat or play once and then stop. 2. Use this emitter property to re-create particles as they die.

M

P **magnitude**   The length of a vector.

map   A bitmap or texture image.

C **map()**   A command used to apply the qualities of a given motion onto another motion.

mass   The illusion of weight created by shading and simulated lighting in 2D displays or drawings. In physics, it's the actual or simulated weight of a given node.

material   The combination of shaders and textures forming surfaces for models.

P **maxSpeed**   The highest speed of particle emission.

P **member**   The member of a texture can be set dynamically to create animated textures.

mesh   The intricate network of triangular polygons that compose a given model's geometry.

P **mesh**   A property of the meshdeform modifier used to grant more detailed access to the properties of the mesh.

K **meshDeform**   A modifier that allows you to manipulate the properties of a given mesh.

P **minSpeed**   The slowest rate at which particles are emitted.

mipmapping   "Mip" is an abbreviation for the Latin *multum in parvo*, meaning many things in a small place. Mipmapping is the process of creating many reduced-size copies of a bitmap used for a given texture in order to make the display of the image more efficient.

P **mode**   1. Either #burst or #stream, this property determines the timing of particle emission. 2. The resolution (#mesh, #box, or #sphere) that will be used to calculate collisions between the mesh and other meshes when each mesh is using a collision modifier.

K **model**   3D element that is composed of one or more meshes.

P **modelA**   A reference to one of the models involved in a collision event.

P **modelB**   A reference to the other model involved in a collision event.

K **modelResource**   The resource information about the geometry used to generate the model.

C `modelsUnderLoc()`   A command that casts a ray from a given 2D location directly back into the Z depth of the screen. A list of intersected models is returned.

C `modelsUnderRay()`   A command that casts a ray from a given vector position in a given direction and returns a list of information about models that were intersected.

C `modelUnderLoc()`   Similar to `modelsUnderLoc`, this command will only return the first model intersected.

C `modelUnderRay()`   Similar to `modelsUnderRay`, this command will only return the first model intersected.

K `modifier`   A 3D element used to enhance the properties of a given node.

P `modifier[]`   Provides access to the *n*th modifier in the nodes modifier list.

P `modifiers`   The list of modifiers assigned to a given node.

morphing   Mesh deformation that blends one model into the shape of the second model over a period of time.

P `motion`   A 3D animation cycle that's either keyframe or bone based.

motion enhancement   Audio cues that reinforce a visual animation effect—a "boing" sound as two objects collide, for example.

motivated   Sounds and lights that appear to be generated by the general environment or by objects within the environment.

motivational   The use of sounds and lights that appear to be generated for the sole purpose of enhancing the emotional effect of the game. This use of such sounds and lights may seem illogical when compared to the logical environment or objects within the environment.

C `multiply()`   A transform command that simulates parenting a transform to another.

multitexture   Using more than one texture in a given shader to accomplish the composite effect.

N-O

n-gon Another way to describe a polygon.

nadir The point directly beneath a given transform in 3D space. The opposite of *zenith*.

P **name** The name of a given node.

narrative The story or plot of a given interactive or dramatic event. The storyline of the game.

P **near** The closest value of the view volume that contains the fog.

P **nearFiltering** A texture property that provides limited smoothing when the texture is displayed at sizes larger than the original image.

P **neighbor** A meshdeform modifier command that returns information about the polygons bordering a given corner of a given face.

C **newCamera()** Used to create a new camera model.

C **newGroup()** Used to create a new group.

C **newLight()** Used to create a new light.

C **newMesh()** Used to create a new mesh.

C **newModel()** Used to create a new model.

C **newModelResource()** Used to create a new model resource.

C **newMotion()** Used to create a new keyframe motion.

C **newShader()** Used to create a new shader object.

C **newTexture()** Used to create a new texture object.

node Any object in the 3D world.

C **normalize()** Used to create a new normalized version of a given vector.

P **normalList** Provides access to the list of normal vectors for each of the faces of a given mesh.

P **normals** Provides access to each of the normal vectors that form the three vertices of the face.

P **numParticles** An emitter property that provides access to the number of particles.

P `numSegments`   The number of subdivisions/vertices that split the height of a given cylinder model resource.

NURBS   Nonuniform rational b-splines. A system of curves used to calculate geometry more efficiently.

P `orthoHeight`   The height, in world units, that is displayed in a camera that is in orthographic projection mode.

P `overlay`   A billboard attached to the near clipping plane of a given camera.

opacity   The visual solidness or lack of transparency of a given model or node.

P

P `parent`   A property that stores a reference to the model that is the hierarchical progenitor of the current object.

P `path`   The path that emitter particles follow over their lifetime, expressed as a linear list of vectors.

P `pathStrength`   The power of the path to pull the particles toward it.

C `pause()`   Halts a current motion.

P `percentStreamed`   The amount of a 3D member file that has been loaded.

C `perpendicularTo()`   The same as `cross()` or `crossProduct()`.

C `play()`   Plays a motion animation sequence.

P `playing`   Determines the active playback state of a given motion.

P `playlist`   The list of motions stacked in the playback queue.

C `playNext()`   Dumps the currently playing motion and then plays the next motion in the playlist.

P `playRate`   The speed at which a motion is played.

plot   See *narrative*.

point   A unique position in 2D or 3D space.

C `pointAt()`   Aims the `pointAtOrientation` axis of a given model or node toward another given node's transform.

P `pointAtOrientation`   The axis angle that is meant to be aimed at another model during a `pointAt()` command.

P **pointOfContact**   A vector representing the point at which the collision of two objects using the collision modifier occurred.

P **position**   The vector representing the parent-relative location of the transform in 3D space.

P **positionReset**   An animation/motion property that restores the node to its initial transform at the end of an animation cycle, when enabled.

P **preferred3DRenderer**   A 3D member property that determines the 3D renderer that should be used if it is available on the target system.

P **preLoad**   Linked 3D files may be preloaded or streamed using this property.

P **primitives**   Returns a list of the primitives that are available on the system.

P **projection**   Determines the mode of projection—either orthographic or perspective.

P **projectionAngle**   See fieldOfView.

Property Inspector   The variable tabbed dialog in Director used to examine the properties of any given selected object.

pitch   The vertical rotation element; the tilt of a given rotation.

polygon   A planar shape defined by more than two edges.

Q-R

quad   A planar shape with four edges.

P **quality**   Provides access to the level of mipmapping.

C **queue()**   A command used to add a motion to the playlist.

P **radius**   The radius of a sphere or cylinder model primitive.

C **randomVector()**   Generates a random unit vector.

ray tracing   A method of calculating the lighting effects and rendering for a 3D scene. Not a real-time feature.

real time   When a player is able to control or modify events without a perceivable delay between user interaction and the system's response.

P **rect**   The display rect of a given camera within the boundaries of a 3D sprite.

P **reflectionMap**   A texture map that provides visual simulation of reflection.

P **reflectivity**   The shininess of the default shader. A property of the member.

P **region**   The point, line, or quad from which the particles of an emitter originate.

C **registerForEvent()**   A 3D command used to register a handler to reply to a given event.

C **registerScript()**   Similar to registerForEvent. Use this version on individual nodes rather than on the 3D member.

P **regPoint**   The registration point of an overlay or backdrop.

C **removeBackdrop()**   A 3D camera command used to remove a backdrop from the 3D world.

C **removeFromWorld()**   Removes the node from the world group.

C **removeLast()**   Removes the last motion from the model's playlist.

C **removeModifier()**   Removes a given modifier from a given node.

C **removeOverlay()**   Removes a given overlay from a given camera.

P **renderer**   Provides access to the current renderer.

P **rendererDeviceList**   A list of the available renderers.

P **renderFormat**   The render format of a given texture expressed as an RGBA color palette.

P **renderStyle**   The style in which you want to draw the given model—either fill, wire, or point.

C **resetWorld()**   A 3D member command used to reset the 3D world and each of its nodes to their original positions after manipulations have been made.

P **resolution**   Controls the number of polygons used to create a sphere or cylinder mesh primitive.

P **resolve**   A collision modifier property. When enabled, this property allows models using the modifier to resolve collisions.

P **resource**   Provides access to a given model's resource.

P **right**   The right side of a box model resource.

P **rootLock**   A switch that locks a model's motion to the `transform.position`.

P **rootNode**   The root node of a camera determines which objects are visible.

C **rotate()**   A command used to rotate a transform.

P **rotation**   1. The angle of deviation of the backdrop or overlay. 2. The angle of deviation of lines on the surface of engraver or shader properties.

S

C **scale**   1. The change in size of the backdrop and overlay. 2. A command that increases or decreases the size of a given object.

score   The animation control interface element in Director.

K **sds**   Subdivision of Surfaces modifier. Used to increase geometric complexity of the meshes dynamically.

P **sendEvent()**   Sends the event to each script registered to receive the event.

C **setCollisionCallback()**   Registers a given event for a callback when a collision occurs.

P **shader**   A simulated surface effect.

P **shaderList**   A list of the shaders assigned to a given model.

P **shadowPercentage**   The percentage of available colors assigned to a toon or painter shader that should be used to render the shadow areas.

P **shadowStrength**   The darkness of the shadows in a toon or painter shader.

shape   An area, such as a triangle or amorphous blob, that is defined by occluding contours or outlines.

P **silhouettes**   Used to turn on and off lines drawn around the 2D projected edges of the model using the toon or inker modifier.

P **sizeRange**   Sets the starting and ending sizes of particles emitted.

P **smoothness**   Control the number of segments used to shape the edges of extruded text.

P **source**   A property that allows you to set the texture to use as the source image for a given overlay or texture.

spec   A document that lists all the technical specifications for a game.

P **specular**   1. A light property that determines whether the highlighted area of a geometric object's surface area will be rendered with the highlights. 2. The color of the highlight of a given shader.

P **specularColor**   The default shader's specular color.

P **specularLightMap**   A light map that simulates the effect of specular light.

sphere of influence   A conceptual sphere that represents a spatial, psychological, or intellectual range of stasis. Interruptions to this stasis cause the character to become agitated.

P **spotAngle**   Determines the angle of the light's projection cone.

P **spotDecay**   A property that determines whether the intensity of the light will diminish over distance.

stage   The window within the Director interface that displays the appearance of the end movie.

P **state**   Determines the readiness of the 3D member.

storyboard   A communication device used by animators and game designers to illustrate moments of a given animation or game.

P **style**   A property of the toon and painter shaders that allows you to set the drawing style.

P **subdivision**   Access to the subdivision of surfaces method of operation. Choose either #uniform or #adaptive.

subtractive color model   Also known as *pigment color theory*. This is the process of mixing colors of pigment wherein the primary colors are red, yellow, and blue and the net result of additional color reduces the reflectivity of the surface.

T

P **tension**   Property of the SDS modifier used to determine how strictly the new polygons conform to the original geometry.

P **texture**   A bitmap or image object–based 3D node that is used to provide surface detail on a given shader.

texture The bitmap that represents the fine detail in the surface of the model's shader.

P **textureLayer** The layers of textures assigned to each shader as properties of the meshdeform modifier.

P **textureMember** See *member*.

P **textureMode** The manner in which a given texture is wrapped around the mesh.

P **textureRenderFormat** The default bit format used by textures when no render format is specified.

P **textureRepeat** Determines whether the texture will repeat (tile) if the scale is less than 1.0.

P **textureRepeatList** The textureRepeat properties of each texture assigned to a given shader in a list.

tiling A repeated display of a given texture image within the confines of a model's surface area.

K **toon** A 3D modifier that adds specialty shader effects.

P **top** The top of a box model resource.

P **topCap** The top of a cylinder model resource.

P **topRadius** The radius of the top of a cylinder or sphere model resource.

transform A mathematical object that is used to calculate and store the rotation, scale, and position data of a given node.

P **translate()** A command that is used to move a transform from one position to another.

treatment A document that outlines the plans for a game's story and playability.

trilinear filtering A method of mipmapping that produces a clean result but is significantly more expensive than bilinear mipmapping.

P **tunnelDepth** The extrusion depth of an extruded model.

U–W

underscoring   The music or other sounds used to enhance the emotional stimulation of a given moment of gameplay.

[C] `update()`   Updates a given model.

[P] `userData`   A property that stores a list of custom data associated with a node.

[C] `useDiffuseWithTexture()`   A command that causes textures in the diffuse channel to be blended with the shader's diffuse color property.

UV coordinates   Coordinates of a texture.

vertex   A single point in 3D space.

[C] `vector()`   A three-item list that contains the Eular coordinates that represent distance and direction.

[P] `vertexList (mesh generator)`   A list of each of the vertices used in a given mesh.

[P] `vertices`   More than one vertex. The points used by a given face.

[P] `visibility`   The visual display mode of a given model—either `#front`, `#back`, `#none`, or `#both`.

[P] `wind`   Determines the movement of particles emitted by simulated wind.

world cognizance   A navigational strategy for intelligent agents in the gamespace that gives the characters the ability to find their way through the space by using a form of virtual vision.

[P] `worldPosition`   The world-relative `transform.position` of a given node.

[P] `worldTransform`   The world-relative transform of a given node.

X–Z

[P] `x (vector property)`   The first element in a vector list.

[P] `xAxis`   The vector that represents the orientation of the x-axis.

[P] `y (vector property)`   The second element in a vector list.

yaw   See *azimuth*.

[P] `yAxis`   The vector that represents the orientation of the y-axis.

P **yon** The farthest visible position of a camera's view volume.

P **z (vector property)** The third element in a vector list.

P **zAxis** The vector that represents the orientation of the z-axis.

Z-buffering Used to determine algorithmically which volumes are visible and which are not (as well as the order of visibility from the front of the viewing volume to the back), given the Z depth of the image and respective models.

zenith The point in space directly above a 3D node; the opposite of *nadir*.

Index

A

M

P

Hey, you've got enough worries.

Don't let IT training be one of them.

Get on the fast track to IT training at InformIT,
your total Information Technology training network.

  | **www.informit.com** | **SAMS**

- Hundreds of timely articles on dozens of topics ■ Discounts on IT books from all our publishing partners, including Sams Publishing ■ Free, unabridged books from the InformIT Free Library ■ "Expert Q&A"—our live, online chat with IT experts ■ Faster, easier certification and training from our Web- or classroom-based training programs ■ Current IT news ■ Software downloads
- Career-enhancing resources

Other Related Titles

3D Graphics Programming: Games & Beyond
Sergei Savchenko
ISBN: 0672319292
$34.99 US/$52.95 CAN

Director's Third Dimension: Fundamentals of 3D Programming in Director 8.5
Paul Catanese
ISBN: 0672322285
$49.99 US/$74.95 CAN

Black Art of 3d Game Programming
Andre Lamothe
ISBN: 1571690042
$49.95 US/$33.90 CAN

DirectX 8 and Visual Basic.NET Development
Keith Sink
ISBN: 0672322250
$39.99 US/$59.95 CAN

Flash Character Animation Applied Studio Techniques
Lee Purcell
ISBN: 0672321998
$54.99 US/$81.95 CAN

ActionScripting in Flash
Phillip Kerman
ISBN: 0672320789
$39.99 US/$59.95 CAN

SMIL: Adding Multimedia to the Web
Mary Slowinski; Tim Kennedy/Nov 12,2001
ISBN: 067232167X
$39.99 US/$59.95 CAN

Sams Teach Yourself Adobe Photoshop 6 in 24 Hours
Carla Rose
ISBN: 0672319551
$24.99 US/$37.95 CAN

Sams Teach Yourself Game Programming with Visual Basic in 21 Days
Clayton Walnum
ISBN: 067231987X
$39.99 US/$59.95 CAN

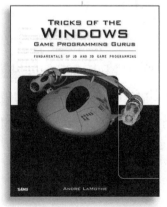

Tricks of the Windows Game Programming Gurus
Andre LaMothe
ISBN: 0672313618
$49.99 US/$74.95 CAN

SAMS

www.samspublishing.com

All prices are subject to change.